Thomas Randolph

A Vindication of the worship of the Son and the Holy Ghost against the exceptions of Mr. Theophilus Lindsey

Thomas Randolph

A Vindication of the worship of the Son and the Holy Ghost against the exceptions of Mr. Theophilus Lindsey

ISBN/EAN: 9783337284343

Printed in Europe, USA, Canada, Australia, Japan

Cover: Foto ©Lupo / pixelio.de

More available books at **www.hansebooks.com**

A
VINDICATION
OF THE
WORSHIP OF THE SON
AND THE HOLY GHOST

AGAINST THE

EXCEPTIONS OF MR. THEOPHILUS LINDSEY

FROM

SCRIPTURE AND ANTIQUITY,

BEING A

SUPPLEMENT TO A TREATISE,

Formerly publiſhed and entitled

A VINDICATION OF THE DOCTRINE OF THE TRINITY.

BY THOMAS RANDOLPH, D.D.
Preſident of C.C.C. and LADY MARGARET's
Profeſſor of Divinity in the Univerſity of *Oxford*.

All Men ſhould honour the Son, even as they honour the Father.
Joh. v. 23.

OXFORD:

Printed for J. and J. FLETCHER, in the TURLE: And ſold by J. and F. RIVINGTON, in St. PAUL's CHURCH-YARD, LONDON; T. and J. MERRILL, at CAMBRIDGE, and J. SMITH, in CANTERBURY. 1775.

A

VINDICATION, &c.

I CAREFULLY read over Mr. *Lindsey's Apology*, soon after it made it's Appearance. I was amazed to see such confident Assertions advanced with such very slender Proof. I examined into such Authorities as he had produced, and drew up some Observations upon them. I afterwards received two excellent Answers to this Work of Mr. *Lindsey*; one written by the ingenious and learned Mr. *Bingham*; the other by a *Layman*, but one *mighty in the Scriptures*, and able to give a good *Reason of the Hope that is in him*. I then threw aside my Papers, as unnecessary in Answer to Suggestions already sufficiently confuted. But having since revised them, I have thought fit to offer them to the Public, and that chiefly for these two Reasons. Some time ago I published *A Vindication of* the *Doctrine of the Trinity*, in Anfwer to a Treatife written by the late *Bifhop of Clogher*, entitled, *An Effay on Spirit*. I therein infifted chiefly on the Proofs of our *Saviour's Divinity*. I had but little Reafon to fay any thing of *the Worfhip of Chrift*, as the *Bifhop* had infifted on this, as ftrongly as I could do. And this has been the Cafe of moft, who have wrote in Defence of the Doctrine of the *Trinity*. None of their Adverfaries denied the *Worfhip of Chrift*; and therefore they thought it fufficient to prove *Chrift* to be truly *God*, and from thence to leave Men to infer the Duty of *worfhipping* him. They proceeded not to give the particular Proofs of this, or to anfwer fuch Objections as might be made againft it. I therefore thought that a Work of this Kind might not be an improper, or ufelefs, Appendix to my *Vindication*.

Another Reafon why I thought fit to undertake this, was the great Importance of the Subject. If any thing is of Importance in Religion, it muft be the *Object of Worfhip*. If our *Saviour* is truly *God*, we cannot without great Impiety with-hold from him the Honour, and Worfhip, due to him as fuch. If he is only a Creature, we cannot worfhip him without *Idolatry*. I thought therefore
that

that such a Point could not be too carefully confidered, nor the Arguments fet in too full a Light. And as I found fome things in my Papers, which I flattered myfelf were of fome Confequence, and which had efcaped the Notice of thofe excellent Writers, who had appeared before me in this Controverfy; I thought my Pains would not be ill beftowed in preparing them for the Prefs. As the Proofs of the *Divinity* of our *Saviour*, and of the *Holy Ghoft*, have been largely fet forth in my *Vindication*, to which this is an Appendix; and as Mr. *Lindfey*'s Objections to this Doctrine have not only been moft of them therein anfwered, but alfo fufficiently confuted, by the able Writers above-mentioned, I fhall confine myfelf chiefly to what he has offered againft the *Worſhip of Jeſus Chriſt*.

To begin with the *Old Teftament*, our *Apologiſt* afferts [a], that *the Hebrews never dreamed of a Plurality in the Deity:* and [b] *that the Law of God given to the Jews by Mofes invariably taught the Unity of God, and appropriated religious Worſhip to God only.* And fo alfo do we, *who worſhip one God in Trinity,*

[a] Page 87. [b] Page 119, 120.

and Trinity in Unity. If the *Jews* were unacquainted with the Diſtinction of *Perſons* in the *Godhead*, they could *worſhip one only God* in the general. But we, who have been taught this Diſtinction, and have been *baptized in the Name of the Father, and of the Son, and of the Holy Ghoſt*, are obliged to worſhip each *Divine Perſon* ſeparately. But have we no Proofs, or Intimations, in the *Old Teſtament*, of *a Plurality of Perſons in the Godhead?* I humbly think that we have a great many. It was aſſerted by the late *Biſhop of Clogher*, in his *Eſſay on Spirit*, and proved to be the Opinion of the ancient *Jews*, that there was a *Second Perſon,* called in the Old Teſtament *Jehovah,* who appeared to *Moſes*, and the *Patriarchs* ; as alſo a *third Eſſence, or Being*, to whom the *Jews* paid divine Honours, though his Lordſhip was not willing to allow this as any Proof of their *Divinity.* It was alſo the conſtant Doctrine of the *Primitive Fathers*, that the *Son of God* was the Perſon who appeared to the *Patriarchs.* And this has been ſince aſſerted, by Biſhop *Bull*, Dr. *Waterland*, Mr. *Allix*, and many others, who have from thence inferred that he was truly, and properly *God.* But our *Apologiſt* is pleaſed to treat this Notion with great Contempt:—

Some

* *Some Christians* (he tells us) *have pretended to gather it from the plural Termination of a Hebrew Word, Elohim, and from the Chaldee Targums.* —— But are these the only Arguments they make Use of? It is a common Artifice of our Author, when he meets with what he thinks a weak Argument in an orthodox Writer, to lay hold of that, and pass by all the rest. The same Dr. *Allix*, whom our Author here refers to [d], and who quotes *Gen.* i. 1. to prove a *Plurality of Persons in the Divine Essence*, in the very next Page quotes *Gen.* i. 26. where we read that *God said — Let us make Man in our Image, after our Likeness —* and also *Gen.* iii. 22. where we are told that *God said --- Behold the Man is become as one of us to know Good and Evil.* See also *Gen.* xi. 7. These Texts our *Apologist* wisely passes by, which plainly denote a *Plurality of Persons* [e]. I shall give the Argument nearly in the Words of a most ancient Fa-

[c] Page 87.   [d] Ch. ix. p. 116.
[e] *Justin. Martyr.* Dial. cum *Tryph.* p. 285, See also p. 359.---*Calvin*, who disallows of the Proof of a *Plurality of Persons* from *Gen.* i. 1. yet enforces strongly the Argument from this Text. And whereas some had pretended that *God* spoke here in the Plural Number, after the Manner of Kings and Princes, *Calvin* adds, that this was a Language of much later Date. See also *Patrick, Ainsworth* Comment.

ther

ther of the Church——*Moses shews by these Words,—Let us make Man in our Image,* &c. *that this Second Person is called God in the same Sense.---Nor can you say that God spake this to himself, or to the Elements, or Earth. For in another Place God says — Behold, the Man is become as one of us, to know Good and Evil. Here at least two Persons are signified, each of them intelligent.* Nor can it be said (adds our Author) *that God spake this to the Angels, or that Man was created by the Angels: but this Offspring, which really proceeded from the Father, co-existed with the Father before all Creatures, and with him the Father here holds Discourse.* --- The same Argument is urged by *Irenæus* [f], by *Tertullian* [g], and by *Novatian* [h].

Nor does the Argument from the Word *Elohim* merit the Contempt here thrown upon it. If indeed our Argument depended wholly on the Plural Termination of the Word, and we had no other Proof of our *Lord's Divinity* from the *Old Testament,* we ought not to lay great Stress on it. But let us consider that the *Hebrew* Language is one of the most ancient Languages in the world. It is thought

[f] L. iv. Præfat. C. 37.   L. v. c. 15.
[g] Adv. Prax. C. 12.   [h] C. 21.

by

by some to be the Original Language of Mankind, taught by *God* himself. How came it then to pass that in this primitive Language a *Plural* Word should be the most common Term used to signify the *Deity?* How came *Moses*, an inspired Writer, to choose out this Word, when another singular Noun might have been had, to describe the Creation of the World by the *Supreme God.* Nay, (what is still more remarkable) he uses this Word in asserting the *Unity* of the Godhead ——— יהוה אחד יהוה אלהינו — [i] *Jehovah our Gods is One Jehovah* ——This, if he did not hereby design to denote a *Plurality of Persons* in the *Godhead,* should seem to be a strange Form of Expression. If therefore this Word is sometimes applied to Creatures, who bear some Similitude, or Relation, to *God*; or if it sometimes denotes one particular Person in the *Trinity,* we may, notwithstanding this, be allowed to conclude, with some Degree of Probability, that it was intended, in it's original Acceptation, to set forth a *Plurality of Persons* in the *Godhead.* To this it may be added, that as we read *Gen.* i. 1. that *God--Elohim--created the Heaven, and the Earth*[k],

[i] Deut. vi. 4.   [k] John i. 1, 3.

so

so we are taught by St. *John* that *the Word was God,* and that *all things were made by him.* It is easy to cavil at Parts of an Argument, when taken to pieces. But I would desire the intelligent Reader to consider all these things together, and judge for himself. We want not this Proof.

As to the *Chaldee Targums,* they are brought only as one Proof out of many, that the *Jews* had a Notion of a *Second Person* in the *Godhead.* In many Places where the *Hebrew* speaks of *God,* these *Targums* render it by *Memra,* or the *Word:* and to this *Word* they ascribe personal Actions. I am sensible indeed that some [l] learned and judicious Writers disapprove of this Argument. They say, that the Word *Memra,* or the *Word of God,* is often used for the reciprocal Pronoun, and signifies no more than *God himself.* But to this it has been answered by [m] Dr. *Allix,* and other learned Men, that if in some Places the Word may have that Sense, in many others it cannot bear such a Sense, but plainly signifies a Person distinct from *God the Father.* I refer

---

[l] *Prideaux* Connect. Part ii. B. 8. p. 431. — *Lud. Capellus* Op. p. 76.   [m] *Allix* Judgment of *Jewish* Church, C. 12, and 24. *Bull* Def. Fid. Nic. Sect. 1. C. 1. n. 19. *Kidder* Demonst. Mess. P. iii. c. 5. — *Grotius, Hammond, Whitby in Job.* i. 1.

for Instances to the Authors cited in the Notes. I shall take Notice only of one produced by our *Apologist*. In *Jonathan's Targum*, cited by *Petrus Galatinus* [n], who lived at the Beginning of the sixteenth Century, and before him by *Raymond Martini* [o], who lived in the thirteenth Century, *The Lord said unto my Lord*, Psal. cx. i. is rendered --- The Lord said unto his Word --- Sit thou on my Right Hand, &c.——Here the *Memra*, or *Word*, is plainly a Person distinct from *the Lord*, who spake to him. And this Person, as our [p] *Saviour* himself and his *Apostles* have taught us, was he, who was afterwards *made Flesh, and dwelt amongst us, Christ the Lord*. Many other Proofs are brought by Dr. *Allix* from other *Jewish* Writers of a Distinction of *Persons* in the *Godhead*. And this is greatly confirmed by the Testimony of *Eusebius* [q], who assures us that the *Jews* had a Notion of a *Second Person* in the *Godhead, whom they called the Image, the Power, the Wisdom, and*

---

[n] Arcana, L. viii. c. 23. L. iii. c. 5. [o] Pugio Fidei, p. 705. This *Targum* is cited also by P. *Fagius* on Deut. v. This is, I believe, not now extant. The *Targums* in *Walton's Polyglott* give quite another Sense to the Psalm, and interpret it wholly of *David*.

[p] Matt. xxii. 44. Acts ii. 34. Heb. i. 13.

[q] Præpar. Evan. L. vii. C. 15. See my *Vindication*, p. 17, &c.

B *the*

the *Word, of God*; and for this he produces the Authority of *Philo the Jew*. He [r] cites a Passage from him, wherein he speaks of a *Second God, who was the Word of the Father of the Universe,* and says, that *the eternal Word of the eternal God is the strongest, and firmest, Support of the Universe.* [s] And as the *Targums* tell us that the *Memra*, or *Word of the Lord, created the Heaven, and the Earth,* so *Philo* says, that the *invisible Logos,* or *Word, is the Image of God,* and that *by him God created the World.* And as they express the Word *Jehovah* in the Appearances of *God* in the *Old Testament* by *Memra,* so *Philo* teaches us that it was the *Logos,* or *Word,* [t] who *appeared to Adam* in *Paradise,* [u] to *Abraham, &c.* [v] and that it was *his true Word, his first-begotten Son, who led the Children of Israel through the Wilderness.*

And St. *John* (as all the best Commentators agree) when he stiled the *Son of God*--- Λογ☉--- or *Word*, spake in the Language of the *Jews* of his Time. He teaches us that— *In the Beginning was the Word, and the Word*

[r] Ib. c. 13. [s] De Mund. Opif. p. 6.
[t] De Somniis, p. 593. [u] Ib. 578. [v] De Agricult. p. 195.

was

was with God, and the Word was God[x]. But our *Apologist*[y] seems willing to infer from his Interpretation of the Word *Memra*, that the *Logos*, or *Word*, in the Text, *is wrongly applied to Christ, and is nothing but a Description, in the Hebrew way, of God himself.* I wish he had given us his Interpretation at length. It should seem to be, according to him---*In the Beginning was God himself, and God himself was with God, and God himself was God.* He ought not to wonder if *many are unwilling to admit* such an *Interpretation*. And I must farther ask him, how he would interpret ver. 14. where we read that *the Word was made Flesh.* Dr. *Clarke*[z], though, both in his *Paraphrase*, and *Scripture Doctrine of the Trinity*, he seems willing to call our *Saviour* any thing but what St. *John* expressly calls him --- God --- yet [a] allows that he *was that visible Person, who under the Old Testament appeared in the Form of God, God the Angel of the Lord*, who appeared to *Jacob*, Gen. xxxi. 12, 13. Gen. xlviii. 15, 16.

This is also the constant Doctrine of [b] *Eusebius*, and all the Primitive Fathers before

---

[x] Joh. 1. i.   [y] P. 89.   [z] See my Vind. P. ii. p. 23, &c.
[a] Script. Doct. No. 535.   [b] Demonst. Evang. L. v. C. 7, 8.

him, that it was the *Son of God*, who appeared to the *Patriarchs*, and was worshipped by them, and they from thence prove his *Divinity*. *Justin Martyr* tells us, that [b] it was *Christ* who *appeared to Moses in the Bush*, who said —— *I am that I am, the God of Abraham, the God of Isaac, the God of Jacob, the God of your Fathers:* and that *this was the Word, the First-begotten of God, and himself God;* —— that *he is the Object of Worship, God, and Christ*; and that [c] *he was the King of Glory, who sat between the Cherubim, whom Moses, and Samuel, and the Children of Israel worshipped as God, and he heard them;* and whom also *all the Angels of God worshipped.* To the same Purpose speaks *Irenæus* [f]. He teaches us that it was *Christ, who with the Father is the God of the Living, who spake to Moses, and was manifested to the Fathers, and worshipped by the Prophets;* [g] that it was he whose *Glory Isaiah saw,* and who appeared to *Ezekiel;* the [h] *God,* who was *known in Judah,* whose *Dwelling-place was in Sion.* [i] In another Place he tells us, that *the Scripture*

[b] Apol. ii. p. 95, 96.   [c] P. 95.   [d] Dial. Tryph. p. 287.   [e] Ib. p. 255, 256. P. 359.   [f] L. iv. C. 11. See also C. 15. 16.   [g] L. iv. C. 37.   [h] L. iii. 9. Psal. lxxvi. 2.   [i] L. iii. C. 6.

no where calls any one God, *but what is truly* God: and yet in the same Chapter he tells us that *the* Son is the Person spoken of by the *Pfalmift, Pfal.* l. and called *the God of Gods,* *Jehovah the God,* who *shined out of Zion.* I might [k] produce similar Instances from almost all the Fathers of the three first Centuries: but this may be sufficient. Nor was this a vain opinion taken up by these Fathers, but what they learnt from the *Scriptures* themselves. As we are told in the *Old Testament,* that [l] *Jehovah appeared to Abraham,* and that he offered up Prayers to him, [m] *so Christ* himself affirms that *Abraham rejoiced to see his Day, and he saw it and was glad:* and he adds --- [n] *Before Abraham was I am.* —— Does the [o] *Old Testament* teach us that *Jehovah led the People of Israel through the Wilderness,* and call him *the* [p] *Rock of Israel?*— St. Paul [q] informs us, that *this Rock was*

[k] Vide *Bull* Def. Fid. Nic. Sect. 1. c. 1.   [l] Gen. xviii.
[m] Joh. viii. 56, &c.
[n] The Context obliges us to interpret this of *Christ*'s Preexistence. This is an Answer to the *Jews,* who asked him, —*Art thou greater than our Father Abraham?*—and wondered how he, who *was not yet fifty Years old,* could have *seen Abraham.*
[o] Deut. viii. 2, 15.   [p] Deut. xxxii. 15.   2 Sam. xxiii. 3.   [q] 1 Cor. x. 4, 9.

Christ,

Chrift, and admonifhes us *not* to *tempt Chrift, as fome of them alfo tempted.* Do we read in the *Old Teftament* that ʳ *Jehovah dwelt between the Cherubim,* and that ˢ *Ifaiah* faw his Glory there? St. *John* ᵗ affures us, that the *Glory,* which he *faw,* was the *Glory of Chrift.* And the fame ᵘ Evangelift teaches us, that *the Word was made Flefh, and dwelt among us*——ἐσκήνωσεν ἐν ἡμῖν — *he pitched his Tabernacle among us: and we beheld his Glory, the Glory, as of the Only-begotten of the Father.* And in Reference to this his Appearance in the Sanctuary *Chrift* is called in the *New Teftament,* ʷ *the Glory of Ifrael,* ˣ *the Lord of Glory,* ʸ *the Brightnefs of his Father's Glory, and the exprefs Image of his Perfon.* ᶻ And he appeared to his Apoftles at his *Transfiguration,* ᵃ and afterwards in a Vifion to St. *John*; in a Glory fimilar to the Defcription of him who *fat on the Throne* in the Prophecies of *Ezekiel* and *Daniel.* We are affured alfo that he will come to Judgment in a Glory exactly correfponding to that which

---

ʳ 2 Sam. vi. 2. Pfal. xcix. 1. ˢ Ifaiah vi. 1, &c.
ᵗ Joh. xii. 41. ᵘ Joh. i. 14. ʷ Luke ii. 32.
ˣ 1 Cor. ii. 8. ʸ Heb. i. 3. ᶻ Matt. xvii. Mar. ix.
ᵃ Compare Rev. i. 14, &c. with Ezek. i. 26. and Dan. vii. 9. See alfo my Sermon on John xii. 41.

appeared

appeared in the Sanctuary. [b] He there manifested his Presence by a visible Appearance of *Glory* encompassed with *Clouds*. [c] He there *sat on a Throne*, attended by his *Angels*. And [d] he himself hath told us, that in the End of the World *he shall come in the Clouds of Heaven with Power and great Glory*; [e] that *he shall come in his own, and in his Father's Glory, and all the holy Angels with him, and shall sit on the Throne of his Glory*. [f] And his Apostle assures that *the Lord Jesus shall be revealed from Heaven with his mighty Angels,* or rather [g] *with the Angels of his own Power.* We find therefore that the Person, who appeared to the Patriarchs, and sat *enthroned in Glory* in the Tabernable, and Temple, was *the Son of God, the Word,* who was afterwards *made Flesh, and dwelt among us.* And this Person is called [h] *Jehovah*, [i] *the Lord of Hosts*, [k] *the God of Gods*, [l] *the most high God*, [m] *the Almighty*. To him the Service of the Tabernacle and Temple was more immediate-

[b] Exod. xl. 34.—1 Kings viii. 10, 11.   [c] If. vi. 1, &c.
[d] Matt. xxiv. 30.   [e] xxv. 31.—Luke ix. 26.   [f] 2 Thess.
i. 7.   [g] Μετ' ἀγγέλων τῆς δυνάμεως αὐτοῦ.   [h] Gen.
xviii. 1.—Psal. xcix. 1.   [i] Psal. xxiv. 10,—2 Sam. vi. 2.
[k] Psal. l. 1.   [l] Psal. lxxviii. 56   [m] Gen. xvii. 1.
xlviii. 3.

ly offered: ⁿ to him Prayer was made, ᵒ Incense offered, ᵖ Sacrifices performed, ᵍ and Vows and Thankſgivings made.

The *Divinity of the Son of God* may be ſtill farther confirmed from Citations in the *New Teſtament* out of the *Old*, where what is ſpoken of *God* in the one is applied to *Chriſt* in the other. Thus we find in the firſt Chapter of ʳ St. *Matthew*'s Goſpel, a Prophecy from *Iſaiah*, which foretells that *a Virgin ſhall be with Child, and they ſhall call his Name Emmanuel, which being interpreted is, God with us.* And, if we look into the Prophet, we ſhall find that this *Son* is not only called *Emmanuel*, but ˢ *Wonderful, Counſellor, the mighty God, the everlaſting Father, the Prince of Peace.* ―― In the ſame Prophecy we read― ₜ *Sanctify Jehovah the Lord of Hoſts himſelf, and let him be your Fear, and let him be your Dread. And he ſhall be for a Sanctuary: but for a Stone of ſtumbling, and for a Rock of Offence to both the Houſes of Iſrael.* ― But

---

ⁿ Gen. xviii. 23, &c. 2 Kings xix. 15, &c· Pſal. lxxx. 1, &c.   ᵒ Exod. xxx. 6, 7.   ᵖ Lev. xvi. 2, &c.
ᵍ Gen. xxviii. 20.―xxxi. 13. Pſal. i. 14.―xcix. 1, &c.―
1 Chron. xvi. 4.   ʳ Matt. i. 23. Iſ. vii. 14.   ˢ ix. 6.
ᵗ viii. 13, 14.

this

this Prophecy is applied to our *Bleſſed Saviour* both by [u] St. *Paul* and [w] St. *Peter*. They teach us that he is *the Stumbling Block and Rock of Offence* here ſpoken of; and therefore he is *Jehovah the Lord of Hoſts, our Fear, and our Dread.*

Again, [x] St. *Mark* in the Beginning of his Goſpel quotes two Prophecies, one from the Prophet *Malachi*, the other from *Iſaiah*. In *Malachi* we read —— [y] *Behold I will ſend my Meſſenger, and he ſhall prepare the Way before me; and Jehovah, the Lord, whom ye ſeek, ſhall ſuddenly come to his Temple.*——But *John the Baptiſt* was this *Meſſenger*, who came to *prepare the Way before our Lord.* It appears therefore that *our Lord* is *Jehovah*, and that the Temple was *his Temple.* The other Prophecy we find in *Iſaiah*, ch. xl. v. 3. It there runs —— *The Voice of him that crieth in the Wilderneſs* --- *Prepare ye the Way of the Lord Jehovah, make ſtraight in the Deſart a Highway for our God.* —— This Prophecy is by [z] all the Evangeliſts ſaid to be fulfilled in *Chriſt.* He therefore is *Jehovah*; he is *our God.* It

[u] Rom. ix. 33.   [w] 1 Pet. ii. 8.   [x] Mark i. 2. 3.
[y] Mal. iii. 1.   [z] Matt. iii. 3. Mark i. 3. Luke iii. 4.
John i. 23.

follows

follows in the Prophet, ver. 5. *The Glory of the Lord shall be revealed, and all Flesh shall see it together.*— He who was *the Brightness of his Father's Glory,* and refided in *Glory* in the *Holy of Holies,* appeared now, and was revealed to all Mankind. In the 9th verse the Prophet, continuing to speak of the same great Event, thus expresseth himself——*Say unto the the Cities of Judah, Behold your God; behold the Lord Jehovah will come with strong Hand, and his Arm shall rule for him: behold his Reward is with him, and his Work before him. He shall feed his Flock like a Shepherd.* —Our Lord *Jesus Christ* therefore, [a] *the great Shepherd of the Sheep,* is *the Lord Jehovah,* is *the God of Judah and Jerusalem.* [b] Another Prophecy we have in St. *Matthew*'s Gospel cited from the *Old Testament,* and applied to our *Blessed Saviour.* We find this in the Prophet [c] *Zechariah.* The whole Prophecy is delivered in the Person of *the Lord God Jehovah.* At ver. 12. we read — *They weighed for my Price thirty Pieces of Silver. And the Lord Jehovah said unto me, Cast it unto the Potter; a goodly Price that I was prised at of them.*——This Prophecy the Evangelist tells

[a] Heb. xiii. 20. [b] Matt. xxvii. 9, 10.
[c] Zech. xi. 12, 13.

us *was fulfilled in Christ*. It follows that he is *Jehovah*, ᵈ *the Shepherd of Israel*, the *God*, *who* ᵉ *had made a Covenant with the People* of the *Jews*.

I am sensible that some learned Writers, who have been zealous Assertors of our *Lord's* true *Divinity*, have either neglected, or spoke slightingly, of the Proofs to be drawn from the *Old Testament*. Others have carried the Matter too far the other Way; and by insisting on Arguments, which will not bear Examination, have thrown no small Discredit on the real Proofs of *our Lord's Divinity*, which may justly be drawn from the *Law, and the Prophets*, especially when compared with the *New Testament*. I have offered such Proofs as seem to me fully to shew that *our Lord* was *the God of Israel*, and the Object of their Worship: and I might have produced many more. I have also shewn that this was the constant Doctrine of the Primitive Church. How far this Doctrine was known to the *Patriarchs* and *Jews* of old, is a Question which I cannot think we are concerned to resolve. It might be sufficient to say, that

---

ᵈ See ver. 7.   ᵉ ver. 10.

many Gospel Doctrines ([i] as particularly that of the calling of the *Gentiles*) were contained in the *Scriptures* of the *Old Testament,* and now appear plainly to be deducible from thence, which yet *in former Ages were not made known unto the Sons of Men.* The Doctrine of a *Trinity* therefore might be wrapt up in the *Scriptures,* and yet remain a Secret, till it was unfolded by the *Revelation* of the *Gospel.* And if this were the Case, we, who *worship one God in Trinity,* worship the same *God,* as those did, who knew not the Distinction of *Persons* in the *Godhead.* But we have no Reason to think this was the Case. [k] Mr. *Lindsey* indeed asserts with great Confidence that *the Hebrews never dreamed of a Plurality in the Deity.* To use his own quaint Expressions, I humbly think that [l] *Jacob dreamt of it* more than once. *Jehovah, the God of Abraham, and Isaac,* appeared to him in *Bethel.* This Person, *Jacob* himself calls [m] *the Angel, which redeemed him from all Evil;* and says the [n] *Angel of God spake unto him in a Dream.* He could not therefore be the same Person with the *God,* whose *Angel* he was. And

[i] Vide Eph. iii. 1, &c.   [k] Page 87.   [l] Gen. xxviii. 12, &c.—xxxi. 11, &c.   [m] Gen. xlviii. 16. [n] xxxi. 11.

yet this fame Perfon calls himfelf *Jehovah the God of Abraham, and Ifaac,* ᵒ *God Almighty.* And ᵖ *Jacob vowed a Vow to him,* and took him for *his God;* ᑫ erected *an Altar,* ʳ and offered *a Drink-offering to him,* ˢ *made Supplication,* and offered up Prayers to him. It fhould feem therefore that *Jacob* more than *dreamt* of a *Second Perfon* in the *Godhead.* And it has been fhewn that *Philo,* and other *Jews* in later Times, had fome Notion of a Diftinction of *Perfons* in the *Deity.* ᶠ It appears alfo from feveral Paffages in the *New Teftament,* that the Title of *the Son of God* was not unknown to the *Jews* in our *Saviour's* Time. ᵗ They accufed him of *Blafphemy,* becaufe he called himfelf *the Son of God:* ᵘ and thought that to *call God his Father* was to *make himfelf equal with God.* But ʷ we are told that *all the Jews of later Times cry out againft fuch an Imputation upon them, and their Anceftors.* Yes: and fo do the *Mahometans.* But we fhall not be fo complaifant, as to give up the fundamental Articles of our Religion to

ᵒ Gen. xxxv. 11.   ᵖ xxviii. 20.   ᑫ xxxv. 7.
ʳ Ib. v. 11.   ˢ xxxii. 9, &c.—Hof. xii. 4.
ᶠ Matt. xiv. 33.   xvi. 16.   John i. 34, 49.   vi. 69.
xi. 27.   ᵗ Matt. xxvi. 63, 65.   John x. 36.
ᵘ John v. 18.   ʷ Page 38.

gratify

gratify either *Jews*, *Turks*, *Infidels*, or *Hereticks*. And whatever thefe *Jews* have advanced, or can advance, has been fully anfwered 1500 Years ago by *Juftin Martyr*, and fince by *Raymund Martini*, *Petrus Galatinus*, Dr. *Allix*, *Bifhop Kidder*, *Grotius*, and many others.

Let us therefore now proceed to the *New Teftament*. And here our *Apologift*'s chief Argument againft the *Divinity*, and *Worfhip* of *Chrift*, and what he repeats in feveral Places, is taken from our *Saviour*'s Behaviour during his Miniftry. [x] He tells us that *Chrift never referred the Jews to any other than the Lord God of their Fathers*; that *he in the moft decifive Terms declares the Lord God to be one Perfon*, Matt. iv. 10. *and fingly exclufive of all others to be the fole Object of Worfhip.* The Words — *One Perfon*---printed in *Italicks*, I find not in the Text cited, nor in any other. We worfhip *One God*, as well as he. [y] But he tells us that *our Saviour himfelf always prayed himfelf, and alfo directed Prayer to be made only to God the Father*; but *he forbad Men's offering Prayers to himfelf*; [z] that *he formally profeffes his Inferiority, and Depen-*

[x] Page 92.   [y] P. 121.   [z] P. 9.

dence;

dence ; that he received his Being, and all his Powers from God, and leads Men by his Precepts, and Example, to look up to God the Father, as the sole Author, and Source of all Blessings to all, and the sole Object of supreme Adoration from all. These Objections have been already sufficiently answered by [a] Mr. *Bingham,* and still more fully considered in my [b] Vindication : and to these it might be sufficient to refer. But as this is the most plausible Argument our *Apologist* has to offer, and the most likely to impose on common Readers, *it will not be grievous to me,* for their Sakes, *to write the same Things again.* [c] Let it then be considered that, when our *Saviour* entered on his Ministry, he found the *Jews* almost universally possessed with false Notions of the *Messiah.* They were all at that Time in Expectation of a temporal *Messiah,* who should deliver them from the Power of the *Romans,* and *restore again the Kingdom to Israel.* And his own Disciples were strongly tinctured with these common Prejudices. Our *Lord* therefore found himself obliged to act

[a] Page 14, &c. [b] Part. ii. p. 37, &c.
[c] See our *Saviour's* Conduct with regard to this Point clearly explained, and justified, in Mr. *Locke's Reasonableness of Christianity.*

with

with great Caution, and Reserve. Had he openly, and publickly, declared that he was the *Messiah*, this would have been, to the Apprehension of the *Jews*, declaring himself a temporal Prince: and all, who were convinced by his Miracles, would have been ready to rise, and take up Arms in his Cause; while on the other Hand the Government would have been alarmed, and proceeded against him as a Traitor, and a Rebel. For this Reason, though he took all Occasions to give full Proof of his Ministry, he chose rather to intimate, than openly declare that he was the *Christ*. In like Manner, and for the same Reasons, we find his *Divinity* rather strongly intimated, than expresly taught. The Title, which he most commonly chose to distinguish himself by, was that of *the Son of Man*. He is generally thought hereby to refer to *Dan.* vii. 13. where the *Messiah* is described as *one like the Son of Man coming with the Clouds of Heaven*, &c. And he seems to have chosen this Appellation, as carrying with it (especially in his Manner of using, and applying it) sufficient Intimation that he was the *Messiah* and yet the most humble Title that he could choose, and that which could give the least Offence. But though he calls himself *the Son of of Man,* he afcribes to this *Son of Man* fuch Actions, and Powers, as plainly denote him to be more than *Man.* ᵈ This *Son of Man came down from Heaven:* ᵉ *he had Power on Earth to forgive Sins.* ᶠ *Angels fhould be feen afcending and defcending on this Son of Man;* ᵍ and he himfelf fhould be *feen afcending up where he was before.* ʰ *No Man* (faith our *Lord* to *Nicodemus*) *hath afcended up to Heaven, but he that came down from Heaven, even the Son of Man, which is in Heaven.* —ⁱ This *Son of Man fhould come in his Glory, and all the holy Angels with him, and fhould reward every Man according to his Works.*——ᵏ This *Son of Man* was alfo *the Son, the Only-begotten Son of God.* And we find that during his whole Miniftry ˡ he fpake with *Authority:* and both delivered Doctrines, and wrought Miracles, in his own Name. ᵐ *Verily I fay unto you*—was the Form, in which he ufhered in his Precepts. And he took on him by his own Authority to explain, and add to, the Laws of *God* himfelf. And in the fame authoritative Manner he wrought his Miracles.

ᵈ John vi. 3, 8. ᵉ Matt. ix. 6. ᶠ John i. 51.
ᵍ John vi. 62. ʰ iii. 13. ⁱ Matt. xxv. 31.—xvi. 27.
ᵏ John iii. 16. ˡ Matt. vii. 29. ᵐ Matt. v. 18. &c.

To the Man sick of the Palsy he said—" *Arise, take up thy Bed; thy Sins be forgiven thee.*—And, when the *Jews* accused him of *Blasphemy*, because he took upon him to *forgive Sins*, which was the Prerogative of *God only*, he answered that by the same Power, by which he wrought his Miracles, he was empowered *to forgive Sins also.* ° To *the Leper*, who said, *Lord, if thou wilt thou canst make me clean,* he said—*I will: be thou clean.*——
ᵖ To the *Dead he said—I say unto thee, Arise.*
ᑫ *He* also *rebuked the Wind, and said unto the Sea---Peace, be still: and the Wind, and the Sea, obeyed him.*—ʳ And he *commanded with Authority even the unclean Spirits, saying, Come out of the Man, thou unclean Spirit.*— And this is a Power, which no Man, either before, or since, either assumed, or exercised.
ˢ Though *Moses* is said to be *made a God to Pharaoh*, yet he wrought no Miracles, and delivered no Doctrines, in his own Name. His Miracles are expresly ascribed to *the Lord*, and his Laws all delivered by *God* himself. The Prophets none of them spake in their own Name, but in the Name of *the Lord*.

ⁿ Matt. ix. 2, &c.—Mar. ii. 3, &c.   ° Matt. viii. 2, &c.
ᵖ Mark v. 41.   Luke vii. 14.   ᑫ Mark iv. 39.
ʳ Mark i, 27.—v. 8,   ˢ Exod. vii. 1.

The

The Form they used was——*Thus saith the Lord.* [t] And the Apostles declare that they wrought their Miracles, *not by their own Power, or Holiness,* but *by the Name of Jesus Christ.* Another Means he used of notifying his *Divinity* was by calling *God* in a particular Manner his *Father* on all Occasions. [u] He calls himself *the Son of God,* [w] *his one Son, his Well-beloved,* [x] *his Only-begotten Son;* and his Apostle calls him *his own proper Son.*

[y] If such Titles as these import not an Equality of Nature, it will be hard to say what Idea they were designed to convey to us. Other Beings may be, and have been, called the *Sons of God* in a figurative, and improper Sense. But he, who is *God's own proper Son, his one, his Only-begotten Son,* is the *Son of God* in such a Sense as no Creature is, or can be. Again, [z] our *Saviour* thus addressed himself to the *Jews,* who accused him

---

[t] Acts iii. 12, &c. [u] Matt. xxvi. 63, 64. Luke xxii. 70. John v. 17, &c.—ix. 35, &c.—x. 25, &c.
[w] Mar. xii. 6. [x] John iii. 16, 18.—ιδιυ υιε, Rom. viii. 32. See also Matt. iii. 17.—xvii. 5. John i. 14, 18. 1 John iv. 9.
[y] See my Vindication, p. 10, 11. *Bull* Judic. Eccl. Cathol. C. v. *Pearson* on the Creed, p. 138, &c.
[z] John v. 17, &c. See my Vindic. p. 38, &c.

of *breaking the Sabbath,* by *healing an impotent Man* on that Day—— *My Father worketh hitherto, and I work*---*The Jews,* offended at this Speech, *fought to kill him, becauſe he not only had broken the Sabbath, but ſaid alſo that God was his Father, his own proper Father*---Πατέρα ἴδιον---*making himſelf equal with God.* [a] That the *Jews* underſtood him to aſſume an *Equality,* not of Power or Authority only, but of Nature, is evident, becauſe their Charge is founded on his calling *God*---ἴδιον Πατέρα --- *his own proper Father.* But what does our *Lord* reply to this? Does he tell the *Jews* that they miſunderſtood him? Does he explain what he meant by calling *God his Father?* Does he deny that this imported an *Equality* with *the Father?* Something of this Kind ſurely it would have been proper, and neceſſary, for him to have done, had he been only a Creature. Inſtead of this he continues to make Uſe of the ſame offenſive Term; and that in ſuch a Manner, as to intimate ſtill more ſtrongly the cloſeſt Con-

---

[a] Dr. *Clarke* allows, that *it is very reaſonable to conceive that Jeſus in this Place, by calling God his Father in ſo abſolute, and particular a Manner might intend to hint to his Diſciples, what they could not then, but were afterwards to underſtand, that he was*—Λογος Θεος—*that Word, which was in the Beginning with God, and was God.* Script. Doctr. N° 580.

junction

junction between him and his *Father* ——— *Verily, verily I say unto you, that the Son can do nothing of himself, but what he seeth the Father do: for what things soever he doeth, these also doeth the Son likewise* ---ὁμοίως--- *For the Father loveth the Son, and sheweth him all things that himself doeth.*—— But does not our *Saviour* here *profess his Inferiority, and Dependence, that he received his Being, and all his Powers from God?* He does *profess an Inferiority and Dependence* with regard to his Office of *Messiah* here on Earth. Our *Lord* acted as *the Father's* Delegate, and Embassador, with regard to his mediatorial Office. He was sent by *the Father;* and did nothing but by his Commission. And this was very proper to insist on in Answer to the *Jews,* who had accused him of Blasphemy, that he had done and said nothing but by Authority, and Commission, from the *Father.* --- *Verily, verily I say unto you, the Son can do nothing of himself, but what he seeth the Father do.*-- And this surely would have been sufficient, had he been only a Prophet, or a created Angel sent on an Embassy to Mankind. To what Purpose then does he add --- *Whatsoever things he doeth, these also the Son doeth likewise --- the Father sheweth him all things that*

that himself doth---*the Son quickeneth whom he will*--*that all Men should honour the Son, even as they honour the Father.* Could a Creature with any Propriety, or Decency, assume to himself so much? Is it indeed possible that any Creature should be enabled to do *whatever the Supreme God doth?* and that too --- ὁμοίως---*in the like Manner*, or that *the Supreme God* should *shew* to a Creature *all things that he himself doth?* Can *Omnipotence*, or *Omniscience*, be communicated? or if they can, why may not also the *Divine Essence* be communicated? Again, would it not have been the highest Presumption in any created Being to require *all Men to honour him, even as they honour the Supreme God?* [b] But we are told that the *Jews*, when they accused our *Saviour* of *making himself God, and equal with God*, meant nothing more than his assuming a divine Power, and Authority, without any Warrant for it. But this is a Sense, which the Words will not bear. A false Prophet, who falsely pretends to speak and act by *God's* Authority, cannot be said thereby to *make himself God*, or *equal with God*. So far from this, that according to our Author himself,

---

[b] Apol. pag. 7.

he

he thereby *formally professes his Inferiority and Dependence upon God.* No: they charged him with *making himself equal with God,* because he *called God his own proper Father.* ^c At another Time they accused him of *Blasphemy, because he being a Man made himself God.* Their Meaning is so plain, that one would think it could not be well mistaken. A false Prophet might justly be charged with Lying, but surely not with *Blasphemy*: nor could he, by falsely speaking in *God*'s Name, be supposed to mean to make *himself God.* And ^d so also, when our *Lord* was brought before *the Chief Priests and Elders,* they charged him with *Blasphemy,* not for teaching *without Warrant,* but because he professed himself to be *the Son of God.* ^e And when our *Lord said unto the Sick of the Palsy, Son, thy Sins be forgiven thee,* the Scribes reasoned *in their Hearts,—Why doth this Man thus speak Blasphemies? Who can forgive Sins but God only.*—It is plain therefore that the *Jews* understood our *Saviour,* as assuming to himself a true and proper *Divinity.*

^c John x. 33.   ^d Matt. xxvi. 63, &c.
^e Mark ii. 5, 6.

But

But what shall we say to those Words of our *Saviour*, ' *that all Men should honour the Son, even as they honour the Father?*——Dr. *Clarke* paraphrases them, *that it is the Will of God the Father that the Son should be honoured with the same Faith, and Obedience* [to which I beg Leave to add--and the same Worship] *which he requires to be paid to himself.* ᶠ But Mr. *Lindsey* tells us, that the *Honour to be paid to him was not so much on his own account, as out of Respect to God, who had sent*

ᶠ *Grotius* thus remarks in his *Annotations* on this Passage— *Ut scilicet homines cognitâ hâc Filii potestate eum colant, ac revereantur* — *Tacite ostendit Christus quam intimus sit Patri : nam Deus honorem suum extraneo non concedit.*——To the same Purpose speaks Dr. *Whitby*, who also quotes a *Socinian* Writer *Woltzogenius*, who proves from this Passage the Necessity of worshipping *Christ*. See also *Waterland*'s Def. of Q. 19.

ᵍ Mr. *Lindsey* quotes *Origen* in Support of his Interpretation. He could not have referred to an Authority more directly against him. *Origen* is here pleading for the Worship of *Christ*, in Opposition to that of *Dæmons* and *Heroes*. He asks *Celsus what Command of God he could produce to honour such as God's*. On the other Hand, he says that *God had commanded Christians to honour the Son even as they honour the Father.*—— Does it not then appear, from Mr. *Lindsey*'s own Quotation, that *Origen* thought *Christ* was to be *worshipped?* But if we look a little farther we shall find him saying — If *Celsus had understood this*—*I and my Father are One*—*he would not have thought that we worshipped any other than the Supreme God*— *we worship therefore One God, the Father, and the Son.*

him.

him. But how does he infer this? If *the Father has sent his Son into the World,* and *he and the Father are one,* the *Honour,* which is paid to one, is paid also to the other, and *he that honoureth not the Son, honoureth not the Father which sent him.* Besides, the Question here is not what the Words, if taken by themselves, might possibly signify, but what they must signify, as here introduced. Our Lord was accused of *making himself equal with God.* If the Charge were false he would doubtless have positively, and earnestly, denied it. Instead of this, such Interpreters represent him as continuing to discourse in equivocal Terms, such as might give his Hearers room to imagine that he was *really equal with God,* only leaving himself a Subterfuge, and Evasion, whereby he might bring himself off: requiring *all Men to honour him, as they honour the Father* — but meaning no more, than what Kings and Magistrates, and all, to whom *Honour* is due, might claim: If we suppose our *Saviour* to be only a Creature, it would be difficult to reconcile such a Procedure, either with his Duty to *God,* or Sincerity to Men. But if he was truly and really *God,* this his Discourse is very proper, and pertinent. He vindicates what he had done by saying that he had not done,

done, nor pretended to do, any thing, but after the Example of, and by Commiſſion from, *God his Father.* And he gives full Proof that he had ſuch Commiſſion. At the ſame Time he departs not from his Claim, but all along gives ſtrong Intimation that he was really, what they accuſed him of *making himſelf, equal with God.*

In the ſame Manner our *Saviour* behaved on other Occaſions—[h] *As the Father knoweth me, even ſo know I the Father*—ſaid our *Lord* to the *Jews.* Again — [i] *My Sheep hear my Voice, and they follow me. And I give unto them eternal Life, and they ſhall never periſh, neither ſhall any one pluck them out of my Hand. My Father which gave them me is greater than all: and none is able to pluck them out of my Father's Hand. I and my Father are One.*——Strange Language this ſurely for a Creature: ſuch as I am perſuaded Mr. *Lindſey* would not uſe with regard to *his Sheep.* And yet he might, if they mean no more than that *God had ſent him,* and would protect him in the Execution of *the important Office committed to him.* The *Jews* certainly

---

[h] John x. 15.   [i] Ibid. ver. 27, &c.

understood him to mean that he was equal to *God the Father*. *They took up Stones to stone him:* and they said, *they stoned him for Blasphemy, and because that he, being a Man, made himself God.* But possibly our *Saviour's* Answer may be thought to imply that he was *God* only in an inferior Sense — [k] *Jesus answered them, Is it not written in your Law, I said, Ye are Gods?*—Had indeed *Jesus* stopt here, or had he gone on to plead that he was *God* only in the same, or a like Sense to that, in which Judges, and Magistrates, are styled *Gods*, there would then have been some Reason to believe that he was only a figurative, or secondary, *God.* And this doubtless, if he had not been really *God,* he would have pleaded. This would, on this Supposition, have been necessary for him to do, and that in express Terms, to avoid giving Offence to the *Jews,* and to clear himself from the Charge of *Blasphemy.* But instead of this, he proceeds still farther to offend them. He gives them to understand that he is *the Son of God* in an higher Manner, than those, *unto whom the Word of God came* of old. *If he called them Gods,* &c. *say ye of him, whom the*

[k] John x. 34, &c.

Father

Father hath sanctified, and sent into the World, Thou blasphemest, because I said, I am the Son of God.—This Answer of our *Lord* is plainly designed to evade the Malice of the *Jews,* and ward off their Accusation: and is yet so worded, as to intimate both his *Messiahship,* and his Superiority over all who are *called Gods.* He tells them that Judges, and others acting under *God's* Commission, are in *Scripture called Gods:* and therefore no Charge of *Blasphemy* could lie against him, because he said, he was *the Son of God.* But then at the same time he signifies to them that he had still a higher Right to this Title, *he whom the Father had sanctified and sent into the World.* He here continues to assert that *God* was his *Father* in a peculiar Manner, and that he was so, before he came into the World — *he whom the Father had sanctified, and sent into the World.* He adds another Reason, not to excuse, but to justify what he had said—*If I do not the Works of my Father, believe me not,* &c. He again calls *God* his *Father,* and appeals to his *Works,* as a Proof that *he and his Father were one.* And from hence therefore, he tells them *that they might know, and believe, that the Father was in him, and he in the Father.* We see here he neither

retracts,

retracts, nor excuses, what he had said before, nor does he say that the *Jews* falsely charged him with *making himself God*. Instead of this, he enforces what he had said in Terms equivalent — *the Father is in me, and I in him*.[1] His Answer therefore taken altogether, instead of a Denial, carries with it a strong Confirmation of his *Divinity*. But it may be said that these Expressions may signify no more than *God*'s Presence, and Assistance, always attending him, as in other Places of *Scripture* Men are said to *dwell in God, and God in them*. It is true that these Phrases, as indeed most others, may, as differently applied, have different Significations. We ought therefore here, as in the former Instance, to consider the Design, and Occasion, on which they were spoken. They

---

[1] This is no novel Interpretation. *Novatian*, an Author of the third Century, gives the same Sense of the Words — *Si illos,* inquit, *dixit Deos,* &c. *quibus vocibus neque se negavit Deum, quin imo se Deum esse firmavit. Nam quia sine dubitatione dixit Deos, ad quos verba facta sunt, multo magis hic Deus qui melior illis invenitur. Et nihilo minus calumniosam blasphemiam dispositione legitimâ congruenter refutavit. — Ita quod ad crimen blasphemiæ pertinet, Filium se, non Patrem dicit, quod autem ad divinitatem spectet ipsius, ego et Pater unum sumus dicendo, Filium se esse et Deum probavit. Deus est ergo.* De Trin. Lib. cap. 23. See also *Bull* Jud. Ecclef. Cath. Cap. v. f. 6. *Maldonat. Whitby* Annot. *Payne* Serm. on *John* x. 36.

were

were spoken by one, who had already given Offence by calling *God his Father*, and saying that *he and his Father were one:* they were spoken to the *Jews*, who accused him of *Blasphemy*, and *making himself God*. In such Circumstances therefore, if he had not been *God*, he surely would not have used such Phrases, as should seem to import his *Divinity*, and as he knew the *Jews* would understand in that Sense. They were, we see, highly offended, and *sought again to take him*. They understood him to mean that he was *equal with God:* nor did our *Lord*, either now, or (as far as we can find) on any other Occasion, vindicate himself, or correct their Mistake.

I shall produce one more Place, where our *Saviour* sets forth his *Divinity* in Terms still more plain. We find in *Joh.* viii. a Dialogue recorded between our *Lord*, and the *Jews*. ᵐ They were much offended at his speaking in such an authoritative Style—— *If a Man keep my Saying he shall never see Death:* and asked him—*Art thou greater than our Father Abraham and the Prophets*—*whom makest thou*

ᵐ John viii. 51, &c.

thyself?

thyself?—*Jesus* denies not the Consequence drawn from his Words, but vindicates it:— *Your Father Abraham rejoiced to see my Day: and he saw it, and was glad.*—The *Jews* understood him to mean that he was actually in Being in *Abraham's* Time. — *They said unto him, Thou art not yet fifty Years old, and hast thou seen Abraham?* Does our *Lord* then correct their Mistake? Does he tell them that he existed only in the divine Decree, as every one of them did? No. He asserts his Pre-existence in still higher Terms --- Verily, verily I say unto you, *Before Abraham was,* I AM. It is introduced with great Solemnity, as an important Truth ---*Verily, verily I say unto you:* --- and the Expression is remarkable--- πριν 'Αβρααμ γενέσθαι, ἐγὼ εἰμι--- Here is plainly an Opposition between γενέσθαι and εἰμι --- *Abraham was made,* was a Creature --- πριν 'Αβρααμ γενεσθαι --- but — I AM — 'Εγὼ εἰμι-- saith our *Lord*. He uses also the Present Tense—I AM—not *I was*—which the *Jews* could not but know was the very Expression which ⁿ *God* himself used to denote his necessary Existence. He could not well have declared to them, both his *Pre-existence* and

ᵃ Exod. iii. 14.

his

his *Divinity* in ſtronger Terms. And they accordingly did ſo underſtand him: *they took up Stones to caſt at him.* Here again then we muſt aſk, if our *Lord* was only a created Being, how came he ſo frequently to uſe ſuch Language, as he muſt know the *Jews* would interpret to be *making himſelf equal with God?* How came he to delight to border ſo near upon *Blaſphemy?* How came he to give ſuch unneceſſary Offence to theſe *Jews*, to exaſperate them againſt himſelf, and his Goſpel, without Cauſe, and ſo often expoſe his Perſon to Danger, without any conceivable Reaſon? If he was *very God of very God*, we need not wonder that he ſhould take all Occaſions of intimating this great Truth. But, if he was only a Creature, I could wiſh that thoſe who think him ſo would give ſome Account of this his Conduct. I ſhould be glad to ſee how they can, on their Principles, vindicate him from the Charge of Folly, and Raſhneſs, not to ſay Arrogance, and Preſumption.

Nay we find him diſcourſing in the ſame Style to his own Diſciples——° *He that hath*

° John xiv. 9. 10, &c.

ſeen

seen me hath seen the Father——*I am in the Father, and the Father in me.*—[p] *All things that the Father hath are mine.*——And, as they acknowledged him to be *the Son of God*, which the *Jews* thought imported an *Equality with God*, he accepted, and approved of, this their Profession. [q] *Nathanael* finding that he knew perfectly what was done in secret, cried out——*Rabbi, thou art the Son of God, thou art the King of Israel.*——[r] *Peter* acknowledged that he was *Christ the Son of the living God:* and our *Lord* approved of this his Confession. [s] *Martha said unto him, I believe that thou art the Christ the Son of God.* [t] *Thomas*, when convinced of the Reality of his Resurrection, *answered, and said unto him, My Lord, and my God.*——Mr. *Lindsey* would willingly explain away this full Acknowledgment of our *Lord's Divinity.* [u] He quotes an anonymous Writer, as saying that this was only an Exclamation of *Astonishment*, or *Thanksgiving to God, who raised Christ from the Dead.* [w] But the Words

[p] John xvi. 15. [q] John i. 49. [r] Matt. xvi. 16. [s] John xi. 27. [t] John xx. 28.
[u] Pag. 27.
[w] Dr. *Clarke* thus paraphrases the Text — *Thou art indeed my Lord, the same that was crucified; and I acknowledge thy*

 Almighty

will not bear this Senſe —— *He anſwered, and ſaid unto Him,* to *Jeſus:* and therefore *Him* he calls *his Lord, and his God.* And this Confeſſion of Faith our *Saviour* accepted, and approved of: by which Acceptance he declared himſelf both *Lord, and God.* ˣ And he himſelf, when interrogated by the High *Prieſt,* whether he were *the Son of God,* aŋſwered, *Ye ſay that I am.* What they meant by the Queſtion is plain. They thought this Confeſſion no leſs than *Blaſphemy.*

From what has been ſaid, we may find an eaſy Anſwer to all that our *Apologiſt* has objected on this Head. If our *Lord* does not ſay in expreſs Terms that he is *God,* yet he gave both his *Diſciples,* and the *Jews,* to underſtand as much, in Language not eaſy to be miſtaken, and which they well underſtood. If he *profeſſes his Inferiority,* and *Dependence,* we have ſeen in what Reſpects, and for what Reaſons he does ſo. He appeared on Earth in *the Form of a Servant,* ſent with a Com-

---

Almighty Power in having triumphed over Death, and adore thee as my God. And thus Dr. *Hammond — I acknowledge that thou art my very Lord and Maſter, and that is an Evidence that thou art the Omnipotent God of Heaven.*——See alſo *Whitby*'s Annot. *Pearſon* on the Creed, Art. ii. p. 131.

ˣ Luke xxii. 70.

miſſion

mission from *the Father* to reveal his Will to Mankind. It was necessary therefore that he should set forth by whose Commission he acted in this Capacity. If he says to his Disciples — [y] *the Father is greater than I* — the Context will shew in what Respect he speaks of himself. These Words were spoken by him to comfort his Disciples, troubled at the Prospect of his approaching Departure. He was now about to leave the World, and *go unto his Father*. He bids them *rejoice* at his Departure, because it would be the Means of advancing him to an higher Condition than that, in which, as Man, he now was. He acted here only in an inferior Capacity, and could do no more than what he was commissioned by the *Father* here to do. His Return to his *Father* would contribute to his Advancement with regard to his mediatorial Office, and enable him to pour forth greater Gifts on his Disciples. As *the Son of Man* therefore, sent by *God*, he was inferior to him that sent him --- *mittens miſſo* ---as *Grotius* expresses it. And in this Capacity it was also necessary for him to pray to the *Father*. *He was made in the Likeness of Man,* [z] subject

[y] John xiv. 28. See *Hammond, Grotius, Whitby* Annot.
[z] Heb. iv. 15.

to all the Wants and Infirmities of human Nature, Sin only excepted. [a] And therefore it became him, *in the Days of his Flesh, though he were a Son, to offer up Prayers and Supplications to the Father.* Nor could he, for the Reasons already alledged, teach or direct his Disciples to worship him, while he appeared here on Earth in the Form of a Man. He directed them to offer up their Prayers to *their Father which was in Heaven:* but we are not therefore to imagine that every thing, which our *Lord*, appearing in our Earth, and acting in his ministerial Capacity, attributes to the *Father*, is so to be appropriated to the Person of the *Father*, as to exclude the other two Persons in the *Trinity*. Nor is the *Lord's Prayer*, though an excellent Form, and Pattern of Prayer, designed to forbid us the Use of any other Form. If it does not direct us to pray to *Christ*, so does it not direct us to offer up Prayers in his Name, which yet Mr. *Lindsey* himself seems to think necessary. [b] But we are told that *our Saviour Christ seems in Words, as express as can be used, to forbid Mens offering up Prayer to himself:* and for this *Joh.* xvi. 23. is quoted —

[a] Heb. v. 7, 8.   [b] Page 121.

In

In that Day ye shall ask me nothing. But the Word in the Original is ἐρωτήσετε. The Verb ἐρωτᾶν, though sometimes it may signify *to petition*, yet in it's most common Acceptation signifies *to interrogate*, or ask a Question. And that it signifies so here is plain from what went before. ⁿ The *Disciples* had Doubts about the Meaning of what our *Saviour* had said to them, and *were desirous to ask him —* ἐρωτᾶν —— *Jesus*, who knew their Thoughts, ---*vi suâ divinâ* --- as *Grotius* says, tells them, that though *they might weep, and lament* at his Departure, yet *their Sorrow would be turned into Joy, and their Joy no Man should take from them.* Then he adds—*In that Day*—ἐμὲ οὐκ ἐρωτήσετε ὀδέν — ᵈ *In that Day ye shall have no Occasion to ask me any Questions.* The Words that follow begin a new Sentence, as appears by the Introduction—*Verily, verily I say unto you---whatsoever ye shall ask the Father* in my Name, he will give it you: and here the Word is not ἐρωτήσετε, but αἰτήσετε. His Design was to comfort his *Disciples*, grieved at the News of his Departure. He tells them that though they could not then apply to him personally for Information, yet they would

ⁿ V. 19, &c.   ᵈ See *Whitby, Hammond* Annot.

have

have free Accefs to the *Father* through his Interceffion, and *he would give them whatfoever they fhould afk.* ᵉ He had faid the fame thing before, and there the Expreffion was— *If ye fhall afk any thing in my Name, I will do it.*---And in this Senfe *his Difciples* underftood him. ᶠ They faid --- *Now are we fure that thou knoweft all things, and needeft not that any Man fhould afk thee* —ἐρωτᾷ— *by this we believe that thou cameft forth from God.*--- As he knew their Thoughts without afking, they were convinced of his Divine Power, and Omnifcience --- *Divinum eft introfpicere cogitata*---again fays *Grotius.*

And, if he gave no exprefs Command to his Difciples concerning his own Worfhip, yet I think it appears that they acknowledged his *Divinity,* and worfhipped him. I know the Word --- προσκυνέω --- often fignifies civil Homage : but what fhall we fay when we find it joined with an Acknowledgment of our *Lord's* divine Power ? ᵍ When our *Saviour* caufed *the boifterous Wind to ceafe, his Difciples, who were in the Ship, came and worfhipped him, faying, Of a Truth thou art*

ᵉ Ch. xiv. 13, 14.   ᶠ xvi. 30.   ᵍ Matt. xiv. 33.

the

the Son of God. ——[h] *The blind Man,* whom *Jesus* healed, when our *Lord* told him that he was *the Son of God, worshipped him.* —— [i] When our *Lord* was taken up into Heaven, and was no longer present with them on Earth, his Disciples *worshipped him.* St. *Thomas's* Confession, if it should not be allowed to be a proper Invocation, yet, as we just now observed, was an Acknowledgment of our *Lord's Divinity,* and accepted by him, as such.

Again, [k] our *Saviour* assures his Disciples, that, where *two or three are gathered together in his Name, there is he in the midst of them.* But our *Apologist* will have this to mean no more than---*it would be the same as if he were amongst them*---But this is not explaining, but adding to, *Scripture.* *I am in the midst of them,* and *it is the same as if I was in the midst of them*--- are two very different Propositions. But we are told *that our Lord could not intend to speak of himself as the God who heareth Prayer, is evident from his speaking of the Father in this very Place, as the Person, who was to grant their Petitions.* Our *Saviour,*

[b] John ix. 38.   [i] Luke xxiv. 52.   [k] Matt. xviii. 20.

as I apprehend, in this Place speaks of himself as Mediator, and of the *Father*, as granting our Petitions through his Intercession. We do not therefore infer immediately from this Place that he is *the God who heareth Prayer*. But we infer from hence his *Omnipresence*. *Wherever two or three are gathered together in his Name*, he is present, and may be applied to, as Mediator between them and the *Father*.

Lastly, [1] Our *Blessed Lord*, when now about to ascend into Heaven, assured his Apostles that *all Power was given to him in Heaven, and in Earth:* and gave them Commission to [m] *make Disciples of all Nations, by baptizing them in the Name of the Father, and of the Son, and of the Holy Ghost*. He here joins himself and *the Holy Ghost* with the *Father* in the same Form of *Baptism*, the most solemn Act of Worship, whereby all Nations were to renounce their false *Gods*, and be initiated into the *Christian* Faith. What must all Nations think was the Import, and Intention, of such a Rite, but that instead of all those *Deities*, which they had before

[1] Matt. xxviii. 18, 19.   [m] Μαθητεύσατε βαπτίζοντες.

bowed

bowed down to, they were now to ferve, worſhip, and adore, *the Father, the Son, and the Holy Ghoſt.* Baptiſm is, as I ſaid, undoubtedly an Act of Worſhip. It is a ſolemn Form of entering into Covenant with *God,* and dedicating ourſelves to his Service. Since therefore we are equally, and indiſcriminately, *baptized in the Name of the Father, of the Son, and of the Holy Ghoſt,* we devote ourſelves equally to the Service of each of theſe three Perſons. Here is no Diſtinction, or Limitation; no Intimation given that leſs Honour, or Homage, was hereby intended to be paid to the two laſt, than to the firſt of theſe three Perſons. I have before urged this Argument at large in my Vindication of the Doctrine of the Trinity, P. ii. pag. 54, &c. It has alſo been frequently inſiſted on by other Writers, as particularly by [n] Biſhop *Stillingfleet,* [o] Dr. *Waterland,* [p] Dr. *Berriman,* &c. See alſo [q] Mr. *Bingham's* Vindication.

And to this our Author has nothing to offer, but only Objections, which have been anſwered over and over again. [r] He ſays that

---

[n] Difcourſe on the Trinity, Ch. ix.   [o] Sermon viii. at Lady *Moyers* Lect.   [p] Sermon vi. p. 116, &c.
[q] Pag. 36, &c.   [r] Pag. 103.

our *Lord had taught his Disciples that there was One God the Father, and none other but he,* Mar. xii. 32. But---*the Father* --- is his own Addition: 'tis not to be found in the Text cited. We all believe there is *One only God, the Father unbegotten, the Son begotten of the Father, the Holy Ghost proceeding from the Father, and the Son.* [*] And with this our Belief of the *Unity,* the Doctrine of the *Trinity* has been frequently shewn to be no way inconsistent.

[†] We are told next, that the *Apostles* frequently *baptized only in the Name of Jesus Christ.* But how does this appear? His Examples from *Scripture* prove nothing. It will not follow, that because the *Name of Jesus Christ* only is mentioned, therefore the two other were omitted in the *Form of Baptism.* Nor can we believe that the Apostles did not obey our *Lord's* express Command, but altered the *Form of Baptism,* which he had prescribed, only because the Form; in which they baptized, is not on every Occasion expressed at large. As Mr. *Bingham* has observed before me, these general Expressions

[*] See particularly *Waterland,* Sermon iv. on this very Text.
[†] Page 105.

of being *baptized into Chrift*, or *in the Name of the Lord Jefus*, are applicable to all of us, who have received the *Chriftian Baptifm*, even when the prefcribed Form was ufed. And he might as well argue that, becaufe the receiving the Communion is fometimes expreffed by *breaking of Bread*, therefore there was no Cup adminiftred. And with the fame ingenious Writer I alfo obferve, that one of thofe very Inftances produced by our *Apologift* affords a ftrong Proof that the Apoftles *baptized in the Name of the Holy Ghoft*. We read, *Acts* xix. that *Paul, finding certain Difciples at Ephefus*, afked them whether *they had received the Holy Ghoft. And they faid unto him, We have not fo much as heard whether there be any Holy Ghoft. And he faid unto them, Unto what then were ye baptized? And they faid, Unto John's Baptifm.*

ᵘ But our Apologift tells us, that *the Nicene Council pronounced Baptifm to be invalid, that was not performed in the Name of the Father, Son, and Holy Ghoft* --- flatly contrary to what appears to have been fometime the Practice of the Apoftles themfelves. What does he

ᵘ Page 106.

mean that this *Council* first *pronounced the Invalidity of such Baptism*. This is contrary to all History. How often has it been proved that this Form of *Baptism* has been invariably retained in the *Christian* Church long before the *Council of Nice*, and always thought to import the *Divinity* of the Persons, in whose Name *Baptism* was administred, and that long before *the Council of Nice*. ^w *Justin Martyr* bears witness, that in his Time *Christians were baptized in the Name of God the Father and Lord of all, and of our Saviour Jesus Christ, and of the Holy Ghost*. ^x He tells us also that *Christians worshipped and adored* these three Persons, and therefore were unjustly called *Atheists*. *Tertullian* has a Treatise on *Baptism*, ^y in which he tells us that in *Baptism our Faith is sealed in the Father, and the Son, and the Holy Ghost*; and that *the Testimony of our Faith, and Covenant of our Salvation, is confirmed by Three*. The same ^z *Tertullian* in his Book against *Praxeas* says, that *our Lord commanded* his Apostles *to baptize in the Name of the Father, and the Son, and the Holy Ghost, and not in one only:* and that it was therefore the Custom of the

^w Apol. ii. p. 94.   ^x Ib. p. 56.   ^y C. vi.
^z C. xxvi.

Church

Church to *dip* the Perſon baptized, *not once only, but three Times, at the Name of each Perſon.* [a] *Hippolytus* in his Book againſt *Noetus* teaches *that we cannot otherwiſe believe in one God, unleſs we really believe in the Father, the Son, and the Holy Ghoſt; and ſays, that our Lord, knowing that the Father would be glorified only in this Manner, delivered, after he was riſen, the Form of Baptiſm to his Diſciples, ſhewing that whoever ſhould leave out one of the Three would not honour God perfectly, for by this Trinity the Father is glorified.*—— Origen [b] ſpeaking of *Baptiſm,* ſays that *it is the Fountain of ſpiritual Gifts, by virtue of the Invocations there made by every one, who dedicates himſelf to the Godhead of the adorable Trinity.* — And in his Comment on *Rom.* vi. 3. he obſerves that *what St. Paul here ſays of baptizing into Chriſt, does not denote any new Form of Baptiſm: for no other Form of Baptiſm was ever thought lawful, beſides that which was given in the Name of the adorable Trinity, according to the Command of Chriſt.* And St. *Paul* (he ſays) *is not ſpeaking of the Form of Baptiſm, but of Chriſt's Death, and our conforming to it, as ſignified in Baptiſm.*

[a] C. xiv. p. 16.   [b] Comment in *Joh.* p. 124.

Cyprian,

Cyprian, in his Epiftle to *Jubaianus*, fays that the *Form of Baptifm implies the Doctrine of the Trinity, in whofe Sacrament Nations were to be baptized.* ᵈ In the fame Epiftle he aſſerts, that *the Baptifm of Hereticks, who baptized in the Name of Chriſt only, was invalid. How* (fays he) *can ſome ſay that a Perſon can obtain Remiſſion of Sins, if he be baptized only in the Name of Jeſus Chriſt, ſince Chriſt commanded all Nations to be baptized in the compleat and undivided Trinity?* And he tells us that when St. *Peter* called upon the *Jews* to be *baptized in the Name of the Lord Jeſus Chriſt*, the Meaning was, *not that the Father ſhould be omitted, but that the Son ſhould be added to the Father*, in whoſe Name alone the *Jewiſh Baptifm* ran. There is another remarkable Paſſage in this ſame Epiftle. ᵉ He aſks *how any Perſon baptized by theſe Hereticks could be ſanctified, and made the Temple of God?* Of what God (fays he) is he made the Temple? *If of the Creator, he cannot be ſo, who doth not believe in him. If of Chriſt, he cannot be his Temple, who denies Chriſt to be God. If of the Holy Ghoſt : but ſince* ᶠ *theſe three are one, how can he be at*

_c Epiſt. 73. p. 200.   ᵈ Ibid. p. 205—6.
ᵉ P. 203.   ᶠ Here is a plain Reference to 1 John v. 7.

Peace

Peace with the Holy Ghost, who is at Enmity with the Father, or the Son? ᵍ It appears then from these early Writers, that the Form of *Baptism in the Name of the three Persons in the Trinity*, was constantly used in the *Christian* Church from the Beginning, and thought to import the *Divinity* of each Person, that it was judged to be the Practice of the Apostles themselves, and that no other *Baptism* was thought valid. And yet our *Apologist* would represent the *Nicene Council* as first pronouncing *Baptism to be invalid*, which was not given in this Form, and runs Riot upon these *Fathers for setting up their Wisdom against that of the Apostles*. But where has he his History? I have looked into the Canons of the *Councils of Nice*, and can find no such Decree. ʰ Nor did *Arius*, or any of his Followers before *Eunomius*, use any other than the common Form of *Baptism*. There is indeed one Canon, the 19th, which ordains that the *Paulianists shall be re-baptized*: but the Reason for this is not specified in the Canon. And they seem to refer to a Decision which had been made before. There

---

ᵍ See also *Bingham* Antiq. B. xi. C. 3. sect. 2, 3. *Waterland* Serm. on Matt. xxviii. 19.
ʰ *Bingham* Ibid. sect. 11.

had

had been a great Difpute in the Church in the preceding Century about the *Re-baptization of Hereticks*. *Cyprian*, and others, had contended that all *Baptifm* given by *Hereticks* was invalid. This Point was fettled in the Council of *Arles*, held before that of *Nice*. They ordained that thofe only fhould be *re-baptized*, who had not been *baptized in the Name of the Father, Son, and Holy Ghoft*. And this, as we have already feen, was always thought neceffary. [i] This is alfo afferted in the *Apoftolical Canons*, which, though not enacted by the *Apoftles*, are judged by learned Men to be more ancient than the *Council of Nice*. They ordain that *the Bifhop, or Prieft, who does not baptize into the Father, and the Son, and the Holy Ghoft, and perform the three Ablutions of one Myftery, but only one Ablution into the Death of Chrift, fhall be depofed. For* (fays the Canon) *our Lord faid not, Baptize into my Death, — but into the Name of the Father, and of the Son, and of the Holy Ghoft.*

We can ftill produce farther Authority from an Heathen Writer. [k] In the Dialogue

---

[i] Canon 41, 42.   [k] See Fabricius Biblioth. Græc. L. iv. c. 16. Voffius de Hiftor. Græc. L. ii. c. 11.

entitled

entitled *Philopatris,* afcribed to *Lucian,* but certainly the Work of an Author of the fecond Century, a *Chriſtian* is in a jeering Manner introduced, as catechifing a *Heathen.* The *Heathen* aſks him — *Whom ſhall I ſwear by?* The *Chriſtian* anfwers — *By the God that reigns on high; the great, the immortal, the heavenly, the Son of the Father, the Spirit that proceedeth from the Father, one of three, and three of one; theſe believe to be Jupiter, theſe eſteem to be God.* ¹ The *Adjuration* plainly refers, either to the Form of *Baptiſm,* or to the Profeſſions of Faith required of *Catechumens* before Baptiſm. And from hence it appears that Perfons embracing *Chriſtianity* devoted themfelves to the Service of the *Father, the Son, and the Holy Spirit;* and that the Doctrine of a *Trinity in Unity* was the received Doctrine among *Chriſtians* in thofe early Times.

ᵐ Nay the Form of *Baptiſm* carried with it fo ftrong a Proof of the Doctrine of the *Trinity,* that many of thofe, who denied this Doctrine, judged it neceſſary to baptize in an-

---

¹ See *Bull* Def. Fid. Nic. Sect. ii. c. 4. No 11. *Waterland* Serm. on Matt. xxviii. 19.
ᵐ See *Bingham* Antiq. B. xi. ch. 3. *Waterland* as above.

H   other

other Form, as particularly *Eunomius*, and probably before him *Paul of Samosata*. ⁿ Some of these *baptized into the Death of Christ:* ᵒ *others in the Name of the Father uncreate, the Son created by the Father, and the sanctifying Spirit created by the Son.* A modern Author, taken Notice of by ᵖ Bishop *Bull*, was pleased to suggest a Suspicion that these Words—*In the Name of the Father, and of the Son, and of the Holy Ghost*——have been added to the Text. And he makes Use of the same Argument, as our Author, *viz.* that *the Apostles baptized only in the Name of our Lord Jesus*. These were more daring, and impious, but yet more open, and consistent, than those, who retain this Form, and yet ᑫ paraphrase it away into no more than *receiving Men to a Profession of the Belief, and an Obligation to the Practice of that Religion, which God the Father has revealed and taught by the Son, and confirmed and established by the Holy Ghost*. And I wonder that Mr. *Lindsey*, who has altered so many things in our Liturgy, should retain this Form, *so flatly con-*

ⁿ *Socrates* Hist. L. v. C. 24.   ᵒ *Epiphan.* Hæres. 76.
ᵖ Posthumous Works Vol. iii. p. 850.
ᑫ Dr. *Clarke*'s Paraph.

trary

trary to what appears to him *to have been sometimes the Practice of the Apostles themselves.*

^r But our *Apologist* does not think that *from the Son, and Holy Ghost, being thus named together with the Father, their Equality to each other may be inferred,* becaufe in fome other *Paſſages of Scripture God and his Creatures are joined together.* To this old Objection I anfwer in the Words of the excellent Biſhop Stillingfleet : ——— ^s " Can any Man of Senfe
" imagine thefe Places contain a Parallel with
" a Form of Words, wherein Men are en-
" tered into the Profeſſion of a new Religion,
" and by which they were to be diſtinguiſh-
" ed from all other Religions ? In the former
" Places the Circumſtances were fo notorious
" as to *God* and the Civil Magiſtrate, that it
" ſhews no more than that the fame exter-
" nal Acts may be ufed to both, but with
" ſuch a different Intention as all Men un-
" derſtood it. What if St. *Paul* name the
" *elect Angels* in a folemn Obteſtation to
" *Timothy,* together with *God,* and the *Lord*
" *Jeſus Chriſt ?* What can this prove but

---

^r Pag. 107.   ^s Difcourfe in Vindication of Doct. of Trinity, C. ix. p. 219. The like Anfwer is given by Mr. Bingham.

" that

" that we may call *God*, and his Creatures to
" be Witnesses together of the same thing?
" And so *Heaven and Earth* are called to bear
" Witness against obstinate Sinners: may
" Men therefore be *baptized in the Name of*
" *God* and his Creatures?— So that these In-
" stances are very remote from the Purpose."

What our Author would infer from 1 *Cor.*
i. 13. I am at a Loss to comprehend. St. *Paul
did not baptize the Corinthians in his own
Name*—therefore—what?— If we had read
that St. *Paul did baptize in his own Name,* this
might have been to his Purpose.

†But our *Apologist* tells us, that his *Interpretation of the baptismal Form is confirmed by those Summaries of Christian Faith drawn up in the first Ages after Christ, particularly that called the Apostles Creed.*— And after quoting some ridiculous Reflections cast on this *Creed* by some foolish *Jesuits*, ⁿ he is pleased to say that *nothing could more expressly condemn the Doctrine of the divine undivided Trinity than this Creed of the Apostles; and hardly shall you meet with two greater Opposites than this Creed, and that which goes under the Name of*

† Page 108. ⁿ Page 112.

Athanasius

Athanasius—And yet he owns that *this Creed was not composed by the Apostles*; and thinks himself at Liberty to leave out of his *Liturgy* such Articles of it as he pleases. [v] In another Place he tells us, that *the Creed called the Apostles, and the other Creeds of those early Times, are a pregnant Proof that all Christian People for upwards of three hundred Years after Christ, till the Council of Nice, were generally Unitarians, what is now called either Arian or Socinian.*—We have here very confident Assertions without the least Proof. I defy him, or the subtlest *Jesuit* upon Earth, to point out any thing in *the Apostles Creed* contrary, either to the *Nicene*, or the *Athanasian Creed:* or shew any one Proposition in these latter *Creeds*, which is *condemned* by the former. If the Doctrine of the *Trinity* is not expressly asserted in *the Apostles Creed*, so neither is the *Unity of the Godhead.*—*I believe in one God* — says the *Nicene* Creed ——— *We worship one God* — says the *Athanasian:* ——— the *Apostles Creed* says not so much. Nor was this *Creed*, as our Author himself owns, composed by the *Apostles.* It is no other than the *Creed* of the *Church of Rome :* and it is

[v] Page 24.

not

not so old in it's present Form as the *Nicene Creed* is, Our *Apologist* refers us to *a Collection of Creeds to be found in* King's *Enquiry into the Worship of the Primitive Church*. I have not that Book by me: but I have the same learned Man's *Critical History of the Apostle's Creed*, where our Apologist may find a full Confutation of all that he has advanced on this Head. ˣ That learned Author has shewn that, though the greatest Part of this *Creed* is of early Date, yet *the exact Form of the present Creed cannot pretend to be so antient as the Days of the Apostles by four hundred Years*. ʸ He proves that this *Creed*, by calling *Christ the only Son of God*, sets forth that he is *the true and natural Son of God, begotten before all Worlds, in such a Way, or Manner, as never any other was, is, or can be*: and that *this Article of the Creed is coeval with Christianity itself, and denotes Christ's divine Nature*. ᶻ *Christ* cannot indeed be called *the only Son of God* in any other respect, but that of his *Divinity*. ᵃ He also says that *the Reason why so little is said of the Holy Ghost in this Creed, is because there was not so great a*

˟ Chap. i. p. 23, &c.   ʸ Chap. iii. p. 131, &c.
ᶻ See *Bull* Jud. Eccl. Cath. Cap. v.   ᵃ Ch. vi. p. 318, &c.

Controversy

Controversy in the Primitive Church concerning the Divinity, and Person, of the Holy Ghost; but that *his Divinity* was intended by the *Creed's* requiring us to believe in him, whereas we are only required simply to believe the other *Articles*..

[b] The learned Mr. *Bingham* in his Antiquities has given us a *Collection of the Creeds of these early Times*. The first I can find is in *Irenæus*. [c] He tells us that *Christians at their Baptism received a certain and unalterable Rule of Faith from the Apostles*, which was to believe *in one God, the Father Almighty, who made Heaven and Earth, and the Sea, and all Things therein; and in one Christ Jesus, the Son of God, who was made Flesh for our Salvation, and in the Holy Ghost, who spake by the Prophets* --- and then follows soon after, in the same *Creed* --- *that every Knee should bow, of things in Heaven, and things on Earth, and things under the Earth, to Christ Jesus, our Lord, and God, and Saviour.* We have several Forms of Faith in *Tertullian*; one in his Book of *Prescriptions against Hereticks*, another in his Book *De velandis Virginibus*. These, though not the same, yet differ but little from the

[b] B. x, C. 4.   [c] L, i. Cap. i. 1, &c.

Apostles

Apostles Creed. But we have still another in his Book against *Praxeas,* which is more full and express. [a] He there sets forth the Faith of *Christians,* as *believing in One God, but under this Dispensation, that the One God has a Son, his Word, who proceeded from him, by whom all Things were made, and without him nothing was made;* that *he was sent by the Father, and born of the Virgin, both Man, and God, the Son of Man, and the Son of God, &c.* that *he sent from his Father the Holy Spirit, the Paraclete, the Sanctifier of the Faith of all those who believe in the Father, the Son, and the Holy Ghost.* --- *This Rule of Faith* (he says) *was delivered down from the Beginning of the Gospel.* And afterwards he adds, that *we must keep the Mystery of the Oeconomy, or Dispensation, which disposes the Unity into a Trinity, the Father, and the Son, and the Holy Ghost---three of one Substance, State, and Power.* --- There is another Form of Apostolical Doctrine collected by Origen in his Book of *Christian Principles.* There, among other things, *Christians* are said to believe that *there is one God, who created all things;* that *Jesus Christ was born of the Father before all Creatures* --- that *being God, he was*

---

[a] Cap. ii.

made

made Flesh, and being Man, he continued the same God that he was before.—Lastly, he says that *the Apostles delivered that the Holy Ghost was associated to the Father and Son in Honour, and Dignity.* We have also among the Works of *Gregory*, commonly called *Thaumaturgus*, ᵉ a *Creed*, which he composed for the Use of his own Church, in which the Doctrine of the *Trinity* is most expresly asserted.—*There is One God, the Father of the living Word—And One Lord, One of One, God of God—And One Holy Ghost, having his Subsistence from God—A perfect Trinity, undivided, unseparated in Glory, Eternity, and Dominion*——— and a great deal more to the same Purpose. We have also another Confession of Faith of *Lucian* the Martyr, recorded by *Athanasius*, *Socrates*, and *Hilary*, which ᶠ (tho' the *Arians* falsely pretended there were some Expressions in it favourable to them,) plainly asserts the *Divinity* of *Christ*. It calls him *the Only-begotten Son of God, the God, by whom all Things were made, begotten of his Father before all Ages, God of God, whole of whole, One of One, Perfect of Perfect, &c.* ——— I

ᵉ See the Genuineness of this Creed vindicated by Bp. *Bull* Def. Fid. Nic. Sect. ii. C. 12. n. 2, 3.
ᶠ Ibid. Sect. ii. C. 13.

I shall

shall mention only one more, and that is the *Creed of the Church of Jerusalem,* as we have it in *Cyrill's Catechetical Lectures.* ᵋ This *Cyrill* was Bishop of *Jerusalem* about the Middle of the fourth Century. This *Creed* must be older than the Lectures, which comment upon it. It differs from the *Nicene Creed.* It has not those Articles, by which the *Nicene* Fathers guarded against the Errors of *Arius,* as — *consubstantial* — *very God of very God;* — and therefore must be more antient than this Council. It is probably the most antient perfect Form of a Creed publickly used in the Church now extant, and had been for some time the *Creed* of the Church of *Jerusalem.* And yet this Creed calls *the Lord Jesus the Only-begotten Son of God, begotten of his Father before all Worlds, the true God, by whom all things were made.* —— These are *the Creeds of those early Times,* which our *Apologist* refers to as *pregnant Proofs, that all Christian People before the Council of Nice were Arians, or Socinians.* ʰ But he thinks it *absolutely necessary that the less learned should be told so.* For these indeed his Performance is calculated. It is

ᵋ See *Bull* Jud. Eccl. Cath. C. vi.

the

the *unlearned and unstable* only that he can hope to beguile. But let me defire this *Instructor of the foolish and unlearned* to *teach himself.* Let him, if it is not too much Trouble, look into some of the Authors cited in the Margin [1].

The fame Writers will inform him, that *Creeds* were originally Confeſſions of Faith made at Baptifm; that in all Probability they at firſt contained no more than the Form of Baptifm itſelf — *I believe in the Father, the Son, and the Holy Ghoſt.* —— And this was more expreſſive of the *Divinity* of each Perſon than the more enlarged *Creeds*, whoſe additional Articles disjoined the Names of the three Perſons, but ſtill retaining the Expreſſion of *believing in* each Perſon. Soon after, other Articles were added, guarding againſt ſuch Errors, as from time to time ſprang up. Some of theſe Articles were probably inſerted in the Days of the Apoſtles themſelves.

[1] *Voſſius* de tribus Symbolis Diſſert. i. *Uſher* de Rom. Eccleſ. Symbol. Apoſt. Vet. *Bull* Jud. Eccleſ. Cath. Cap. iv. iv, v, vi. *Bingham* Antiq. B. x. Ch. 3 & 4. *King* Crit. Hiſt. of the Apoſtles Creed. *Wall* Hiſt. of Infant Baptiſm, P. ii. Ch. 9. ſ. 10, &c. *Stillingfleet* Vindic. Doct. Trin. Ch. ix. *Waterland* Sermon Matt. xxviii. 19. Import. Doct. Trin. Ch. vi.

These *Creeds* were different in different Churches. In the *Roman Creed* the Article of—*Maker of Heaven and Earth*—was probably designed to guard against those who held that the World was made by Angels, or by some evil Being. The several Articles relative to our *Lord*'s Birth, and Crucifixion, might be designed to exclude those Hereticks, who denied our *Lord* to be really Man. In this *Creed* they thought it sufficient to set forth our *Lord's Divinity*, by calling him *the only Son of God*; a Title, which can belong to no Creature. In the *Oriental Creeds*, as in those Parts Hereticks arose, who denied the *Divinity* of our *Saviour*, this Doctrine appears to have been more explicitly expressed. The same Doctrine is contained in all the antient *Creeds:* and the latter are only explanatory of the former. We acknowledge then the *Apostle's Creed* to be an excellent Summary of the *Christian Faith*, but we cannot argue from it negatively. We cannot conclude that nothing is necessary to be believed, but what is fully, and explicitly, therein contained: nor any Error dangerous, but what is therein expressly condemned. Our *Apologist* might as well tell us that this *Creed* condemns the *Protestant* Religion, because the Errors of Popery

Popery are not therein so particularly guarded against, as in our Articles, and other *Protestant* Confessions of Faith.

I have now followed our *Apologist* through the *Gospels*: I come now to the *Acts*, and *Epistles*. The *Divinity* of our *Blessed Saviour* is set forth in many Texts there, and the Proofs thereof set forth by many excellent Writers; and our Author's Exceptions sufficiently obviated by Mr. *Bingham*, and the learned *Layman*. I shall therefore confine myself to such as relate to the *Worship of Christ*. We have already seen that *the Disciples worshipped him* on his *Ascension into Heaven*: and soon after we find them offering up a Prayer to him — [k] *They prayed, and said, Thou Lord, which knowest the Hearts of all Men, shew whether of these two thou hast chosen.* [l] This Prayer is, I think, addressed to *Christ*, not only because the Word, *Lord*, was the usual Appellation, by which they were wont to address him, but because [m] the *Apostles* were his Messengers, and it was he,

---

[k] Acts i. 24.

[l] See *Whitby*'s Annotat. who brings Proof of this from *Woltzogenius*, a *Socinian* Writer.

[m] Matt. x. 1, &c.—John xx. 21.

and

and he alone, who appointed them. And therefore he was the proper Perſon to apply to, to fill up the Vacancy. ⁿ And afterwards St. *Paul* was ordained *Apoſtle* by the ſpecial Appointment of *Chriſt* himſelf, who appeared to him. ᵒ Accordingly in the Beginning of almoſt all his *Epiſtles*, he ſtyles himſelf *an Apoſtle of Jeſus Chriſt*, ᵖ and declares that from him he *received Grace and Apoſtleſhip*. And ᑫ St. *Peter*, and ʳ St. *Jude*, call themſelves *the Apoſtles of our Lord and Saviour Jeſus Chriſt* ˢ But to this our *Apologiſt* has two Objections; *firſt, becauſe in a ſimilar Paſſage that follows ſoon after, the ſame Apoſtles addreſs their Prayer in the ſame Terms to* God *the Father, Acts* iv. 24, 29. But there is not in this Prayer one *Term*, nor one Word, the ſame, but only the Appellation of *Lord*. And ſurely it will never follow, that becauſe the *Apoſtles* ſometimes addreſſed their Prayers to *God the Father* particularly, and called him *Lord*, therefore they never called *Chriſt Lord*, and never addreſſed their Prayers to him. But, ſecondly, *Grotius* is quoted, as concluding that this Prayer is addreſſed to

---

ⁿ Acts ix. 1, &c.   ᵒ 1 Cor. 1, &c. &c.
ᵖ Rom. i. 5.   ᑫ 2 Pet. iii. 2.   ʳ Jude 17.
ˢ Page 128.

God

God the Father, and not to *Chrift*, becaufe the Perfon here addreffed is faid to *know the Hearts of all Men*. But *Grotius* draws no fuch Conclufion. He fays indeed on this Paffage---*It is the Prerogative of God only to judge certainly of the Hearts of all Men*. And that is all he fays: he does not fpecify to whom he thinks this Prayer addreffed. *Grotius* moft certainly acknowledged both the *Divinity*, and the *Omnifcience*, of our *Bleffed Saviour*: and in his Comment on *John* ii. 25. where *Jefus* is faid to *know what was in Man*, he fays, that is, *in the inmoft Receffes of the Heart, which is the peculiar Prerogative of God*.—Nay, our Author himfelf acknowledges that *Chrift faith of himfelf*, Rev. ii. 23. *I am he, which fearcheth the Reins, and Hearts* —but then he adds, that *this is a derived Power*. And what then? If *Chrift* had this Power, whether *derived* or *underived*, there is an End of his Objection. He might be the Perfon, to whom this Prayer is directed. Nay, if *this Power was entrufted with him for the Government of his Church*, he muft be able to hear the Prayers of his *Church*. But I muft carry this Argument ftill farther. ᵗ *Chrift* had

---

ᵗ See Matt. ix. 4.—xii. 25. Luke ix. 47. John ii. 24, 25. vi. 64.

the

the Power of *knowing Mens Hearts, and Thoughts*, long before his Afcenfion. ᵘ He had juſt before given his Apoſtles Proof, and they had acknowledged that *he knew all things*. And therefore it is from hence moſt probable that he was the Perſon, whom they here addreſſed under the Character of him, who *knew the Hearts of all Men.* And we are not only taught in *Scripture* that *Chriſt* is *omnifcient*, but he in an emphatical Manner ſays of him-ſelf—ʷ *I am he which ſearcheth the Reins and Hearts*.— This Text our Author quotes, and at the ſame time acknowledges that it is *the Prerogative of God alone to ſearch the Heart of Man. Chriſt* is therefore *God* by his own Con-feſſion. I muſt indeed own myſelf at a Loſs to comprehend how the peculiar *Prerogatives of God* can be communicated to a Creature. If theſe Attributes are derived to the *Son*, ſo muſt alſo be his *eternal Power and Godhead:* and we muſt acknowledge him to be *God of God, Light of Light, very God of very God.*

The next Prayer addreſſed to *Chriſt* was by St. *Stephen* at his Martyrdom, ˣ when *he called upon Chriſt, ſaying, Lord Jeſus, receive*

ʷ Rev. ii. 23.   ˣ Acts vii. 58.

my

my Spirit. Our Author acknowledges it to be *unqueſtionable* that St. *Stephen addreſſed this Prayer to the Lord Jeſus.* But he is ready at an Evaſion: he tells us that *he ſaw him with his Eyes.*—But where did he ſee him? not on Earth, but in *Heaven*—what a Space between?——(to uſe his own Words) *He ſaw him with his Eyes*—but could he hope that *the Son of Man,* with ſuch *a Space between,* could hear him with his Ears.—A proper Anſwer this to ſuch a trifling Objection.—But to be ſerious. If our *Lord* could *hear in Heaven, his Dwelling-Place, the Supplications* made to him here on Earth, what better Proof can we deſire of his *Divinity?* It muſt be equally eaſy to him to hear thoſe who *ſee him not, yet believing* addreſs themſelves to him. Beſides this Viſion appeared to St. *Stephen* on the finiſhing his Speech. They afterwards *ran upon him, and caſt him out of the City, and ſtoned him.* This muſt take up ſome Time: and we have no Reaſon to ſuppoſe that the Viſion continued to appear to him at this Diſtance of Time, and Place, or that his *Lord Jeſus* was in Sight, when he addreſſed his Petition to him. But St. *Stephen calls him the Son of Man.* And

K   ſo

so do all of us call him. [y] But this *Son of Man* was also *the Only-begotten Son of God, perfect God,* as well as *perfect Man.* No other *Son of Man* could hear, or grant, such a Petition — *Lord Jesus receive my Spirit* — Was this a Prayer to be addressed to a mere Man? It was a Prayer, that none was able to grant, but *the God of the Spirits of all Flesh.* It is the same Prayer, which our *Lord* himself made to his *Father,* when, now expiring on the Cross, [z] *he cried with a loud Voice, Father into thy Hands I commend my Spirit.*— And what adds great Confirmation to what is here said, is that [a] it was customary for the *Christian* Martyrs to direct their last Prayers personally to *Christ,* after the Example of St. *Stephen.*

[b] By the same Evasion our *Apologist* would explain away another Passage of *Scripture* where Worship is offered to our *Blessed Saviour* in the fifth Chapter of the *Revelations.* But did he never read the whole Chapter? How then came he to pass by v. 8, where we read that *the four Beasts, and the four and twenty Elders, fell down before the Lamb,*

[y] *Joh.* iii. 14—16.   [z] *Luk.* xxiii. 46.
[a] *Bingham.* Antiq. B. xiii. Ch. 2. S. 3.   [b] P. 130.

having

having every one of them Harps, and golden Vials full of Odours, which are the Prayers of Saints. Here we fee both Worſhip, and Prayer, offered to the *Lamb, the Prayers of all the Saints*—And at v. 13. the fame Worſhip is offered indifcriminately, both unto *him that ſitteth upon the Throne, and to the Lamb,* by all the *Angels and every Creature, which is in Heaven, and on the Earth—Bleſſing, and Honour, and Glory, and Power be unto him that ſitteth upon the Throne, and to the Lamb for ever and ever:*—*And the four Beaſts ſaid Amen.*—— But *this* our Author tells us *is no more than a Declaration of their Reverence of him.* No. *If falling down before him,* offering him up *Prayers,* afcribing to him *Honour* and *Glory* in the moſt folemn Manner, and jointly with *God Almighty,* is not *divine Worſhip,* it is not eaſy to fay what is *divine Worſhip.* 'This Viſion of St. *John* anſwers to the Appearance of *God* in the *Tabernacle,* and *Temple,* and is nearly the fame, which appeared to the Prophets [d] *Iſaiah,* [e] *Ezekiel,* and [f] *Daniel. God* is repreſented as *ſitting on his Throne in Heaven. Chriſt* is repreſented under his Character of Mediator by the Figure of

[c] See my Sermon on *Job.* xii. 41.   [d] *Iſ.* vi. 1, &c.
[e] *Ezek.* i, &c.   [f] *Dan.* vi. 9, &c.

a Lamb

a Lamb that was slain. His Exaltation under that Character is here represented, and the Homage and Worship paid him on that Occasion by Men, and Angels. But it is observable that, though he stands in that Capacity distinguished from him who sat on the Throne, yet equal Worship is paid to both without any Distinction. And the like Titles, and Appellations are given to both. Is *he who sat on the Throne* said to live for ever and ever? [g] so our *Lord* saith of himself — *I am alive for evermore.* As *the four Beasts* style *him who sat on the Throne Lord God Almighty, which is, and which was, and which is to come* [h], so our *Lord* assumes to himself the same Titles. As we read that *there were seven Lamps of Fire burning before the Throne, which are the seven Spirits of God,* [i] so in the preceding Chapter we read that our *Lord* is styled *he that hath the seven Spirits of God* [k]. Nay, *the Throne itself is called the Throne of God, and of the Lamb.*

[l] In the same Manner St. *Paul,* speaking of our *Lord,* says, that *God had highly exalted*

[g] Ch. i. 18.   [h] i. 8, 11, 17.   See Dr. *Waterland*'s Sermon on *Joh.* xvi. 15. P. 217, &c.   [i] iii. 1.
[k] xxii. 1.   [l] *Phil.* ii. 9, &c.

him,

him, and given him a Name, which is above every Name: that at the Name of Jesus every Knee should bow, of things in Heaven, and things in Earth, and things under the Earth; and that every Tongue should confess that Jesus Christ is God, to the Glory of God the Father. This Text so expressive of the Homage, and Worship, paid to our *Lord* by all Creatures both *in Heaven, and Earth*, Mr. *Linsey* only barely refers to. I shall therefore content myself with referring him to Dr. *Waterland*'s excellent Sermon on this Text.

And that our *Lord* was to be *worshipped* by *Angels*, as well as Men, appears from another remarkable Passage of *Scripture*, which our *Apologist* has wholly omitted. The Dignity of the *Son*, and his Superiority to the *Angels*, is asserted in very full and strong Terms in the first and second Chapter of the Epistle to the Hebrews [m]. He is said to be *the Brightness of his Father's Glory, and the express Image of his Person.* He is expressly called *God*, said to have *laid the Foundation of the Earth*, and created *the Heavens*; and to *uphold all Things by the Word of his Power.*

[m] *Heb.* i. 3, &c. See *Waterland*'s Sermons at Lady *Moyer*'s Lectures. P. 62, &c.—154, &c.

And

And *all the Angels of God* are called on to *worship him*. Afterwards we read——*thou madest him a little lower than the Angels*—or, as the Words may better be rendered—[n]*for a little Time lower than the Angels.*—*The Son of God* therefore was before his *Incarnation* superior to all *Angels*, and consequently no *Angel:* but was *God*, and *worshipped by all the Angels.* And if the *Angels* were bound to *worship* him, much more we, who bear a nearer Relation to him, he being our Redeemer, as well as our Creator.

The Apostles in their Epistles have not given us any particular Forms of Prayer, nor have we perhaps any direct Invocations of *Christ* in them: and nothing less it seems will satisfy Mr. *Linsey.* But we have full Proof that the *Christians* in those Days did worship *Christ*. *Christians* are described by the Title of *those who call on the Name of our Lord Jesus Christ* 1 Cor. i. 2. [o] But our *Apologist* has found out another way of translating this Term. He renders it, *all them that are called by the Name of our Jesus Christ*—and he has luckily the Authority of an able Commenta-

---

[n] Βραχύ τι. See *Grotius, Hammond.*   [o] P. 133.

tor,

tor, Dr. *Hammond*, to fupport him. But he might have known that this Interpretation of the Text is fully confuted by Dr. *Whitby* in his Annotations. One need indeed only turn to the Texts cited by Dr. *Hammond*. The Word ἐπικαλύμενος by itfelf indeed fignifies *called*, or *named*. And out of five Texts which the Doctor has produced, four prove no more, as *Matt.* x. 3.—*Luk.* xxii. 3.—*Acts* i. 23.— iv. 36.—And the fifth—*Acts* vii. 59. —proves directly againſt him. The Word— ἐπικαλύμενον is there plainly uſed not in the *Paſſive*, but the *Middle Voice*, and fignifies actively, *calling upon*, or *invoking:* and is by Dr. *Hammond* himfelf rendered—*He continued in Prayer to God*. And our *Apologiſt*, though he would expunge the Word *God*, yet allows it to be a *Prayer*, or *Invocation*. But the fame Verb ἐπικαλέομαι — with an *Accuſative* Caſe following it, ought, according to all the Rules of *Grammar*, to be conſtrued in an *Active* Senfe. Accordingly it always in *Scripture* fignifies, either *calling upon in Prayer*, or *appealing to*, as a Witneſs, or Judge. The learned Doctor has fucceeded very happily in interpreting the *New Teſtament*, by Compariſon with the *Old*, and with the *Septuagint* Tranſlation. I wiſh he had taken the ſame

Method

Method here. *To call upon the Lord,* or *upon the Name of the Lord,* is a common Phrase used in the *Old Testament* to signify *the Worship of God:* and is expressed in the *Septuagint* by the Verb—ἐπικαλέομαι—in the *Middle Voice.* Thus we read, *Gen.* xii. 8. *that Abraham built an Altar unto the Lord, and called upon the Name of the Lord*—ἐπεκαλέσατο ἐπὶ τῷ ὀνόματι Κυρίȣ—and so again—xiii. 4. and xxi. 33.—where it is expressed—ἐπεκαλέσατο το ονομα Κυρίȣ—*Isaac also built an Altar, and called upon the Name of the Lord,* as we read, *Gen.* xxvi. 25. where again it is translated—ἐπεκαλέσατο τὸ ονομα Κυρίȣ—[p] The same Phrase of *calling upon the Name of the Lord* is used in the same Sense in many other Places. Ἐπικαλεῖσθαι τὸν Κύριον, or τὸν Θεὸν is also used in many Places in an *Active* Sense to signify the *Worship of God.* The like Phrase is used in the same Sense in many Places of the *New Testament,* and particularly in those, on which the Doctor would put another Interpretation: and so he himself in his Paraphrase acknowledges. We have already seen this in *Acts* vii. 59. Again [n] St. *Peter* quotes the Pro-

---

[p] 1 *Kings* xviii. 24—1 *Chron.* xvi. 8.—*Psal.* lxxix. 6.—lxxx. 18.—xcix. 6.—cv. 1.—cxvi. 4. 17.—*If.* lxiv. 7.—*Jer.* x. 24.—*Lam.* iii. 54.—*Joel.* ii. 32.—*Zech.* xiii. 9.   [n] *Acts* ii. 21.

phecy

phecy of [r] *Joel*, and applies it to the Times of the *Gospel*——Πᾶς, ὃς ἂν ἐπικαλέσεται τὸ ὄνομα Κυρίȣ σωθήσεται — *Whosoever shall call upon the Name of the Lord shall be saved.*—In the Prophet the Phrase plainly signifies (as it does in all other places of the *Old Testament*) *the Worship of God:* and therefore must signify the same in the Citation. The same Prophecy is also cited by St. *Paul, Rom.* x. 13. another Text produced by Dr. *H.* which proves directly against him. For St. *Paul* applies this particularly to *Christ*. He was before speaking of *Faith in our Lord Jesus Christ*, v. 9, &c. and then adds, v. 12. *The same Lord over all is rich unto all that call upon him.* Then follows this Quotation from *Joel*. And in the next Verse the Apostle adds—*How shall they call on him, in whom they have not believed?*——The *Apostle* is here speaking of *Christ*. To *call upon him* is therefore something different from, and subsequent to, *believing in him*; and can scarce signify any thing else but *worshipping him*. And Dr. *H.* renders it—they shall *constantly confess, pray, and adhere to Christ*. There cannot indeed well be a fuller Proof of the *Divinity of*

---

[r] *Joel.* ii. 32.

Christ,

Chrift, and the *Worſhip* due to him, than this Paſſage. The Prophecy of *Joel* is here applied to *Chrift*. He therefore is *Jehovah*: and it is our Duty to *call upon his Name*, and worſhip him. And he is here ſaid to be *Lord over all, rich unto all that call upon him:* ready to hear, and to grant the Prayers of all his faithful Servants. There is one more Text produced by Dr. *H.* where he would interpret the Word in a Paſſive Signification, *viz. Acts* ix. 14. where *Ananias* ſays to the *Lord*, who appeared to him,—*Here he (Saul) hath Authority from the Chief Prieſts to bind all that call on thy Name* — τῶς ἐπικαλουμένους τὸ ὀνομάσω—But the Doctor himſelf renders this Paſſage—*all that publickly avow the Worſhip of Chrift.*—And he refers to the ſame Phraſe, *Acts* xxii. 16. where he paraphraſes it—*joining with the Church in Performance of all Chriſtian Duties of Devotion to God.* It cannot here, nor at v. 21. ſignify *thoſe who were called by the Name of Chrift:* ‘for *the Diſciples* were not *called Chriſtians* till ſome Time after at *Antioch.* And for the ſame Reaſon in the laſt-cited Text, *Acts* xxi. 16. where *Ananias* bids *Saul ariſe and be baptized, and*

‘ *Acts* xi. 26.

waſh

wash away his Sins, calling on the Name of the Lord—ἐπικαλεσάμενος τὸ ὄνομα τοῦ Κυρίȣ— muſt ſignify in an *Active* Senſe——*worſhipping the Lord.* Again, "*they that call on the Lord out of a pure Heart,* is a Phraſe uſed by St. *Paul,* 2 *Tim.* ii. 22. where the Word cannot well bear a *Paſſive* Signification, or ſignify any thing elſe but *the Worſhip of the Lord*[u]. The ſame Verb alſo --- ἐπικαλεῖσθε --- is uſed by St. *Peter,* to ſignify the *Worſhip of God.* In ſome other Places, both of the *Old* and *New Teſtament, the Name of God* is ſaid to be *called on* Perſons, or Things devoted to his Service: but here the Phraſe is different. The Word — ὄνομα — is here a nominative Caſe prefixed to the *Verb.* But, where the *Verb* — ἐπικαλέομαι---is followed by an *Accuſative Caſe,* it always ſignifies to *invoke,* or *worſhip,* excepting only where it ſignifies to *appeal to.* I know that Dr. *Clarke* would conſtrue it, as ſignifying only *believing in Chriſt, and acknowledging him as our Saviour.* But, if we conſider that the Phraſe in the *Old Teſtament* always ſignifies *the Worſhip of God,* and that in ſome of the Texts cited, as *Acts* ii. 21.— xxii. 16.—*Rom.* x. 12, 13.—2 *Tim.* ii. 22.—

---

[u] 2 *Tim.* ii. 22.   [w] 1 *Pet.* i. 17.

it cannot well bear any other Senſe, then we have the greateſt Reaſon to interpret this Text of 1 Cor. i. 2. in the ſame Senſe. And if ſo, we have not only one, but many Texts of *Scripture*, to ſhew that it was the Practice of *Chriſtians*, in the Days of the Apoſtles, to *call upon the Name of Chriſt, and worſhip him ;* and that this was the diſtinguiſhing Character, and Denomination, of *Chriſtians.* --- And what adds ſtill farther Confirmation to our Interpretation of this Text is, that in the Verſe immediately following St. *Paul* implores *Grace* to the Diſciples, *and Peace from God the Father, and from the Lord Jeſus Chriſt*. And not only here in this Epiſtle, but in every one of his Epiſtles he begins with this, or the like, Benediction. And he concludes his ſecond Epiſtle to the *Corinthians* with this ſolemn Bleſſing --- *The Grace of the Lord Jeſus Chriſt, and the Love of God, and the Communion of the Holy Ghoſt, be with you all. Amen.* ---[x] St. *John* alſo uſes the like Form. [y] Our *Apologiſt* may call theſe *pious Wiſhes:* but I muſt beg leave to call them ſolemn Benedictions. That St. *Paul* ſhould ſo conſtantly join *our Lord Jeſus Chriſt*

[x] 2 *Joh.* 3. [y] P. 132.

ſo

so closely with *God the Father*, and implore *Grace*, *Mercy*, and *Peace*, not only by him, but *from him*, seems to me to carry a strong Proof that he was the Author of *Grace* and *Peace*; and that *from him Christians* might, and ought, to ask these Blessings. But to this our Author objects, that *Rev.* i. 4. St. *John* prays for *Grace* and *Peace*, not only *from God the Father, and Jesus Christ*, but *from the seven Spirits which are before God's Throne*. But surely the Evidence arising from such solemn Benedictions, so frequently repeated, cannot be set aside by one obscure Passage in the *Revelations*. It is much questioned what is to be understood by these *seven Spirits*. [z] Dr. *Lightfoot*, and other learned Men, are of Opinion, that the *Holy Ghost* himself is here meant, who is called so in respect of his manifold Gifts, and Operations. *Grotius* thinks that *Grace, and Peace,* are here prayed for from *God,* operating by *seven,* or many, different Ways [a]. The learned Mr. *Mede* supposes these *seven Spirits* to be the *seven Archangels,* who more immediately attend *the Throne of God.* Dr. *Hammond* also gives the like Interpretation. If our *Apolo-*

---

[z] Vol. I. P. 341. See also *Poole's Synops.*
[a] Disc. x. P. 40, &c.

gist

gift is of the fame Opinion, yet let him remember that our *Lord* himself styles himself---*he that hath the seven Spirits of God*---[b] and *the Lamb* is described as *having seven Eyes, which are the seven Spirits of God:* and then let him consider who must he be who hath Power over the highest Angels.

The same Interpretation our *Apologist* puts upon 1 *Thess.* iii. 11. and 2 *Thess.* ii. 16. These are only *pious Wishes*. But are not these spiritual Blessings, which are here implored? and is not *God* the sole Author of such Blessings? Who can *direct our Way, make us to increase, and abound in Love, and stablish our Hearts unblameable in Holiness,* but *God* alone? Who can *give us everlasting Consolation and good Hope through Grace? who can comfort our Hearts, and stablish us in every good Word, and Work,* but *God* alone? And are not these Blessings equally implored of *God our Father, and the Lord Jesus Christ?* and are not they joined together in close Conjunction, as equally the Authors of these Blessings.

[b] *Rev.* iii. 1.   [c] V. 6.

(87)

To thefe we muſt add (though our *Apologiſt* has not thought fit to take any Notice of them) Forms of *Adjuration,* or *calling Chriſt, and the Holy Ghoſt, to witneſs* to the Truth of what is ſaid. [d] This has been always eſteemed an Act of religious Worſhip, and an Acknowledgement of the *Divinity* of the Perſon thus adjured. Thus ſaith St. *Paul*——[e] *I ſay the Truth in Chriſt, I lie not, my Conſcience alſo bearing me Witneſs in the Holy Ghoſt.* --- This Text Dr. *Whitby* thus paraphraſes --- *I call Chriſt and the Holy Ghoſt to bear Witneſs with my own Conſcience that I only ſpeak the Truth* --- And his Note upon it is --- *An Oath being an Act of religious Worſhip, in which God is called upon as Witneſs to the Truth, or an Avenger of the Falſehood, of what we teſtify, or promiſe, by ſwearing by our Lord Chriſt, and the Holy Ghoſt, the Apoſtle muſt perform an Act of religious Worſhip to them, and by that agniſe their Divinity*——*And by calling to them to bear Witneſs to the Secrets of his Heart, and Conſcience, he muſt aſcribe to them the Knowledge of the Secrets of the Heart of Man, which is the Property of God alone.*---And ſo alſo Dr. *Ham-*

---

[d] *Sanderſon* de Juram. oblig. Prelect, I. Sect. 3 & 4.
[e] *Rom.* ix. 1.

mond paraphrases it ---*I protest before Christ, and testify to you that Truth, of which mine own Conscience, in the Presence of the Holy Ghost, (that is privy to, and Searcher of Hearts) is Witness to me.*---To the same Purpose *Erasmus* ---*Quod res est loquar, teste Christo omnium conscio, neque quicquam mentiar, teste mihi meâ conscientia, cujus autor et inspector est Spiritus Sanctus* --- *Grotius* also interprets it to be *an Oath by Christ:* ᶠ and so do the Commentators in general. In like Manner St. *Paul* calls *Christ* to witness 2 Cor. xii. 19: ---*We speak before God in Christ.*---And again, 1 Tim. ii. 17.---*I speak the Truth in Christ, and lie not.* ᵍ Dr. *Clarke* interprets this ---*We speak in the Presence of God, Christ being our Witness.*

But farther, we have, I think, 2 *Cor.* xii. 8. an Instance of the Apostle's direct Invocation of *Christ* in Prayer---*For this Thing* (says St. *Paul*) *I besought the Lord thrice that it might depart from me.*---ʰ Here our *Apologist* tells us positively that St. *Paul appears here to have directed his Prayer to God the Father*: but how it so *appears* he tells us not. Dr. *Clarke*

ᶠ See *Poole*'s Synopsis.
ᵍ Script. Doct. Trin. Nº. 698, 707, 735, 167.
ʰ Page 132.

is

is more modeſt. He ſays that *the Word is ambiguous, ſignifying either Chriſt, or God the Father.* But he allows that *it ſeems from the following Verſes rather to be underſtood in this Place of Chriſt.* I humbly think it more than ſeems ſo. For in the next Verſe we read thus —that *the Lord ſaid unto me, My Grace is ſufficient for thee: for my Strength*— ἡ δύναμις μȣ—is made *perfect in Weakneſs.* And then it follows —*Moſt gladly therefore will I rather glory in my Infirmities, that the Strength*— ἡ δύναμις —*of Chriſt may reſt upon me.* It was then *the Power of Chriſt,* that *was made perfect in his Weakneſs.* And therefore it was *Chriſt,* to whom he prayed, and who anſwered his Prayer [k].

[k] But our *Apologiſt* would form an Argument againſt our *Lord's Divinity* from his being *a Mediator between God and Man.* I ſhould draw juſt the contrary Inference. [l] *He is now paſſed into the Heavens:* and if we cannot apply to him there, how can he be our *Mediator?* How can we *have an Acceſs to the Father by him,* if we can have no *Acceſs* to him himſelf? [m] *He ever liveth to make In-*

---

[i] See *Grotius, Whitby* Annot. *Poole*'s Synopſis.
[k] P. 26.　　[l] *Heb.* iv. 14.　　[m] vii. 25, &c.

terceſſion

tercession for us: but how shall he *intercede for us,* if he can neither hear our Prayers, nor be sensible of our Wants? The *Jewish High Priests* could not *continue by Reason of Death:* but *the Son* is *consecrated for evermore.* ⁿ *He is entered into Heaven,* and *appears in the Presence of God for us,* and offers up our Prayers to him there. As our *Mediator,* and *High-Priest,* he is a distinct Person from *God the Father.* But he is *the Son of God, God of God.* And as such °he *is a Discerner of the Thoughts and Intents of the Heart:* and *all Things are naked, and opened to his Eyes.* As *Man* he was subject to the Infirmities of human Nature: and as *God,* he knows all our Wants, and Infirmities. ᵖ And therefore we are encouraged to *come boldly unto the Throne of Grace, that we may obtain Mercy, and find Grace to help in Time of Need.*

But there is another Species of Worship besides that of Invocation. ᑫ We find in the Book of *Revelations* all Creatures *worshipping him that liveth for ever and ever, by giving Glory, Honour, and Thanks to him.* For *Worship* is paid to *God,* and his *divine* Perfections

---

ⁿ Heb. ix, 24.   ° iv. 12, 13.   ᵖ v. 16.
ᑫ Rev. iv. 9, 10.

acknowledged,

acknowledged, as much by giving Praise, and Glory, to him, as by offering him Prayers, and Supplications. And accordingly *Doxologies* have had a Place in all *Liturgies:* and been generally put at the Conclusion of Hymns, and Prayers. The Apostles probably established Forms of Worship in every Church: but we have none delivered down to us in *Scripture*. We have *Doxologies:* but they run in different Forms: and so I suppose they did in the antient *Liturgies*. We have already had Occasion to take Notice of a very full one *Rev.* v. 13, where we find the whole Creation joining in giving *Blessing, and Honour, and Glory, and Power, unto him that sitteth upon the Throne, and unto the Lamb, for ever and ever.* And so again Chap. vii. 9. we are told that *a great Multitude of all Nations cried with a loud Voice, saying, Salvation to our God which sitteth upon the Throne, and unto the Lamb.* — St. *Paul* in his Epistles uses different Forms of giving *Glory to God.* ʳ Sometimes he gives *Glory to God in general,* ˢ sometimes to the *Father* in particular, ᵗ sometimes to the *Father through the Son.* ᵘ In other Places it is uncertain whether the *Father* is

---
ʳ *Rom.* xi. 36. — 2 *Tim.* iv. 18.   ˢ 1 *Phil.* iv. 20.
ᵗ *Rom.* xvi. 7. — *Eph.* i. 21.   ᵘ *Gal.* i. 3.

spoken of, or the *Son*. But in some Places *Glory* is given to the *Son* only. Thus *Heb.* xiii. 20, 21. — *The God of Peace make you perfect in every good Work to do his Will, working in you that which is well-pleasing in his Sight through Jesus Christ, to whom be Glory for ever and ever, Amen.* —— These last words must in all reasonable Construction be referred to the immediate Antecedent — *Jesus Christ.* — St. *Peter* is still more plain — " *Grow in Grace, and in the Knowledge of our Lord and Saviour Jesus Christ. To him be Glory both now, and for ever, Amen.* — And so also *Rev.* i. 5, 6. we have this *Doxology* — *Unto him that loved us, and washed us from our Sins in his own Blood, and hath made us Kings and Priests unto God, and his Father, to him be Glory, and Dominion, now and for ever. Amen.* — But here we are told that *there are so many different Readings of this Passage, that no certain Conclusions can be drawn from it.* — I have looked into Dr. *Mill's New Testament*, and can find no various Readings that much alter the Sense, excepting one, and that is only in one MS. which reads — τῦ ἀγαπήσαντος ϗ λύσαντος — And even according to this Reading the *Doxology* more

properly

---

w 2 *Pet.* iii. 18. It ought not however to be concealed that some MSS. add here — καὶ Θεῦ Πατρος.

properly belongs to *Chrift* the Perſon ſpoken of before, and alſo in the Words immediately following — *Behold he cometh with Clouds,* &c. — The *Doxology* alſo 2 *Tim.* iv. 18. according to Dr. *Clarke,* ſeems rather to be meant of *Chrift.* And ſo, I think, is that which we have *Jud.* 25. But theſe I paſs by as ambiguous.

ˣ If we enquire into the *Doxologies* uſed in the ancient Church, we ſhall find them different in Form : but all, or moſt of them, addreſſed to the *Son,* and to the *Holy Ghoft,* as well as the *Father.* The moſt ancient Form ran — *To the Father, and to the Son, and to the Holy Ghoft.* — ʸ *Clemens* Biſhop of *Rome,* ᶻ St. *Paul's Fellow-labourer,* thus expreſſes himſelf — *We who fly to his (God's) Mercies through Jeſus Chrift our Lord, to whom be Glory, and Majefty throughout all Ages.* —— The antient Account we have of the Martyrdom of *Ignatius* concludes thus — *Jeſus Chrift our Lord, by whom, and with whom, be Glory and Dominion to the Father, with the Holy Ghoft for ever, Amen.* In like manner con-

---

ˣ See *Bingham.* Antiq. L. xiv. Ch. 2. S. 1.
ʸ Epiſt. i. ad *Corinth.* S. 20.   ᶻ *Phil.* iv. 3.

cludes ᵃ the Epiſtle of the *Church of Smyrna* concerning the Martyrdom of St. *Polycarp — Jeſus Chriſt, to whom be Glory, with the Father, and the Holy Ghoſt, throughout all Ages.* — And in the ſame Epiſtle we have a Prayer, which *Polycarp* offered up to *God* at his Martyrdom, which concludes thus —— *I praiſe, and glorify thee, with the eternal and heavenly Jeſus Chriſt, thy beloved Son, with whom to thee, and the Holy Ghoſt, be Glory both now, and for evermore. Amen.* — In the *Apoſtolical Conſtitutions,* which (though we do not, with Mr. *Whiſton,* ſuppoſe them to be written by the *Apoſtles,* nor by St. *Clement* of *Rome)* ᵇ are by the beſt Criticks ſuppoſed to contain the antient Offices of the Church, we find ſeveral *Doxologies.* In the 8th Book Ch. 12. the *Oblation Prayer* concludes thus — *To thee be all Glory, Worſhip, Thankſgiving, Honour, and Adoration, to the Father, to the Son, and to the Holy Ghoſt, both now, and for ever, and to infinite, and endleſs Ages, and let all the People ſay Amen.* — In the 13 Chapter of the ſame Book the *Prayer for the faithful* is thus concluded—*by thy Chriſt, with whom be Glory,*

ᵃ This Epiſtle is quoted, and no ſmall Part of it recited by *Euſebius* Hiſt. Eccleſ. L. iv. Ch. 15.   ᵇ *Cave, Du Pin, Beveridge, Bingham* Antiq. B. xiii. Ch. 5. Sect. 7.

Honour,

Honour, Praise, Doxology, and Thanksgiving to thee, and the Holy Ghost, for ever. Amen. —— In the 15th Chapter the *Invocation after the Communion* ends thus —— *To thee be Glory, Praise, Majesty, Worship, and Adoration, and to thy Son Jesus Christ, our Lord, and God, and King, and to the Holy Ghost now and for ever. Amen.* —— And most of the Prayers there are concluded with the like *Doxologies*. Again, *Clemens* of *Alexandria* thus concludes his last Book of his *Pedagogue* —— *Let us give Thanks to the only Father and Son, to the Son our Pedagogue and Teacher, with the Holy Spirit, one in all Respects, in whom are all Things, by whom all Things are one, by whom is Eternity, whose Members we all are, whose is the Glory, who is in all Things good, fair, wise, and just; to whom be Glory now, and for ever. Amen.* —— There follows an *Hymn to Christ*. [c] But, when the *Arian* Controversy arose, those of that Persuasion would use no other Form of *Doxology* but —— *Glory be to the Father, by the Son, and by the Holy Ghost* —— [d] St. *Basil* in his Treatise on the *Holy Ghost* proves at large that though this Form was sometimes used, and was very proper, when

---

[c] *Bingham*. Antiq. B. xiv. Ch. 2. Sect. 1. *Berriman* on Primitive Doxol. [d] Cap. vii, xxv & xxix.

rightly

rightly underſtood, yet the other was more common, and uſed by all the antient Churches. ᵉ What Reaſon then has our *Apologiſt* to quarrel with the Form of *Doxology* uſed in our Church? and what Occaſion has he to fall upon Arch-Bp *Secker*, who has given him no Provocation. The Arch-Bp in the Place cited ſays not a Word in behalf of our Form of *Doxology:* he pleads only for the repeating our Praiſes to *God* often; and to that End very properly introduces *Eph.* v. 20, where the Apoſtle exhorts us to *give Thanks always for all Things to God and the Father in the Name of our Lord Jeſus Chriſt.* But what Authority our Author has to add the Word — *only* — to the Text, or how he would infer from hence that no *Thanks* are to be given to the *Son,* or the *Holy Ghoſt,* I know not. Theſe *tacit Condemnations* and negative Arguments, I cannot comprehend the Force of. ᶠ As to the latter Clauſe of our *Doxology* — *As it was in the Beginning* &c. it was not ſo ſoon introduced, nor is it certainly known when, or where, or on what Occaſion it was firſt uſed: it appears however to have been at leaſt 1200 Years old. But ᵍ Our *Apologiſt* makes it ſtill

ᵉ P. 117.　　ᶠ See *Bingham* as above.　　ᵍ P. 113.

older,

older, and falls foul upon St. *Jerom* for *composing it:* and tells us that it *had an unchristian, and uncharitable, Origin*. But he should have known that these Epistles between Pope *Damasus* and *Jerom* are rejected as spurious by all learned Men. And, if it be *unchristian, and uncharitable*, to exclude *crafty Hereticks* from our Communion, who hold *the Son of God* to be a Creature, I am afraid the Charge will lie not only against those who added this Clause, but against the *Council of Nice*, all the *Ante-Nicene* Fathers, and St. *John* himself. Nor can I find what Right, or Reason, he has to find fault with this Clause. It is composed in the very Words of *Scripture*. —[1] *In the Beginning was the Word*, (saith St. *John*) *and the Word was God*. And therefore most certainly *in the Beginning Glory* was given to him. [k] Nay he himself hath told us that he *had Glory with the Father before the World was*. [l] And the same St. *John* has represented the whole Creation as giving *Blessing, and Honour, and Glory, unto the Lamb, for ever and ever*. Nay, he himself owns it to be reasonable [m] *to declare our Reverence, and high Esteem of him, and on all proper Occasions to join*

[h] See *Bingham* as above. xvii. 5.   [i] *Job*. i. 1.   [k] *Joh*.
[l] *Rev*. v. 13.   [m] P. 131.

with

with his Apostle in saying—*To him be Glory both now and for ever.* — Why does he then refuse to declare this? — Why does he strike out of the *Liturgy* almost every Clause that gives *Glory* to his *Saviour?* Why does he expunge this *Doxology*, which he might explain to his own Sense much more easily, than he can the first Verse of St. *John's* Gospel, and many other Parts of *Scripture?* [n] But we are told that it matters not much to inquire when this Doxology *was first used, or how long it had been used, if it is not in the New Testament.* —— I know of no Form of Prayer enjoined *in the New Testament*, but only the *Lord's Prayer*: and therefore according to this Rule we ought to use no other. But it has been shewn that in the *New Testament Glory, and Praise*, are offered up to our *Blessed Saviour*. And, if in some of these Places there be some Ambiguity, what better Method can we take of clearing up these Ambiguities than by enquiring into the Practice of the antient Church? This at least appears from the Examples produced that the first *Christians* worshipped *Christ*, and offered up their *Doxologies*, and gave *Glory to the Father, Son, and Holy Ghost.*

[n] P. 118.

And

(99)

*And yet our *Apologist* has the Assurance to tell us that all Christian People for upwards of 300 Years *after Christ, till the Council of Nice, were generally Unitarians, what is now called either Arian, or Socinian.*— ᵖAnd in another Place he is pleased to tell us that *it was the universal Practice of the Christian Church, with little or no Variation, for the three first Centuries, to address all religious Worship only to God the Father.*—— But herein he contradicts, not only all History, but himself too. ᑫFor he says that *Irenæus, and Justin Martyr,* two Writers of the second Century, *contributed to bring into Christianity the Platonick Doctrine of a second God:* ʳ and that *the Word Trinity was first used by Theophilus,* who wrote in the same Century. But what Proof does he bring of these confident Assertions? none from any of the Works of the most antient Writers. But he appeals to the antient *Creeds*, and to Dr. *Whitby*, who, if, you will believe him, *has confuted the Objections of Bull, and Waterland, with accumulated Evidence.* It has been already, I trust, fully shewn that all the Remains we have of ancient *Creeds* prove the

* P. 24. ᵖ P. 147, 8. ᑫ P. 158. ʳ P. 12.

direct contrary of what our Author here alledges them for. As to Dr. *Whitby* he was in the Vigour of his Age a zealous Affertor of the Doctrine of the *Trinity:* and in his Annotations has vindicated feveral Texts of *Scripture* from the Mifconftructions of *Socinus*. Some of his Comments I have had Occafion to refer to. He lived to a great Age: and in his latter Days, when Dr. *Clarke* wrote his *Scripture Doctrine of the Trinity*, he fided with him, and wrote a Treatife entitled —— *Difquifitiones modeſtæ in Bulli defenſionem Fidei Nicenæ*, —— wherein he paffes Cenfure on a Book, ᵃ which he had before in a Treatife on *Chriſt's Divinity* cried up as a moſt excellent Performance. Dr. *Whitby* was a Man of Learning, and had done good Service to the Church, and to the learned World. But we muſt appeal from Dr. *Whitby* in his Dotage to Dr. *Whitby* in his fober Senfes. As to this Treatife of his, I have it not, nor have I been able to obtain a Sight of it. I believe it is out of Print, and long ago buried in Oblivion. But this I find, that it has been fully anfwered by ᵇ Dr. *Waterland* in his Firſt Defence of his

---

ᵃ Opus ære perennius ad doctorum invidiam, et novatorum cordolium fummo judicio et induſtriâ peregit. P. 59.

ᵇ Q. xxvi. P. 399, &c.

Queries

Queries. The Dr. has therein fully expofed his notorious Fallacies, Mifconftructions, and falfe Quotations, as any one may fee, who will take the Pains to look into that Treatife. The Dr. thus concludes his Remarks — *You may perceive by this Time that Bp Bull's Book is like to ftand, till fomething much more confiderable appears againft it. Several Attempts of this Kind have been made before: but to as little Purpofe. And if there be ever fo many more, by ever fo good Hands, I'll venture to fay, they will fucceed no better. The Book will ftand as long as clear Senfe, found Reafoning, and true Learning have any Friends left. The main Subftance of it is not to be confuted, any more than you can extinguifh Truth, or put out the Light of the Sun.* I think that Dr. *Whitby* made fome Reply to this: but whatever he had to fay has been fully anfwered by Dr. *Waterland*. When our *Apologift* then will produce this *accumulated Evidence*, it will be then Time enough to confider it. But by what I have feen of it in the Treatife above-cited, it feems to deferve very little Notice. — "But our *Apogift* refers us to *Dr. Clarke's Obfervations on Dr. Waterland's fecond Defence of his Queries,*

[u] Page 66.

which,

which, it seems, fully confuted Dr. *Waterland*, and closed the Controversy. But he is much mistaken. These *Observations* were not, I think, Dr. *Clarke*'s, but Mr. *Jackson*'s, and were fully answered by Dr. *Waterland* in a Pamphlet entitled, *A farther Vindication of Christ's Divinity* — to which I do not find that the Author made any Reply.

But we need not rely on the Authority of Dr. *Whitby*, Dr. *Waterland*, or Bp *Bull*. We have the Works of the *Primitive Fathers* before us. ʷ It has been already shewn that they held that it was the *Son of God*, who appeared to the *Patriarchs*, and was worshipped by them, and they from thence infer his *Divinity*. We have seen also that they looked on the *Form of Baptism* as a Profession of their Belief in the *Trinity*; that their antient *Creeds* teach the same Doctrine, and that their *Doxologies* were addressed in the most solemn Manner to the *Son*, and the *Holy Ghost*, as well as to the *Father*. But for the farther Information of *the less learned*, the Rev. Mr. *Lindsey* himself amongst the rest, I shall add a few more Proofs from some of the most early

---

ʷ Page 11, &c.

Writers.

Writers. [x] *Clemens* Bp of *Rome* thus begins his second Epistle to the *Corinthians* — *Brethren, We ought to think of Jesus Christ, as of God, as of the Judge of quick, and dead, nor ought we to think meanly of our Salvation.* — *Ignatius* addresses the Church of *Ephesus as elected by the Will of the Father, and Jesus Christ our God:* [y] and in other Parts of the same Epistle he calls *Christ our God.* In the Preface of his Epistle to the *Romans, Christ* is twice called *our God.* And in the same Epistle S. 4. he desires the Brethren to *pray unto Christ for him.* He thus begins his Epistle to the Church of *Smyrna* —— *I glorifie Jesus Christ our God, who hath given us such Wisdom.* — And thus he closes his Epistle to *Polycarp* —— *I wish you all Happiness in our God Jesus Christ, in whom continue in the Unity, and Protection of God.* [z] And the antient Relation of this Saint's Martyrdom informs us that just before his Death *he prayed to the Son of God for the Churches.* — *Polycarp* in his Epistle to the *Philippians* prays that *the God and Father of our Lord Jesus Christ, and he himself the eternal High Priest, the Son of God, even Jesus Christ,*

---

[x] The Genuineness of this Epistle has been sufficiently vindicated by Bp *Bull*, Dr. *Cave*, and others. The Genuineness also of *Ignatius*'s Epistles has been vindicated by Bishop *Pearson*, and others. [y] S. 4, 15. S. 6. [z] S. 12.

would build them in *Faith*, and in *Truth*, &c. This is not only a *pious Wish*, but a Prayer to the *Son* jointly with the *Father*, and represents him, as well as the *Father*, as the Giver of all good Gifts. And the Epistle of the Church of *Smyrna*, which gives us an Account of the Martyrdom of this good Man, tells us that his Persecutors, *at the Instigation of the Jews, took care that no Remainder of his Body should be left, lest the Christians, forsaking him that was crucified, should begin to worship this Polycarp;* not knowing (say they) *that we can never forsake Christ —— nor worship any other. —— For him indeed, as being the Son of God, we worship. But the Martyrs we worthily love, as the Disciples and Imitators of the Lord.* —— ᵇ *This*, as the learned Mr. *Bingham* observes, *is an unanswerable Testimony, to prove both the divine Worship of Christ, as the true Son of God, and that no Martyr or other Saint was worshipped in those Days.*

Not long after lived *Justin Martyr*. ᶜ We have already seen that he held *Christ* to be the Person, who appeared to *Abraham*, and the *Patriarchs*, whom *Moses*, and the *Children of Israel* worshipped, and whom all the *Angels* adored.

ᵃ S. 17.   ᵇ Antiq. B. xiii. Cap. 2. S. 2.   ᶜ P. 11.

adored. ᵈ I have in my Vindication brought many Proofs of his Belief of our *Lord's Divinity*. I shall here content myself with citing a few, which bear Testimony to the *Worship of Christ*. ᵉ In his Dialogue with *Trypho*, after having brought several Proofs of the *Divinity* of our *Saviour* from the *Old Testament*, he adds — *These Words plainly shew that he is the Object of Worship, both God, and Christ* —— ᶠ Again in the same Dialogue he thus bespeaks *Trypho* — *Do you think that there is any other said in Scripture to be the Object of Worship, Lord, and God, but he who made the Universe, aud Christ, who is proved by so many Texts of Scripture to have been made Man?* — ᵍ Once more he says — *When David taught that he was begotten before the Sun and Moon, according to the Will of his Father, he shewed that Christ was the mighty God, and the Object of Worship.* — ʰ But we are told that *these early Fathers contributed to bring into Christianity the Platonick Doctrine of a Second God, which they had learnt before their Conversion to Faith.* ⁱ I know this has been said by *Le Clerc*, and others.

ᵈ Pt. iii. p. 28, &c. ᵉ P. 287. ᶠ P. 293.
ᵍ P. 302. ʰ P. 158. ⁱ See this Point accurately handled in a Dissertation by a learned Friend of mine in my Vindic. Doct. Trin. Pt. iii. P. 50, &c.

others. But I never yet could see any sufficient Proof that *Plato,* or any of his Followers before *Christ,* held the Doctrine of *a Trinity in Unity.* Nor does it appear that *these Fathers* were all, or most of them, *Platonists. Justin* himself had, in Quest of Truth, applied to all the chief Sects of Philosophy, [k] as he himself tells us. Nor did they bring their philosophical Notions into *Christianity.* On the contrary they on all Occasions very severely censure these Philosophers. And *Justin,* though he speaks honourably of *Plato,* [l] yet very freely censures his absurd Notions of the *Deity.* But if *Justin's* Authority may be questioned in Matters of Faith, yet surely he must be allowed to be a competent Witness of plain, and notorious, Matter of Fact. And he bears full Testimony that the *Christians* in his Days worshipped both the *Son,* and the *Holy Ghost.* [m] In his Second Apology, to wipe off the Charge of *Atheism* brought against the *Christians* by their Enemies, he answers that they could not be called *Atheists, who worshipped, and adored, God the Father, the Son,*

---

[k] Dial. *Tryph.* sub init. &c. 21. [l] Ad Græcos Cohort. P. 6, [m] P. 56. See this Passage quoted at large, and vindicated against all Exceptions, by Bp *Bull* Def. Fid. Nic. Sect. ii. Cap. 4. N. 8.

who

who came from him, and the prophetick Spirit.
— [n] And in the same Apology in Answer to the same Charge he replies as before, that as *they worshipped God the Creator of all Things,* so *they paid Honour to Jesus Christ in the second Place, knowing him to be the Son of God, and to the prophetick Spirit in the third Place.*

Athenagoras, a Writer nearly of the same Age, to the same Charge makes the same Answer — [o] *Who would not wonder* (says he) *to hear those called Atheists, who call the Father God, the Son, and the Holy Ghost God, shewing their Power in Unity, and their Distinction in Order.* — And again, [p] *We are not therefore Atheists, honouring as God the Maker of this Universe, and the Word, who proceeded from him.*

Nay, *Heathen* Authors also bear Witness to the Practice of the *Christians* in those Times. *Pliny,* who lived in the Beginning of the second Century, [q] in an Epistle to the Emperor *Trajan* tells him that, having taken a Confession of some *Christians, they declared to him that they used to meet on a certain Day before*

[n] P. 60.   [o] P. 11.   [p] P. 34.   [q] Lib. x. Ep. 97.

it was light, and sing an Hymn to Christ, as to God. And *Lucian,* who lived in the same Century, in his *Philopatris* ridicules the *Christians,* as swearing by the three Persons in the Trinity. And again in his *Proteus* he charges the *Christians* with *worshipping a crucified Impostor,* as he blasphemously terms our blessed Lord. [r] And we find that *Celsus* afterwards brought the same Charge against *Christians.*

Irenæus, who flourished about the middle of the second Century, 'tells us that *Christ with the Father is the God of the Living, who spake to Moses, who appeared to the Patriarchs, and was worshipped by the Prophets.* [s] The same Father speaking of the Miracles then wrought by *Christians,* and particularly in *casting out Devils,* says that they *did it not by Invocations of Angels, or Inchantments, or other evil and curious Arts, but clearly and openly directing their Prayers unto the Lord who made all Things, and calling on the Name of our Lord Jesus Christ.*

And that they called upon him by Prayer appears from *a Prayer for Persons possessed* preserved in the [v] *Apostolical Constitutions*

[r] *Origen.* contra Celf. L. iii. P. 131. Lib. iv. Cap. 11, [t] Lib. ii. Cap. 57.
[s] Contra Hæref. [v] Lib. viii. C. 7.

addressed

addressed to *Christ*. It calls him among other honourable Appellations him *whom the Angels worship,* and concludes thus ——— *O only-begotten God, Son of the great Father, rebuke the evil Spirits, and deliver the Works of thy Hands from the Power of the strange Spirit. For to thee is Glory, Honour, and Majesty, and by thee to the Father, in the Holy Ghost, for ever, Amen.*

Towards the Close of this Century lived *Clemens* of *Alexandria,* who bears full Testimony to the *Worship* of Christ. In his *Admonition to the Gentiles* he thus expresses ᵘ himself *Believe, O Man, in him who is both Man and God; believe, O Man, in him who suffered, and is worshipped, the living God.* — ʷ Again in his *Stromata* — *We are commanded to worship, and honour, him, whom we believe to be the Word, our Saviour, and by him the Father.* — I have already taken Notice of his *Doxologies* at the End of his *Pedagogue.* There is indeed there a direct Prayer addressed to the *Son* jointly with the Father in these Words — *Be merciful to thy Children, O Master, O Father, the Guide of Israel, Son, and Father, both One* — and the whole is concluded with an *Hymn to Christ.*

ᵘ P. 66.   ʷ Lib. vii. C. 7. P. 719.

About

About the same Time flourished *Tertullian*. [x] We find that it was then a common Objecjection against *Christians*, that *they worshipped a Man condemned to Death by the Jews.* —— *Tertullian* does not answer this Charge by denying that they *worshipped Christ*, but by justifying this *Worship. They knew him to be begotten of God, and therefore called the Son of God, and God, by Unity of Substance. For God was a Spirit — and the Son was Spirit of Spirit, and God of God, as Light is of Light — so what proceeds from God is God, and the Son of God, and both One —* [y] In his Treatise against the *Jews* he boasts that *the Kingdom, and Name, of Christ is spread every where, is believed every where, he is worshipped by all the Nations abovementioned, reigns, and is adored every where — is God and Lord to all.* [z] Again in his Treatise *ad Uxorem* he dissuades *Christian* Women from marrying *Unbelievers*, and uses this Argument among others, that in such a Family there could be *no Mention of God, no Invocation of Christ.* [a] Lastly in his Book against *Praxeas*, who denied the Distinction of *Persons* in the *Trinity*, he argues thus — *Therefore they pre-*

[x] Apol. Cap. xxi.   [y] Cap. vii.   [z] Lib. ii. Cap. 6.   [a] Cap. 3.

tend

tend that we preach two, nay three, Gods, but they are the Worshippers of one only God (and so also pretends Mr. *L.*) *as if the Unity absurdly collected might not make an Heresy, and the Trinity rationally understood might not constitute the Truth.* [b] And he there explains how these *Three* are *One* ──── viz. *of one Substance, Condition, and Power.* ── Nor have we here only *Tertullian*'s own private Opinion, but his full Testimony that the *Worship* of the *Trinity* was the Practice of the *Christian Church* in his Days, and that their Enemies reproached them with it.

In the next Century lived *Novatian*, and, though he stands charged with some Errors and Misdemeanors, yet his Testimony is of Force with regard to the Practice of the Church in his Time. We have extant of his a Treatise on the *Trinity*. [c] Among many other Arguments for the Divinity of *Christ* he uses this ── *If Christ is only a Man, how can he be present in all Places to those who call upon him, since it is not the Nature of a Man, but of God, to be present in all Places?* And he argues farther, in direct Opposition to Mr. *L.*

---

[b] Cap. 2.   [c] Cap. xiv.

— *If Chrift be only a Man, why do we call upon him as a Mediator, as the Invocation of a mere Man muft be thought of no Efficacy to Salvation?*

Cotemporary with *Novatian* was *Cyprian*. Many Paffages might be produced from him in Proof of our *Lord's Divinity:* I fhall felect only two or three relating to his *Worfhip*. In his eleventh Epiftle he exhorts Men *to be inftant in Prayer, and firft to pray to our Lord, and then by him to God the Father*. Again, in his 61ft Epiftle he thus befpeaks *Lucius* — *In our Sacrifices, and our Prayers, we ceafe not to give Thanks to God the Father, and to his Son Chrift our Lord, and to make Prayer, and Supplication, that he who is perfect, and makes us perfect, would keep and perfect in you the glorious Crown of your Confeffion*. Laftly, in his Treatife on the *Benefit of Patience* he tells us that *God the Father has commanded his Son to be worfhipped*, and the *Apoftle Paul*, mindful of the divine Precept, fays — *God hath exalted him, and given him a Name, which is above every Name, that at the Name of Jefus every Knee fhould bow, of Things in Heaven, and Things in Earth, and Things under the Earth*.

Arnobius,

Arnobius, another *Ante-Nicene* Writer, [d] in Anſwer to the *Heathens*, who objected to the *Chriſtians* that *they worſhipped a Man, who was put to Death on the Croſs, and contended that he was a God, and believed that he was ſtill alive, and worſhipped him with daily Sup- plications*, firſt retorts their own Objection upon them, [e] and then anſwers more cloſely, that *he not only might be called God on account of his Services to Mankind*, but that *he was truly and undoubtedly God, and therefore they could not deny that he was a proper Object of Worſhip*. And though an *angry Heathen* might *rave* at his being called *God, yet they muſt an- ſwer that he was God, and God too of the in- terior Powers of the Soul*. We have ſeen the ſame Objection anſwered in like manner by *Tertullian*, and ſo it is by *Minucius Felix*, *Ori- gen*, and *Lactantius:* but their Evidence ſhall be conſidered hereafter.

We have farther Proof from *Euſebius*. [f] He has given us a Fragment from *Caius*, a Ro- man Preſbyter, who lived in the Beginning of the third Century. He informs us that there

[d] Lib. i. P. 30. [e] P. 36. [f] Hiſt. Eccleſ. Lib. v. Cap. 28.

P   were

were in his Time *antient Pfalms*, and *Hymns*, in the Church *written by the Faithful,* ^g *praifing Chrift the Word of God, and attributing Divinity to him*.

The same *Eusebius* has given us an Epistle from the *Council of Antioch*, which censured *Paul of Samosata* for denying the *Divinity* of *Chrift*, in which among other Things they charge him with *forbidding the Ufe of the Pfalms, which ufed to be fung in Honour of our Lord Jefus Chrift*.

We learn also from the same Writer, as we do also from others, that it was usual for the Martyrs at their Death to invoke *Chrift* after the Example of St. *Stephen*. ^h He informs us that *Blandina*, at her Martyrdom, *had familiar Converfe with Chrift*; ⁱ that *feveral Chriftians in Phrygia* suffered Martyrdom ^j *calling on Chrift the God over all*; and lastly, that ^k *Porphyrius* the Martyr expired in the Flames, *calling on Chrift the Son of God to help him*. To this I may add *Eufebius's* Testimony concerning his own Times. ^l He tells us that *the*

---

g τὸν Λόγον τῶ Θεῶ ὑμνῶσι θεολογῶντες.   h Lib. v. Cap. 1.
i L. viii. Cap. 11.   j He refers, I presume to Rom. ix. 5.   k De Martyr. Palæst. Cap. 11.   l Eccl. Histor. Lib. x. Cap. 4.

higheft

highest Powers on Earth *confessed Christ, not as a common King made of Men, but worshipped him as the true Son of the Supreme God, and God himself.*

Thus have I deduced the Proofs of the *Worship* of the *Son*, and *Holy Spirit*, through all Ages from the Days of the Apostles down to the Time of the *Council of Nice*. And I think it fully appears how little Reason our *Apologist* has so confidently to assert that *religious Worship was in those Days addressed to the Father only*. The *Heathens* constantly objected to them the *Worship* of a Man put to Death on the Cross: from whence it is plain that it was their Practice to *worship Christ*. And this is the Reason that they principally insist on *his Worship*. And, whereas our Author pretends that *the Holy Ghost* was never worshipped till after the *Council of Nice*, the contrary is evident from the Quotations from *Justin Martyr, Lucian's Philopatris, Tertullian*, and other Places cited before with regard to the *Baptismal Form*, and antient *Doxologies*. And all this our *Apologist* might have learnt from [m] Mr. *Bingham*'s

[m] Antiq. B. xiii. Ch. 2.

Antiquities, and other Authors. I might have added Proofs from the ancient Liturgies, in all of which are Prayers to the *Son*, and to the *Holy Ghost*. ⁿ But as it does not appear when these Liturgies were committed to writing, and as it is probable that they have undergone Reviews, and received several Additions, since they were first composed; and as I have confined myself chiefly to such Writers, as lived before the Council of *Nice*, I do not think proper to insist on them, though it is probable that most of the Prayers therein contained are the Prayers of the antient Church.

· But what has he to say in Opposition to this full Evidence? ᵒ We have (what is indeed very strange) the Testimony of Bp *Bull*, that able *Defender of the Nicene Faith*. Two Passages of his are quoted from Dr. *Clarke*, to prove an Assertion directly contrary to what he has maintained most strongly, and proved most incontestably, in several learned Treatises. In Opposition to the Bp of *Meaux*, who pleaded for the Invocation of Angels, he says that *in the first and best Ages the Churches of Christ directed all their Prayers to God only through*

ⁿ Ibid. Ch. v. S. 3.   ᵒ P. 148, 9.

the Mediation of Jesus Christ. And, again in his Sermon on *the Existence of Angels* he says that *in the Clementine Liturgy* [p] *there is not one Prayer made either to Angel, or Saint: but all the Prayers are directed to God, in the Name of his Son Jesus Christ, as they are in our Liturgy.* His Meaning is plain. His Design could not be to exclude the *Worship of Christ,* but only that of all Creatures, *Saints,* and *Angels.* The Bp well knew, and [q] has shewn, that in the *Clementine Liturgy* many of the *Doxologies* are offered up jointly to *the Father, Son, and Holy Ghost,* as they are in our *Liturgy,* and one long Prayer at least personally addressed to *Christ.* [r] And he himself has explained his Meaning in his *Defence of the Nicene Faith. Origen* had been accused of *Arianism* for using the like Expressions. Bp *Bull* vindicates him by saying that *Christ* may be considered either as *God of God,* or as *Mediator* between *God and Man.* In the latter Capacity all Prayers are to be offered to *God the Father* through him : in the former he is himself the Object of *Worship.* Dr. *Clarke* has given us

[p] This Clause is omitted both by Dr. *Clarke,* and our *Apologist.* [q] Def. Fid. Nic. Sect. ii. C. 3. N°. 6.
[r] Sect. ii. Cap. 9. N°. 15.

a Quotation

a Quotation from this very Place, immediately before the two other Quotations: but gives us such Part only as might seem to make for him, and leaves out what goes before, and what follows after, where the Bp explains himself, and fully answers the Objection.

However our Apologist has produced two Testimonies on his Side from *Origen*, and *Lactantius*, neither of whom wrote before the third Century, and therefore can scarce be allowed competent Witnesses of the Practice of the Church for the first three Centuries. [s] As to *Origen*, it is well known that he has been accused of holding heretical Doctrines, and particularly those of *Arianism*, both by Antients, and Moderns, and powerfully vindicated by others. It must be allowed, that as he is a voluminous, so is he an hasty, and inacccurate Writer; and has expressed himself very incautiously, not only with regard to the Doctrine of the *Trinity*, but with regard to other important Points. It is also generally supposed that many of his Writings

---

[s] See *Cave*'s Life of *Origen*—Idem Hist. Lit.—*Du Pin* Biblioth. Auth. Eccl.——*Bull* Def. Fid. Nic. Sect. ii. Cap. 9. *Waterland*'s 2d Defence, P. 247, &c. ——*Fabric*. Biblioth. Græc.

have

have been interpolated, and corrupted by evil Hands. ᵗ The Passage cited in the *Apology* must be allowed to be very exceptionable. I do not well understand the good Father's Meaning. He had in the Words immediately before this Passage said that *it is our Duty to give Thanks to Christ, who hath by the Will of his Father bestowed upon us such great Blessings, and also to make Intercession to him, as St. Stephen did, saying, Lord lay not this Sin to their Charge, and, after the Example of the Father of the Lunatick, saying, I pray, Lord, have Mercy on my Son, or myself, or any one else.* —— He here plainly teaches us to give Thanks, and *pray* to *Christ*, and yet in the Words immediately following seems to say that *Prayer* is to be offered not to the *Son*, but to the *Father*. ᵘ It should seem that *Origen* had a Notion that there was some peculiar Kind of Prayer, perhaps Petition for the Forgiveness of Sins, which was to be addressed, not to the *Son*, but to the *Father* himself through the *Son*. If *Origen* here meant to deny that any *Worship* was to be paid to the *Son*, he must contradict himself in the same Breath. He must also contradict his own plain

ᵗ P. 142.   ᵘ Annot. in loc. Oxon. Ed.

Doctrine

Doctrine in other Parts of his Works. [w] In his Book against *Celsus*, which is allowed to be the most valuable Part of his Works, he tells us that *the wise Men, or Magi, conceiving our Lord to be greater than all their Gods, resolved to worship him; and that coming into Judæa they offered Symbols to him, who (if we may so speak) was compounded of God and mortal Man, Gold as to a King, Myrrh as to one who was to die, and Frankincense as to God.* —— *And, as he was God superior to the assistant Angels, being the Saviour of Mankind, the Angel rewarded their Piety in worshipping Jesus, by warning them not to return to Herod.* —— [x] Again, he says that *though Angels are sometimes in Scripture called Gods, yet we are not commanded to worship, or adore, them — but to offer up all Prayer, Supplication, Intercession, and Thanksgiving, to the God over all by the High-Priest, who is above all Angels, being the living Word, and God. And we must also pray to the Word himself, and make Intercession to him, and give Thanks, and make Supplication to him,* [y] *if we can but understand how*

---

[w] Lib. i. P. 46.   [x] Lib. v. P. 233.   [y] See this last Clause explained, and its Sense vindicated by Bp *Bull* Def. Fid. Nic. Sec. ii. C. ix. N. 15. Dr. *Waterland*'s 2d Defence, Q. xvii. P. 399.

Prayer

Prayer is taken in Propriety of Speech, or in an improper Sense. ᵃ Farther, as *Celsus* had objected to *Christians* the Worship of *a mortal Man*, he makes the same Answer as other *Christian* Apologists do, not by denying the Fact, but vindicating it, saying that *they believed, and were fully perswaded, that this Jesus was from the Beginning God, and the Son of God,* ᵃ *the very Word, the Wisdom, and the Truth.* — ᵇ And, again in Answer to the same Objection he says — *If Celsus had understood this — I and my Father are One — and what is said by the Son of God in his Prayer — as I and thou art One — he would not have thought that we worshipped any other than the Supreme God. For he saith ——— The Father is in me, and I in the Father — We therefore, as I said, worship one God, the Father, and the Son, and our Reasoning stands in full Force against others, and we do not worship an upstart Being, who never existed before: for we believe him, who said — Before Abraham was I am.* ——— And after more to the like Purpose he says ———

ᶻ Lib. iii. P. 135.   ᵃ ὁ αὐτόλογος ϗ ἡ αὐτοσοφία, ϗ ἡ αὐτοκλήθεια.   ᵇ Lib. viii. P. 385, 6. See this Passage cited at Length, and explained by *Bingham* Antiq. B. xiii. C. 2. P. 566. See also *Origen*'s Doctrine fully set forth by Bp *Bull* Def. Fic. Nic. Sect. ii. C. 9.

We worſhip one God, and his only Son, and Word, and Image, with Supplications, and Prayers, to the utmoſt of our Power, offering up our Prayers to the God over all, by his Only-begotten Son, to whom firſt we offer them, beſeeching him —— as our High-Prieſt, to offer them to the God over all. —— Here we ſee a full Declaration of *Origen*'s Opinion concerning the *Divinity* of our *Bleſſed Saviour*, and the *Worſhip* due to him. Nor have we here only his private Opinion, but the full Teſtimony both of *Celſus*, and *Origen* himſelf, to plain Matter of Fact, that *Chriſt* was then worſhipped by all *Chriſtians*. *Celſus*, and other *Heathen* Writers, perpetually charged *Chriſtians* with worſhipping a dead Man. *Origen,* and all the other *Apologiſts*, do not deny this Charge. They do not ſay that no *Worſhip* was paid to *Chriſt*, as they certainly would have done, if none had been paid: but ſay that they *worſhipped Chriſt*, becauſe he was God, one God with the Father. [c] *Origen* alſo himſelf, in the Remains we have of his *Homilies*, offers up Prayers, and Ejaculations to *Chriſt*. And whereas our *Apologiſt* roundly aſſerts that no Worſhip was paid to the *Holy*

---

[c] See ſeveral Inſtances in *Bingham* as above.

Ghoſt

Ghost till *the latter End of the Fourth Century*, to the Proofs, and Instances already produced, we may add that of *Origen*. In the first Book of his Commentary on the Epistle to the *Romans* he says — *It is the Property of those only to dishonour their Bodies, who serve Idols.* —— *As for us, who worship and adore no Creature, but the Father, the Son, and the Holy Spirit, as we do not err in our Worship, so neither let us offend in our Actions, and Conversation.*

As to *Lactantius*, the like Exceptions lie against him, as against *Origen*, and still more strongly. ᵈ Our *Apologist* indeed sets him forth as *a fine Writer, a Teacher, and Example of Religion*. We allow him to be an eloquent, and able, Defender of the *Christian* Faith. ᵉ But he was, in the Estimation of the best Judges, more an Orator, than a Divine. He was but little skilled either in the sacred Writings, or in the Doctrines of the Church. Hence he has run into the grossest Mistakes, and advanced the wildest Notions. ᶠ He seems, to have held two Principles, a good, and an

---

ᵈ Pref. P. iv. Cap. x. N. 20, &c.

ᵉ See *Bull* Def. Fid. Nic. Sect. iii. *Du Pin* Biblioth. *Cave* Hist. Lit. *Waterland* 2d Defence.

ᶠ Institut. L. ii. C. 9.

evil one. [g] And yet Mr. *L.* think *he needs no Apology for producing* a long Quotation from this Writer. Mr. *Bingham* has already fully answered him, and has shewn that this Passage, though very inaccurately, and improperly expressed, is capable of a good Sense. It is indeed plain that *Lactantius* did not here design to deny our *Lord's Divinity* as the Title of the Chapter immediately preceding is ——*De Jesu Deo et Homine*—and in that Chapter, and the preceding, he frequently calls him *God*; and proves from the Prophecies of the *Old Testament*, that he was to be both *God* and *Man*, particularly from *Isaiah* vii. 14 — ix. 6 — xlv. 14 &c. — *Psal.* xlv. 6 — cx. 1. But the fullest Answer to the Inferences drawn by Mr. *L.* from this Passage of *Lactantius* he himself has furnished us with in another Passage, [h] which he has cited from this *fine Writer*. But he there gives us the Objection made to *Christians* by the *Heathen,* and leaves out *Lactantius's* Answer, which is full, and strong, against him. He first proposes this Objection in the 16th Chapter. — *They reproach the Christians* (says he) *as worshipping a Man, who was grievously punished,*

[g] P. 122.   [h] P. 147. *Lactant.* Instit. L. iv. C. 29.

and

and tortured by Men. He, like *Origen*, and other *Christian* Writers before him, does not answer this by denying the Fact, but by justifying it. He spends several Chapters on the Incarnation, Sufferings, and Death of our *Blessed Saviour*, in which he frequently calls him God, and shews that it was no way absurd that *God* should take upon him human Nature, and suffer Death on the Cross. —— [i] *The Jews*, he says, *condemned their God*. — [k] *God was crucified by the Worshippers of God* [l] *No Man could be a perfect Teacher, unless he were also God*. — [m] *He was therefore both God, and Man, being made a Mediator between God and Man — He therefore came as a Mediator, that is, God in the Flesh*. —— At last in the 29th Chapter he repeats the Objection proposed before, [n] which our *Apologist* hath been pleased to quote: but there stops without giving us *Lactantius*'s Answer, which follows immediately after — *When we call the Father*

---

[i] Cap. xviii. [k] Ib. [l] Cap. xxiv. [m] Cap. xxv.
[n] And even this he mistranslates. *Lactantius* says that the *Christians* were charged with *holding two Gods, God the Father, and God the Son,* our Translator says they only *seemed to believe* this. *Lactantius* says that the *Christians* were accused of *calling the same God eternal and mortal. The* Translation says that *they held a second God, and him also a mortal one.*

God,

God, and the Son God, we do not call them different Gods, nor do we separate the one from the other: because the Father could not be without the Son, nor can the Son be separated from the Father — Since therefore the Father makes the Son, and the Son the Father, there is one Mind, one Spirit, one Substance to both. —— He afterwards declares that *the Father and Son are One God*, and concludes thus — *The one Supreme God cannot be worshipped but by the Son, He who thinks to worship the Father alone, as he worships not the Son, so neither does he worship the Father. But he, who receives the* Son, *and bears his Name, he with the Son worships also the Father* — There could not be a fuller Proof not only that *Lactantius* himself, whatever crude Expressions may sometimes have dropt from him, believed that *Christ* was truly *God*, and that *Worship* was due to him as such, but that this was the Doctrine, and the Practice of the Church, in his Time. And this strong Proof must have stared our *Agologist* in the Face, if he would have been at the Pains of reading the whole Chapter he quotes. But he takes this extraordinary Quotation at second Hand from one *Ben Mordecai*, so that whether he is the Deceiver, or the deceived, I cannot say. Nor do I know who this *Ben Mordecai*

Mordecai is: but take him to be one of his own Fraternity who has perfonated a *Jew*, the better to attack the Doctrine of the *Trinity*. Let me advife him to confult the Authors he quotes himfelf, and not to depend on others, not even on Dr. *Clarke* himfelf. But perhaps he would infer from hence at leaft that the *Worfhip of the Holy Ghoft* was then unknown, becaufe the *Heathen* objected againft the *Worfhip* only of *two Gods*. The Reafon is plain. They did not object againft a *Plurality of Gods*: for this they held themfelves. They objected to the *Chriftians* that they worfhipped, and called *God*, a Man put to an ignominious Death. And therefore the *Chriftian Apologifts* mention, and defend, only the *Worfhip* of the *Son*: the Objection did not lead them to fay any Thing of the *Holy Ghoft*. What we would conclude then from fuch Defences is that the *Worfhip of Chrift* was then the Practice of the Church: and this is a Conclufion which cannot be contefted. But that they did alfo worfhip the *Holy Ghoft* full Teftimony has been produced.

But our *Apologift* is pleafed to repeat P. 161. what he told us before that *the whole Chriftian Church in the Apoftolick Age, made up* up of *Jews* and *Gentiles*, *was entirely Naza-rene, or Unitarian, and that the Truth of the Gospel, as they held it, was preserved to the Time of Victor Bishop of Rome*: nay *that these Jewish Believers subsisted till the 5th Century.* But for this he brings no Proof: he only refers to two Authors, *Mosheim*, and *Eusebius*, who both, by his own Confession, deny, and disprove, these bold Assertions.° That there were *Hereticks* in the first Ages of the Church, who denied the *Divinity* of *Christ*, such as *Ebion*, *Cerinthus*, &c. History informs us. But the same Histories teach us that these were always condemned, and censured, as *Hereticks*, and their Doctrines rejected by the Church. ᵖAnd the same *Primitive Fathers*, who condemn those who denied our *Saviour* to be a real Man, censure as freely those who deny his *Divinity*. It is indeed strange that our *Apolo-*

° See this fully proved by Bp *Bull*, Jud. Eccl. Cath. Cap. ii. — *Waterland* Import. Doct. Trin. Ch. vi. P. 245, &c. —
ᵖ *Iren.* Lib. i. Cap. 25, 26. Lib. iii. C. 2, 21. Lib. iv. C. 59. — *Ignat. ad Ephes.* Cap. vii. — *Justin.* Martyr Dial. *Tryph.* P. 253. — We have a Book of *Tertullian* entitled, *De Præscriptionibus adversus Hæreticos*, wherein he thus expresses himself — *Johannes in Epistolâ eos maximè Antichristos vocat, qui Christum negarent in carne venisse, et qui non putarent Jesum esse Filum Dei, illud Marcion, hoc Hebion vindicavit.* Cap. xxxiii. see also C. xlviii.

gist

gift should, without any Proof, and in Contradiction to all History, revive this idle Story of the *Nazarenes*, advanced not many Years ago by some *Socinian* Writers, and by the Infidel Writer *Toland*. Those were fully confuted by [q] Bp. *Bull*, and by *Mosheim*, the Author Mr. *L.* refers us to. He wrote an Answer to *Toland* — entitled — *Vindiciæ antiquæ contra Toland*—And in his *Ecclesiastical History* he tells us that *the Term Nazarene was originally given to all Christians, and that it was afterwards appropriated to those Christians of Jerusalem, who considered the Observance of the Mosaical Rites as necessary to Salvation. These were distinct from the Ebionites, and were not placed by the ancient Christians in the heretical Register, while the latter were considered as a Sect, whose Tenets were destructive of the fundamental Principles of the Christian Religion. But, after the second Destruction of Jerusalem by Adrian, they deserted the ordinary Assemblies of Christians, and were then reckoned a distinct Sect, but yet were treated by other Christians with great Gentleness, as agreeing in the main Doc-*

[q] Jud. Eccl. Cath. Cap. ii. Sect. 10, &c.—Prim. et Apost. Trad. Cap. i. Sect. 6, &c. [r] B. i. P. 2. C. 5. P. 70. Cent. 11. Pt. B. 11. C. 5. P. 106.

trines of *Christianity*. — This is Mr. *Mosheim's* Account of these *Nazarenes:* how totally different from that in our *Apology?*

But, it seems, he *wrongly understood* the Matter. Mr. *L.* understands it better. He has met with an *anonymous Writer*, * in *Eusebius, about the Year* 200, *who bears these Jewish Christians this Testimony?* But what *Christians?* and what *Testimony?* Not a Word does this Author say of any *Jewish Christians;* he speaks, as our Author himself tells us, of the Followers of *Artemon,* who is said to be a Native of *Pergamus*. And what *Testimony* does he bear? full *Testimony* against our *Apologist*. He does indeed say that these *Hereticks* pretended *that all the Antients, and the Apostles themselves held and taught the same Doctrines which they did, and that the Truth of the Gospel was preserved till the Days of Victor Bp of Rome, but was corrupted by his Successor Zephyrinus*. — Thus far Mr. *L.* gives us: but, though he tells us that *this Writer would invalidate* these their Pretensions, yet he, rather prudently, than honestly, has suppressed his Answer. I must beg leave to supply this Omission. This

* Hist. Ecclef. L. v. Cult.

antient

antient Writer, suppofed to be *Caius* Prefbyter at *Rome*, tells us that this their vain Affertion *was contradicted*, not only by *Scripture, but by the Writings of Authors more ancient than Victor, as Juftin, Miltiades, Tatian, and Clement, and many others, who, as every one knows, teach that Chrift was both God and Man.* † He refers alfo to *Pfalms*, and *Hymns* of the Church, *wrote long ago from the Beginning by the Faithful, celebrating Chrift the Word of God, and calling him God.* And he wonders at their *Impudence* in pretending that *Victor held their blafphemous* Doctrines, *who excommunicated Theodotus the Author of this God-denying Herefy, who held that Chrift was a mere Man.* I will not exprefs my Wonder at Mr. *L's Impudence*, but return him my Thanks for referring us to this fine Remnant of Antiquity, which affords us the ftrongeft Evidence againft him, which we could defire. We have here the Teftimony of an Author, who lived about the Year 200, that the *Divinity of our Bleffed Saviour* was taught by the moft refpectable Writers of that Age, and thofe preceding; that in the moft antient Pfalms and Hymns of the Church *Chrift* was celebrated as *God*, and

---

† This Paffage I have quoted above P. 113.

R 2 that

that those who denied his *Divinity* were accounted Hereticks, and cast out of the Church. What becomes then of his confident Boastings that *the whole Christian Church were then Arians, or Socinians?* He stands convicted by his own Witnesses.

ᵘ The same *Eusebius* assures us that there was, before the Destruction of *Jerusalem* by *Adrian, a Succession of fifteen Bishops there, who were Jews by Descent, and held the true Faith of Christ.* —— What he esteemed *the true Faith of Christ* may be seen from the above Quotation, as also from what he says of the *Ebionites*. ʷ *These,* he says, *believed Christ to be only a common Man, born of Joseph and Mary. But there were others also called by the same Name, who, though they observed the Ceremonies of the Mosaical Law, yet, avoiding their absurd Notions, believed the Pre-existence of Christ, and that he was God, the Word, and Wisdom of the Father* —— These are plainly the *Nazarene,* or *Jewish Christians,* here mentioned by our *Apologist,* and we have here the full Testimony of *Eusebius,* that they believed

---

ᵘ Ecclef. Hist. Lib. iv. C. 5, ʷ L. iii. C. 27. See *Bull* as above,

our

our *Lord's Divinity*. The fame is attefted alfo by *Sulpitius Severus,* a creditable Hiftorian of the fourth Century. [x] He tells us that *the Emperor Adrian placed a Guard to keep the Jews out of Jerufalem, which was of Service to the Chriftian Faith: for they almoft all, together with the Obfervance of the Law, believed Chrift to be God.* —— To this we may add the Teftimony of St. *Auftin.* [y] He diftinguifhes the *Nazarenes* from the *Cerinthians,* and *Ebionites*. Thefe, he fays, *held that Chrift was only a Man:* but the *Nazarenes*, though they obferved *the Precepts of the Law,* yet confeffed that Chrift was the Son of God. I muft therefore take the Liberty, with Bp *Bull*, to call this our *Apologift's* Story of the *Nazarene Chriftians—puditiffimam atque impudentiffimam fabulam.*

I muft again thank our *Apologift* for another Citation from *Juftin Martyr*, which bears full Teftimony to our *Lord's Divinity*. To what purpofe he cites this Paffage I cannot tell, nor where he had his Tranflation: it differs totally, from the Original. Whatever he has to fay has been fully anfwered by Mr.

---

[x] Sac. Hift. Lib. ii. C. 45. C. 8, 9, 10,

[y] Lib. de Hæref.

Bingham.

Bingham. [z] The Paſſage has been conſidered at large, and what Obſcurities may be therein fully cleared up by Bp *Bull,* and Dr. *Waterland.* I need add but little more. But as our Author has miſerably curtailed, and miſtranſlated this Paſſage, I ſhall give Dr. *Waterland's* Tranſlation, which he has vindicated from all Exceptions. — *Trypho the Jew* (ſays the Doctor) *in the Dialogue, having a little before told Juſtin that his Doctrines concerning Chriſt (that he was God before the World, and afterwards became Man, and of a Virgin) appeared to him a great Paradox, and contrary to common Senſe, Juſtin replies as follows, I am very ſenſible that this will look like a Paradox, and more eſpecially to thoſe of your Nation, who are in no Diſpoſition either to apprehend, or follow, the Things of God, but the Dictates only of your own Rabbins, as God himſelf proclaims. Nevertheleſs (ſaid I) O Trypho, my Argument does not fall, as to his being the Meſſiah of God, though I ſhould not be able to prove that the Son of the Maker of the Univerſe pre-exiſted, being God, and was born a Man of the Virgin, but after it has been once fully proved that he is*

---

[z] *Bull* Jud. Eccl. Cath. Cap. vii. — *Waterland* Import. Doct. Trin. Ch. vi. P. 382, &c. — See alſo *Thirlby* Annot. and my Vind. Doct. Trin. Pt. 3. P. 40.

the

the Messiah of God, *(whatever else he be)* tho' I should not farther demonstrate his Pre-existence, and condescending to become Man of like Passions with us, taking Flesh upon him according to his Father's good Pleasure, all that you can justly say is, that I am so far in an Error; but you should not hereupon deny that he is the Christ,[a] *appearing as a Man born of human Parents, and approving himself as the chosen Messiah. For (said I) my good Friends, some there are of our Profession (or of your Nation) who acknowledge him to be the Messiah, yet conceive of him, as of a Man born of human Parents, whom however I assent not to, no not though there were ever so many concurring to tell me so, since we are commanded by Christ himself not to submit to the Doctrines of Men, but to what the holy Prophets have delivered, and himself hath taught us.* —— I hope the Reader will pardon this long Quotation, as it will appear from hence how grievously Mr. L. has mangled poor *Justin*, and not only how little it is to his Purpose, but how strongly it proves against him. This Passage fully

---

[a] I should rather translate this — *although he should appear to be a Man born of human Parents, and appointed by Election to be the Messiah.*

shews that *Justin*, and other *Christians* in his Time, the second Century, (the *Ebionites* only excepted) firmly believed that *Christ pre-existed, as God, before the World began*; that they looked upon this as the Doctrine of the *Prophets*, and of *Christ himself*; and that it appeared otherwise only to those, *who were in no Disposition, either to apprehend, or follow, the Things of God.*

[b] His Pretence that *these early Fathers brought their Platonick Doctrines into Christianity has* been already considered. He brings indeed no Proof of it, but only a general Reference to *numerous Instances in their Writings*. Pray did he ever read these Writings? From his Citations, which we have examined, we have Reason to believe, and ought charitably to hope, that he never did. The Reverse of this is most true. In the Passage just cited from *Justin*, we are told that *Trypho*, and his Brethren, could not receive the Doctrine of the *Incarnation*, because *it appeared to them paradoxical, and contrary to common Sense.* [c] And *Irenæus* tells us that the *Hereticks* of his Time borrowed many of their wild No-

[b] P. 158.   [c] Adv. Hæref. Lib. ii. Cap. 19.

tions

tions from *Plato*, and other heathen Philosophers. [d] *Tertullian* also says that the *Heresies* of his Time, among which he reckons those of *Ebion*, and *Cerinthus*, who denied our *Lord's Divinity, took their Rise from Philosophy*; and that the *Hereticks* were Followers of *Plato, Aristotle, Zeno*, or *Epicurus*. And the Writer cited by *Eusebius*, as above, ascribes the Errors of the *Anti-Trinitarians* in his Time to their Attachment to *Philosophy*. I entirely agree therefore with our *Apologist* that [e] *Science falsely so called first led Men into Errors concerning the true Person, and true Character, of our Saviour Christ*. The Divinity, and Incarnation of the *Son of God* are taught in *Scripture* in plain Terms — [f] *The Word was God* — and — *The Word was made Flesh*. — If Creeds were added, it was to guard the Truth against the Evasions of those who would explain away the plain Truth; [g] and *through Philosophy and vain Deceit deny the Incarnation of Christ, in whom dwelleth all the Fulness of the Godhead bodily*.

[h] Another Topick of Declamation in the *Apology* is that *human Authority was a prin-*

---

[d] Præscript. adv. Hær. Cap. vii. &c. [e] P. 153. [f] *Joh.* i, 1. 14. [g] *Coloss.* ii. 8, 9. [h] P. 162, &c.

cipal *Source of the Corruption of the true Chriſtian Doctrine and Worſhip*. For *Victor Biſhop
of Rome* excommunicated *Theodotus*, a *Jewiſh
Chriſtian, for not coming up to his own Opinion
concerning Chriſt*, which was that afterwards
called *Arian*, and happened then and there
chiefly to prevail.—— This is far above my
Comprehenſion. Pray, good Sir, who was the
Arian, Victor, or *Theodotus?* and whoſe, and
what, *Opinion then and there prevailed?*
This *Theodotus*, as we learn [i] from *Euſebius*,
[k] and other Authors, was no *Jewiſh Chriſtian*,
but a Citizen of *Byzantium*, who had denied
Chriſt in Time of Perſecution, and afterwards
going to *Rome* became the Ringleader of a
Sect, who, among other ſtrange Doctrines,
held *Chriſt* to be a mere Man. Him *Victor*
caſt out of the Church: and ſo, I humbly
apprehend, he was authorized to do, by the
conſtant Practice of the Church, [l] and the
Apoſtles themſelves. But how ſhall we reconcile theſe Matters? Our Author has given us
a third hand Quotation from *Euſebius*, which,
if it proved any Thing, would prove that *the*

---

[i] Eccleſ. Hiſt. L. v. C. 28. [k] *Theodorit.* Hæret. Fab.
L. ii. C. 5. *Epiphan.* Hær. liv. 1. [l] See *Tit.* iii. 10 —
e *Job.* 10.

whole

whole Chriſtian Church was entirely Unitarian till the Times of *Victor*'s Succeſſor *Zephyrinus,* who is ſaid to be *the firſt who corrupted the Truth.* And now we are told that *Victor* himſelf *excommunicated* theſe *Unitarians,* and ſo eſtabliſhed *his own Opinion.* But a little before we were told that *thoſe very early Fathers, Irenæus, and Juſtin Martyr, brought into Chriſtianity the Platonick Doctrine of a Second God* half a *Century* before *Victor*'s Time. Here then we have three Stories, all of them falſe: and, as they are not eaſily reconcilable with one another, ſo are they all utterly inconſiſtent with our Author's main Poſition, that *all Chriſtian People, for upwards of three hundred Years after Chriſt, till the Council of Nice, were generally Unitarians, what is now called either Arian, or Socinian.*

But perhaps he may have more Reaſon to complain of the Exerciſe of Authority, *when the Emperors had embraced Chriſtianity.* [m] A heavy Charge we have indeed againſt theſe *Chriſtian Emperors:* but with very little Proof to ſupport it. I find quite a different Account in the learned Mr. *Bingham*'s Antiquities. [n]

[m] P. 164, &c.   [n] Antiq. B. xvi. Ch. 2. Sect. 4. — See alſo *Moſheim* Cent. iv. P. 220.

After setting forth at full the Imperial Laws against *Heresy*, he thus concludes —— *Now from all this it is plain that whatever Favour, or Assistance, the ancient Church required of the Civil Magistrate to back her Discipline with against Hereticks, or other Delinquents, she never desired them to unsheath the Sword in her Cause, or punish them with Death; but always interposed in their behalf, that they might have the Favour to live, and repent, if ever any sanguinary Laws (which were very rare, and no ways encouraged, or approved, by the Church) were made against them. The Discipline of Fire and Faggot and Inquisitions, and a thousand other Tortures, which under Pretence of Mercy has spilt so much Christian Blood, are Inventions of later Ages, and more corrupt and degenerate Times, when Men had forgot the Spirit of Christianity, and the Character of our Blessed Lord, who came not to destroy Men's Lives, but to save them.*—Where then are we to find these *sanguinary Laws of the Emperors against those who differed from them from Constantine inclusive*, which our Author complains of? There is not one to be met with in the whole *Code* till *Theodosius*'s Time. He first made a Decree, not against the *Arians*, but against some particular Sects of the *Manichees*, that they should be punished with Death.

This

This Law may be supposed to have been made upon some particular Provocation of their Enormities, such as these *Manichees* were guilty of. Nor can I find any Instance, before *Priscillian*, of any *Heretick* suffering Death: and he too was accused of other wicked and lewd Practices.º Nor was he an *Arian*, but a Kind of *Manichee*. He was charged with holding several wild, and impious Tenets. As to the Doctrine of the Trinity, he is said to have been a *Sabellian*. He was put to Death about A. D. 385, but not by any *Christian Emperor*, but by the Usurper *Maximus*. He suffered indeed by the Prosecution of *Ithacius*, a Bishop, but of no very good Character: but the Fact was greatly condemned by all orthodox *Christians*, and particularly by *Martin* Bp of *Tours*, who besought *Maximus* to abstain from the Blood of this poor Man, for Expulsion from the Church, by the Sentence of the Bishop, was fully sufficient. In the same Sentiments were the other *Christian* Fathers. ᴾ St. *Chrysostom* tells us that *Christ hath forbid us to put Hereticks to Death, but not to restrain them,*

o *Sulpit. Sever.* Hist. Sacr. Lib. 2. — *August.* de Heres. 70. Leo. Magn. Epist. xv. vel xciii. — *Cave* Hist. Lit. — *Du Pin.* Nouv. Biblioth.   ᴾ Hom. xlvi. in Matt. xiii.

or *stop their Mouths, or forbid their Meetings.* ᵠ St. *Austin* in his Epistle to *Dulcitius* tells *him that he did not receive the Power of the Sword, nor was by any Laws, or imperial Injunctions, commanded to put Hereticks to Death.* ʳ And in his Book against *Cresconius* he says that, *no good Men in the Catholick Church are pleased to have any one, though an Heretick, prosecuted to Death.* But I suppose our *Apologist* will call all Kinds of Laws to restrain *Hereticks* by the Name of Persecution. ˢ He has quoted *Mosheim* to shew that *Theodosius the Great raised the secular Arm against the Arians with a terrible Degree of Violence:* and we are told in a Note, that *Amphilochius,* whom in Derision he calls a *Saint, instigated him to this inhuman Work.* What *inhuman Work?* ᵗ Did this *Saint Amphilochius instigate the Emperor* to proceed with Fire and Faggot against these *Arians,* or any way to injure their Persons, or Properties. No: he only desired him to forbid their Meetings. Nor did the Emperor at his Instigation put any *Arian* to Death, or raise any Persecution against them. He only

ᵠ Epist. lxi.   ʳ Lib. iii. C. 50.   ˢ P. 25.
ᵗ See *Sozomen* Hist. Eccl. Lib. vii. C. 6. — *Theodoret.* L. v. C. 16.

forbad

forbad their Conventicles, which has been the Practice of all *Christian* States from the first Establishment of *Christianity* to this Day. I cannot indeed but think the learned *Mosheim* to blame for speaking in such high Terms of the Proceedings of *Theodosius* against the *Arians*, and passing over so slightly the Severities of *Constantius*, and *Valens*, against the *Catholicks*. ᵘ *Theodosius the Great* is allowed by all the best Historians to have been an excellent Prince, and eminent not only for his Piety, but for his great Moderation, and Clemency. When he came to the Throne he found the Church rent by Divisions. Those who adhered to the *Nicene* Faith had been cruelly persecuted by *Valens*, and deprived of their Bishopricks. *Theodosius* took great Pains both to enquire into the Truth, and to settle Matters between the contending Parties. When he found this could not be done, being himself convinced of the Truth of the *Nicene* Faith, he restored the orthodox Clergy, turned out the *Arians*, and forbad their meeting in Conventicles. And when they still continued obstinate, and raised Disturbances in the Church, though he had at first treated them

---

ᵘ *Socrat.* Hist. Eccl. Lib. v. — *Sozomen* Lib. vii. — *Theodorit* Lib. v.

with

with great Lenity, he enacted some severe Laws against them. But these, as *Sozomen* assures us, he never put in Execution, but designed them only *in terrorem*. However, as I am no Friend to Persecution, so I am not disposed, nor think myself concerned, to vindicate every Decree, which the *Christian* Emperors published against *Hereticks*, nor all Measures taken by the orthodox Clergy, [x] especially as our *Apologist* is so just as to own that both Parties were guilty of these Practices, *Arian*, as well as *Homoousian*. [y] And Mr. *Mosheim* tells us *that unjustifiable Measures were taken, and great Excesses committed on both Sides*. And he thinks it *difficult to determine, which of the two exceeded most the Bounds of Probity, Charity, and Moderation.* — I cannot think so. Whoever reads the Acounts given by Ecclesiastical Historians of the Persecutions raised [z] against *Athanasius*, and his Adherents, by the *Arian* Party, the Severities exercised by [a] *Constantius*, and [b] *Valens*, who persecuted

---

[w] Lib. vii. C. 12.   [x] P. 165.   [y] Cent. iv. C. 5.
[z] *Socrat.* Hist. Eccl. Lib. i. C. 27, 28, &c. — *Sozomen* Lib. ii. C. 22, &c. — *Theodorit.* L. i. C. 26, &c.   [a] *Socrat.* Lib. ii. C. 16, 26, &c. — *Sozomen* Lib. iii. C. 5, &c. L. iv. C. 2, &c. — *Theodorit.* Lib. ii. C. 13, &c.   [b] *Socrat.* L. iv. C. 2, &c. 16, &c. — *Sozom.* Lib. vi. C. 7, &c. — *Theodorit.* L. iv. C. 13, &c.

the

the *Homooufians* even to Death; [c] and the Cruelties practifed by the *Goths*, *Vandals*, and *Hunns*, and that on account of Religion, will eafily judge on which Side the greateft Exceffes were committed. This at leaft he will fee how little Reafon our Author has to inveigh fo bitterly againft the Emperor *Theodofius*, and how little Pretence he has to afcribe the Prevalence of the *Nicene Faith* to the Perfecutions of the *Arians*. And this efpecially if we confider [d] what *Mofheim* tells us, that, *when thefe Ravages were over, in the Days of Juftinian, the Arian Sect declined apace, and could never afterwards recover any Degree of Stability.*

But our *Apologift*, not content with the Alliance of the *Goths*, *Vandals*, and *Hunns*, is eager to lift into his Party all that he can lay hold of, and compel them to come in. [e] *The Neftorians*, he tells us, *were in general Unitarians, and are now in great Numbers all over the Eaft*. And for the Truth of this he quotes *Mofheim*, who fays the direct contrary in the

---

[c] *Evagr*. Scholaft. Eccl. Hift. L. iv. C. 14.—*Victor Vitenfis* de Perfecut. Afric.—*Procop*. de Bell. Vandal. L. 1. C. 8.
[d] Cent. vi. P. 2. C. 5. [e] P. 27.

very Sentence here quoted. But he gives us only one little Scrap of this Sentence. He might probably hope to perſwade *the leſs learned* Reader that, as *Neſtorius* denied *the Virgin Mary* to be *the Mother of God*, he alſo denied *Chriſt* to be *God*. [f] But Mr. *Moſheim* ſeems to think that *Neſtorius* was rather hardly uſed, and that *the Difference* between him, and his Adverſaries *was only in Words* — He concludes with the Sentence, of which Mr. L. gives us only the latter Part — *The Doctrine of the Neſtorians was, that in the Son of God there were two Perſons, or Ὑποϛάσεις, of which the one was divine, even the eternal Word, the other, which was human, was the Man Jeſus, that theſe two Perſons had only one Aſpect, that the Union between the Son of God, and the Son of Man, was formed in the Moment of the Virgin's Conception, and was never to be diſſolved, that it was not an Union of Nature, or of Perſon, but only of Will and Affection: that Chriſt was therefore to be carefully diſtinguiſhed from God, who dwelt in him, as in his Temple, and that Mary was to be called the Mother of Chriſt, and not the Mother of God.* — I have quoted this Sentence

---

[f] Cent. v. P. ii. C. 5. P. 268.

at large, to shew how very unfair our *Apologist* is in his Quotations. It appears from this very Passage that, according to *Mosheim*, *Nestorius* held both the *Eternity*, and the *Divinity*, of the *Son of God*. The like Account of his Tenets is given both by ᵍ Dr. *Cave*, and ʰ *Du Pin*. ⁱ *Socrates* also informs us that *Nestorius* was not only no *Arian*, but a violent Enemy to all the *heretical* Sects, the *Arians* in particular; that he instigated the Emperor to persecute them, and that he himself attempted to pull down a Church of the *Arians:* and he blames him for his persecuting Spirit. ᵏ *Socrates* farther tells us that, though some of his Enemies accused him of making *Christ* a mere Man, the contrary appeared from his Writings, and from the Testimony of his Followers. His Error consisted not in denying the *Divinity* of Christ, but the Union of the *divine* and *human* Nature in him. And against this Error that Article of the *Athanasian Creed* seems to have been levelled — *Who, although he be God and Man, yet he is not two, but one Christ*. ˡ There are also seve-

ᵍ Hist. Lit. L. vii. C. 29, 31.   ʰ Nouv. Biblioth. ᵏ Ib. C. 32.   ⁱ Hist. Eccl.   ˡ See many of these Fragments among the Works of *Marius Mercator*, published by *Garnerius*.

ral Fragments of *Neſtorius* extant, in which he expreſsly affirms the *Divinity* of *Chriſt*, declares his Aſſent to the *Nicene Faith*, and condemns *Arius*, and his Doctrines. And that the *Neſtorians* now in the Eaſt hold the ſame Doctrines with their Founder, I refer him for Proof to the ſame learned ᵐ *Moſheim*, and the Authors cited by him.

Againſt this full Proof, which our *Apologiſt* might, or rather muſt, have ſeen in the very Author he quotes, he has given us in a Note a moſt curious Argument to prove that the *Neſtorians could not well be other than Unitarians*. *Theodore Biſhop of Mopſueſtia* would not allow the Confeſſion of St. *Thomas* to *Chriſt*, *Joh.* xx. 28. to be a Proof of our *Lord's Divinity*. But *Neſtorius*, and his Followers, *ſtrictly adhered to and reverenced his Name and Writings*. Therefore *Theodore* himſelf, and all theſe his Admirers, muſt be *Arians*. And for this he quotes Dr. *Lardner*. But if we look into Dr. *Lardner*, we ſhall find that he does not quote this from any Work of *Theodore* now extant: but from *the Acts of the Council of Conſtantinople*. And he tells us *they are alledged*

ᵐ Cent. xvi. C. 2. S. 3.

in

in the Way of Reproach, and are among Charges brought againſt him. And perhaps the Quotations are not quite exact and fair. —— But all this our *Apologiſt* has wiſely omitted. It is ſurely, neither reaſonable, nor poſſible, to judge of any Man's Opinion from ſuch an Extract as this is. Suppoſing, the moſt that can be inferred from this Paſſage, that *Theodore* really put *this fine Interpretation* on this Text of *Scripture*, it will not follow that he did not believe our *Lord's Divinity*. He might infer this from many other Texts. Much leſs will it follow that all who *reverenced his Name were Arians*. I have ſhewn above that this Confeſſion of St. *Thomas* was a full Proof of *Chriſt's Divinity:* but I don't call every one, who thinks otherwiſe, an *Arian*. I have alſo proved the Worſhip of *Chriſt* from 1 *Cor*. i. 2. but though Dr. *Hammond* gives another, and I think, a very wrong, Interpretation of this Text, I am well aſſured he was neither *Arian*, nor *Socinian*. The Truth of the Matter is that both *Neſtorius*, and *Eutyches*, had greatly diſturbed the Church by their curious Queſtions, and idle Diſputes, about the Union of the two Natures in *Chriſt*, and Things were carried with great Heat,

and

and Animosities, on both Sides.[n] This Council of *Constantinople* seems to have acted with more Zeal, than Prudence, or Temper. They were not content with condemning *Nestorius*, but proceeded against all who bore any Relation to him, and from Extracts out of their Writings charged them with heterodox Opinions, which they themselves never dreamt of. And therefore we can form no Judgment of any Man's Opinions from such partial Extracts. Does Mr. *L.* consult Authors only to pick out such little Scraps, as may seem to favour his Opinion? He might have learnt from this Account of *Theodore* by Dr. *Lardner*, which he refers to, that he lived and died in the Communion of the Church; and that he was in high Esteem among all his Cotemporaries. [o] *Socrates* tells us that he was a Friend and Companion of St. *Chrysostom.* [p] *Sozomen* says the same, and commends him as *a Man well versed in Scripture, and other Parts of Learning, and Philosophy.* [q] *Theodoret* tells us that he was *an eminent Teacher, and had vigorously opposed all the Crews of Hereticks;*

[n] *Mosheim* Cent. vi. P. 2. C. 3. [o] Hist. Eccl. Lib. iv. C. 3. [p] Hist. Eccl. Lib. viii. C. 2. [q] Lib. v. C. 27, 40. See also *Cave* Hist. Lit. —— *Du Pin.* Nouv. Biblioth.

that

that he continued *Bishop* 36 *Years*, contending against the Followers of *Arius*, *Eunomius*, and *Apollinarius*. Nor was this *Theodore* ever accused of *Heresy* in his Life-time. And, when after his Death this Charge was brought against him, he was powerfully vindicated by *Vigilius*, and *Facundus*. ʳ *Facundus*'s Vindication is now extant: in which he proves from *Theodore*'s own Works that he was orthodox in the Doctrine of the *Trinity*. I shall quote only one Passage out of many. He says that *Christ was both God and Man, both according to Nature the true God, and essentially the true Son of the true God*. *Theodore* also wrote against *Eunomius*, and *Apollinarius*, and an *Exposition of the Nicene Faith*. We have also his *Confession of Faith* preserved by *Marius Mercator*, who wrote against him. There he says, *We confess the Father to be a proper Person, and so likewise the Son, and so likewise the Holy Ghost, and preserving the Word of Godliness, we do not think the Father, the Son, and the Goly Hhost to be three different Essences, but one in the Unity of the Godhead*. If therefore we may judge of the Faith of these *Nestorians* from the Writings either of *Nestorius*,

---

ʳ *Facund.* Lib. ix. C. 2. P. 132.

or his Master *Theodorus,* they were indeed *Unitarians,* and so I hope we are all, but not in Mr. *L*'s Sense of the Word. They received the *Nicene Faith,* and held the Doctrine of a *Trinity in Unity.*

* Our *Apologist* skips from the fourth Century to the tenth, where he can find no Associates but some *Lombards,* and other *barbarous Nations.* Towards *the Close of the eleventh Century* he claims *Roscellin Canon of Compiegne,* and quotes *Mosheim* for it. † But as *Mosheim* tells us that he was charged not with Arianism, but Tritheism, so his learned Commentator Mr. *Macklaine* acquits him of this Charge. He observes that it must be considered that *the learned Men now mentioned, (Fulco and Anselm) were the inveterate Enemies of Roscellin, and that they perhaps comprehended his Meaning imperfectly, or perverted it willingly. Several Circumstances prove that some of his Adversaries were in one, or the other, of these two Cases. Anselm himself furnishes sufficient Grounds for this Suspicion, since, notwithstanding his Aversion to the Nominalists, of which Roscellin was the chief, he grants that the Opinion*

* P. 28.   † Cent. xi. P. 2. Ch. 5. P. 548.

of

of his Antagonist may be admitted, or at least tolerated, in a certain Sense, and even that he is not perfectly assured of understanding fully his Meaning, and that he believes the Sentiments of that Ecclesiastick to be less pernicious than his Accusers have represented them.

"In the same Manner our *Apologist* takes his Account of *the famous Abelard's* Tenets from *the Charge brought against him* by his Enemies. And yet from this very *Charge* it appears, that he was not so *completely an Unitarian* as our Author would wish him. If *he corrupted the Doctrine of the Trinity*, he must believe a *Trinity*. If *he entertained unworthy and false Conceptions of the Union of the two Natures in Christ*, he must believe that *the two Natures*, divine and human, were in some sort *united in him.* But *Mosheim* himself, from whom our *Apologist* takes his Account, vindicates him from this Charge, in the Words immediately following, which Mr. *L.* with his usual Unfairness has thought proper to pass by. —— "*It must be confessed* (says he) *by those who are acquainted with the Writings of Abelard, that he expressed himself in a very singular, and incongruous Man-*

u P. 29. w Cent. xii.

ner upon several Points of Theology, and this indeed is one of the Inconveniences, to which subtle Refinements upon mysterious Doctrines frequently lead. But it is certain on the other Hand, that St. Bernard, who had much more Genius, than Logick, misunderstood some of the Opinions of Abelard, and wilfully perverted others. ˣ The like Account is given by all the best Historians. And his Apology is now extant, in which, after some Excuses made for some crude Expressions, he denies every Part of the Charge brought against him, and declares, amongst other Things, that he believes that *Jesus Christ is the true and only Son of God, born of the Substance of the Father before all Ages*; and that *the Holy Spirit is the third Person of the Trinity, who proceeds from the Father, and the Son*. There is also among his Works a short Exposition of St. *Athanasius's Creed*, in which he professes his Assent to that *Creed*, and says that *we not only believe, but worship three Persons in the Unity of the*

ˣ See *Du Pin*. Nouv. Biblioth. — *Cave* Hist. Lit. — Mr. *Bayle* in his Dictionary tells us that his Enemies *had caused a Belief that he admitted three Gods. Yet 'tis very certain that he was very orthodox on the Doctrine of the Trinity, and that all the Processes made against him on that Matter are pitiful Cavils, that proceeded either from Malice, or Ignorance.*

Godhead.

Godhead. This is Mr. *L's complete Unitarian,* as *complete* an one as *Athanasius* himself. But he chooses to give us his Doctrines, not from himself, but from the *colouring, and Representation of his Adversaries.* And this he takes from *Mosheim,* but takes no Notice of the Paragraph immediately following, where *Mosheim* in great Measure acquits him from this Charge. Such reasoning really deserves no better Name than, what Mr. *Bayle* calls it, *pitiful Cavilling.*

ʸ I shall leave our *Apologist* in quiet Possession of his *Pasaginians,* an obscure Sect, of whom I can find but little Notice of in History. ᶻ *Mosheim* tells us that *their two chief religious Tenets were, first that the Observation of the Law of Moses was obligatory on all Christians, in consequence of which they circumcised their Followers, &c. Secondly, that Christ was no more than the first, and purest Creature of God.* And, he also tells us, that this wild Sect expired soon after their Birth.

I do not find that our *Apologist* any where lays claim to the *Waldenses,* as complete Unita-

---

ʸ P. 31.   ᶻ Cent. xii. P. 2. C. 5. P. 618.

rians: [a] but he has given us at the End of his Appendix *their Confeſſion of Faith, which was preſented to Francis* I. 1541. which he extolls highly for its *admirable Simplicity, and Conformity to Scripture.* This he has taken from [b] Mr. *Morland*'s Hiſtory of theſe Churches. But with what View he has inſerted it I know not. Would he from hence infer, or inſinuate, that theſe Men were of the ſame Principles with himſelf? Was this the only *Confeſſion of Faith,* which we have of theſe *Waldenſes?* No. [c] The ſame Mr. *Morland* but a few Pages before gives us *an antient Confeſſion of Faith of theſe Waldenſes out of certain Manuſcripts bearing Date A.D.* 1120. The ſecond Article of which is—*We do believe there is one God—Father, Son, and Holy Spirit*—[d] And a few Pages after we have *an Abbreviation of their Confeſſion of Faith which was preſented to Ladiſlaus King of Bohemia* A. D. 1508. by ſome of his Subjects of the ſame Faith with theſe *Wal-*

---

[a] P. 175. [b] We are obliged to our Author for referring us to this curious Book of Mr. *Morland*'s, where may be ſeen an Account of the Antiquity of theſe Churches of the *Waldenſes*, their Faith and Practice; how many Years before *Luther* they oppoſed the Errors of the *Church of Rome*, and what cruel Perſecutions, and Maſſacres, were brought on them by the Inſtigation of the *Popes of Rome*, to the eternal Infamy of that Church. [c] P. 30. [d] P. 43.

denſes,

denses, wherein they declare that *they taught that God is known, by Faith in the Scriptures, to be One as to the Substance of the Divinity, and three Persons, viz. Father, Son, and Holy Spirit; that as to the Persons there is a Difference, but as to the Essence and Substance, Coequality, and Indistinction.* ᵉ And they refer to the *Nicene*, and *Athanasian*, *Creed*. The same Author has given us *a Confession of Faith published by the reformed Churches of Piemont A. D.* 1658, the first Article of which is that *there is one only God, a spiritual Essence, &c. and that there are three Persons in that one, only, and simple, Essence, the Father, the Son, and the Holy Spirit.* ᶠ In the same Book we have an Account of *the ancient Discipline of the Evangelical Churches of the Valleys of Piemont, extracted out of divers authentick Mascripts written in their own Language several hundreds of Years before either Calvin, or Luther.* Amongst the rest we have *the Catechism of these antient Waldenses.* One Question is — *Whereby canst thou know that thou believest in Christ?* --- The Answer is --- *By this that I know him to be true God, and true Man* --- Another Question is. — *Dost thou believe in*

ᵉ P. 61.　　ᶠ Chap. 5, P. 72, &c.

the

the Holy Spirit? Anſw. —— *Yes, I do believe. For the Holy Spirit proceeds from the Father, and the Son, and according to the Divinity is equal to the Father, and to the Son.* Laſtly, We have an Extract from *ſeveral Treatiſes of theſe Evangelical Churches,* [g] in one of which they declare againſt all *Invocation of Saints,* and ſay that *no Man bodily born whoſoever, but Chriſt, ought to be adored;* [h] and again, *that it were far more expedient to adore Chriſt alone of all Men, he being abſolutely the beſt and kindeſt Mediator.* From all this it appears abundantly how little Mr. *L's* Quotation from their *Confeſſion is to his purpoſe.* They could never mean to exclude the *Worſhip of Chriſt.* They believed him to be *God, adored him,* and thought his *Worſhip comformable to Scripture.* [i] As to their *Confeſſion of Faith preſented to Francis* I, the Deſign of it was to vindicate themſelves from the Calumnies of their Enemies, who threatened them with a Perſecution. It is a very ſound one. They declare their Belief that *in Jeſus Chriſt dwelleth all the Godhead bodily.* If it is not ſo explicit with regard to the *Doctrine of the Trinity,* as ſome of their other Confeſſions are, it might be

[g] Ch. vii. P. 169. [h] P. 171. [i] See *Thuan,* Hiſt. Lib. vi. P. 189. — *Sleidan* Hiſt. Lib. xvi. P. 347.

becauſe

because they were never accused by their Adversaries of denying this Doctrine. *k* The Popish Inquisitors, who drew up Articles against them, never charged them with this. *l Reinerius*, a Popish Author, who wrote against these *Waldenses*, and is cited by A-Bp *Usher* in his Treatise *de Christianarum Ecclesiarum successione et statu*, complains that *this Sect of the Waldenses was the most pernicious of any, because they carried with them a great Shew of Godliness, as they lived honestly with Men, thought well in all Things of God, and believed all the Articles of the Creed, only they blasphemed, and hated the Church of Rome*.

I shall readily indeed acknowledge that there have been in all Ages of *Christianity*, from the Days of the Apostles down to the present Times, Persons who have denied the Doctrine of the *Trinity*, and the *Divinity* of our *Blessed Saviour*. Such were *Ebion*, and *Cerinthus* in the *Apostolick* Age, against whom, ⁿ as we are told by good Authority, St. *John*

---

k *Morland* B. ii. C. 1.   l Cap. vi. P. 151. See also *Cave* Hist. Lit. — *Mosheim* Cent. xii. P. 2. C. 5. P. 616. — *Allix*'s Hist. of the Churches of *Piemont*.   m *Iren.* L. iii. C. 11, 18. — *Tertull.* Præscript. C. 33. —— *Hieron* de viris illustr. Prolog. in *Matt.* —— *Epiphan.* Hæref. L. ii. P. 423. See *Waterland* Import. Doct. Trin. Ch. vi.

wrote both his *Gospel,* and *Epistles,* [n] and he calls them *Deceivers,* and *Antichrists.* Such there were also in the following Ages, both before, and after, the *Council of Nice.* But they have been always condemned as *Hereticks* by the *Catholick Church,* and cast out of her Communion. But, that *religious Worship is to be paid to God the Father only, and not to our Lord Jesus Christ,* I do not find that any of them ever held. [o] And this was the bold Assertion, which our *Apologist* undertook the Proof of. But he will not find among them all any such *complete Unitarians* as himself. His *Nazarene Christians, the Church of Jerusalem,* and all other *Christian* Churches, both before, and since *the Council of Nice,* have thought it their Duty to worship the *Son of God.* Not only *Nestorius,* and his Master *Theodorus, Roscellin, Abelard,* and the *Waldenses,* but *Arius* himself, and all his Followers, in *Asia, Africa,* and *Europe,* and among the *Goths, Vandals, Hunns,* and *Lombards,* were *Worshippers of Christ.* And so have been our modern *Arians,* and *Socinians.* [p] His great Apostle Dr. *Clarke* expressly teaches us that

---

[n] 1 *Joh.* ii. 22. — iv. 3. — 2 *Joh.* 7.   [o] P. 119, 147.
[p] Script. Doct. Trin. Pt. ii. Sect. 50.

Worship

Worſhip is to be paid to the Son, by offering him *Praiſe and Thankſgiving, invocating him in Prayer*, &c. And the late *Bp of Clogher* in his *Eſſay on Spirit* calls our *Lord* the *ſecond Jehovah*, and pleads ſtrongly for *Worſhip* due to him as ſuch. *Socinus* alſo, though he held *Chriſt* to be not *God*, but only *Man*, yet held *Worſhip* to be due to him, q as our Author himſelf tells us. And when *Franciſcus Davides*, and ſome others in *Tranſylvania*, more dangerous, but more conſiſtent, *Hereticks*, denied the *Worſhip of Chriſt*, r *Socinus* was greatly provoked, wrote againſt him with great Bitterneſs, and called him a *Blaſphemer, more than an Heretick, and unworthy the Name of a Chriſtian*. And the *Socinians* depoſed theſe Men, and caſt them out of their Communion. And *Davides* was at their Inſtigation caſt into Priſon, where he died a miſerable Death. Accordingly in the *Racovian Catechiſm* we find the *Worſhip of Chriſt* defended on the ſame Principles, as the *Romaniſts* defend the *Worſhip of Saints, and Angels.* s And to the Queſtion

---

q P. 138. r *Socin.* contra Vujek Ch. 2. — *Moſheim* Hiſt. Eccleſ. Cent. xvi. Sect. iii. Pt. 2. Ch. 4.

s *Quid vero ſentis de iis hominibus, qui Chriſtum non invocant, nec adorandum cenſent ? — Prorſus non eſſe Chriſtianos ſentio, cum re ipſâ Chriſtum non habeant, et licet verbis id negare non audeant, re ipſâ negent tamen.*

—— *What think you of those who hold that Christ is not to be worshipped* —— The Answer is *I think they are by no means Christians.* In vain then does Mr. *L.* look out for *his complete Unitarians* either in ancient, or modern Times. He has, I believe, the Honour of being the Author of the first Sect (unless perhaps these *Transylvanians*) who called themselves *Christians*, and yet denied that any *Worship* was due to *Christ*, and his *Liturgy* is the first *Liturgy*, wherein *the Worship of Christ* was omitted.

It does not fall within the Compass of my Design to follow him any farther. I could point out gross Misrepresentations in his *English* History. But I think I have followed him far enough, and I believe the Reader will think so too. I shall not therefore attempt to derogate from the Character of his Martyrs, and Confessors, but leave him to enjoy his good Opinion of them. Nor do I approve of any *sanguinary Laws,* or Persecution for Conscience sake. I shall not justify, or apologize for, *Calvin's* Treatment of *Servetus,* or any other like Severities. Only one Thing I would observe to him, that those, who were condemned for *Heresy* here in *England* in the first Ages of

the

the Reformation, did not suffer merely for denying the *Divinity of Chrift*. They were *Anabaptifts* from *Germany*, as Bp *Burnet*, and our Author from him, tells us. Let him then look into *Sleidan, Seckendorf*, and other Historians of thofe Times, and he will find that they not only held the moft dangerous Tenets fubverfive of all Government, but were guilty of the groffeft Enormities, had raifed the moft dangerous Seditions, and fubverted whole States. It is no Wonder then, that the Government fhould be very jealous of fuch Enthufiafts, and think it neceffary to proceed againft them with great Severity, for Reafons of civil Policy.

But why all this Outcry againft *Perfecution?* Surely there was never lefs Reafon to complain, or be afraid, of it. Never were Diffenters of all Kinds treated with greater Lenity. ᵗ The *Church of England* fets not up herfelf as *Lord over the Faith, and Confciences of others;* nor does fhe *dictate, or prefcribe, to others what they are to believe.* She claims only a Right to declare her own Terms of Communion, a Right, which every petty Society lays Claim to, and to judge of the Qualifications to be

ᵗ P. 163.

required

required of her own Ministers, a Power essential to the very Being of a Church. Those who cannot comply with these Terms have free Liberty to worship *God* in what Manner they please. Mr. *L.* himself, who exclaims against this *Monster of human Authority*, has (ᵘ as an ingenious Writer has observed before me) Reason to acknowlege that our Church is no very fierce *Monster*. If these *Unitarians* should ever gain an Establishment (which I trust they never will) I very much doubt whether we should meet with the like Indulgence. In the last Century, when the *Sectaries* got the upper Hand, they treated the Members of the *Church of England* with greater Severity, than they themselves had felt in the Days of A-Bp *Laud*. We have seen that of old *Constantius*, and *Valens*, and after them the *Goths* and *Vandals*, grievously persecuted the Church of *God*. We have seen too that in later Times the *Socinians* proceeded with great Rigour against *Davides*, and his Adherents. And I fear, if these *complete Unitarians* should prevail, they would not want Pretence from *Scripture* to prohibit what they must call *Idolatry*, and perhaps extirpate all those *who served other Gods*.

ᵘ *Layman*'s Script. Confut. P. 217.

Far

Far be it from me to desire to persecute them, or injure them in the least, in their Persons, or Possessions: but surely we may exclude them from our *Communion*, and much more from our *Ministry*, without any Breach of Charity. How can there be any Communion between Persons of Sentiments so diametrically opposite? how can they join in Worship, who have not the same Object of Worship? If Persons of these Principles petition for Relief, and call upon us to repeal our *Articles*, and new model our *Liturgy*, I humbly think they merit very little Regard.

THE END.

As I was unwilling to fwell this Pamphlet with Quotations at length from the Original, I have here added the Editions of the antient A U T H O R S herein cited.

Clemens Romanus
Ignatius
Polycarp } per Cotelerium 1724.
Conftitut. Apoftol.
Juftin Martyr.
Athenagoras } Par. 1615.
Theophilus
Irenæus per Grabe, Oxon. 1702.
Clemens Alex. per Sylburg. Par. 1629.
Tertullian } per Pamel. Rotomag. 1662.
Novatian
Hippolytus per Fabricium, Hamburgh, 1716.
Cyprian per Fell, Oxon. 1682.
Origen Opera, per Huet. 1668.
——— contra Celf. Cantab. 1658.
——— De Oratione, Oxon. 1686.
Arnobius, Hannov. 1603.
Lactantius, Lugdun. 1548.
Eufebius, &c. Ecclef. Hift. per Valef. Par. 1678.
Philo Judæus, Par. 1640.
Bafilius, Par. 1638.
Chryfoftom per Savil. Eton. 1612.
Auguftinus Hipp. Baf. per Froben. 1569.
Epiphanius, Par. 1622.
Sulpitius Severus, Lugd. Bat. 1654.
Victor Vitenfis, Par. 1610.
Procopius de Bell. Vandal. Par. 1662.
Facundus, Par. 1679.
Thuanus Hift. Aurel. 1620.
Sleidan Hift. tranf. by Bohun, 1689.
Pearfon on the Creed, Fol. Lond. 1715.
Prideaux Connect. Fol. Lond. 1718.
Bingham Antiquities, Fol. Lond. 1726.
Mofheim Eccl. Hift. tranf. by Macklane, Lond. 1765.

Lately printed by J. and J. FLETCHER, in the Turle, Oxford;

THE Reasonableness of requiring Subscription to Articles of Religion from Persons to be admitted in Holy Orders, or a Cure of Souls, vindicated in a Charge delivered to the Clergy of the Diocese of Oxford, in the Year 1771.

The Certainty of a Future State asserted and vindicated against the Exceptions of the late Lord Bolingbroke. —— A Sermon preached before the University of Oxford.

An Answer to a Pamphlet, entitled, Reflections on the Impropriety of Lay-Subscription to the 39 Articles, in the University of Oxford. Addressed to the Author.

An Answer to a Pamphlet, entitled, Considerations on the Propriety of requiring a Subscription to Articles of Faith.

The Excellency of the Jewish Law considered. In Two Sermons preached before the University of Oxford. To which is added an Appendix: And also a short Comment on Psalm CIX. and LV. wherein they are shewn not to be Imprecatory but Prophetical.

Christ the Lord of Glory. —— A Sermon before the University of Oxford, with Additions, confirming and enforcing the Doctrine.

The Use of Reason in Matters of Religion stated and explained. —— A Sermon before the University of Oxford.

Jephtha's Vow considered. —— A Sermon before the University of Oxford. With an Appendix, &c.

The Witness of the Spirit —— A Sermon before the University of Oxford.

The Doctrine of Justification by Faith, explained in a Sermon before the University of Oxford.

A Vindication of the Doctrine of the Trinity, from the Exceptions of a late Pamphlet, entitled, an Essay on Spirit, in three Parts, with an Appendix.

* The above are all by the Rev. THOMAS RANDOLPH, D. D. President of C. C. C. Lady Margaret's Professor of Divinity, and Archdeacon of Oxford.

A

SCRIPTURAL CONFUTATION

OF THE

ARGUMENTS

AGAINST THE

ONE GODHEAD

OF THE

FATHER, SON, and HOLY GHOST,

PRODUCED BY

The Reverend Mr. LINDSEY

In his late APOLOGY.

By WILLIAM BURGH, Esq.

THE SECOND EDITION.

OMNES AD SACRAS LITERAS SUNT DUCENDI, UT INDE TALIA HAURIANT, QUÆ, NISI DEO SEMET PATEFACIENTE, COGNOSCI NEQUEUNT.
GROTIUS.

YORK:

Printed by A. WARD, for the AUTHOR, and sold by W. NICOLL, in St. Paul's Church-Yard, London; and by all Booksellers in Town and Country.
MDCCLXXV.

[PRICE THREE SHILLINGS.]

to draw their own inferences, without being distracted by the intervention of such as are altogether foreign to the subject. I have gone yet farther, and, reasoning on the principles I had set down, have supplied them with such arguments as were amply sufficient to my own conviction; and which, had I not believed them to be sufficient to theirs, I never should have given to the world.

But, as I was new, both to that world, and myself as an author, it was natural in me to wish to obtain its sentiments as speedily as possible. To this purpose (which was all that an anonymous writer could do) I directed my printer to present copies of my book to a select number of persons, who might reasonably be supposed to lead the sentiments of the public: Persons on whom, either an exalted station, or something better than an exalted station had conferred consequence. I flattered myself that I should the more readily learn their opinion of my work, (if a favourable one) by taking this method of soliciting their perusal of it. I was not disappointed; for though I have not much to boast of any approbation personally addressed to myself, from those who have drawn their honours from the royal fountain, yet I was not unnoticed by others, who derive theirs from the clear and unpolluted spring of merit. Amongst the first of these, Sir, I was favoured

DEDICATION. iii

ed with your sentiments, delivered to me thro' the medium of my bookseller's conveyance, in the speediest and most polite manner. Let then a Layman, writing on a most important religious subject, make his boast, that he can, at least, produce credentials in his favour from a layman, and that layman Mr. Edmund Burke.

To have found an ally in a person who had himself maintained the establishment of the church; who, as a friend to truth, and as an investigating Christian, had already so ably, so eloquently, so zealously combated in her cause, must, in any situation, have been a pleasing circumstance. In mine it was much more; for when I perceived myself abetted by your favourable judgement, it gave me the fullest reason to hope, that my well-meant endeavours, to satisfy the scruples of men, who object upon one particular ground, would be attended with success; especially as I might now take the liberty of inscribing that work to you, from whose approbation alone it could derive the confidence to claim your patronage.

When I have thus made it known to the world that you have borne me a favourable testimony, I may add, that I republish with a certainty of being useful. I may indeed consider myself as having answered Mr. Lindsey's book in a manner originally foreign from my intention,

intention, and thrown a weight into the opposite scale, sufficient to preponderate against his
huge mass of human authority. I have the
honour to be,

Sir,

With the greatest respect and esteem,

Your much obliged,

And most obedient, humble servant,

WILLIAM BURGH.

Advertisement.

IN the following sheets, which I am desirous of rendering universally useful, I have taken care to write the third and fourth chapters in such a manner, as that they may be read separately by persons to whom the preceding part of the work might be difficult or unnecessary.—The plan I have pursued throughout is as follows.——Having, as I think, set aside Mr. Lindsey's foundation of argument in the introduction, and shewed the fallacy or inconclusiveness of what he builds most upon, I have in my first chapter stated the proper premises upon which our reason is at liberty to act with respect to scripture truths. In my second, I have endeavoured to shew the nature of the evidence which is borne to that great scripture truth to which our faith is required. And in the subsequent parts of the work have shewed what the evidence itself is.— I have but one request to make of my reader, which is, that he will do by me as I did by Mr. Lindsey; and when he is reading my book, that he will place the

Bible beside him; for, by my agreement, with that only do I desire to stand; nay, if I shall be found to disagree, I wish to fall. In some few instances, for the sake of continuing a sentence, I have changed the person used in a scripture precept, and, instead of absolutely adhering to such words as *do ye*, have sometimes said *we are desired to do*, &c. and in a few instances have omitted a multitude of nominatives, where one answered the purpose full as well, as in Rev. vi. 15, 16, where it is said that *the kings of the earth, and the great men, and the rich men, and the chief captains, and the mighty men, and every bond man, and every free man hid themselves in the dens, and in the rocks of the mountains*; in such cases I have used only the first. Of this I think it necessary to apprize my reader, lest he should charge me with inaccuracy in my quotations; whereas I will promise him that, throughout the whole work, he will not find the smallest alteration made in the sense. The passages with which I have taken this liberty are but very few also; but let him lay the Bible before him, and there is no great danger of his being misled.—— Sometimes instead of quoting I have para-

phrased;

phrafed; but that will always appear in the inftance. — In the 66th page I have made a comment upon John viii. 58, and confuted an objection brought againft it by an author who ftyles himfelf " a Lover of the Gofpel." The paffage which I have treated of was pointed out to me; it remained on my mind, and by miftake I have afcribed it to Mr. Lindfey. This is but of fmall importance. I mention it only that I may apologize to him for it.

A

SCRIPTURAL CONFUTATION, &c.

INTRODUCTION.

THE conduct of Mr. Lindfey, in refigning the vicarage of Catterick on certain fcruples, excited my curiofity to know what his particular objections to the fubfcription of the articles of the church of England were. His refignation was foon followed by a book under the captivating title of "The Apology of Theophilus Lindfey, A. M. on refigning the vicarage of Catterick, Yorkfhire." With this book, which was greedilybought up, I alfo furnifhed myfelf. What I expected to have found in it, is of no confequence to the public; but I did indeed find a much "larger circuit taken" than the title promifed, and that "the defign was not barely to offer a vindication of the motives and conduct of a private perfon," but to affail every fundamental doctrine of the church, from the miniftry of which he had retired; to degrade the God of our falvation; to fnatch from us the object of our religion; and to evince, that Jefus Chrift is not one, with the Father and the Holy Ghoft, God. Upon what foundation he has raifed the flimfy fuperftructure of his own doctrine, or rather with what engines he has endeavoured to fubvert the fixed fabrick of our religion, and force it from the bafis of revelation, I fhall proceed to fhew; and without infinuating

nuating pretenſions to divine aſſiſtance, from the grant of which it might be inferred, that my cauſe had the particular favour of heaven, I hope to evince the divinity of our bleſſed Lord and Saviour Jeſus Chriſt, and, in oppoſition to all the human authority convened by Mr. Lindſey, to ſhew that God himſelf has borne teſtimony to it; and if, from his revelation, it be clearly ſet forth that Jeſus Chriſt is both God and man, I hope and believe the poſition will be acceded to, however unable reaſon may be to comprehend it, or how numerous ſoever the voices may be which have lifted themſelves up againſt it.

Before I enter upon the ſubject propoſed, I think it neceſſary to remove ſome prejudices which favour Mr. Lindſey's cauſe, prejudices ſo natural to the mind of man, that he has been aware of their uſe, and, with ſuperfluous diligence, beſtowed near half his book to inſtill them. The influence of theſe upon my readers I muſt, however, try to avert before I can hope for an impartial hearing; for I have reſigned no vicarage; I have puſhed from me no worldly advantages; I have given no proofs that a little, with a ſettled conſcience, is preferable, in my eyes, to great riches retained by acquieſcence in that which I do not believe; all of which he has done, and for which let me freely pay him the tribute of my praiſe; let me declare that I honour the ſincerity which ſuch a conduct demoſtrates; but let me never ſay that, from the rectitude of his heart, I can deduce the rectitude of his opinions. Such proofs of my ſincerity, it is true, I have it not in my power to produce; but even Mr. Lindſey has borne ſuch teſtimony to the troubles of an unquiet ſpirit, that no man will conceive that I ſhould ſeek to incur them by a voluntary engagement in the cauſe of falſehood, or look upon the ſalvation of my immortal ſoul as a matter of

ſo

so little importance to me, that I should maintain a doctrine, connected as this is with the felicity of a future state, if I were not clearly convinced of its truth.

Unless then I am to consider it written with a view to prejudice the Reader, the aim of the long chapter of sufferers for the maintenance of Mr. Lindsey's doctrine is altogether inexplicable to me, because I am unable to deduce the truth of a system from any other source than that of reason or fair argument. Submission to misery, in preference to the concession of an opinion, does indeed prove the sincerity of the sufferer, but by no means the opinion for which he has suffered; it may prove the weakness of his understanding, but by no means the strength of his cause. In India the distortions of the Bramin are the testimony of the divinity of his Ixora; in the holy office, the submission of the Jew to the extremest tortures, is the testimony that our Saviour had not even divine assistance; and now in England we find a number of unhappy wretches suffering under equally unjust and cruel inflictions, to prove a negation of our Saviour's divinity; and this list of miserable creatures is held out to the public by a gentleman who has voluntarily added himself to the number. I have already said that I considered such a conduct as a proof of sincerity, but I cannot submit to allow it the name of martyrdom, or in the least degree a proof of the justice or truth of the opinion for the maintenance of which it is sustained; doctrines the most contradictory would else be true. Papal supremacy and regal supremacy have almost mingled their blazing testimonies, and were they both truly to be maintained? What horrible proofs have been given to the world that flour and water are flesh and blood; and will any man declare that the contrary doctrine has derived validity from equal, nay greater, streams of blood

poured

poured out to teftify that they were flour and water ftill? No man, furely; becaufe this is a pofition, the proofs of which are fubmitted to all men, and a ftronger degree of teftimony, than my ftedfaftnefs, may be and is borne to it by the fenfes of all mankind. Both fides of this queftion have had their bleeding advocates, and are they therefore both true? I will go yet farther and fay, that were I to undergo the fharpeft afflictions for entertaining the oppofite doctrine to that of Mr. Lindfey, (and I would undergo them rather than depart from the belief for which I think I have fo fufficient grounds) yet I fhould not conceive that I had added even the flighteft proof of the truth of it. My fincerity the world would, I believe, allow, but what could my fincerity evince? I fuffer for a pofition, and becaufe I have believed it upon arguments feeming fufficient to me; if they be in fact fufficient, I have done well to adhere to them, and they were as valid before my fuffering as afterwards; and if they are defective, my miferies cannot alter the conclufions following from them. Their truth or falfehood, the juftice or injuftice of the inference are pre-exiftent to my teftimony, and fo abfolutely independent of my belief, or any proofs that I may give of the fincerity of my belief, and are fo far from deriving ftrength from my fuffering in behalf of them, that they would have been precifely the fame though I had never been born, as if I had made my exit at a ftake. I am anxious to eftablifh this point, and therefore dwell upon it, for I fear that too eafy credit may be yielded to a doctrine held forth by a claimant to martyrdom; the feal of blood has given a feeming validity to many a pofition, from which the affertors had before derived no glory; the ftake, where it has been the only argument, has fometimes been confidered as a very convincing one; and a departure in flames has been thought to have re-

vealed

vealed the angel, where the precepts for which they are sustained had perhaps only shewed forth the contemptible man: But martyrdom is not now to be deduced from sincerity, which is all that can be concluded from strenuous suffering. The apostles indeed were martyrs, they bore testimony to facts submitted to their senses, and had even a sensible perception of divine assistance, of which also they gave proofs to the world: They bore testimony, and they would not recede from it; what they testified they knew, and promulgated by extraordinary aid, of which they were eminently conscious; what they knew, not what opinions they formed without divine assistance, was their doctrine; and from the testimony of what they knew they would not be deterred; they suffered, and their constancy was a proof of their sincerity: But they were sincere, not in the maintenance of dubious controvertible doctrines, but in having testified, that what they had preached they had known. As then they were sincere, and had proved themselves so, we must conclude that they did know what they had preached, and consider their stedfast adherence to what they had set out with as an exceedingly strong testimony borne to the truth of it; and such a testimony as this is what is properly called martyrdom. I hope that this may be sufficient to warn my readers from looking upon sincerity as a proof of the opinion sincerely believed; let it recommend the heart, but by no means the head, the errors of which may be as sincerely believed as the best established maxims.

The prodigious number of names, only pretending to human authority, which are produced by Mr. Lindsey to support his doctrines, might perhaps be well opposed by citing as great a multitude of eminent men, who have agreed with the church of England, and ascribed divinity to our blessed Saviour. Were it only to

satisfy

satisfy him, with whom, I fear, the authority of the scriptures will signify but little, I would pursue this course of argument (if argument it may be called); but I scorn any other foundation than that of God himself, whose written word, not seen through the medium of a comment, is alone evidence to me; let it not therefore be inferred, that I am unable to meet him upon his own ground, because I choose that which is better; for I could, to him, oppose as good human authority to maintain my belief as any ten Dutch women in Europe, however strenuously they might have sustained and suffered for the doctrines of Anabaptism.

The dispositions of mankind lean toward those who flatter their reason, and endeavour to reduce all things to her comprehension, or to those who abet that pride with which she is desirous of rejecting whatsoever she cannot comprehend; from this principle it is that they who familiarly illustrate the most unfamiliar difficulties, or flatly deny the existence of that which transcends the faculties of man, are heard with partial ears. Against this prejudice also, in favour of Mr. Lindsey, I am obliged to guard; for he has declared, that " our Saviour Christ teacheth no mysterious doctrines". As I have already said, that the scriptures shall be my only appeal; to this denial of a mystery, nay to that ridicule with which the word *Mystery* is treated throughout Mr. Lindsey's book, I shall oppose the serious declaration of St. Paul, who, speaking of the gospel of Jesus Christ and him crucified, and that not with enticing words of Man's wisdom, but in demonstration of the Spirit, that our faith might stand not in the wisdom of man, but the power of God, declares, " we speak the wisdom of God in a mystery"; and this he says he does " by the Spirit of God, by which alone the deep things of God are searched"; and he farther declares, that

that "the fpirit compares fpiritual things with fpiritual; but that thefe things are foolifhnefs to the natural man who receiveth not the things of the Spirit of God." See 1 Cor. ii.

Will Mr. Lindfey now perfevere to fay, that the doctrine of Chrift is not myfterious? The moral doctrines delivered by himfelf I grant, indeed, are not fo; but on the contrary moft perfpicuoufly clear; but a manifeftation of him who delivered thofe doctrines, and a revelation teftifying of him, and fetting forth who he was, and is, and fhall eternally be, and that " in him dwelleth all the fulnefs of the Godhead bodily," Coloff. ii .9. Is not this a myftery? " Now, without controverfy, great is the myftery of godlinefs; God was made manifeft in the flefh, juftified in the Spirit, feen of angels, preached unto the Gentiles, believed on in the world, received up into glory," 1 Tim. iii. 16. Let us then beware of the philofophy of the natural man, of the enticing words of man's wifdom, which St. Paul has warned us againft, becaufe he well forefaw that it would ftand in the way and preclude " the acknowledgment of the myftery of God, and of the Father, and of Chrift," Coloff. ii. 2. This warning to beware of the deceits of philofophy is given at fuch a time, and in context with fuch a doctrine, as makes it utterly aftonifhing to me how any man in his fenfes fhould attempt to warp it to the purpofes of overturning our Saviour's divinity: We are defired to beware of it, becaufe it might be oppofite to the declaration which immediately follows, that " in Chrift dwelleth all the fulnefs of the Godhead bodily;" that " Chrift is all in all;" that " Chrift forgave us all;" that " of the Lord we fhall receive the reward of the inheritance, for we ferve the Lord Chrift;" that " whatfoever we do, we fhould do it heartily, as to the Lord, and not unto man."

man." In short, St. Paul has given us this warning in the midst of his epistle to the Colossians, to which I refer as a most explicit declaration of our Saviour's divinity throughout. Let us just consider now, whether this warning can have any other object in view. Mr. Lindsey's principal objection to the Godhead of Christ, is, that it is not reconcilable to reason; St. Paul says, that the Greek requires wisdom. Mr. Lindsey says, that it is a doctrine fraught not only with impiety but absurdity; St. Paul says, that it is to the Greek foolishness. Of what doctrines, of what philosophy now was St. Paul afraid? Will Mr. Lindsey say, that he feared that the Greeks would, from their demand for a reasonable doctrine, adopt a doctrine contrary to what he thinks reasonable himself? Or will he say that the apostle apprehended, from their aversion to that which was foolish, their adoption of a doctrine which he himself declares to be foolish? If this be his mode of reasoning, it is so self-subverted that it requires only to be read for its own confutation. His assertion, that the Trinity is an idea adopted from Plato, is full of impiety, and so extreamly weak, that I am sorry to see any man capable of promulgating it; and, were I not assured of this gentleman's sincerity, from the proof which he has given to the world, that upon the whole he disbelieves our Saviour's divinity, I should incline to conceive that he meant to impose this on mankind upon the faith of a martyr. I will now advance one of the like nature, and assure Mr. Lindsey that the idea of the Unity of God is derived from the philosophy of Socrates, who, notwithstanding his having been educated in a country where such a doctrine was esteemed impious, yet dared to preach this imagination of his own brain. How does this sound? Just as well as the other, and is advanced with fully equal truth. For my own part, I must now declare to this gentleman, that (so far from

having

having drawn my faith in the Trinity from Plato, the only book I have ever read on the fubject, (except his own, which I was led to look into by my curiofity to fee the motives of his uncommonly confcientious conduct) is the Bible. That I have thence deduced the doctrine of the Trinity; that both the Old and the New Teftaments evince it; the Old by typical and verbal prophecies; and the New, by the events which juftify the prophecies; that our Saviour's life and leffons teach it; and that the more explicit teftimony of the Holy Ghoft declare and enforce it; that, in the epiftles of St. Paul, evaded or trifled with, it is delivered in nearly fo many words. But I muft farther declare, that though it be not precifely fo denominated there, or in any part of the fcriptures, I cannot form an idea why I am not at liberty to give a name to that, which another fhall fo defcribe as to put it into my power to give it a name for the benefit of communication. The Godhead of the Father, and of the Son, and of the Holy Ghoft, is a doctrine which I deduce from the facred writings, and to thefe three perfons I am furely at liberty to give a name that fhall at once comprehend them all, and ferve the purpofe of more expeditioufly conveying my mind on the fubject, whenfoever I fhall fall upon it, without levity. From the fame fource alfo I deduce the being of but one God; and as I have before given the name of Trinity to the three Perfons, to this Godhead I give the name of Trinity in Unity; and what fhall preclude my giving a name where the fcriptures have given the fubftance, I own I do not fee; nor can I conceive this objection to the Trinity of perfons, and the Unity of the Godhead, to be a bit better grounded than that of the Quakers to the ufe of the word *you*, becaufe the term is not to be found in the Bible. It is objected alfo to the doctrine of the Trinity, that the word was not formed till

B late

late in the second century. As to the date of a word I cannot see it to be of any sort of consequence, if the idea to which it is annexed be but conveyed by it. If we had not been termed Christians by the people of Antioch, and that the professors of Christ's religion had, as yet, continued without a name, would posterity deny the existence of Christianity, or dispute the propriety of the term, because it was of the eighteenth century? The word *Christians* was equally applicable to us before we were called by it at Antioch, as after; and the word *Trinity* was equally applicable to the three persons of the Godhead before mankind agreed to call them by it, as after.

But if the name only were in debate, I should be but very little concerned about it, the Unity of the Godhead, and the Divinity of the three Persons being allowed, I care not by what appellation they are called: But I am sorry to see, at a time when I believe the *doctrine* is what Mr. Lindsey would confute, that he is weak enough to conceive that a disapprobation of the *name* will in the least contribute to his purpose; for either he must conceive that it does, and so trifle; or not conceiving so, acknowledge that he is talking about words only; and surely nothing can be more uncandid than such a process. He must assuredly know that his delicate conduct will procure him more readers than he could with modesty have hoped for, had his book been put forth without such a concomitant circumstance; and also that, in the multitude of his readers, understandings of every size must be numbered; and it is therefore impossible but he must have foreseen that some will be of so contracted dimensions, as to reckon the dislike of the word among the arguments against the substance named. To what purpose else than that of deception is it advanced, that to Luther " the word

Trinity

Trinity founds oddly, and is of human invention, and that it were better to call Almighty God, God, than Trinity." And that Calvin says " I like not this prayer, O holy, blessed, and glorious Trinity, it favours of barbarism." Are Luther and Calvin among the opponents of the doctrine of the Trinity? No such thing; and Mr. Lindsey himself shall tell you that they were well known and warm contenders for what is called the doctrine of the Trinity, though they expressed such a dislike of the word itself. I cannot see his inference, unless he would insinuate that a dislike of the word, is a dislike of the doctrine, and therefore avail himself of the authority of these " virtuous holy" men: But that authority is altogether against him, as himself acknowledges; and Calvin, by a horrible instance, proved the sincerity of his belief in the Trinity, for he actually brought Servetus to the stake for opposing it.

If this delicacy of Calvin, concerning the barbarism of a term, be admitted in argument, I see no reason wherefore we should reject a classic mythology; or why, when we speak of our Saviour's incarnation, we should not use the words with which Erasmus ridiculed the fastidious wits of Leo's polished court, and say, " E cœlo descendit filius Jovis." In short, I can see no reason wherefore we should not, like Leo himself, pass judgment upon the whole of the sacred writings, declare them barbarous, and never read the Bible for fear of spoiling our taste. And with respect to what is said concerning Luther, however it may be asserted that he prefers the calling upon God, by the name of God, to the calling upon him by the name Trinity, it is deducible from this assertion, that he looked upon the two words as synonimous, and consequently that the word *Trinity*, though it might found oddly, was expressive of the idea, which he chooses rather to express by the term

term God; a term perhaps more pleasing to his ear.

Thus far I have written, not with a view of derogating from the real worth of Mr. Lindsey, nor of lessening the value of such worth in the eyes of mankind; but with a purpose of preventing the merits of the honest conscientious man being carried over to his cause, and concluded to be the merits of his argument. I am myself desirous that the favour which is due to his virtue should attend his person, but not be converted into partiality for his cause. I seek not to obtain the favour of the public to myself, but their unprejudiced ear, and that men should yield their convictions to truth only, and not take prepossessions for conviction. Preliminaries being, I hope, settled, I shall now no longer withhold my reader from that line of argument, by which alone it seems to me possible to inquire into the subject before us, and by the pursuit of which, I trust, I shall be able to evince the Divinity of our Lord and Saviour Jesus Christ.

CHAP.

CHAP. I.

On the Province of Reason, with Respect to its Enquiry into Scripture Truths.

MR. Lindsey commences with an assertion, that "the unlearned reader sees at once, that the God who made him, and whom he is to adore, is one, without multiplicity or division, even as he knoweth himself to be one, being one person and not many;" and on this position he proceeds to argue. If Mr. Lindsey means by the unlearned reader, the reader of his book, who has never read the Bible, perhaps he is right; but I believe that every reader, who has read the Bible, will see the fallacy of this great foundation of all that follows in confutation of a trinity of Persons in the Godhead. On a supposition that nature has suggested, and philosophy refined upon the suggestion of a God, I do not doubt that natural religion might acquiesce in this assertion; but are we to come to the scriptures, which all men allow to be the foundation of our religion, with a religion already formed, and to judge of the revelation made by the God of truth, according to its correspondence with our previous persuasions? Are we to exalt our own reason, and say, that it is a standard whereby to measure the infinite extents of power and wisdom? or are we to set bounds to infinity, and annihilate all that stretches beyond the grasp of our limited comprehension? The short-sighted man may, with equal truth, and equal wisdom, deny the existence of all objects beyond the reach of his vision. And yet one of these consequences must be inferred from the assertion, either that our reason is infinite

nite to meafure infinite wifdom; or that the wifdom of God is finite, and narrowly limited, in order to be conformable to our reafon; for the faculty muft be commenfurate to the object, before it can take it into obfervation and determine upon it.

I fhould be forry to have it underftood, that I wifh to fet up one boundary which original nature has fuffered reafon to pafs. I think, however, that, as there are boundaries already formed, beyond which fhe is not permitted to expatiate, it is an object of confequence to mankind to find where they are fixed; for, by an acquaintance with our limits, we fhall alfo poffefs a definite idea of that which is within our comprehenfion; and fo, inftead of idly fquandering our ufeful hours in purfuit of knowledge that is too high for us, and which, when we conceive that we have attained unto it, terminates not in conclufion, but at the very beft in fpecious fallacy, we fhall turn the force of our faculties againft objects which muft yield to our vigorous exertions, atchieve that which, retained, may be ferviceable to ourfelves, or, communicated, prove beneficial to our fellow creatures.

My purpofe is only to inquire into thofe limits by which reafon is circumfcribed with regard to fcripture truths, and into the proper conduct of reafon within thofe limits.

By the word *Reafon*, I mean that faculty of the mind by which it perceives the relative qualities of the objects of our perception; by which it compares the objects of our perception; and, upon comparifon, fees the conclufions, of whatfoever nature they be, which refult.

The

The word *Comparison* I use in an extensive sense, for every manner of laying together the relative qualities in order to infer; and I choose to say, that reason sees rather than forms the conclusions, because I suppose them to have been formed, and existing at all times, whether observed or not, and no more to be annihilated by my withdrawing my observation, than Mr. Hume is by my blowing out the candle, by the light of which I had (according to his own philosophy) seen him into existence.

That great truth of Scripture which I wish to hold forth for the assent of mankind, and which I wish also to prescribe and pursue a proper manner of inquiring into, is, that Jesus Christ is one with the Father and the Holy Ghost, God.

It has often been asserted, that reason absolutely contradicted the possibility of such a union of divine perfection and human imperfection, and thence the impossibility of such a union is inferred, and the Godhead of Jesus Christ denied upon this unweighed assertion; whereas, were it considered, that the relative qualities of God and of Man are the objects of comparison, and that the incompatibility of these two natures, upon a perception of the qualities of each, must be seen from the comparison, perhaps men who deny our Saviour's divinity would hesitate a moment before they would even pronounce that their reason had, upon natural premises, given any testimony whatsoever concerning him; for, in the process, it must be enquired into, whether the objects of the comparison be really the objects of their perception, how far even the nature of man is within their comprehension, and how far the nature of God is beyond it; and if, upon enquiry, it be found, that the relative qualities of the two natures are altogether unknown, reason must be declared incompetent competept to make a comparifon, and confequently to fee any conclufion whatfoever. Reafon, therefore, can never have denied, that Jefus Chrift is both God and Man, however ignorance and prefumption may, under her refpectable name.

I do not defire, on the other hand, to conclude a belief in fcripture truths from the unaffifted light of reafon; I only defire to put that religion, which we may imagine nature has found by that light, out of the queftion; and then firft to call for the obfervation of reafon, when maxims, whence argument may proceed, are eftablifhed; when we firft find objects which we may compare, and from the comparifon of which we may conclude: But till fuch are found, and agreed upon, we muft walk upon uncertain ground; and if we fhould happen to come right in the end, it muft be by ways of which we could not have been certain while on our progrefs. To fabricate maxims is not the office of reafon, but to obferve upon fuch as are ready made and fubmitted to her cognizance, I therefore afk no aid to my caufe from any fuggeftions that fhe may be fuppofed to have made, nor will I allow that fhe can have afforded any to infidelity. I wifh only to diffuade from looking upon a negative as proved, becaufe the affirmative does not follow from premifes not cognizable: From fuch premifes we never can argue to any conclufion whatfoever; for no relation being vifible, no refult can iffue. A declaration from natural religion that God is omnipotent and all-wife, can by no means fet afide a declaration that he has done that which to us may appear weak and foolifh; we muft be competent to judge of infinite power and infinite wifdom before we can compare the act with the agency; and we muft be very fure that the act which is inconfiftent with our degree of wifdom, muft be inconfiftent with a greater height than our own,
before

before we can pronounce that it is impoffible for infinite wifdom to fee a reafon for fo acting. Even in the courfe of worldly tranfactions, how often has a man of fenfe accounted for imputed abfurdity of conduct, and, by fhewing us the grounds of his action, extorted our applaufe where we had before been too liberal of our cenfure? The reafons which influence man are intelligible to man, and therefore, when affigned, may indemnify his act; but the reafons of the conduct of our infinite Maker muft be incommunicable, becaufe unintelligible to our faculties, unlefs our minds were enlightened above our fphere; that is, unlefs mankind were placed higher in the chain of intellectual beings, which fomewhere requires the exiftence of fuch a creature, and fo fhould not be man. We cannot then argue, from any idea we are able to form of any attribute of God, to the action properly proceeding from it; and therefore can never deny an act, by himfelf afcribed to any of his attributes. Has infinite mercy let loofe the bloody tyrant to fcourge mankind? Or does infinite juftice choofe to afflict the meek and benevolent heart? Can the affumption of flefh, and fubjection to the infirmities of man, be imputed to the wifdom of God? Or does infinite power and glory beam from a helplefs bleeding body hanging on a crofs? And yet as reafonably may thefe two latter inftances of impotence and folly be afcribed to infinite extents of power and wifdom, as the two former, the profperity of the wicked, and the broken heart of the benevolent, to the infinite extents of mercy and juftice. If then the conduct of the affairs of this world be not reconcilable to our ideas of infinite faculties, we muft, if we interpret from the act to the agent, difprove the exiftence of thofe attributes with which we cannot reconcile fuch conduct, and confequently the exiftence of the being in which we had before conceived them inherent; fo that returning to God by the fame road by which we defcended from him,

him, we no more find him, and the infinitely great Creator of all things we then difcover to have been a meer Creature of our own imaginations.

Such is the procefs of unconducted reafon: With the fame arguments fhe conceives and annihilates her God: At every turn fhe finds and lofes him, yet ftill regrets the lofs, and though fhe cannot maintain the poffeffion, relinquifhes it with reluctance. If from our longing after immortality, our immortality is to be concluded, from our longing after an acquaintance with an intimated God, we may likewife infer the reafonablenefs of a revelation admitting us to that acquaintance, and helping us to a permanent idea, which nature was never enabled to acquire of herfelf. It feems then an act confiftent with our previous perfuafions, in which even reafon acquiefces, that a God, endowed with benignity, fhould ftretch forth his hand to mankind thus wandering in eternal intricacies, mercifully vouchfafe himfelf to become his guide, lead him to truth, and make his own way ftrait before him. This mode of argument, however, I do not infift upon, I make ufe of it rather to illuftrate than infer. I can do without any conceffions from reafon; for, at all events, I am certain, that, if fhe does not affirm, fhe cannot, upon the principles which I have already laid down, deny the confiftency of fuch an act with the agent of whom it is fuppofed; but if the ftrongeft external teftimony bear witnefs, that God has revealed himfelf, and that reafon be incapable of producing any evidence to the contrary; nay, if a revelation be what reafon might have herfelf prefcribed, and hoped as a guide to her own errors, wherefore fhould we not acquiefce in it when related, and look upon it as a fact, that God has actually revealed himfelf? The nature and validity of the teftimony, upon which the affertion is made, is extreamly well worth

enquiry,

enquiry, and certainly fhould be inveftigated by all who entertain any doubt of the fact afferted. For my own part, I am fatisfied; and Mr. Lindfey has exempted me from the neceffity of going into the enquiry here; having acknowledged that God has revealed himfelf, that the fcriptures are his revelation, that they afford " an evidence which no fair mind can refift," and that they are " the only rule of faith and confcience to Chriftian men:" In all of which I perfectly and entirely agree with him. The credibility of God, whom all allow, and who has pronounced himfelf to be the God of truth, is a ground whereon to build our faith in whatfoever he fhall relate of his own incomprehenfible majefty; and, as I have faid before, that the conduct of God can never be meafured by his attributes, fo I now fay, that there lies no appeal from his credibility, from his truth to the infcrutable nature; we muft acquiefce in that which he has faid; it muft be; it is true.

Having admitted the fcriptures to be the word of God, and that whatfoever is fet forth in them is true, we are not yet to conceive that he has fo far fubmitted himfelf to our faculties as to enable us to draw any argument from him; for we are not yet to compare his conduct, as revealed therein, with God himfelf, nor to judge of the confiftency of any act therein declared to be his, with the infinite Agent ftill left incomprehenfible; for to render him otherwife to us, the enlargement of our faculties muft attend upon a revelation of all his glory, and therefore a revelation of all his glory is not to be required. Perhaps the diftinction is not here fo clearly marked as I could defire, and that what I have laft written may feem to be only a repetition of what immediately precedes it; it is not fo; what I wifh to inculcate is briefly this, that, as in natural religion, no comparifon can be had between the attributes of God, and the moral evils of the world submitted to our observation, and yet that we do not quite consent to annihilate an original to nature, because his government seems to argue against him; so we should not, when revelation declares a course of conduct, which we cannot reconcile with the attributes ascribed to him, any more deny that course of conduct, from its irreconcileableness with God, than we should deny the existence of moral evil, because we had by nature pronounced that Original to be great, wise, and good: For if moral evil were incapable of rooting out the acknowledgment of the existence of a cause supremely good; so a conduct, not understood to be wise, should not be admitted an argument against the existence of a revealed God; but we cannot deny the existence of moral evil, and yet nature says there is a good God; wherefore then should we conceive, that an acknowledgment of a conduct confessedly not understood, and therefore not to be reprehended, can militate against the acknowledgment of the God who has revealed himself? Let us then, if we admit a good cause consistent with moral evil, not argue against the consistency of an incomprehensible God, and an unintelligible conduct: There may subsist an unseen relation in this latter case; whereas an eventual evil, resulting from a supreamly good cause, seems actually to contradict our reason. The purpose for which I have written this, is to put men upon their guard against any suggestion, that the revelation of God, made by himself, should convey an adequate idea of his great glory. That it should do so to man I have shewed to be impossible. It has indeed declared him infinite, but a declaration that God is infinite, is a declaration that he is incomprehensible: An indefinite majesty is all that can possibly be ascribed to God; and, in the conduct of incomprehensible wisdom, it is not probable that much can occur exactly conformable to our faculties. If then,

even

even a revelation be unable to make him comprehended, we are still to consider him beyond the reach of reason; and when he relates his own actions, still conceive that the agent is not cognizable, that he should be compared with them. To make us better men upon hope grounded on his mercies, is the most beneficial purpose for which we can conceive it possible for God to reveal himself; and to this very purpose we find a revelation made, wherein that providence which extends to us is declared. To what end should God lay before our eyes the government of all that we are not concerned in? That he has created and redeemed us, is a motive to gratitude and to brotherly love; it is sufficieut to shew in him a power to be feared for its extent, and adored for its beneficent exertion. To evince that he has promised to every man the reward of his works, and pointed out those works which lead us to hope in him that is faithful, is a fully sufficient motive to faith, hope, and charity; that he bears the relative superiority of a creator over his creature, is a sufficient motive to us to pronounce him our God, and ascribe to him all honour and glory, without seeking for a farther revelation of the exertion of his infinite power, which we are not concerned to know. But in the government of the universe, it may be said, he has selected this little orb, rolling through infinite space, as a scene of a most wonderful transaction in which we are certainly concerned; for it is asserted that our salvation is the consequence, and was the end proposed; and are we not yet to comprehend him? By no means; the infinite wisdom which dictated and knows wherefore such a transaction is the fittest means of our salvation, has not yet submitted itself to our investigation, nor directly told us why this was the most adequate means to so beneficent an end; he still remains incomprehensible, and that transaction by which we are become partakers of eternal life, being revealed,
amounts

amounts only to a foundation and motive for us to rely upon God, and act according to his will thereby declared to us, and not to a difplay of all that muft neceffarily exceed the limits of our perception. We are not called upon to account for his conduct; but we are required to love him, to hope and to truft in him. A declaration of his power, and the exertion of fo much of it as bears relation to us, is all then that was neceffary for thofe ends; thefe are beft declared by a revelation of the conduct of God towards man. Such a revelation is made, and there is much in it that we cannot underftand; and fuch muft ever be the cafe, for in whatfoever action we look upon, proceeding from a higher intellect than our own, we fhall fee fomewhat not intelligible till the grounds of it are communicated. In whatfoever action of God, made perceptible to us, we look upon, we fhall fee fomewhat which muft eternally continue unintelligible; for it proceeds from infinite heights of intellect, and confequently muft be incommunicable.

Reafon is, as it were, the eye of the mind; and as the eye is incapable of comparing invifible things, or vifible with invifible, fo is reafon incompetent to bring together objects not perceptible, or to compare that which it can perceive with that which is beyond her perception. A view into that which is invifible, is not neceffary to give exiftence to that which the eye has feen; neither is the comprehenfibility of objects not perceptible, neceffary to the exiftence of that which is fubmitted to the perception of reafon.

Having, as I hope, now proved that there can fubfift no vifible relation between the conduct of God and the uncomprehended God of natural religion, and therefore that reafon cannot deny that he has revealed himfelf;

and

and having farther shewed, upon the supposition that he has revealed himself, that it was neither necessary nor possible for him to render himself comprehensible to our faculties; and therefore that his conduct, as revealed, cannot be brought into comparison with himself, that it should be denied of him by reason; we must come to this conclusion, that God is not an object of our perception, and consequently his faculties are not a ground whence argument can proceed, that which is incomprehensible not being to be brought to the test of reason, nor by her made a measure for any thing which may be asserted concerning them. About matters which we do not comprehend, it is obvious that we cannot with certainty say any thing. The incomprehensible attributes of God then are not fit premises, no conclusion possibly following, from any comparison of them with whatsoever may be revealed to have been effected by them.

The infinite and incomprehensible majesty of God then is an object beyond the limits of reason; we are incapable of forming any idea of him; and consequently, from whatsoever ultimate maxims reason may proceed with relation to scripture truth, she is debarred of any appeal to God himself, or to any imagination she may conceive herself able to entertain of him.

But the scriptures are admitted to be the word of God, and whatsoever is set forth in them is admitted to be true; henceforward reason may proceed. The scriptures are that ultimate, that axiom, beyond which we are not to seek for the grounds of whatsoever is asserted in them; they are the word of God, and they are true. This is granted, and from this datum there lies no appeal.

Come

Come on then, for reason has now found a commencement to her work; and first she says, the scriptures, being true, contain no contradictions, the truth of contradictories being impossible: Her business then it is to reconcile what seem to be contradictions, to compare, one with another, the passages which lead to particular conclusions, and to yield her assent to that which she cannot understand, referring it only to the credibility of him who is the author of it; to acquiesce in the conduct of infinite wisdom, and not seek for principles beyond her own limits. By such a process she will never pronounce any thing to be impossible, the impossibility of which she does not see upon a comparison of perceptible qualities; but, acknowledging herself incapable of giving counsel to her Maker, believe that he has employed means for our salvation which we cannot look into; trust him with the means who has so graciously employed them for such an end; look upon the end not with vain and impious curiosity, but with unbounded gratitude; habituate our minds by such a prospect to love him, and from love and gratitude ascend to the desire to please him; seek from himself the means of pleasing him, and with renewed love and gratitude learn that to bear good will towards man, is the conduct most conformable to his will, that by which we shall best ascribe glory to God on high, and by which we shall procure to ourselves eternal happiness through Jesus Christ our Lord and Saviour. Is this a conduct beneath the dignity of reason? It is a glorious undertaking which is committed to her charge.— Let us now come more directly to the point.

If then the testimony of our Saviour be allowed, and the testimony of the Holy Ghost, to which he refers enquirers into his nature, be admitted as credible; and if by these it be declared that Jesus Christ is God from everlasting,

everlasting, I see not how a doubt is to be entertained that he is God, one with, and equal to, the Father: But if his having appeared clothed with flesh among men, as a man; if his sympathetick tears; if his apprehensive agonies and prayers to have the cup of evil put away from him; if his having fallen under the severest afflictions, and even having suffered an ignominious death, added to his own testimony and that of the Holy Ghost, be admitted as evidence that he was man, I see not how a doubt can be entertained that he was Man, inferior to God, as we are inferior to him: and if these be both admitted, it must necessarily follow, that Jesus Christ is both God and Man: But if both God and Man, I do not see the force of the objection to his Godhead, that he has acted and suffered as Man; that he refers the preservation of his human nature to the power which is alone equal to the preservation of it; that he prays as man for the world, which he sympathizes with; that he declares his human nature and the man Jesus to be a messenger to man, and acting with power derived of God. For as I believe that men, who make a difficulty of believing that any union between the two natures is possible, will hardly insist upon their own capacity to explain the manner of it, or to shew that, upon such an union, so much of the divinity is derived to the manhood of Christ, as to render it independent of God, and able to act for its own purposes, without farther application than the exertion of this derived power: so I will not admit of their explanations of our blessed Saviour's prayers, and declarations that he was sent; for these prayers were breathed by the man Jesus; and this commission to die for and to adopt a world, was given to the human nature by God, and not to the divine nature of Christ, which was itself the power, one with the Father, God Almighty, which had so sent forth this man to atone for us.

us. I am far from saying that I am myself able to explain this union, God forbid; but that I am not able to explore the ways of an Almighty God, whose little creature I am, is not a reason why I should doubt his word, when he is pleased to reveal any part of them to me. We are told, that the ways of God are not as our ways, nor his thoughts as our thoughts: And shall we attempt to contradict the declarations of his power, because we cannot exert the like? Or question the wisdom which we cannot comprehend, merely because we cannot comprehend it? Were God pleased to open the stores of his wisdom to our eyes, but not to open our eyes to look upon them with more extended faculties than we now enjoy, is it to be imagined that we should comprehend them? Surely not; and wherefore should we reject the belief of that wonderful exertion of his power for our redemption, which he has laid open to us? It is a way of God, and not of man; and is its being wonderful a cause? It is a way of God, and not of man; and is its exceeding the limited comprehension of our faculties a cause? It is not to comprehend that we are required, but to believe; and to yield that degree of assent which we call belief, is certainly the best, nay the only exertion of our reason in the case before us; for, having granted that God is true, and that he has spoken, the inference is, that what he has spoken is true; and as his power is adequate to all things, no exercise of it can oppose the conclusion drawn; as his wisdom is infinite, no dictate of it is referred to our judgment; and therefore our judgment must retire from giving any decision upon other premises than those laid down; and consequently, instead of opposing, must abet the conclusion that follows from those which are stated. If our blessed Saviour himself, though in union with Godhead, was humble, and referred all to God, I should conceive that, instead of arrogantly op-

posing,

posing, we should cultivate in ourselves that mind which was in Christ Jesus, and humbly submit to his will, who has in part revealed, and in part reserved for future revelation, the mystery of our redemption, for a mystery I must agree with St. Paul in calling it, rather than with any mere human authority in denying it to be such.

Mr. Lindsey says, That, in a multitude of passages to which he refers, "Jesus Christ formally professes his inferiority and dependence, that he received his being and all his powers from God." It is of no consequence whether the passages referred to prove it or not, for I readily grant him this position, "There is one God, and one mediator between God and Men, the man Christ Jesus," 1 Tim. ii. 5. And when I have granted it, what will he infer more than I have already laid down, that, as Man, the man Jesus Christ (evidently intended here to be distinguished from God by that name only, and therefore in other respects implied to be one with the father, God) was inferior to God; that is, that having two natures, one was greater, and consequently one less than the other. Were I in the midst of an argument, proving the immortality of the soul of man, to declare, that I laboured under a lingering disease of which I feared that I should die, would even Mr. Lindsey say, that I had confuted my own doctrine of the soul's immortality? Would he pronounce that I meant my soul should die? And yet he might as well, as in the case before us, declare, that when Jesus Christ speaks as Man he denies his Godhead.

I do not mean to say, that there exists any analogy between the union of spirit and flesh in man, and the union of God and Man in Christ; for I do not at all
                                                                understand

understand how the union of soul and body exists, and consequently cannot compare it with that which I as little understand, for I cannot say that I understand it less; and how, if I am absolutely unacquainted with an union, which not only subsists in every person I hourly converse with, but even in myself, how, I say, am I to declare that an union between God and Man, of which but one instance has ever offered itself to human observation, is impossible? And I refer it to Mr. Lindsey, or any of his disciples, to explain the nature of Spirit, and to shew its compatibility with Flesh; or that of Flesh, and to shew its compatibility with Spirit; and if my request be not complied with, from their absolute and entire ignorance, I must then request farther that they will desist from denying the compatibility of Natures, which they must allow they as little understand. They yield their assent in the one case, because daily observation confirms the existence of an animal in which spirit and flesh are conjoined, and they take their assent to be a conclusion from premises supplied by reason; but because Christ is but one, they have not had an opportunity of analysing him, as they think they have done by their own nature, and so deny what they could never have understood, had there been as many Christs as Men. Would they desire such an intimacy? would they desire such a multiplication? see where the impious tenet ends, " Jesus Christ once crucified is not a sufficient atonement for the sins of mankind." I shall make no farther comment than to declare, that whensoever reason withholds belief in that which it comprehends not, merely because it is beyond the reach and comprehension of reason, the union of the body and soul in man must be denied; for it never can be proved by reason, which must understand the compatibility of both before the union can be declared to exist. I would then advise every man not determined to be a

sceptic,

sceptic, whom I will not hesitate to pronounce a fool, to look upon a revelation of one, the sufficiency of which precludes the necessity, and consequently the existence of more, to be adequate to a fuller view of that which admits of a fuller view. In short, my recommendation amounts to no more, nor less, than the old established maxim, that proofs, and consequently our credit, are to be deduced from the best evidence the nature of the case admits of.

The best evidence then, which the nature of the case before us admits of, is the revelation of God, allowed to have been made by him, and admitted incontrovertibly true. Whatsoever is related therein, is advanced upon authority sufficient to warrant our assent; but as the revelation is not itself supported by an equally strong evidence as that which, upon admittance, it affords to whatsoever it testifies, we are not required to yield more than belief to the assertions contained in it; were it as certainly the word of God, as the word of God is certainly true, we should possess little less than certainty of the facts revealed therein; but being allowed, upon that evidence which is unquestionably sufficient to induce credit, it remains to be enquired into, whether it bears testimony to the divinity of our blessed Reedeemer Jesus Christ, or not?

As I have now reached the threshold, and am just entering into the proofs, and the nature of the proofs, which the scriptures afford of the truth of this great mystery, once more let me warn, and deeply inculcate the warning, to beware of the delusions of natural religion, if such a religion there be, and if that which we conceive to have been derived from nature, be not rather a residuum, after our pride has rejected whatsoever is revealed beyond its reach.

The

The Chinese philosopher believes, that the earth stands upon the back of an elephant, which stands upon the back of a tortoise, which stands upon the back of, &c. &c. &c. Now, suppose this same philosopher to be instructed in the Copernican system, and that he had, upon full consideration, yielded his assent to the great probability of its truth; would it not rather seem absurd in him, after a time, to recur to his old tenets, because the sufficiency of the sun's attractive power to support this world, was inconsistent with the occupation of his old elephant and tortoise, and that he could not see how it should be possible for animals so loaded, and of themselves none of the swiftest, to carry the earth, whirling through its orbit with such astonishing velocity? Just so absurd shall we be, if, after our assent to the truth of God, and admission that he has revealed himself, we suffer any one previous persuasion to recur, and require that scripture should be consonant to it, after we have admitted that the word of God is true, whether it be consonant to any previous persuasion or not. The sensible Chinese would surely reject his ancient tenets upon the admission of that which he had assented to, because of the value of those arguments which had induced his assent; let us then, upon the admission of the scriptures as the ultimate boundary of argument, reject whatsoever seems to make against their ceded truth; howsoever we may persuade ourselves that reason had supplied it to us, we must have expatiated beyond her limits to seek for the tenet, for within her proper province it is not to be found.

CHAP. II.

Of the Nature of the Evidence of our Saviour's Divinity afforded by the Scripture.

THE full effulgence of the Gospel did not burst suddenly upon mankind. That sun of righteousness, by the light of which we are enabled to walk, did not at once reach its meridian height; so exceedingly gradual was its progress, that, when first it dawned upon the world, its rays were not discernible; "it shone in darkness, and the darkness comprehended it not;" it encreased in splendor, but was not sufficient to be the "light of those who come into the world; at length the day-star arose, and a light shone forth to lighten the Gentiles, and the day-spring from on high hath visited us, to give light to them that sit in darkness, and in the shadow of death, to guide our feet into the way of peace."

To drop the metaphor. We find the prophecies of our blessed Saviour, from great obscurity, become more and more explicit as they approach the great event: At the first they were extreamly indefinite, and such only as were adapted to the purposes for which they were pronounced. The first hope of redemption to mankind accompanied the sentence of condemnation, and was graciously conveyed by God himself, who comforted the forlorn state of our fallen parents with a promise conceived in general terms, that the seed of the woman should bruise the head of the serpent which had beguiled her.

Noah is afterwards taught by the Spirit to hope, and to exclaim, "blessed be the Lord God of Shem." To
shew

shew that this blessing is a prophecy, it is enough to say, that Noah spoke it in a train of prophecy concerning the future state of his own sons and their posterity. From Shem descended Abraham, to Abraham was the promise made, and from Abraham, as concerning the flesh, Christ came. From the manner in which the blessing upon Shem is pronounced, I incline greatly to believe that this descent was the object of Noah's prophetic vision; it seems to have been the result of his having foreseen, that, in the progeny of Shem, all the families of the earth should be blessed: and let it be remembered, that Noah was no unconcerned prophet in whatsoever should happen to any future inhabitants of the earth; for all were then equally to descend from him as their common parent; and well might he rejoice and bless the God of Shem, by one of whose line he foresaw that all his posterity should be blessed.

To Abraham, because he had obeyed the voice of the Lord, it is foretold, (and this is by the New Testament declared to be spoken of Jesus Christ) that in his seed all the nations of the earth should be blessed; and this promise is from time to time renewed in that line of which our Saviour was to be born; to Isaac, in preference to Ishmael; to Jacob, in preference to Esau; and to Judah, in preference to his eleven brothers. To Judah, indeed, there is somewhat of more particular revelation made, for the length of time during which he shall bear the sceptre (that is, continue a tribe) is made commensurate with the coming of Shiloh, upon which the sceptre is to depart from him. Judah alone continued to be a tribe after the Assyrian Captivity, and then only ceased when Christ came; whence, however difficult it may be to explain this passage with certainty, it is to be presumed that the prophecy of Jacob, concerning the sceptre of Judah and its time

of

of departure, bears reference to the coming of the Messiah.

Moses, who is the relater of what was spoken before his day, in his own person also often speaks of a future prophet: And in the compelled prophecies of Balaam, when he poured forth blessings from a heart replete with curses, and in spight of that indignation with which he ascended the rock to denounce evil, fore-shewed the future brightness of the star that shall come forth out of Jacob, there is something which, however obscure it may be, is certainly referable to our Lord.

David hoped for one of his seed to sit upon his throne; and though he looked for a descendent from himself, he has nevertheless "in spirit called him Lord." That our Saviour was the object of David's expectation, though he knew not why he called him Lord, and only trusted that some great good was promised to him, the declaration of the angel to the Virgin Mary evinces, who says to her of the child which she is to bear, and whom she is to call Jesus, "He shall be great, and shall be called the Son of the Highest; and the Lord shall give unto him the throne of his Father David, and he shall reign over the house of Jacob for ever, and of his kingdom there shall be no end," Luke i. 32, 33.

Every succeeding prophet throughout the Old Testament found a consolation to the several troubles of Judea, in looking forward to that which was revealed to them in a general way by the spirit of Christ; but the full declaration of that which was so revealed was withheld from them; they understood it not themselves, and even when they spoke of the divinity of our Saviour,

E   like

like Balaam, they spoke it constrainedly; they uttered only the word which the Lord had put into their mouths. If they who spoke it were ignorant of its meaning, it is no great wonder that they who heard did not understand the full force of the prophecy of the Godhead of him who was to come; nor is their misapprehension a reason why we should doubt that the prophets foretold it. The purpose of prophecy is "to tell before it come to pass, that when it come to pass we may believe," John xiv. 29. And the object of the prophecy of the Old Testament is the coming of a great deliverer, of whom such seeming contrarieties are declared, that it is not possible the Jews could ever have formed a definite idea of the expected Messiah. It is foreshewn of our Saviour, (whom all allow to be the Christ) that he was to be a King of the seed of David, and to sit upon his throne; that he was to be cut off, but not for himself; that he was to be exalted and extolled, and to be very high; oppressed, afflicted, bruised and put to grief, numbered with the transgressors, taken from prison, and from judgment, and cut off out of the land of the living; ruling the nations, &c. Isaiah lii. and liii. With such irreconcileable declarations were the hopes of the Jews kept alive; but in all this there is nothing that could have suggested an expectation that God himself would come; for how should the idea of his infinite majesty unite itself with that of a man of sorrows and acquainted with grief, having a cheek turned to the scorner? and how, indeed, could even such an idea as this agree with the expectation of a great King, to overcome all their enemies? It cannot, therefore, be admitted in argument against the divinity of Jesus Christ, that it was not understood by the Jews; for how should they understand it, when the prophets, who prophesied of the grace that should come unto us, have enquired and

searched

searched diligently of this salvation, " searching what, or what manner of time, the spirit of Christ which was within them did signify, when it testified beforehand the sufferings of Christ, and the glory that should follow. Unto whom it was revealed, that, not unto themselves, but unto us, they did minister the things which are now reported unto you by them that have preached the gospel unto you, with the Holy Ghost sent down from heaven; which things the angels desire to look into, 1 Pet. i. 10, 11, 12. and that many prophets have desired to see these things which our Saviour shewed forth, and have not seen them."

To us then, who have come after the event, it belongs to explain the prophecy, as that which is foretold is come to pass; and therefore we must cease to look for such testimony from the prophets as should have explained the fact, to such as had never seen it: of the sufferings of Christ, and the glory that should follow, they could form no certain idea whatsoever, nor did the prophecy put things into that order, as to impart a notion that the glory was to be subsequent to the sufferings; and this I assert, notwithstanding that Isaiah had said " he shall divide the spoil with the strong: because he hath poured out his soul unto death," Isa. liii. 12. For even the expectation of a man to arise from the dead, never seems, by the history of the Jews, throughout the Old Testament, in the least degree to have suggested itself to them; for if it had, Christ crucified could not have been to the Jews a stumbling block; and it is even probable, that such a fact, clearly understood, might have withheld their hands from inflicting that death whereby " Christ was perfected."

Still nearer to the manifestation of Christ the Angel has declared, that the Prophet, who should be the

preparer

preparer of the ways of the Lord, fhould be filled with the Holy Ghoft, even from his mother's womb; and Zacharias, upon the birth of John, breaks that filence which had been impofed upon him becaufe of his unbelief, and, being filled with the Holy Ghoft, cried out, "Bleffed be the Lord God of Ifrael, for he hath vifited and redeemed his people, and hath raifed up an horn of falvation for us, in the houfe of his fervant David; as he fpake by the mouth of the holy prophets, which have been fince the world began," Luke i. 67, 68, 69; and then fpeaking of his own fon, who was the appointed harbinger of the Chrift, whom he has already called the Lord God of Ifrael, he fays, "and thou child fhall be called the Prophet of the Higheft; for thou fhalt go before the face of the Lord to prepare his ways," Luke i. 76. The angel faid alfo to the Virgin Mary, when he gave her affurance of the birth of her fon to be called Jefus, "He fhall be great, and fhall be called the Son of the Higheft; and the Lord God fhall give him the throne of his father David;" and "that Holy Thing which fhall be born of thee, fhall be called the Son of God," Luke i. 32, 33, 35. The babe leapt in the womb of Elizabeth for joy upon the falutation of Mary, and Elizabeth afks this remarkable queftion, fimilar in expreffion to the prophecy of David already cited, "whence is this to me, that the mother of my Lord fhould come to me?" Luke i. 43. The fhepherds are told by an angel, "unto you is born this day, in the city of David, a Saviour, which is Chrift the Lord," Luke ii. 11. At the prefentation of the infant Redeemer in the temple, Simeon, to whom it was revealed by the Holy Ghoft, that he fhould not fee death before he had feen the Lord's Chrift, taking the babe in his arms "bleffed God, and expreffed his contentment to depart then, his eyes having feen the promifed fource of falvation,"

Luke

Luke i. 28, 29. And subsequent to these mysterious predictions concerning the supposed child of a carpenter, came forth a prophet, cotemporary in birth with Jesus Christ, appointed to be his immediate forerunner, to prepare the way of the Lord, and to make his paths straight, and he declared of him that " he that cometh from above, is above all;" and that " he that believeth on the Son, hath everlasting life," John iii. 31, 36.

Thus, from the first obscure hint of salvation to our first parents, do the prophecies gradually approximate to an explanation of the great glory which should in the end be revealed; but by no means have they become so explicit yet, as to render a revelation unnecessary; nay, there is yet to proceed a new species of previous intimation to makind of " the salvation of God which all flesh shall see," Luke iii. 6; and accordingly now came forth the great subject of all that had been testified, but not yet to be declared, nor yet indeed the full subject of the prophecy, nor of the subsequent testimony of the spirit, having before him that mighty work to do, toward which the hopes of the prophets looked as the source of deliverance, in vain searching into what the manner of it was to be; a work by which we have received the atonement, and obtained reconciliation, the word and ministry of which was afterwards to be committed by God to those who were to be the appointed witnesses of our Lord: and this ministry of reconciliation is that which alone can be, according to the scriptures, pronounced the manifestation of Jesus Christ; and therefore I consider himself, even the Lord of glory, who was crucified, who arose from the grave, and ascended into heaven, as only bearing, by his miracles, a practical testimony during his stay on earth; to that which should be revealed

vealed of him when his work should be finished. This, indeed, I admit to be a much closer evidence of the Godhead than any given before; and that, perhaps, by which the minds of men should be led to look upon the expected King of the Jews in a much more exalted light than the former prophecies had instructed them to do. It is such an evidence as, when referred to, might well provide credit, when it should come to pass, for that which before it came to pass it had foreshewn. Our Saviour himself, for the most part, declines bearing witness to himself, but refers both to the scriptures which had now begun to be fulfilled, and which he desires to have diligently sought into as about to receive their full completion, and to the testimony of the Holy Ghost hereafter to be given for the purpose of manifesting him; and whenever he does bear record, it is rather such as he would have second to that which should follow the finishing of his work here, thence to derive its explanation, than such as he would have principal in the line of evidence.

Had our blessed Lord and Saviour borne any ultimate testimony to the Jews that he was God, they would have known this hidden mystery; and, " had they known it," says St. Paul, " they would not have crucified the Lord of glory," 1 Cor. ii. 8; and so the very end of his coming in the flesh would have been defeated; mankind must still have remained due to the justice of God, without the atonement which we have received by the death of Christ. The blood of our gracious Redeemer was to be the price of our salvation, and would it have been consistent with wisdom to take measures to prevent the shedding of it? It was enough that his miracles should testify of him to those who were afterwards to preach him, and offer them to mankind as marks of a life consistent with what they should

relate

relate concerning his death, resurrection, and ascension, which were the great persuasives to believe in his Godhead, and in that mighty work which he came in the flesh to do for our sake.

Our Saviour, I say, did not frequently bear record to himself; but continuing the train of prophecy of that by which we also have become the children of Abraham, the Israel of God, even of that which all the prophets had in view, the redemption of makind, he very frequently foretells his own sufferings, that " the Son of man shall be lifted up as Moses lifted up the serpent in the wilderness;" that " he will raise the temple in three days, and this he spake of his body;" and " that he will go before us into heaven." That this great event, attended by such mighty consequences to us, consolatory in every woe of Israel, and making all men heirs of salvation, should be the object of prophecy, and of the subsequent testimony of the Holy Ghost, no man surely can doubt, when, in order to enable us to become partakers of the benefits thence derived to mankind, it is necessary that we believe in Christ, " who gave himself a ransom for all, to be testified in due time," 1 Tim. ii. 6. " How beautiful then upon the mountains are the feet of those who bring good tidings of good!" A preacher, even the Holy Spirit, has instructed us in the salvation which is of God, and " said unto Zion, thy God reigneth."

This then is the line of testimony; this the object of revelation, namely, that " Christ, by being made perfect, has become the author of eternal salvation unto all them that obey him;" that he hath been the Redeemer of mankind by the full accomplishment of all that he came to do for us; and not, according to Mr. Lindsey, that he has merely come into the world as a teacher,

teacher; the truth of whose doctrines were to be witnessed by his death. And let not this be considered as an unsupported suggestion of my own, it is authorised by St. Luke in the first chapter of the Acts; where, speaking of that history which he had before set forth of the life of our Saviour, he is so far from considering it as the manifestation of Christ, that he says, "The former treatise have I made, O Theophilus, of all that Jesus *began* both to do and to teach, until the day in which he was taken up:" so that all the life of our Lord in the flesh was but a commencement of that which was afterwards to be revealed. In the moment of his ascent too, the same apostle presents Christ telling his disciples that " ye shall receive power after that the Holy Ghost is come upon you: and ye shall be witnesses unto me, both in Jerusalem, and in all Judea, and in Samaria, and unto the uttermost part of the earth," Acts i. 8. Of what were they to be witnesses unto him? of that which he had already died to testify? Was his death then so defective a testimony to those who had seen it in Jerusalem, and who had also seen his resurrection? If these were intended but as a mere testimony that he had lived, wrought miracles, and taught among them, we must declare that they have come very short of answering the purpose, if there still remained a necessity of appointing farther witnesses to concur in proving their object. Was it ever before heard of, that the breathless corpse of a man is a better evidence of his having been born into the world than his living and active body, that our Saviour's death should be considered only as a proof of his life? Did a continued series of miracles, performed before the eyes of the multitude, stand in need of one more, to prove, to those who had seen them, that they had been performed? or are those moral doctrines, which our blessed Redeemer delivered to mankind, of such a dubious

nature,

nature, that any man should entertain a doubt of their justice, requiring so strong an engine as the death and resurrection of the preacher, in order to remove it? No, but on the contrary, so obvious is their rectitude, so far from requiring any testimony whatsoever to their indisputable truth, that many who never became Christians allowed their value; and even Trajan, who persecuted those "who called upon Christ as God," adopted from his sermons that charitable doctrine of returning good for evil. But of what were they to be witnesses unto him? of his death and resurrection? What? to Jerusalem, and all Judea, and to Samaria? did Christ hang invisible on a cross at Jerusalem, that a witness shall be wanting to testify it? or was his death and resurrection a transaction carried on in secret? On the contrary, at the very time when he was dragged " from judgment to pour out his soul unto death; when he was numbered with the transgressors, and made intercession for the transgressors," Isaiah liii. all Judea were eye-witnesses of the fact; for it was at the time of the passover, when all Judea had come up to Jerusalem, the scene of the transaction, to celebrate that feast: nay, farther, where all Judea, as if to fill up the measure of her rebellions, and justify her approaching desolation, had, with one voice, cried out, "crucify him, crucify him." Of this then they were not to be witnesses unto him; but of that which the prophets had not made manifest, of that which the life and lesions of our Saviour himself had not made manifest, without farther explanation. They were to be witnesses unto him that he was the expected Christ, and that the Christ was the " mighty God, the everlasting Father, the Prince of peace;" that the Godhead of him, whom their own eyes had seen, so far from being a great king, that he was actually in " the form of a servant," and an ignominious sufferer, was the royalty

F which

which they had looked for in the expected king of Israel; that he was indeed a "king who had all things put under his feet, who had led captivity captive, and hath given to us the victory over death and the grave; a king, whose throne endureth for ever, and the sceptre of whose kingdom is a right sceptre." To these witnesses of Jesus Christ the Holy Ghost was given, even the spirit of truth, to shew forth the means of our redemption, by which his infinite mercy had reconciled mankind to his infinite justice: whatsoever the prophets had said was given to them to understand, to open, and to reconcile: and whatsoever our Lord had done and said in the flesh, was given to their remembrance to corroborate that which they should themselves declare; and these they have accordingly called upon, and shewed to be a testimony bearing toward the truth, which it was their appointment to render fully manifest, even this great truth, that the blood which streamed from a supposed malefactor, dying for imputed blasphemy upon a cross, was the blood of God himself, Acts xx. 28. " poured out for our transgressions," and " by which we have received the atonement." This is the full manifestation of Christ to mankind; till the work was finished it could not be related, and, when done, so portentous was the deed in itself, so above the reach of all human intellect, that it required and obtained a miraculous testimony; a testimony precisely adequate to that which is required of those who receive it, our belief, which alone is called for as the terms upon which this great salvation is offered to us, " that eternal salvation of which, by being made perfect, he became the author unto all them that obey him," Heb. v. 9.

The prophecies waited for their explanation till all which they had predicted should have come to pass;

and

and therefore were not evidence to thofe who lived before the event. The four gofpels relate, that a man had come into the world endowed with a power of working miracles, which he was perpetually exerting in acts of benevolence; inftructing mankind in virtue, by leffons fuperior to thofe of any other man; fpeaking of the kingdom of God, and faying, that he was the door by which it was to be entered; inculcating faith in God, and the hope in his mercies, arifing from the cultivation of piety toward him, and goodwill toward man; teftifying that he was the object of former prophecy; forefhewing things which the hearers remembered, when they came to pafs, to have heard of, but not to have underftood before; dying upon a crofs, arifing from the grave, and afcending into heaven; that is, the gofpels relate the hiftory of Jefus Chrift in the flefh, but have by no means revealed him, nor declared finally who or what he is, wherefore he died, arofe, and afcended. They tell us that he did the work for which he came, but the full import of this work, and why undertaken by this man who finifhed it, was not the object of the hiftorian to reveal; and till it was finifhed it could not be revealed to what end it had been done. From our Saviour we are not to expect this revelation, for his afcenfion into heaven being a part, the final part of his work, he continued not among men to declare its end. Another teftimony then muft be found, and that fuch as muft be very powerful; we accordingly now find the apoftolic body come forth in the ftrength of the Lord, endowed with miraculous powers to be exerted before all hearers, and bleffed with elocution in every language, that all hearers might underftand and believe; and thus the end of all that has been done is declared; that our falvation was the object is revealed; that for our fins Chrift died, and that for our juftification he rofe again;

F 2   that

that he has taken our nature into heaven, "having appeared to put away sin, by the sacrifice of himself," Heb. ix. 26. and, "by his own blood entered in once into the holy place, having obtained eternal redemption for us," Heb. ix. 12. that, because he can have a feeling of our infirmities, having been in all points tempted like as we are, he is now our high-priest and intercessor; and that, for the same gracious reason, he is to be our judge, when, in the last day, he shall come forth in his glory, and all nations shall be gathered before him, even before their God.

I hope and believe now that I have pointed out the degrees of proof which have been afforded to the world, that the Lord of life, Jesus Christ, who redeemed it, is the God of our salvation; and having shewn by what light he has been manifested, even that which has come from himself after his ascension and resumption of his former glory, it is easy to see that the prophets and evangelists are to be read by that light only: by this alone the expectations of Israel are to be reconciled, and the prophets found to have spoken consistently; and what other circumstances could have reduced their predictions to good sense, but a revelation of the glory that has followed the sufferings of our Lord and Saviour Jesus Christ? what other circumstances than the death, burial, resurrection, and ascension of a man revealed to be the "King of kings, and Lord of lords," Rev. xix. 16; "who has become the captain of our salvation, who shall come once again with power and great glory, sitting upon the throne of his glory, bringing his reward with him, to judge all men, could reconcile the expectations which the prophets had imparted, that the Messiah should be a King, sitting on the throne of David for ever; that he should be a great deliverer, subduing

all

all nations under them; and also, that he should be a man despised and rejected of men, wounded for our transgressions, and bruised for our iniquities, upon whom was the chastisement of our peace, and by whose stripes we are healed?" Isa. liii. 5. for such were the indefinite hopes of the Jews, and therefore their ignorance is never to be considered as of any weight in argument against the Godhead of Christ, nor a defect of testimony in the Old Testament taken by itself, and not explained by the subsequent revelation, as any ground for denying that which it was never written with a view of ultimately proving. The same thing may be asserted of the four evangelical histories of our Lord and Saviour Jesus Christ, they were not intended to have been ultimate; and, consequently, if partial quotations do not evince his divinity to partial enquirers, it is not in the least degree an argument that he was not one with the Father and the Holy Ghost, God. Those histories, I have said already, were written with a view of setting before all men the works which our blessed Redeemer did, in evidence of a power concerning which he withheld his own testimony, but for the promulgation of which he refers to the scriptures already written, and to the testimony of the Holy Ghost hereafter to be afforded, the truth of which, he foresaw, would be less liable to doubt than that of his own record, which he therefore declined bearing, saying, that it would not be received as true. Had our Lord therefore been wholly silent upon this head, not even his absolute silence would have derogated from the evidence of his divinity. "He came not to bear witness of himself," "but to be testified in due time;" and he even saw that his testimony, had he attempted to have borne it, would be rejected, as an evil interpretation was put upon the most benevolent exertion of his power; that the faith

of

of even his perpetual hearers was defective, and that they had fallen from him, becaufe they could not comprehend him. He therefore looked for the belief of mankind from a miraculous declaration and teftimony of his Godhead, to be borne, not after a partial, but a full execution of that great work which he took our nature upon him to do; and faw that Godhead would be more readily acquiefced in, as in union with a man who fhould be teftified to have rifen from the dead, and afcended into heaven, than with one, the courfe of whofe innocent life was feemingly unable to refift perfecutions and forrows, nay the infliction of an ignominious death. An acquaintance with grief, a cheek turned to the fcorner, the grave and the fhadow of death, which he had often (and even with agonies which certified his feeling of our infirmities) predicted to be all before him, were fo far from conveying an idea of divinity, that they afforded but a very humiliating picture of humanity. The belief of mankind was not required from fuch circumftances, and they who inflicted thofe miferies upon him were forgiven, for they knew not what they did. It is at the fame time true, that Jefus Chrift has not left us without a record of himfelf, as I fhall hereafter have occafion to fhew, but it was carried only fo far as to become a teftimony, when explained afterwards, otherwife they who crucified him muft have known what they did. On the day on which our Lord was betrayed, knowing that his hour was come, he fays to his difciples "I have yet many things to fay unto you, but ye cannot bear them now. Howbeit, when he the fpirit of truth is come, he will guide you into all truth: for he fhall not fpeak of himfelf; but whatfoever he fhall hear, that fhall he fpeak: and he will fhew you things to come. He fhall glorify me: for he fhall receive of mine, and fhall fhew it unto you.

you. All things that the Father hath, are mine: therefore said I, that he shall take of mine, and shall shew it unto you," John xvi. 12, 13, 14, 15. What is this but saying, that as they are as yet unable to bear the full revelation of his nature, he will in a future time shew it to them by the spirit who shall speak as he shall receive of Christ. And that it is the full declaration of the Godhead, which, he says, they are as yet unable to bear, and which he will reveal by the spirit who shall testify of the truth, is evident from the testimony which he proceeds to say this spirit shall bear to him; for " he shall glorify him," having received that which he is to shew from Christ, whose it is, and from the Father, whose it is, equal possessors of the glory which shall be revealed. A triumph over death, and an ascent into heaven, were first to intervene; and these, added to every miracle performed in the presence of multitudes, were facts, which, when referred to, were fully sufficient to shew forth a power that none could doubt to be the power of God; and if the Holy Ghost, by miracles subsequent to such an act as that of rising from the darkness of the grave to the mansions of light, should testify of him who had so acted, that he was God, I see not how a more proper line of evidence could have been adopted, or a more certain means of spreading information among men, not hardened against the receipt of it, devised; nor do I see it to be less than an impious presumption to deny the attested fact, because we have not ourselves had the conduct of the evidence, and therefore do not find it where it is not reasonably to be expected.

The doctrine of Christ's godhead then may be considered as imparted to us by four different sorts of revelation; first, by the prophecies and the law, or in general terms that which was called the scriptures, before

fore the writing of the New Testament, to which we are referred, and told that "they are they which testify of me;" secondly, by the testimony of our blessed Saviour himself, whether by words or works, throughout the writings of the evangelists; thirdly, by the testimony of the apostles, confirmed by the Holy Ghost, to which our Saviour usually referred enquirers into his nature, whether delivered by them in the gospels; which were written after the Holy Ghost had been given to the writers, or by their explanation of the nature and the purposes of his having come and suffered in the flesh, in their sermons throughout the Acts, and in their epistles; and fourthly, by the testimony of Christ himself, after his ascension and reassumption of that glory wherewith he had been glorified before the world was, delivered by his having sent the comforter according to his frequent promises that he, and that the father (promiscuously named) would send him, by his compliance with the prayers of the apostles, his appearance in divers circumstances, and by the vision shewed to St. John in the revelation, in which he speaks of himself in the same terms, as God, before his incarnation, had spoken to the prophets.

This is the order in which the evidence is placed before us, and in which I shall therefore produce it in the following chapter. Were it to be stated according to the degree of its strength, it ought to be reversed.

There is yet another species of testimony borne to the divinity of our gracious Redeemer, resulting from the reconcileableness of the whole of sacred writ, upon the adopting this proposition as a datum, namely, that Christ is God. Were a subject to be treated so enigmatically by a man of sense, as that it should escape the understanding of all his readers, and yet leave them convinced upon the credit of the author, that the book itself was worth study and labour; were there scarce an intelligible sentence contained in the book, and yet a certainty that it contained much matter; and were there at length to arise a man whose ready faculties should alight upon one proposition by which that whole book should be explained, to which every obscure assertion should be referred, and by the reference to which they should become clear and perspicuous; and therefore it should appear, that this proposition was the object of every sentence, the darkness of which it dispelled; could any man pretend that this was not the object of the writer; or conceive that any one point, thus borne down upon by every argument, was not the point intended to be illustrated and proved? certainly not. And if, on the other hand, the contradictory of that proposition was a point to which the process of the argument so little referred, as that it should still continue obscure when referred to it; would any man say that this was the writer's object? certainly not. Exactly such is the state of the Bible; every position falls into sense, the tenour of it becomes a course of argument the instant that the divinity of our Saviour in union with manhood is acknowledged to be its object; whereas, upon a denial of this proposition, there is not on earth a book so fraught with contradictions and irreconcilable absurdities, as that which is acknowledged to be the word of the God of truth. Partial quotations therefore, and passages taken from the whole consistent word of God, are to be considered as of no value whatsoever in argument; they cannot afford any proof of any thing: and nothing contained in the sacred writings is to be explained but as it stands in context with the whole. Nothing less therefore than the whole of the Bible is to be considered as the gospel of Christ; and from the whole, taken together, his almighty Godhead is to be deduced.

CHAP. III.

The Evidence of our Saviour's Divinity afforded by the Scriptures.

AS I have already said that the Old Testament affords but a very small part of the testimony of the Godhead of Jesus Christ, I shall produce but few separate passages from it, under the head of prophecy: such as receive their explanation from the New Testament, being better brought under that head. It is not to shew that the prophets have foretold our Lord and Saviour that I am engaged, for that were an easy office; but to shew that they have foretold his divinity; and that the expected Messiah was, though ignorantly, by them declared to be God himself.

From the prophecies of the Old Testament I take the following proofs of the Godhead of Jesus Christ.

I.

" Therefore the Lord himself shall give you a sign, behold a virgin shall conceive, and bear a Son, and shall call his name Immanuel," Isaiah vii. 14. This prophecy is referred to by St. Matthew, declared to be of our Saviour, and the name interpreted to be " God with us."

II.

" For unto us a child is born, unto us a Son is given, and the government shall be upon his shoulder: and his name shall be called, Wonderful, Counsellor, the mighty God, the Everlasting Father, the Prince of Peace," Isai. ix. 6.

III.

" Thus saith the Lord the King of Israel, and his Redeemer the Lord of Hosts, I am the first, and I am the laſt, and beſides me there is no God," Iſai. xliv. 6. This aſſertion is made by God to Iſaiah, and by Jeſus Chriſt (verbatim) to St. John, Rev. ii. 8. God, in the ſubſequent verſes, declares his prerogatives to the prophet; the ſame are applicable to the ſame firſt and laſt, " is there a God beſides me? yea there is no God, I know not any." This God then is Jeſus Chriſt.

IV.

"Awake, awake, put on ſtrength, O arm of the Lord; awake, as in the antient days, in the generations of old. Art thou not it which hath dried the ſea, the waters of the great deep, that hath made the depths of the ſea a way for the ranſomed to paſs over?" Iſai. li. 9. 10. The anſwer to this call has the following words in it, " But I am the Lord thy God, that divided the ſea, whoſe waves roared: the Lord of Hoſts in his name," Iſai. li. 15. To this entire chapter, and the two following, I refer for the explanation of theſe texts which I have brought to evince the divinity of Jeſus Chriſt, and which I take to be even of themſelves ſufficient for that purpoſe. The arm of the Lord is here invoked, and in making anſwer, the arm of the Lord declares " I am the Lord thy God." The arm of the Lord, and the Lord God, are then with Iſaiah ſynonimous terms; but he afterwards ſays " the Lord hath made bare his holy arm in the eyes of all the nations, and all the ends of the earth ſhall ſee the ſalvation of our God," Iſai. lii. 10: and again, " Who hath believed our report? and to whom is the arm of the Lord revealed?" Iſai. liii. 1. To the former of theſe two texts St. Luke refers, and declares expreſsly that it is ſpoken of Jeſus Chriſt, for he relates that they were uttered by St. John the Baptiſt, whoſe office was to be the forerunner of our Saviour, Luke iii. 6. To the latter St. John refers, chap. xii. verſe 38, where he quotes the verſe at large concerning the unbelief in

Chriſt,

Chrift, and fays, "thefe things faid Efaias, when he faw his glory, and fpake of him," John xii. 41. Here then is the fame arm of the Lord, which is fynonimous with God, declared to be Jefus Chrift, whofe name is therefore fynonimous with God, one with him who is the " Lord thy God." St. Paul alfo intimates, that Chrift was the leader of the Ifraelites through the wildernefs, faying, " neither let us tempt Chrift, as fome of them alfo tempted," 1 Cor. x. 9; to which I refer.

V.

The arm of the Lord is thus foretold again, " behold, the Lord God will come with ftrong hand, and his arm fhall rule for him: behold, his reward is with him, and his work before him. He fhall feed his flock like a fhepherd," Ifa. xl. 10, 11. In the Revelation, our Saviour fays to St. John, " behold, I come quickly; and my reward is with me," Rev. xxii. 12: And in the gofpel he fays, " I am the good fhepherd," John x. 11. St. Paul fays of him, " now the God of peace that brought again from the dead our Lord Jefus, that great fhepherd of the fheep, through the blood of the everlafting covenant, make you perfect in every good work to do his will, working in you that which is well-pleafing in his fight, through Jefus Chrift; to whom be glory for ever and ever. Amen." Heb. xiii. 20, 21. Here we find Ifaiah's words concerning the arm of the Lord (the fame as God) pronounced by our Saviour concerning himfelf, both in earth and in heaven, and alfo teftified of him by St. Paul, whofe doxology affifts us to pronounce of Jefus Chrift, in the words of Ifaiah immediately preceding the text before us, " behold your God."

VI.

" How beautiful upon the mountains are the feet of him that bringeth good tidings, that publifheth peace, that bringeth good tidings of good, that publifheth
salvation,

salvation, that saith unto Zion, thy God reigneth!" Isai. lii. 7. St. Paul, speaking of the necessity of a preacher to instruct men in the belief on Christ, that they may call upon him and be saved, directly applies these words of Isaiah, as being prophetick of a preacher who should publish salvation, and say unto Zion, "thy God reigneth," Rom. x. 15. If then the promulgation of the gospel of our blessed Lord and Saviour be correspondent to this prophecy, the preacher of Christ is surely he who says " thy God reigneth."

VII.

" Out of the mouth of babes and sucklings hast thou ordained strength," or " perfected praise," (which is the interpretation of the New Testament) Psa. viii. 2. These words David directs to God, whose name he declares to be excellent. When children in the temple cried " Hosanna to the Son of David," and the Chief Priests and Scribes were displeased at them for it, our Saviour himself justified the children by assuming the direction of these words to himself, and declaring them a prophecy of his praise, to be perfected by the mouths of babes and sucklings; so that we find a prophecy, that the praise of the Lord, " who had set his glory above the heavens," Psa. viii. 1. is declared to be fulfilled by the direction of praise and hosannas to the Son of David, who must therefore be one with the Father, God, Mat. xxi. 16.

VIII.

" For thy sake are we killed all the day long; we are counted as sheep for the slaughter," Psa. xliv. 22. These words directly addressed to God, by David, are by St. Paul declared to be a prophecy of the perseverance of the apostles in the love of Christ, of which he says, " Who shall separate us from the love of Christ? shall tribulation, or distress, or persecution, or famine, or nakedness, or peril, or sword?" As it is written,
" for

" for thy fake, &c." Rom. viii. 35. For whofe fake? certainly Chrift's, one with the Father, God.

The prophecies afforded by the New Teftament, I have already ftated in the preceding chapter, and fhall not trouble my reader with a repetition of them.

The following proofs are taken from the teftimony borne to our blefled Lord's divinity in the writings of the four evangelifts.

IX.

" Thy kingdom come," Matth. vi. 10. " Thine is the kingdom, and the power, and the glory, for ever and ever. Amen." Matth. vi. 13. That our Saviour's command to the difciples, is to addrefs thefe words, and the prayer in which they occur, directly to God, is not only granted but contended for: but let us fee now who is this God, who is this king of glory. " Then (in the laft day) fhall all the tribes of the earth mourn, and they fhall fee the Son of man coming in the clouds of heaven, with power and great glory. And he fhall fend his angels, &c." Matth. xxiv. 30, 31. " When the Son of man fhall come in his glory, and all the holy angels with him, then fhall he fit upon the throne of his glory. And before him fhall be gathered all nations; and he fhall feparate them one from another, as a fhepherd divideth his fheep from the goats; and he fhall fet the fheep on his right hand, but the goats on the left. Then fhall the King fay unto them on his right hand, come, ye blefled of my Father, &c." Mat. xxv. 31, 32, 33, 34. Here we fee the coming of the kingdom, and we fee alfo whofe is the kingdom, and the power, and the glory. Wherefore then fhould we fay that Jefus Chrift, in prefcribing this form of prayer, forbad worfhip and application to be made to him, whom we find to be the very being

defcribed

described and pointed out as the proper object of our adoration? It is manifestly his command that we should worship him; and hence it follows, that he is one with the Father, God Almighty. He says in another place, "whosoever shall be ashamed of me, and of my words, in this adulterous and sinful generation, of him also shall the Son of man be ashamed, when he cometh in the glory of his Father, with the holy angels," Mark viii. 38. On which I remark, that the glory of the Father, and of the Son, is but one glory, one Godhead; for we see our blessed Lord coming in his own glory, and in the parallel passage, in the glory of his Father. The following texts evince this, and also ascribe the kingdom and the glory to Jesus Christ. "The Son of man shall send forth his angels, and they shall gather out of his kingdom all things that offend, and them which do iniquity," Mat. xiii. 41. "The Son of man shall come in the glory of his Father, with his angels; and then he shall reward every man according to his works," Mat. xvi. 27. "Whosoever shall be ashamed of me and of my words, of him shall the Son of man be ashamed, when he shall come in his own glory, and in his Father's, and all the holy angels," Luke ix. 26. "No whoremonger, &c. hath any inheritance in the kingdom of Christ, and of God," Ephes. v. 5. "Jesus Christ, who shall judge the quick and the dead at his appearing, and his kingdom," 2 Tim. iv. 1. "The everlasting kingdom of our Lord and Saviour Jesus Christ," 2 Pet i. 11. Our Saviour, in answer to the demand of the Pharisees, (Luke xvii. 20 to 30) "when the kingdom of God should come," tells them, "the kingdom of God cometh not with observation;" or as it is translated in the margin of the Bible, "with outward show;" and then, addressing himself to his disciples, continues to declare, that no prognosticks shall foreshew his day; but that,

as

as the flood was not preceded by any signs that it was at hand, but found men eating and drinking, and altogether unprepared, so should it be " in the day when the Son of man is revealed." From the continuance of the discourse, and applying still the coming without observation, to the coming of the kingdom of God, and to his own day; which is often spoken of as synonimous with the day in which the Son of man shall come in power and glory, sitting on the throne of his glory to judge the world, we may, without in the least straining for an inference, say, that the day of which he speaks to the disciples as coming unobserved, and the kingdom of God, of which he asserts the same thing to the Pharisees in the same conversation, are one and the same thing; and if the day of Christ be the same as the kingdom of Christ, the kingdom of God is here declared to be the kingdom of Christ; therefore one with the Father, on that day, on the coming of that kingdom to be fully revealed to be God.

X.

The incomprehensibility of the Father and the Son, except to each other, is a mark of equality of Godhead, which alone can be the subject of the following words of our Saviour himself. " No man knoweth the Son but the Father: neither knoweth any man the Father, save the Son, and he to whomsoever the Son will reveal him," Matth. xi. 27. Many a man had known Jesus Christ as Man; but as God, he was known then to the Father only, with whom he was one God. The parallel passage says, " No man knoweth who the Son is, but the Father, &c." Luke x. 22. Mr. Lindsey says he does, but I cannot think it. How shall he, who is known by all his disciples to be a man, say he is unknown to all but the Father, if he speak not of a nature not human, and of so high a rank as to be comprehensible to the Father only, even his Godhead?

When

XI.

When our blessed Lord, just before he ascended into heaven, was sending forth his disciples to baptize all nations in the name of the Father, and of the Son, and of the Holy Ghost, and to teach them to observe all things which he had commanded them, he gives them a promise of his own assistance in the performance of their mission, saying, " And, lo! I am with you alway even unto the end of the world," Matth. xxviii. 20. We accordingly find that, upon his ascent, " they went forth, and preached every where, the Lord working with them, and confirming the word with signs following," Mark xvi. 20. " How then shall we escape if we neglect so great salvation, which at the first began to be spoken by the Lord, and was confirmed unto us by them that heard him; God also bearing them witness, both with signs and wonders, and with divers miracles, and gifts of the Holy Ghost, according to his own will?" Heb. ii. 3, 4. Here we find that the testimony of signs and miracles wrought to confirm what is preached by the apostles, is borne by God, and by the Lord Christ, therefore one, with the Father, God.

XII.

It is evident what was the faith of the father of the sick child, who " cried out, and said with tears, Lord, I believe; help thou mine unbelief," Mark ix. 24. So strong was his faith already, that he looked upon our Lord as possessed of power to assist his spirit, and supply whatsoever was defective in his belief. This application was approved and confirmed to be right by our blessed Saviour himself, who granted the distressed father's prayer, and healed his sick child.

XIII.

Upon hearing Jesus Christ say to the sick of the palsy, " Man, thy sins are forgiven thee," I cannot wonder at the remark of the Scribes, who said, " Who can forgive sins but God alone? For their law had shewed them that God had made an exclusive claim to the forgiveness of sins, saying, "I, even I am he that blotteth out thy transgressions for mine own sake, and will not remember thy sins," Isai. xliii. 25. But our Saviour perceived their thoughts, and healed the sick man, in order to shew "that the Son of man hath power upon earth to forgive sins," Luke v. 20, 25. But God, whom Nehemiah, ix. 17, beautifully, calls "a God of pardons," has an exclusive right in the forgiveness of sins; the Son of man who exercises that right, even Jesus Christ, is therefore one with the Father, God.

XIV.

"Blessed are ye when men shall hate you, and when they shall separate you from their company, and shall reproach you, and cast out your name as evil, for the Son of man's sake. Rejoice ye in that day, and leap for joy: for behold your reward is great in heaven: for in the like manner did their fathers unto the prophets," Luke vi. 22, 23. If the happiness of the disciples, to whom our Saviour addresses the words above, be not to proceed from the reproach, but from the cause wherefore they are to undergo it, there is no similitude between their case and that of the prophets, unless the prophets also suffered for the sake of the Son of man, and for the testimony which they bore to him; and that this was really the intention of our Lord's words, the following text, spoken by St. Stephen, will evince, "Which of the prophets have not your fathers persecuted? And they have slain them which shewed before of the coming of the just one; of whom ye have now been the betrayers and murderers," Acts vii. 52. Stephen was, at the time when he uttered these words, under the persecution which our Saviour had foretold to his disciples that they should sustain for his sake; he therefore reflected on the circumstance pointed out by him,

him, as a means of happiness and blessing, in their afflictions, and considered that, with the prophets, he was " a partaker of Christ's sufferings; that when his glory shall be revealed, he might be glad also with exceeding joy. If ye be reproached for the name of Christ, happy are ye; for the Spirit of glory, and of God resteth upon you: on their part he is evil spoken of, but on your part he is glorified," 1 Pet. iv. 13, 14. Let us just turn then to the relation of the sufferings of this authentic martyr of Christ, and see whether, upon the reproach incurred for his sake, the glory of God, and of Jesus sitting at his right hand, was not revealed to him; and whether the Spirit, which proceeds from the one glory, the one Godhead of the Father and the Son, did not rest upon him, even the Holy Ghost, with which he was comforted, and by which he cried, " Lord Jesus receive my spirit," Acts vii. 51 to 59.

XV.

" Jesus sent him away, saying, Return to thine own house, and shew how great things God hath done unto thee. And he went his way, and published throughout the whole city, how great things Jesus had done unto him," Luke viii. 38, 39. According to a command, to shew what God had done, the man who had been healed testified what Jesus had done. I do not look upon the evidence of this man as of any great weight in the argument; but there is certainly some testimony borne to our Saviour's divinity, by the manner in which the fact is related by an apostle filled with the Holy Ghost, for the purpose of preaching Christ with precision, and who has, nevertheless, repeated the same words concerning the name of God and of Jesus Christ. It is somewhat remarkable also, that in the relation of the same fact made by St. Mark, the command to the man is said to have been, " go home to to thy friends, and tell them how great things the Lord hath done for thee," Mark v. 19; and the man's publication is exactly as related by St. Luke, " how great things Jesus had done for him." The title of Lord is so very often, nay, so almost peculiarly ascribed to our Saviour, throughout the New Testament, that the use of it here seems an argument for looking upon our blessed Redeemer to have been intended by it: if Jesus Christ then be the Lord intended here, and that the title of Lord be of the same import as the name of " God," for which it is used by St. Mark, then we must acknowledge, that Christ is the Lord, and the Lord he is God. There is a farther circumstance favouring the position that Jesus Christ is the person named here by the appellations of Lord and God, which is, that the man whom he had healed is desired to add to a declaration of what the Lord had done for him, " that he had compassion on him," which certainly must bear reference to that tenderness with which he felt our infirmities, that sympathy with which " Jesus wept," John xi. 35, for the afflictions of those who called upon him even at the moment that he was in act to wipe away the tears from their eyes.

XVI.

I should not look upon the application of the dying thief to our Saviour, hanging also upon a cross, to be any proof that Jesus Christ is the object of prayer, but for the answer made by him, who immediately granted that which was asked, and by admission into paradise, in consequence of a petition preferred to him in an hour, when, of all others, he seemed least able to assist in the time of trouble, exalted the last words of this poor penitent into an incontrovertible testimony that his is the kingdom, that " by suffering he was about to enter into his glory," and that

that he is therefore the Lord, one with the Father, God, Luke xxiii. 42, 43, and xxiv. 26.

XVII.

"Jesus answered and said unto them, destroy this temple, and in three days I will raise it up," in saying which "he spake of the temple of his body," John ii. 19, 21. Here Jesus Christ declares that he will himself raise his body from the grave; but in the grave that body lay truly dead and incapable of any agency: but here he says, that he will act, he must therefore speak of some very extraordinary power remaining to him. But we are often told, that God raised the body of our Saviour from the grave. "This Jesus hath God raised up," says St. Peter, Acts ii. 32; wherein it is observable, that the union of the two natures being suspended during the death of the body, God is spoken of as distinct from Jesus, whose body only is intended by that name: this distinction Peter seems to have had in view throughout the Acts. That which Christ engaged to do, most assuredly he did. He engaged to raise his own body, therefore he did raise his own body. But "this Jesus hath God raised up." Jesus Christ is therefore one with the Father, God.

XVIII.

"Jesus answered and said unto her, If thou knewest the gift of God, and who it is that saith to thee, give me to drink; then wouldest thou have asked of him, and he would have given thee living water," John iv. 10. "Whosoever drinketh of the water which I shall give him, shall never thirst," John iv. 14. Here Jesus Christ gives the gift of God, more properly the gift of Jesus Christ, who gives it, and only reconcilable to sense, by acknowledging him to be one with the Father, God. "They have forsaken the Lord, the fountain of living waters," Jer. xvii. 13.

"And

"And he shewed me a pure river of water of life, clear as chryſtal, proceeding out of the throne of God, and of the Lamb," Rev. xxii. 1. "Let him that is athirſt, come: and whoſoever will, let him take of the water of life freely," Rev. xxii. 17. This invitation ſo mercifully made to all mankind, and in the power of all to accept, is made by Jeſus Chriſt; he therefore who gives ſuch " water ſpringing up into everlaſting life," John iv. 14, is aſſuredly the " Lord, the fountain of living waters;" which Jeremiah declares God to be. "Ho! every one that thirſteth, come ye to the waters," Iſai. lv. 1; " for I will pour water upon him that is thirſty, and floods upon the dry ground: I will pour my ſpirit upon thy ſeed, and my bleſſing upon thine offspring," Iſai. xliv. 3. " Jeſus ſtood and cried, ſaying, If any man thirſt, let him come unto me, and drink. He that believeth on me, as the ſcripture hath ſaid, out of his belly ſhall flow rivers of living water. (But this he ſpake of the ſpirit, which they that believe on him ſhould receive,") John vii. 37, 38. This laſt text clears up and explains the figure, and ſhews what is all along meant by living waters. But " God ſhall pour his ſpirit upon him that is thirſty;" and according to this prophecy, Jeſus Chriſt is to give this water ſpringing up into life, which is the ſpirit. But theſe waters are ſaid to proceed from God; Jeſus Chriſt therefore, from whom they proceed, is one with the Father, God. Let us then with gratitude come upon the invitation to believe; let us confeſs that the blood which was ſhed for us is the blood of God himſelf, Acts xx. 28, ſhed for our redemption; acknowledge " Chriſt the Saviour of the world," John iv. 42, and " with joy draw water out of the wells of ſalvation," Iſai. xii. 3.

"My

XIX.

"My Father worketh hitherto, and I work. Therefore the Jews fought the more to kill him, becaufe he not only had broken the fabbath, but faid alfo that God was his Father, making himfelf equal with God, John v. 17, 18. As the Hebrew idiom of the fcripture language is urged as a reafon for doubting of our common acceptation of the affertions made in the New Teftament, we muft certainly admit the Jews to be the beft verbal interpreters of fuch phrafes as were peculiar to themfelves, and here they have taught us to underftand that whenfoever our Saviour, or any witnefs of his gofpel, declares him to be the Son of God, they intended thereby to convey an affurance that Jefus Chrift is equal with the Father, and with him one God. The fubfequent verfes fay that "what thing foever the Father doeth, thefe alfo doeth the Son likewife." "As the Father hath life in himfelf: fo hath he given to the Son to have life in himfelf; and hath given him authority to execute judgment alfo, becaufe he is the Son of man," John v. 26, 27. Here he fpeaks of himfelf both as God and man ; he declares the felf-exifting life equal with that of the Father; declares the derivation of that to his manhood, with which it was united by the will of God and the Father ; and he declares alfo the reafon wherefore the fecond perfon of the Godhead is to have the execution of judgment to be, " becaufe he is the Son of man." And St. Paul has explained the force of this reafon, " for that he himfelf hath fuffered, being tempted, he is able to fuccour them that are tempted," Heb. ii. 18. " That he can be touched with a feeling of our infirmities ; having been in all points tempted like as we are," Heb. iv. 15; and in the next verfe we

are

are called upon to approach the throne of grace boldly, becaufe that Chrift is the Son of man, having taken on him the feed of Abraham, and has called us brethren, and can have compaffion upon fuch infirmities as he was himfelf fubject to in the flefh: fo that whenfoever we hear our gracious Lord and Saviour call himfelf the Son of man, we may look upon it as an inftance of tendernefs, and that he ufes that name, in order to infpire a confidence in mankind, his brethren, to approach his throne without diftruft in his mercy. Whenfoever he fpeaks of coming to judgment, he qualifies the terrors of that dreadful day by faying, that it is before the Son of man that all nations are to be gathered; and in the paffage before us, declares the reafon wherefore all judgment is committed to the Son to be, becaufe he is the Son of man. Our Saviour, after having faid that " the Father quickeneth the dead," John v. 21, proceeds to tell us, that on that day " the dead fhall hear the voice of the Son of God: and they that hear fhall live," John v. 25. And farther, that " the hour is coming, in the which all that are in their graves fhall hear his (the Son of man's) voice," John v. 28: fo that here, they that are in their graves, live, being called upon by the Son of man, becaufe they have heard the voice of the Son of God, the Father being he who quickeneth the dead. Can this be reconciled to any fenfe, if it be not granted that Jefus Chrift, the Son of God, and alfo the Son of man, is equal to, and one with the Father, God? And this once granted, is any pofition more reconcilable to reafon? Refift this who can, for my part I am unable to ftand againft it; but verily " believe, and am fure that thou art that Chrift, the Son of the living God," John vi. 69; words, which I am bold to ufe, as expreffive of an equality between

tween the Son and the Father: nay farther, of an identity and unity of Godhead. As poſſeſſed of this Godhead " I believe on him, and I worſhip him," John ix. 38.

XX.

" He that believeth on him that ſent me, hath everlaſting life, and ſhall not come into condemnation," John v. 24. "He that believeth on him, (the Son) is not condemned; but he that believeth not, is condemned already, becauſe he hath not believed in the name of the only begotten Son of God," John iii. 18. If there be no condemnation for thoſe who believe in the Father, how is it neceſſary to believe in the Son in order to indemnify? It can only be ſo, becauſe that the Son is one with the Father, God; and the two paſſages then convey the ſame inſtruction. In context with the laſt aſſertion, our Saviour, ſpeaking of himſelf, uſes the following very remarkable words, " the Son of man which is in heaven," John iii. 13. This is a very expreſs declaration of his Godhead, the ubiquity of which was by no means affected by its union with the Son of man; for whilſt he was ſpeaking to Nicodemus he could be on earth only as a man, and as God only filling immenſity could he at that moment of time have been in heaven. He declares alſo, that " he came down from heaven," in the ſame verſe; and St. John Baptiſt, ſpeaking of Jeſus Chriſt, teſtifies, that " he that cometh from above is above all," John iii. 31. The pre-exiſtence of our Lord in heaven is expreſsly declared by himſelf in the following words alſo, " What and if ye ſhall ſee the Son of man aſcend up where he was before?" John vi. 62. This muſt refer to his Godhead, as it is no where aſſerted that his fleſhly body had ever been in heaven before his final aſcent. But when he declares, " I came forth from

I the

the Father, and am come into the world: again, I leave the world, and go to the Father," "his disciples said unto him, lo, now speakest thou plainly, and speakest no proverb," John xvi. 28, 29.

XXI.

"Jesus said unto them, verily verily I say unto you, before Abraham was, I am," John viii. 58. There is a very remarkable distinction in this passage between the words *was* and *am*. By the former, the existence of Abraham is marked to have had a commencement, and to have been finite; whereas, by the latter, the eternity of Jesus Christ, as God, is strongly pointed out. The word *am* bears reference to a life in every moment extended to all eternity; which, as the presence of the Almighty fills infinite space, stretches itself at once through all duration, and is at all periods to be spoken of in the present tense, as all periods are present to it at once; a life "which is, and which was, and which is to come," Rev. i. 4. Jesus Christ here makes use of the same expression which God had declared to be his name to Moses, and given to him as a token whereby he should make himself known to the children of Israel, to have come from God, Exod. iii. 14; and it can hardly be conceived that he does so without an intention of marking his divinity, and declaring himself to be that God, and that he it was who led the forefathers of those with whom he spoke, out of the land of Egypt by the hand of Moses. In some passages, ending in a declaration, "*I am*" in the original, the translation has supplied the word *he*; because a relative pronoun, the expression of which the Greek tongue can dispense with, is necessarily to be expressed in ours, in order to make good sense of the passage in English, which is good sense in Greek without it. For instance: the woman of Samaria tells our Saviour,

that

that " when Chrift comes, he will tell us all things:" to which he anfwered, " I that fpeak unto thee, am," John iv. 26; fo it ftands in the original, and requires no more words to convey the idea that he was Chrift of whom fhe fpake; whereas it is indifpenfibly requifite that the tranflator fhall add a pronoun referring to what had been faid before, and turn the paffage, as our Bible has it, " I that fpeak unto thee am *he*." From this circumftance it is urged, that no inference, favouring our Saviour's divinity, is to be drawn from the paffage before us, becaufe (as is alledged) it is only of the fame ftamp of the others. Without going farther into grammatical difquifitions, let us try the experiment upon it, and write it accordingly, " Jefus faid unto them, verily verily I fay unto you, before Abraham was, I am *he*." Who? Abraham? Will any man infift on this? The word *am* in this verfe fignifies, I exift, in a neuter fenfe, and fo cannot require a relative pronoun to follow it. The context alfo requires the interpretation which I have put upon thefe words; our Saviour declares to the Jews, " I am," in anfwer to their objection to the poffibility of his having feen Abraham, not being yet fifty years old. Upon the whole, I look upon this to be a very explicit declaration of his Godhead and pre-exiftence to the time of his having come into the world, a teftimony borne to it by the author of our falvation himfelf, and therefore I muft yield my affent to his words, that he is one with the Father, God.

XXII.

" I and my Father are one," John x. 30. When our Saviour made this very literal declaration, the Jews ftoned him, and gave as a reafon, " becaufe that thou, being a man, makeft thyfelf God," John x. 33. This fhews how they underftood him; and the anfwer of our Saviour to their charge fhews alfo that they were right, for, inftead of retracting, he refers them to the teftimony of his works; " that ye may know and believe that the Father is in me, and I in him," John x. 38: words, which, however they might admit of a figurative interpretation in any other paffage, being here fpoke to confirm what he had before declared, muft be interpreted by that declaration, and mark a mutual relation, refulting only from the poffeffion of one Godhead with the Father.

XXIII.

" Philip faith unto him, Lord, fhew us the Father, and it fufficeth us. Jefus faith unto him, have I been fo long with you, and yet haft thou not known me, Philip? He that hath feen me, hath feen the Father: and how fayeft thou then, fhew us the Father? Believeft thou not, that I am in the Father, and the Father in me? The words that I fpeak unto you, I fpeak not of myfelf: but the Father that dwelleth in me, he doeth the works. Believe me that I am in the Father, and the Father in me: or elfe believe me for the very works fake," John xiv. 8, 9, 10, 11. The interpretation of this paffage may be drawn from the remark made upon the texts laft cited, for our Saviour teftifies, that he is in the Father, and the Father in him, in order to evince, that Philip, in having known him, had known the Father. As our Lord could not mean that Philip's acquaintance with the Father was the fame as his acquaintance with himfelf, in the flefh, he has pointed out, that the means whereby he had known the Father, in having known him, was by his knowledge of thofe words which he had fpoken, and thofe works which he had done by the operation of his Godhead,

head, one with that of the Father. These had been often cognizable by Philip; he therefore in having known the Son, who had said and done such things in testimony of what he was, might well be said to have known the Father, with whom our Lord and Saviour was, in that respect which was pointed out, one and the same God.

XXIV.

" I go unto my Father. And whatsoever ye shall ask in my name, that will I do, that the Father may be glorified in the Son. If ye shall ask any thing in my name, I will do it," John xiv. 12, 13, 14. I believe no man will deny that a petition is to be made to him who is to grant it. Jesus Christ here declares to his disciples, that he will fulfil their prayers, and do that which they shall ask in his name; who then can hesitate to pronounce this doctrine of our Saviour a command to ask of him, a declaration that he is the God of our salvation, from whom cometh help? " With Melancthon, (as quoted by Mr. Lindsey, but for what purpose I cannot comprehend) I take refuge in those plain declarations of scripture, which injoin prayer to Christ, which is to ascribe the proper honour of divinity to him, and is full of consolation." And with Mr. Lindsey himself I observe, 1st, that this eminent person thought, and justly as it should seem, that prayer is the highest act of worship, the proper honour of God, and peculiar to him alone. And, 2dly, that the principal argument for Christ's divinity was to be fetched from religious worship, and prayer being addressed to him." Apology, p. 135. Mr. Lindsey's candour is such that I rely upon his not starting from this conclusion, which he admits as necessarily following from Christ's being proved the object of prayer and religious worship. I shall therefore, if the above texts afford a

proof,

proof, or many others, which I shall call up in evidence of this fact, testify that Christ is properly to be adored, demand and peremptorily insist upon Mr. Lindsey's acquiescence in this position, that Jesus Christ is one with the Father, God. It is a certain fact, even upon a supposition that our Saviour was no more than man, that he was "without sin," and, consequently, that he did not in any instance contradict himself, whereby he must have once spoken that which was not true; but he says to his disciples, "And in that day ye shall ask me nothing: verily verily I say unto you, whatsoever ye shall ask the Father in my name, he will give it you;" John xvi. 23. As our blessed Redeemer cannot mean here to say that he had before spoken an untruth, these words must have exactly the same meaning as those before us; for, if not, they flatly contradict them. That I will grant your prayers, and that the Father will grant your prayers, must therefore signify that the one Godhead of the Father and the Son will grant them; and therefore it follows, that the Father and the Son are one God. "If ye shall ask any thing, in my name, I will do it," says our Saviour; whence I have inferred, that he it is of whom the demand is to be made: But I foresee a possible objection to be made to this inference, which I shall endeavour to obviate. It is, that in this case Jesus Christ has commanded prayer to be preferred to himself in his own name; to which I answer, that so to have done is exactly correspondent to the conduct of God, so long as he had a selected nation his worshippers, and dealt by them as a peculiar people to call upon his name; and that therefore, when they were to cease to be peculiar, and that a whole world was to be adopted, there is no force in the objection, which only shews God governing his additional adorers, as he had governed their predecessors,

Before

Before God was to be adored through Christ, he was to be adored through those benefits which he had conferred upon the children of Israel; before the name of Christ was given, through which he was to be invoked, his innumerable mercies were commanded to be held in remembrance, and in the name of them he was to be called upon; and accordingly we find the Hebrews adored him as the God of Abraham, the God of Isaac, and the God of Jacob, the God of their fathers, to whom he had promised, and frequently renewed the promise of a blessing to proceed from them to all nations of the earth. They adored him as the God of their fathers, who had led them out of the house of bondage into a land flowing with milk and honey; and, as the God who had dealt thus graciously by them, he prescribed to them, and prefaced the decalogue with a claim to their obedience, and to their worshipping him only, grounded upon that debt of gratitude, which they owed for the protection and deliverance that he had vouchsafed them; and he has expresly commanded them to call upon him as the God of their fathers, and made this " his name for ever, and his memorial unto all generations," Exod. iii. 15. But he has since been pleased to hold out a light to lighten the Gentiles, and, remembering his mercies, hath holpen his servant Israel, according to his promises; wherefore then shall we refrain from offering up the sacrifice of praise and thanksgiving to God, in the name of his mercies vouchsafed to us by his having taken our nature upon him? in the name of that man in whose flesh he was manifested *, and in which our eyes have seen, and our hands have handled the word of † life, even that word which is ‡ God? Wherefore, in remembrance of so great benefits, should we not
say,

* 1 Tim. iii. 16.   † 1 John i. 1.   ‡ John i. 1.

say, " by thine agony and bloody sweat, by thy cross and passion, by thy precious death and burial, by thy glorious resurrection and ascension, good Lord deliver us?" The sense, in which I understand the words calling upon God in the name of Christ, is calling upon God to assist us, whom he had already thought worthy of so great benefits, in memory of those benefits which he suffered in the flesh, in order to confer. And surely in this sense, it is perfectly conformable to the course of God's government, that our Saviour should desire us to call upon his Godhead in memory of what he has done for us as man, having already declared that he had, in remembrance of his former mercies, holpen us.

XXV.

" It is expedient for you that I go away: for if I go not away, the Comforter will not come unto you; but if I depart, I will send him unto you," John xvi. 7. " The Comforter, which is the Holy Ghost, whom the Father will send in my name, he shall teach you all things, and bring all things to your remembrance, whatsoever I have said unto you," John xiv. 26. Here Jesus Christ sends the Holy Ghost, and the Father at the same time sends the Holy Ghost; therefore the Father and the Son are one God, from whom the spirit is to proceed. He says in another passage; " but when the Comforter is come, whom I will send unto you from the Father, even the Spirit of Truth, which proceedeth from the Father, he shall testify of me," John xv. 26. The Holy Ghost here proceedeth from the Father only; we find that the same witness of Christ preceded his coming, and testified of him beforehand, as well as after his ascent; " For the prophecy came not in old time by the will of man: but holy men of God spake as they were moved by the Holy Ghost," 2 Peter i. 21. But we find the prophets themselves, who spake as they were

were moved by the Holy Ghost, " searching what, or what manner of time the spirit of Christ which was in them did signify, when it testified beforehand the sufferings of Christ, and the glory that should follow," 1 Pet. i. 11; so that the apostles, filled with the Holy Ghost, have here expressly declared what glory that is which should be testified after the sufferings of Christ, even that the spirit which proceedeth from the Father is the spirit of Christ, therefore one with the Father, God. But our Saviour himself, as if determined to put the matter out of doubt, by preparing the ears of his audience to hear the testimony of the Holy Ghost concerning him, declares that " he shall glorify me: for he shall receive of mine, and shall shew it unto you. All things that the Father hath, are mine: therefore said I, that he shall take of mine, and shew it unto you," John xvi. 14, 15.

XXVI.

Our blessed Lord and Saviour, having taken our nature upon him, and having been in all points tempted like as we are, on the approach of that hour in which he was to be made perfect by suffering death for all men, and in which he was to finish the great end of his having come in the flesh, consoles himself by looking beyond his grave, and contemplating the glory that should follow; and as a man about to endure great afflictions, and, surmounting them, to take our nature " into heaven itself, now to appear in the presence of God for us," Heb. ix. 24. addresses himself to that Being to which, as Man, he was inferior, saying, " Father, the hour is come; glorify thy Son, that thy Son also may glorify thee," John xvii. 1. " And now, O Father, glorify thou me with thine own self, with the glory which I had with thee before the world was," John xvii. 5. " For thou lovedst me before the foundations of the world," John xvii. 24. The pre-existence of our Saviour is exprefsly declared here, and the identity of that Godhead with which he and the Father are mutually to glorify each other; that glory which the Son had in all refpects equal with the Father, before he had, for the fake of mankind, taken upon him that nature whereby he was, upon earth, inferior to him.

XXVII.

" Pilate therefore faid unto him, art thou a king then? Jefus anfwered, thou fayeft that I am a king. To this end was I born, and for this caufe came I into the world, that I fhould bear witnefs unto the truth. Every one that is of the truth, heareth my voice," John xviii. 37. Thefe words are preceded by a declaration made by our Saviour, that, " my kingdom is not of this world;" and the whole together is faid by St. Paul to be " a good confeffion witneffed before Pilate," 1 Tim. vi. 13. That Nathanael, an Ifraelite indeed, in whom was no guile, underftood the prophecies of our Saviour's kingdom in this fenfe is evident, for, upon feeing him an unattended man, he pronounced him " the King of Ifrael," which he muft have feen that he was not in any other acceptation of the terms than as he was the " Son of God," John i. 49. and this interpretation he put upon the prophecies, upon feeing our Saviour poffeffed of an extraordinary knowledge. Greater things have been referved for us to fee than Nathanael faw; why then fhall we hefitate to fay, according to the teftimony which this great witnefs of the truth bore to himfelf, " thy kingdom is not of this world," and with Nathanael, " thou art the King of Ifrael, the Son of God;" words which I have already fhewed, when fpoken by a Jew, to mean, thou haft equality of Godhead with the Father.

" And

XXVIII.

"And Thomas answered and said unto him, my Lord, and my God. Jesus saith unto him, Thomas, because thou hast seen me, thou hast believed," John xx. 28, 29. To call this saying of Thomas an exclamation, is a poor and disingenuous evasion of the Bishop, quoted by Mr. Lindsey; for it is declared to be *an answer* and *an address* to our Saviour, who had convinced him that he was the same Jesus who had been dead and was alive again; an argument which I should conceive sufficient to evince the truth of doctrines which Thomas had heard before, but through a defective faith did not understand; and to induce that confession which he now makes, saying unto him, "my Lord and my God." When Mary, ver. 16, saw and knew our Lord after his resurrection, she made no exclamation, but directly addressed herself to him, saying, "Master," acknowledging him to whom she spoke. Mary had not been a witness of all the declarations of his own nature which he had made to his apostles, who were to be witnesses unto him; she acknowledges him as she had known him before; but Thomas, who considered a resurrection from the dead to be a conclusive proof of the truth of what he had often heard, instantly draws the natural inference, and acknowledges him to be his Lord and his God. If the works of this bishop of *Mopsuestia*, which have not reached us, be of the same stamp as the fragment quoted by Mr. Lindsey, we have no great reason to regret the loss, or condemn our ancestors for having consigned the rest of them to oblivion. The poor bishop himself must also be obliged to those who have redeemed him from our censure.——

Next in order follows the testimony borne to the divinity of Jesus Christ by the apostles, men appointed to be his witnesses, on whom "he breathed and said,"

" receive ye the Holy Ghoſt," " the ſpirit of truth, he will guide you into all truth ;" " he ſhall teach you all things, and bring all things to your remembrance, whatſoever I have ſaid unto you ;" " he will ſhew you things to come; he ſhall glorify me." Men, " whoſe underſtanding he opened that they might underſtand the ſcriptures," " holy men of God who have made known unto us the power and coming of our Lord Jeſus Chriſt, for they were eye-witneſſes of his Majeſty." To perſons thus qualified, ſpeaking as they were moved by the Holy Ghoſt, coming in due time to ſpeak of him who had given himſelf a ranſom for all, " underſtanding the myſtery of Chriſt, which in other ages was not made known unto men, as it is now revealed unto his holy apoſtles and prophets by the Spirit ;" taking the prophecies from a dark place to ſpread abroad their radiance, and render their ſure word a light to us; to ſuch men we ſhall do well that we take heed; to their teſtimony it is eſſential to our own eternal happineſs that we give credit, and not that we look upon all ſuch things as occur in their writings, which are " hard to be underſtood, as given to our ignorance and inſtability to wreſt to our own deſtruction ;" they have pointed out the way to a bleſſed immortality; it is our duty to ſearch into what they have ſaid, and where we cannot underſtand to confide. From the apoſtles we are to expect the manifeſtation of ſpiritual things, and as ſuch are certainly beyond the reach of our farther enquiry, it is but reaſonable to truſt thoſe who were permitted to look into them, and to promulgate ſo much as concerns us to know.

XXIX.

" And they prayed, and ſaid, thou Lord, which knoweſt the hearts of all men, ſhew whether of theſe two thou haſt choſen, that he may take part of this miniſtry and apoſtleſhip," Acts i. 24. This prayer

is

is preferred to the Lord who had sent forth his disciples, saying, " ye shall bear witness, because ye have been with me from the beginning," John xv. 27. " Go ye into all the world, and preach the gospel to every creature," Mark xvi. 15; and by whom, St. Paul says, " we have received the apostleship," Rom. i. 5; to that Lord, who knew to whom he should commit himself, " because he knew all men, and needed not that any should testify of man; for he knew what was in man," John ii. 25. And the petition is that out of two men, namely, Justus and Matthias, selected from those " who had been with our Saviour from the beginning," " which have companied with us, all the time that the Lord Jesus went in and out among us, beginning from the baptism of John, unto that same day that he was taken up from us," Acts i. 21, 22; he should ordain one to be a witness of his resurrection in the place of Judas, who had fallen by transgression. That it is addressed to Jesus Christ, not only the context, but the following circumstance may thoroughly demonstrate: The very same call being to be made of another apostle, as the Lord is now desired to make, a light shone from heaven round about Saul, and of the voice which spoke it is thus declared: " the Lord said, I am Jesus whom thou persecutest:" " and the Lord said, arise, and go into the city, and it shall be told thee what thou must do," Acts ix. 5, 6. But when Saul, according to this commandment, came into Damascus, " he is met and received by a certain disciple named Ananias, to whom said the Lord in a vision, Ananias. And he said, behold I am here, Lord. I have heard by many of this man, how much evil he hath done to thy saints at Jerusalem: and here he hath authority from the Chief Priests, to bind all *that call upon thy name*. But the Lord said unto him, go thy way:

way: for he is a *chosen* vessel unto me, to bear my name before the Gentiles and Kings, and the children of Israel," Acts ix. 13, 14, 15. That the vessel which was to bear the name of Christ before the Gentiles, &c. was to be chosen by him is here evident; and St. Paul himself farther says, " Christ sent me (not to baptize, but) to preach the gospel," 1 Cor. i. 17. To him who was to *choose*, it is therefore to be concluded the petition was preferred that he would shew whether of these two he had *chosen* to preach his gospel, and take part of that ministry to which " the wisdom of God," Luke xi. 49, even " Christ," Mat. xxiii. 34; said, " I will send them prophets and apostles:" so that here is an instance of adoration incontrovertibly offered up to Jesus Christ; therefore one with the Father, God, the proper object of prayer and religious worship.

But, throughout the relation, there is a farther testimony to be found of the adoration of Jesus Christ; for Ananias, himself a disciple, declares, that Saul was a persecutor of those *who called upon the name of Christ*, and " the disciples of our Saviour were therefore afraid of him when he assayed to join himself unto them," Acts ix. 26; for " all that heard him preach Christ in the synagogues were amazed, and said, is not this he that destroyed them which *called on this name* in Jerusalem, and came hither for that intent, that he might bring them bound to the Chief Priests?" Acts ix. 20, 21. We have here direct proof that the disciples of Christ called upon his name, both from those who did, and those who did not call upon it.

I shall in this place take notice of Mr. Lindsey's assertion, (supported by quotations from various authors) that to call upon the name of Jesus is the same as to be be called by the name of Jefus, or to have the name of Jefus called upon the fubject fpoken of. This declaration he has made in his very extraordinary comment upon 1 Cor. i. 2. Apology, p. 132. And he farther declares, that Stephen's calling upon the name of Jefus, is the only paffage in which thefe words mean directly the fame as invoking him. Notwithftanding that the name of that great critick in the Greek language, Dr. Clarke, is produced in evidence of this affertion, I own I am not convinced of its truth; nor can I fee a reafon why the identical word, fignifying an invocation in one place, fhall be denied to have the fame fignification in another, where the context is exactly fimilar to that in which it is allowed to have that meaning, and indeed in which it requires to be fo interpreted, in order to its bearing any meaning at all. But, with refpect to the paffage before us, it is a little remarkable that the name of Chrift had not yet been called upon his difciples, and that for want of a name to comprehend them all, the commiffion to Saul is couched in the following aukward terms: " that if he found *any of this way,* he might bring them bound unto Jerufalem," Acts ix. 2. In the execution of this warrant from the priefts it was, that Saul was chofen to bear *the name* of Jefus Chrift to the Gentiles; and this happened exactly two years after the afcenfion of our Saviour, whereas it was not till ten years after that event that the difciples were firft called chriftians at Antioch. How difingenuoufly then do men deal, not only with the world, but with themfelves alfo, in wrefting words from their true meaning, to the fupport of their own fuggeftions. If one man, filled with the Holy Ghoft for the purpofe of " guiding him into all truth," has invoked Jefus Chrift, is not fuch an act, once fo performed, fufficient to evince the propriety of the invocation, and to eftablifh the right of Je-

fus

sus Christ to be invoked? And if adoration then be the due of Christ, why should we deny a literal interpretation to words by which it is asserted, that the disciples of our Lord rendered him that praise and adoration to which he is entitled? Is it meant that the disciples contradict the testimony of the Holy Ghost by which Stephen called upon the Lord Jesus? They were themselves filled with the Holy Ghost; and is the Spirit of Truth divided against himself? If this be the assertion, either Stephen, or the disciples, or Dr. Clarke, or Mr. Lindsey, are guilty of an impious and absurd blasphemy, and I leave it to my reader to choose the blasphemer. "He is a chosen vessel unto me," says Jesus Christ to Ananias, Acts ix. 15. "The God of our Fathers hath chosen thee," says Ananias to Saul, Acts xxii. 14. Who can now withhold the application of the following address to the Lord Jesus, or his concurrence with me in saying to him, "Lord thou art God."

There is yet another circumstance in the passage before us, which proves that the prayer was addressed to Jesus Christ. Peter, (who had, upon his own appointment to the ministry, taken our Lord to witness that he loved him, and would with fidelity discharge the trust of feeding his sheep committed to his keeping, saying, "Lord, thou knowest all things; thou knowest that I love thee," John xxi. 17.) was certainly the chief speaker, and the person who preferred the prayer of this venerable assembly. It is therefore highly probable, that he who had accepted of his own apostleship with such an acknowledgment of our Saviour's omniscience, repeated the like acknowledgment when calling upon him to choose another to associate with them, who should also love him, and faithfully acquit himself of a part in the same apostleship. When Peter spoke
those

those words to Jesus Christ in his own case, he certainly alluded to his knowledge of the heart, for "he was grieved;" and well he might upon recollection of the event which induced the declaration, for he had an aching memory of our Lord's more intimate knowledge of his own heart than he was himself possessed of, when upon his confidence of his own faith, saying, "I will lay down my life for thy sake, Jesus answered him, wilt thou lay down thy life for my sake? verily verily I say unto thee, the cock shall not crow, till thou hast denied me thrice," John xiii. 37, 38. This he knew to have been truly spoken by his Master, and for him, whose own particular experience had taught him that Jesus Christ was acquainted with man, and needed not that any should testify of man, it is exceedingly natural that he should on such an occasion say to him " who knew all things," " Lord which knowest the hearts of all men, &c."

XXX.

When Peter and John had, " in the name of Jesus Christ of Nazareth," healed the lame man at the gate of the temple, the people who saw it ran together greatly wondering; "and when Peter saw it, he answered unto the people, ye men of Israel, why marvel ye at this? or why look ye so earnestly on us, as though by our own power or holiness we had made this man walk?" Acts iii. 12. " Be it known unto you all, and to all the people of Israel, that, by the name of Jesus Christ of Nazareth, whom ye crucified, whom God raised from the dead, even by him doth this man stand here before you whole," Acts iv. 10. Upon which, the Rulers, having threatened Peter and John, were obliged to let them go, " for all men *glorified God for that which was done,*" Acts iv. 21. Peter, when he restored Eneas to health at Lydda, called him from his bed

bed in the following remarkable terms: "Eneas, Jesus Chrift maketh thee whole: arife, and make thy bed," Acts ix. 34. He arofe immediately, and the confequence was, that "all that dwelt at Lydda, and Saron, faw him, and *turned to the Lord*," ver. 35.

XXXI.

"When they heard thefe things, they were cut to the heart, and they gnafhed on him (Stephen) with their teeth. But he being full of the Holy Ghoft looked up ftedfaftly into heaven, and faw the glory of God, and Jefus ftanding on the right hand of God, and faid, behold, I fee the heavens opened, and the Son of man ftanding on the right hand of God. Then they cried out with a loud voice, and ftopped their ears, and ran upon him with one accord, and caft him out of the city, and ftoned him: And the witneffes laid down their clothes at a young man's feet, whofe name was Saul. And they ftoned Stephen, calling upon *God*, and faying, Lord Jefus receive my fpirit. And he kneeled down, and cried with a loud voice, Lord, lay not this fin to their charge," Acts vii. 54, 55, 56, 57, 58, 59, 60.

Mr. Lindfey's remark upon this paffage is fo very particular, that I will give it at large, and then proceed to fhew its futility to the very few of my readers, who fhall not have found it out of themfelves. "There is no doubt but Stephen made this requeft, addreffed this prayer to the Lord Jefus. But this can be no precedent for directing prayer to him *unfeen*, or addreffing him as God, whom the bleffed Martyr declares *he faw with his eyes*, and calls him "the Son of man ftanding on the right hand of God." Calls him *the Son of man*, in this his higheft ftate of exaltation. *Son of man, and God moft high: what a*

fpace

space between?" Apology, p. 129. Does this gentleman conceive that the actions of an almighty God are circumscribed by the limits appointed to his comprehension, that the space beyond which his imagination cannot pass, is equally an obstruction to the will of him to whom " all things are possible," and that the Omnipotent is to pause in his progress, till Mr. Lindsey shall have leisure to come up with him and mark his footsteps? I hope I have already evinced the absurdity of this appeal from the written word to natural religion, and shewed that the scriptures only are the fountain from whence the course of our argument is to flow; they are granted to be true, and to be ultimate, and if from them I find that God has put his own nature into union with that of man, I will believe that he has done so; that he has formed us a creature, with whom it was possible for him who had " put all things into his own power" to come into union; notwithstanding that neither Mr. Lindsey nor I know any thing of the manner. The space between God and man may be utterly unsurmountable to our conceptions, but shall it therefore impede the Almighty? It is not reason which stands in the way of our belief, but the impious pride of ignorance, " speaking evil of that which it understands not," " beguiling unstable souls," " withdrawing from the knowledge of the Lord and Saviour Jesus Christ, by which we had before escaped the pollutions of the world," 2 Peter. ii. Mr. Lindsey having allowed that " the principal argument for Christ's divinity is to be fetched from religious worship and prayer being addressed to him," Apology, p. 135, is most exceedingly distressed at the passage before us, and accordingly uses his utmost diligence to extricate himself from the melancholy necessity of yielding up his spirit into the hands of his Redeemer, his Mediator, and his Judge; and left it should follow

follow that he who " bought us with the price of his own blood," " and so loved us that he gave himself a ransom for all," has any right in his purchase, or should " in due time be testified," by the invocation of St. Stephen, to be one with the Father, God, recourse is had to an expedient, the most singular perhaps that ever was made use of to any purpose whatsoever, and it is asserted that this first Martyr of our Saviour having *seen* the Lord Jesus *with his eyes* when he prayed, affords no precedent for directing prayer to him *unseen*. The very fact, as stated by Mr. Lindsey, is disputable; for although it be said that Stephen, while before the council, and under their displeasure, so long as he looked up stedfastly into heaven saw Jesus Christ, it by no means follows that the vision continued, or that he could conveniently keep his eyes fixed stedfastly upon it at the time when they ran upon him, cast him out of the city, and stoned him; that is, at the time when he called upon the Lord Jesus. But I will, for argument's sake, admit that Stephen still continued to have his eyes upon him, and that, " being filled with the Holy Ghost, he *still* saw the glory of God, and Jesus Christ standing at the right hand of God." Is not God himself here equally before the eyes of the blessed Martyr as the Son of man? why then should his view of the one induce prayer more than his view of the other? Nay, wherefore should he pass down from God most high through that immense space which lay between him and the Son of man, unless that, conducted by the Holy Ghost, sent " to guide him into all truth," John xvi. 13. he saw that Father and Son were not one and another, but one and the same God, and that there was no space between the Son of man and God most high? unless indeed he saw the Lord Jesus, into whose hands he commended his spirit, to be the almighty God to whom David had said " into thine hand

hand I commit my spirit: thou haft redeemed me, O Lord God of truth?" Pfalm xxxi. 5. Will Mr. Lindfey perfift to fay that the Holy Ghoft had led him into error? and yet into an error he has led him, if Jefus Chrift, even in this his higheft ftate of exaltation, be but his fellow creature. But becaufe Jefus was in fight he was to be worfhipped; and there is nothing wrong in worfhipping a vifible creature. If the command be, and if the duty of a chriftian therefore be to worfhip God only, I own myfelf too blind to difcern how the vifibility of any Creature fhould fuperfede the commandment, and alter the unalterable law of God. The Angel was vifible to St. John, Rev. xxii. 9. yet reftrained him from worfhip, which Chrift did not do by his adorer; but he, who was equally vifible to Stephen as the Son of man, winked at the difrefpect with which he paffed by his own glory, and addreffed himfelf to the Lord Jefus; and by a difplay of that glory teftified in the higheft his approbation of that addrefs which was preferred to the Son of man by this holy Martyr, " with the Spirit of Truth," as being confiftent with the command, as a direct obedience to his will declared in thefe words, " Thou fhalt worfhip the Lord thy God, and him only fhalt thou worfhip." " Worfhip God," faid the Angel to St. John; our Saviour faid no fuch thing to Stephen, nor referred him to that God whofe glory was before his eyes. I therefore think it evident, that God, and God only, Stephen did worfhip, in the perfon of Jefus Chrift, one with the Father, God. I grant Mr. Lindfey's affertion, that the word " God" is fupplied in the 59th verfe, " calling upon God, and faying Lord Jefus receive my fpirit." It is of no confequence if it be omitted, for then the invocation is made directly to Chrift, and remains a proof that he is God, though he be not addreffed by that name. The word " God" being inferted by the tranf-
lators,

lators, shews how they understood the passage before us, and though I do not choose to make use of human authority, I cannot help this once saying that I look upon this conclusion, drawn by men of great abilities, and employed in the most diligent perusal of the whole Bible, as more than a balance to every quotation produced by Mr. Lindsey from men pursuing systems, and wresting half sentences to their own particular purposes. Upon the whole, unless it be admitted that being visible is a reason for addressing prayer to any thing we are looking at, here is an instance of adoration, a precedent of religious worship preferred to our Lord and Saviour, and, if " religious worship and prayer be a proof of Godhead," I demand Mr. Lindsey's acquiescence in this conclusion, that Jesus Christ is one with the Father, God; who has said, " am I a God at hand, and not a God afar off?" Jer. xxiii. 23.

I mean now to resume what for a time I admitted, that Stephen had Jesus Christ before his eyes when he was cast out of the city and stoned. The scriptures are seldom so vague as to require our belief of that which is not particularly revealed. The star which appeared to the wise men is never withdrawn from before their eyes till it stood over the house where the young child was. The evangelist has constantly kept it in view, whereas there is no mention made that the heavens continued open to Stephen, from the time he was taken from before the council; and therefore we have no reason to affirm that they did. The very prayers which our Lord and Saviour, suffering in the flesh, preferred, are preferred by Stephen, who therefore must be aware of the force of example; or, if not so acute himself, must have known by the Spirit of Truth that future times would refer themselves to the conduct of this martyr; and that men, like him, in articulo mortis,

would

would commend their spirit to the Lord Jesus. Did the spirit mean to deceive? It surely has not guided to all truth, if it did not, and that Mr. Lindsey's hypothesis be true; and therefore even the Holy Ghost comes under this gentleman's charge of incompetency to be a witness to the great preserver of all spirits.

Before I dismiss this subject I shall add one more remark, which, if it do not afford conclusive proof of what has been advanced already, must be allowed greatly to corroborate the force of it.

"Behold," says Stephen, "I see the heavens opened, and the Son of man standing on the right hand of God; then they cried out with a loud voice, and stopped their ears, and ran upon him with one accord, &c." Acts vii. 56, 57. "Hereafter," says our Lord, "shall ye see the Son of man sitting on the right hand of power, and coming in the clouds of heaven: then the high priest rent his clothes, saying, he hath spoken blasphemy," "then did they spit in his face, and buffeted him, &c." Matth. xxvi. 64, 65, 67. "Art thou the Christ, the Son of the blessed? and Jesus said, I am. And ye shall see the Son of man sitting on the right hand of power, and coming in the clouds of heaven. Then the high priest rent his clothes, and saith, What need we any farther witnesses, ye have heard the blasphemy? what think ye? and they all condemned him to be guilty of death, and some began to spit on him, &c." Matth. xiv. 61 to 65. When Jesus said, "before Abraham was, I am," "the Jews took up stones to cast at him;" when he said, "I and my Father are one, they took up stones again to stone him," saying, "because that thou being a man makest thyself God." The Jews also sought to kill him, "because he said that God was his Father, making himself
equal

equal with God." Here the ground of the Jewish resentment appears, they were Unitarians, and looked upon an equality or unity of Godhead between the Father and Son as the greatest indignity to the God of their fathers. To the words for which our Saviour was condemned by the high priest and his council, we may therefore ascribe the same meaning, and conclude that they were designed to convey the same idea of our Lord's equal and one Godhead with the Father. The very same thing which Jesus here says they shall hereafter see, St. Stephen declares to the very same tribunal to be now before his eyes; and the very same consequence attends his declaration; so that we may consider Stephen as having in this respect also borne his testimony to the one Godhead of the Father and of the Son of man.

XXXII.

After Peter had healed Eneas at Lydda, saying, " Jesus Christ maketh thee whole, arise," the friends of Tabitha, who was sick, and had died at Joppa, in the neighbourhood of the town where he had wrought this miracle, solicited his immediate attendance; upon which he arose and went with them, and coming into the chamber where they had laid her body, and having put forth all those who stood weeping by, " he kneeled down and prayed, and turning him to the body, said, Tabitha, arise. And she opened her eyes: and when she saw Peter, she sat up," Acts ix. 40. " And it was known throughout all Joppa; and many believed in the Lord," verse 42. The words which Peter spoke to Eneas were addressed to him in order to induce his faith, and that of those who saw the work which he had done, in the Lord. But in the case of Tabitha, where he had put forth those whose clamorous grief might interrupt the fervour of his devotion, and remained alone with the dead body,

such

such language being absolutely unneceffary, it is very probable that Peter did not ufe it on that account; but as there is no doubt that the fame Jefus Chrift, who had made Eneas whole, now called Tabitha back to life, it is furely to be inferred that the prayer of Peter was preferred to him; and this is the more probable, when we fee that the confequence of her revival on the call of Peter was, that " many believed on the Lord," for many who faw what had been done to Eneas " turned to the Lord."

XXXIII.

" When God had to the Gentiles alfo granted repentance unto life," " fome of the difciples which were come to Antioch, fpake unto the Grecians preaching the Lord Jefus. And the hand of the Lord was with them: and a great number believed, and turned unto the Lord:" upon which, when the church at Jerufalem heard it, " they fent forth Barnabas, that he fhould go as far as Antioch. Who, when he came, and had feen the grace of God, was glad, and exhorted them all, that with purpofe of heart they would cleave unto the Lord," Acts xi. 18, 20, 21, 22, 23. Upon the hand of the Lord being with them, Barnabas is glad to have feen the grace of God; or, he was glad upon having feen the " grace of God, who hath to the Gentiles alfo granted repentance unto life:" " but we believe that through the grace of the Lord Jefus Chrift, we fhall be faved even as they," Acts xv. 11. Here the grace of the Lord Jefus, and of God, are one and the fame, the fame alfo is the one Godhead of the Father and of the Son.

XXXIV.

That our Saviour was not intended " to be a light to lighten the Gentiles," and confequently, that the full manifeftation of his Godhead was delayed till after

after his ascension, as I have already shewed, is evident from the following words of St. Paul to the Jews at Antioch, who were contradicting and blaspheming, because he gratified the request of the Gentiles, and on the sabbath day preached to them also " the word of God." " It was necessary," said he and Barnabas, " that the word of God should first have been spoken to you: but seeing ye put it from you, and judge yourselves unworthy of everlasting life, lo! we turn to the Gentiles. For so hath the Lord commanded us, saying, I have set thee to be a light of the Gentiles, that thou shouldest be for salvation unto the ends of the earth," Acts xiii. 45, 46, 47. These words were spoken by the Lord to Isaiah, when he asked him, was it a light thing that he appointed him to be his servant, and " for a light to the Gentiles, that thou mayest be my salvation unto the end of the earth?" Isa. xlix. 6. These words evidently spoken by God to Isaiah, and as evidently alluded to by St. Paul, who declares them a prophecy of the appointment made by the Lord Jesus Christ to his Apostles, whom he had commanded " to go forth and preach his name to all nations, and to be his witnesses unto the uttermost parts of the earth," to teach repentance and remission of sins among all nations in his name, " and to bear his name to the Gentiles," are an uncontrovertible evidence that the Lord, who commanded the apostles, saying, " I have set, &c." is the same God who had before spoken by his holy prophet. It is farther remarkable, that our Saviour then first " opened their understanding that they might understand the scriptures, and see the necessity there was that Christ should suffer and rise from the dead the third day, when he was about to commission them to go forth and preach him to the Gentiles, which was not till after his resurrection, not indeed till the moment preceding his ascension.

fion. "He was not fent but to the loft fheep of the houfe of Ifrael," Matth. xv. 24. "for it was neceffary that the word of God fhould firft have been fpoken to them;" "but when they had put it from them," and offered up this great facrifice for the fins of the whole world, hanging upon a crofs "the Lord of glory," we find that, after he was made perfect by fuffering death, and, by his fuffering, had atoned for and adopted all nations, he was to be preached to the Gentiles, fo that the whole which he came to do according to the fcriptures, by which it was feen that it behoved him to die and rife again from the dead, could not have preceded his death, for fo the profit had been only to Ifrael; to them were his life and leffons, but to the whole world his falvation, which was to be promulgated after he had died for it; he therefore now fent out the apoftles to hold forth this great light to lighten the Gentiles alfo, according to the prophecy before, certifying to them, "that they fhould be for falvation unto the ends of the earth." Paul and Barnabas continued fome time at Antioch, preaching the "word of God," "and when the Gentiles heard this, they were glad, and glorified the word of the Lord: and as many as were ordained to eternal life, believed. And the word of the Lord was publifhed throughout all the region," Acts xiii. 48, 49. The Jews having ftirred up the honourable women, and raifed a perfecution againft them, they proceeded to Iconium, where they "fo fpake, that a great multitude, both of the Jews, and alfo of the Greeks, believed," "long time therefore abode they, fpeaking boldly in the Lord, which gave teftimony unto the word of his Grace, and granted figns and wonders to be done by their hands," Acts xiv. 1, 3. What Paul and Barnabas preached is to be collected from its being faid, that both Jews and Greeks believed. The God of the Jew and of the Unitarian is the same; it was not therefore the God of the Jews, that the Jews were now firſt induced to believe; the Jews preached not their Jehovah, they ſought not to make proſelytes, it was not therefore in the God of the Jews that the Greeks believed; but Paul was ſent " to bear the name of Chriſt to the Gentiles, and to all nations, beginning from Jeruſalem;" that the ſecond perſon of the Godhead was then the object of Paul's doctrine to thoſe who needed not a teacher of the one Godhead, but knew nothing before of the three Perſons in that Godhead, is evident hence; and therefore we may, with thoſe believing Jews, lay aſide the Unitarian ſyſtems of Mr. Lindſey, and believe, that Jeſus Chriſt, who, according to his promiſe that " he would be with them alway, even unto the end of the world," Matth. xxviii. 20. " continued working with them, and confirming the word with ſigns following," Mark xvi. 20. " and who now gave teſtimony unto the word of his grace, and granted ſigns and wonders to be done by their hands," Acts xiv. 3. is one with the Father, that " God who bore them witneſs, both with ſigns and wonders, and with divers miracles, and gifts of the Holy Ghoſt, according to his own will," Heb. ii. 4. " that God who wrought ſpecial miracles by the hands of Paul" before thoſe " who heard him preach the word of the Lord Jeſus, both Jews and Greeks," Acts xix. 11, 10.

XXXV.

When the ſame Lord, who, juſt before his aſcenſion, had " opened the underſtanding of his diſciples, that they might underſtand the ſcriptures," Luke xxiv. 45. had opened the heart of Lydia, a ſeller of purple, at Thyatira, that ſhe attended unto the things which were ſpoken of Paul, and conſtrained him to abide with her; a damſel, poſſeſſed with a ſpirit of divination, " followed Paul, and us, and cried, ſaying, theſe

these men are the servants of the most high God, which shew unto us the way of salvation," Acts xvi. 14, 15, 16, 17. Jesus Christ, when veiled in the flesh, " suffered not the devils to speak, because they knew him," Mark i. 34; even the testimony of this spirit of divination then is to be admitted, and it has called Paul, who declares himself to the Romans i. 1. to be " a servant of Jesus Christ," " a servant of the most high God." The space contracts itself exceedingly between Son of man and God most high. Paul has himself addressed not the Romans only, but the Philippians, under the title of the servant of Jesus Christ," Philip. i. 1. and to Titus he commences his epistle by the name of " Paul, a servant of God," Titus i. 1. These terms are therefore synonimous.

XXXVI.

The doctrine of Paul and Silas to the Keeper of the prison at Philippi, and the consequence of it, are remarkable. The keeper said to Paul and Silas, his prisoners, " Sirs, what must I do to be saved? and they said, believe on the Lord Jesus Christ, and thou shalt be saved, and thy house. And they spake unto him the word of the Lord, and to all that were in his house. And he took them the same hour of the night, and washed their stripes; and was baptized, he, and all his, straightway. And when he had brought them into his house, he set meat before them, and rejoiced, believing in God with all his house," Acts xvi. 30 to 34. Here is a very rapid transaction. Paul and Silas being at prayer, and singing hymns at midnight, the foundations of the prison are shaken, the doors fly open, and the bands of the prisoners are loosed; the keeper, terrified at the probability of their escape, falls into despair; and, about to take away his own life, is restrained by Paul, who, to his astonishment, shewed himself and the rest undismayed, without chains, and yet not making use

of

or so favourable an opportunity. Convinced that some power controlled the ordinary course of nature, and had interfered in behalf of his prisoners, the man immediately applies to them to know what he should do to be saved: and here the apostles preach to a heathen, that his salvation is to be the consequence of his belief in the Lord Jesus Christ; and accordingly we find him, even at the same hour of the night, rejoice, and indeed believe in the Lord Jesus Christ, one with the Father, God.

XXXVII.

In the Acts, St. Luke says, that " because Paul preached Jesus to the Athenians, they said he seemed to be a setter forth of strange gods," Acts xvii. 18. On this they questioned him, and his answer was, that having seen among them an altar inscribed TO THE UNKNOWN GOD, " whom therefore ye ignorantly worship, him declare I unto you," ver. 23. Here, upon a call to explain himself, and answer the charge of setting forth strange gods, in having preached Jesus, he avows, that he whom he had preached was that God whom they knew not, but worshipped ignorantly: but he had preached Jesus; therefore Jesus Christ was that God hitherto unknown to them, and one with the Father. The attributes with which the apostle proceeds to characterize the God, to whose worship he is persuading the Athenians, are as follow, and, in apposition to them, I will put those attributes which are by the same preacher ascribed to Jesus Christ; and if upon comparison it be found that he has arrayed him with the same power and glory as he proposes to the Athenians to invite their adoration to God, we may, we must say, that he is that God, and that honour and religious worship are his due who is possessed of the same glory to excite them.

Of God whom he preached at Athens, even Jesus, he says,	Of Jesus Christ, expressly so named, he says,
"God that made the world, and all things therein, seeing that he is the Lord of heaven and earth," ver. 24; "for in him we live, and move, and have our being," ver. 28.	"By him were all things created that are in heaven, and that are in earth, visible and invisible, whether they be thrones, or dominions, or principalities, or powers, all things were created by him, and for him. And he is before all things, and by him all things consist," Coloss. i. 16, 17.

If then the exclusive prerogatives of God be in Jesus Christ, and that we see him clothed in that glory of which God has spoken, saying, "I am the Lord, that is my name, and my glory will I not give to another," Isaiah xlii. 8. we must surely say of him who wears it, that he is one with the Father God. That which is but one, even the glory, and which the declaration of God had made incommunicable, must be a distinguishing mark of him who has declared that he will not impart it. Jesus Christ has this glory: the declaration therefore came from that Godhead which is his equally as the Father's.

XXXVIII.

"And Crispus, the chief ruler of the synagogue, believed on the Lord with all his house: and many of the Corinthians, hearing, believed, and were baptized. Then spake the Lord to Paul in the night by a vision, be not afraid, but speak, and hold not thy peace: for I am with thee, and no man shall set on thee,

thee, to hurt thee: for I have much people in this city. And he continued there a year and six months, teaching the word of God among them," Acts xviii. 8, 9, 10, 11. That they who were baptized believed upon Jesus Christ, on hearing him preached, is evident from the necessity of that belief to baptism: that it was Jesus Christ whom Paul preached, is therefore evident also, for " how should they believe without a preacher." But Paul is in a vision called upon by the Lord to persevere without apprehension of danger, and accordingly we find him continue to teach the word of God among them, the same doctrine that he had before held forth that they might believe and be baptized. Lest it should be doubted who the Lord was who spake to him, I will remind my reader of a similar vision, wherein " in the night." " the Lord stood by him, and said, be of good chear, Paul: for as thou hast testified of me in Jerusalem, so must thou bear witness also at Rome," Acts xxiii. 11. As we know well whose name Paul was chosen to bear before the Gentiles, and that he was the Lord who spake to him now, we have no reason to doubt that it was the same Lord Jesus Christ who cheared him in the instance before us, and allayed the apprehensions which a man, who had undergone such persecutions for the sake of Christ, might reasonably entertain, if he persevered in the maintenance of his testimony.

XXXIX.

That the prophecies were in themselves insufficient to make a perfect revelation of Christ, nay, that the baptism of John was not sufficient to make him known, is evident from the case of Apollos, " a man mighty in the scriptures, fervent in spirit, who spake and taught diligently the things of the Lord, at Ephesus;" but that these were a strong assistant testimony to the manifestation of his Godhead, afterwards by the spirit
of

of truth, is evident alſo from the doctrines of the ſame man, who, "knowing only the baptiſm of John, was inſtructed by Aquila and Priſcilla; who expounded unto him the way of God more perfectly," upon which "he helped them much which had believed through grace; for he mightily convinced the Jews, and that publickly, ſhewing by the ſcriptures, that Jeſus was Chriſt," Acts xviii. 24 to 28.

XL.

Paul having continued, by the ſpace of two years, daily diſputing in the ſchool of one Tyrannus, "all they which dwelt in Aſia, heard the word of the Lord Jeſus, both Jews and Greeks," Acts xix. 10. And having manifeſted that God bore witneſs to that which he teſtified by ſpecial miracles wrought by his hands, "fear fell on them all, and the name of the Lord Jeſus was magnified. Many alſo of them which uſed curious arts, brought their books together, and burned them before all men: and they counted the price of them, and found it fifty thouſand pieces of ſilver. So mightily grew the word of God, and prevailed," Acts xix. 17, 18, 19, 20. But it was the word of the Lord Jeſus which they had heard; therefore it was his word that grew and prevailed; his name therefore is worthily magnified, being one with the Father, God.

XLI.

When Agabus foretold to Paul, that he ſhould be bound at Jeruſalem, and delivered into the hands of the Gentiles, the diſciples "beſought him not to go up to Jeruſalem. Then Paul anſwered, what mean ye to weep, and to break mine heart? for I am ready, not to be bound only, but alſo to die at Jeruſalem for the name of the Lord Jeſus. And when he would not be perſuaded, we ceaſed, ſaying, the will of the Lord be done," Acts xxi. 11, 12, 13, 14. The context here ſhews, that the Lord, to whoſe will the apoſtles resigned themselves, was the Lord Jesus, for whose name Paul was ready to resign himself, not to bonds only, but to death. This example therefore authorises us to address to the Lord Jesus that expression of our submissiveness to his pleasure in the Lord's prayer, " thy will be done in earth," Matth. vi. 10.

XLII.

" Arise, and be baptized, and wash away thy sins, calling on the name of the Lord," Acts xxii. 16. Belief in the Lord Jesus Christ is throughout the scriptures made necessary to baptism; and the testimony of Saul's belief, which is required by Ananias here, in order to his being baptized, is nothing less than invocation itself.

XLIII.

" And it came to pass, that when I was come again to Jerusalem, even while I prayed in the temple, I was in a trance: and saw him saying unto me," Acts xxii. 17, 18. Whom did Paul see? the pronoun *him* has no antecedent substantive to which it should be referred, though it be made the subject of a long subsequent detail; the antecedent then must be sought for from the meaning of the sentence altogether; but it is therein declared that Paul prayed. The object of his adoration then is the subject of the proposition, and this subject is then found to be the antecedent to this pronoun. But of this object of Paul's religious worship, it is said, that he " saw *him* saying unto him, Make haste, and get thee quickly out of Jerusalem: for they will not receive thy testimony concerning me. And I said, Lord, they know that I imprisoned, and beat in every synagogue them that believed on thee. And when the blood of thy martyr Stephen was shed, I also was standing by, and consenting unto his death, and kept the raiment of them that slew him," Acts xxii. 18, 19, 20. That it was of Jesus Christ Paul was to bear testimony, ny, is a well-established fact; and that it was of Jesus Christ that the Jews would not receive Paul's testimony, is clear from this, that they were very ready to receive an Unitarian doctrine. That Stephen, at whose blood-shedding Paul stood by, consenting to his death, was the martyr of Christ, is also certain; for the word martyr signifies no more than witness, and it was for the testimony of Christ that he died. That Jesus Christ, upon the whole, was the object of Paul's religious worship in the temple, is evident; and therefore Mr. Lindsey himself must conclude him, one with the Father, God.

XLIV.

Paul charged before Felix with "having gone about to profane the temple," and being "a ringleader of the sect of the Nazarenes," Acts xxiv. 5. declares himself not guilty of any profanation of the temple; but to the other part of the accusation he answers, "But this I confess unto thee, that, after the way which they call heresy, so worship I the God of my Fathers, believing all things that are written in the law and the prophets," Acts xxiv. 14. The scriptures, that is, the law and the prophets, " are they which testified of Christ," John v. 39. according to that testimony, which Paul's " understanding was opened that he might understand," this bold apostle of our Lord declares himself a worshipper of the God of his Fathers; but this he acknowledges he is, according to the charge before Felix, that he was a ringleader of the sect of the Nazarenes. Jesus Christ of Nazareth is here therefore pronounced by Paul to be the God of his Fathers, even one in Godhead with Jehovah, the Father.———

XLV.

St. Paul commences his epistle to the Romans thus, " Paul, a servant of Jesus Christ, called to be an apostle, and separated unto the gospel of God," Rom. i. 1.

and then making a declaration of his great good-will towards them, he says, " For God is my witnefs, whom I ferve with my spirit in the gofpel of his Son, that without ceafing I make mention of you always in my prayers," Romans i. 9. So that here, in the fame breath, this great apoftle of our Lord and Saviour declares himfelf the fervant of Jefus Chrift, the preacher of the gofpel of God, and the fervant of God, the preacher of the gofpel of Jefus Chrift. One only is the Mafter whom Paul ferved, and he, whofe gofpel Paul preached, but one, even Jefus Chrift one with rhe Father, God.

XLVI.

" Thinkeft thou that thou fhalt efcape the judgment of God?" Rom. ii. 3; but " the Father judgeth no man, but hath committed all judgment unto the Son," John v. 22. who " fhall reward every man according to his works," Matth. xvi. 27. Who then is that God whofe judgment is inevitable? certainly Jefus Chrift one with the Father, that " God, who will render to every man according to his deeds," Rom. ii. 6.

XLVII.

" Or defpifeft thou the riches of his goodnefs, and forbearance, and long-fuffering; not knowing that the goodnefs of God leadeth thee to repentance," Rom. ii. 4. to " repentance unto life," Acts xi. 18. " Howbeit," fays the fame apoftle, " for this caufe I obtained mercy, that in me firft Jefus Chrift might fhew forth all long-fuffering, for a pattern to them which fhould hereafter believe on him to life everlafting," 1 Tim. i. 16. We muft then " account that the long-fuffering of our Lord is falvation; even as our beloved brother Paul alfo, according to the wifdom given unto him, hath written," 2 Pet. iii. 15. Who then is this Lord, who, " is long-fuffering to us-ward?" " not willing that any

any should perish, but that all should come to repentance," 2 Pet. iii. 9. Certainly he is the same Lord Jesus Christ who mercifully shewed all long-suffering to Paul, for a pattern to them who should hereafter believe on him to everlasting life; one, with the Father, God, the riches of whose goodness, and forbearance, and long-suffering, leadeth to repentance unto life.

XLVIII.

The argument carried on through the latter part of the third, and the whole of the fourth chapter of St. Paul's epistle to the Romans, affords a strong proof of the Godhead of Christ. Abraham was faithful in God, his faith was imputed to him for righteousness, and the promise was therefore made to him; he believed in God; and was justified by his belief; but God is declared to be the "justifier of him that believeth in Jesus," Rom. iii. 26. The faith of Abraham, and the fruits of it are set forth as a pattern and persuasive to us to have faith in Jesus; but the faith of Abraham, whereby he was justified, was in God. Were Jesus Christ therefore other than God, he could not have been held out to us by this eloquent preacher of his gospel, as an object of faith after the example of Abraham. The same mode of argument is carried through the 11th chapter of Hebrews, and in the 12th we are told that Jesus Christ is the object of faith.

XLIX.

"Ye are not in the flesh, but in the spirit, if so be that the spirit of God dwelleth in you. Now, if any man have not the spirit of Christ, he is none of his," Rom. viii. 9. Here the context, and the course of St. Paul's argument, put it out of controversy, that the spirit of God and the spirit of Christ are synonimous terms; but of him, whose this spirit is, it is said, that "he raised up Jesus from the dead," Rom. viii. 11.

which

which affords an apoſtolical expreſſion of that which I have already laid down, that the one Godhead of the Father, and of the Son, was indeed the power which raiſed up the man Jeſus from the dead; for though I aſſert that Chriſt is God, I never yet denied that he was alſo a Man, and that his manhood was inferior to that Godhead which was in the fleſh, and upon which the ſtate of man is neceſſarily dependent.

L.

"Whoſe are the Fathers, and of whom as concerning the fleſh Chriſt came, who is over all, God bleſſed for ever. Amen," Rom. ix. 5. As it is not a very common caſe for men to come of their fathers as concerning any thing elſe than the fleſh, St. Paul has uſed an expreſſion concerning Chriſt, which implies, that he had come of ſome other origin than of the Jews, and in ſome other manner than as concerning the fleſh, and therefore has rendered an explanation neceſſary, which he accordingly proceeds to make; and in order to ſhew what that nature of Chriſt was, from which he had diſtinguiſhed his fleſh, he directly aſſerts in ſo many expreſs words, that "he is over all, God bleſſed for ever. Amen."

LI.

"For the ſame Lord over all, is rich unto all that call upon him. For whoſoever ſhall call upon the name of the Lord, ſhall be ſaved. How then ſhall they call on him in whom they have not believed? and how ſhall they believe in him of whom they have not heard? and how ſhall they hear without a preacher?" Rom. x. 12, 13. St. Paul is here preaching Jeſus, of the confeſſion of whom cometh ſalvation, and in whom, he ſays, whoſoever believeth ſhall not be aſhamed: and, as a reaſon for what he had ſaid, declares him rich to all that call upon him, and that ſalvation is the fruit of invoking him. Here Mr. Lindſey muſt confeſs him

one

one with the Father, God. He is here preaching to the Jew as well as the Greek; and to the Jew a preacher was surely not wanting to induce his belief in Jehovah, the God of the Unitarians.

LII.

" He that eateth, eateth to the Lord, for he giveth God thanks; and he that eateth not, to the Lord he eateth not, and giveth God thanks. For none of us liveth to himself, and no man dieth to himself. For whether we live, we live unto the Lord; and whether we die, we die unto the Lord: whether we live therefore or die, we are the Lord's. For to this end Christ both died, and rose, and revived, that he might be Lord both of the dead and living," Rom. xiv. 6, 7, 8, 9. St. Paul here makes our eating " to the Lord" depend upon our giving God thanks, which are therefore a dedication of the act; but this dedication of the act is to God, whereas the act itself is, in consequence of it, " to the Lord:" the Lord therefore to whom we find it to be done must be the same God, to whom by thanksgiving it had been addressed. But who that Lord is to whom we eat or eat not, to whom we live or die, and whose we are, the following verses render very certain; and he it is who died, and rose, and revived, even Jesus Christ, over all, one with the Father, God, blessed for ever, the proper object of our gratitude and thanksgiving, " to whose glory, whether we eat, or drink, or whatsoever we do, we should do all," 1 Cor. x. 31: " for the earth is the Lord's, and the fullness thereof," 1 Cor. x. 28.

LIII.

" For we shall all stand before the judgment-seat of Christ. For it is written, As I live, saith the Lord, every knee shall bow to me, and every tongue shall confess to God. So then every one of us shall give account of himself to God," Rom. xiv. 10, 11, 12. Here, in
bowing

bowing the knee to Jesus Christ, we fulfil the prophecy that is expresly spoken to Isaiah, by God, of himself, "I have sworn by myself, the word is gone out of my mouth in righteousness, and shall not return, that unto me every knee shall bow, every tongue shall swear," Isaiah xlv. 23. If this then be fulfilled by the bowing the knee to Christ, Christ is that God who spoke this prophecy. I must then refer to the whole chapter, every declaration in which is made of him who has so spoken, even Jesus Christ: "there is no God else beside me, a just God, and a Saviour, there is none beside me. Look unto me, and be ye saved, all the ends of the earth: for I am God, and there is none else," Isaiah xlv. 21, 22. Besides this circumstance, every man is here confessing to God before the judgment-seat of Christ, therefore that God, (one with the Father) before whom they are confessing, "for we must all appear before the judgment-seat of Christ; that every one may receive the things done in his body, according to that he hath done, whether it be good or bad. Knowing therefore the terror of the Lord, we persuade men," 2 Cor. v. 10; and surely when arrayed in all the terrors with which he will come to judgment, "it is a fearful thing to fall into the hands of the living God," Heb. x. 31.

LIV.

"I know, and am persuaded by the Lord Jesus, that there is nothing unclean of itself," Rom. xiv. 14. We do not find any particular revelation made to Paul that there is nothing unclean: he must then have had it from Peter, to whom it was revealed, and who says, "God hath shewed me, that I should not call any man common or unclean;" and this the Lord had shewed him by a vision in which Peter is called upon to eat things heretofore common and unclean, but now cleansed by God. If Paul therefore was persuaded by Jesus Christ,

through

through the relation made by Peter, we find him look upon our Lord to be the God which had fhewed the vifion to him; or, if Paul had a like vifion, it is very probable that it was prefented to him and to Peter by the fame agent: but as Paul is not faid to have had fuch a revelation himfelf, the former fuppofition is moſt to be relied on. But if it be infifted on that Paul was perfuaded by the Spirit, with which he was full, it muſt follow, that the Holy Ghoſt, proceeding from the Fa-ther, proceeds equally from the Son, by whom Paul declares himfelf to be perfuaded.

LV.

"That I ſhould be the minifter of Jefus Chriſt to the Gentiles, miniftering the gofpel of God," Rom. xv. 16. He goes on to fay, that, according to this appointment, "from Jerufalem and round about unto Illyricum, I have fully preached the gofpel of Chriſt," Rom. xv. 19; but he declines boafting of the mighty figns and wonders which he did in confirmation of this gofpel by the power of the fpirit of God. The grace which was given to him, that he ſhould be a minifter of Chriſt, is that wherein he fays he may glory, and not in the miracles he had wrought, which, however, he declares to be the work of Chriſt by the hands of thofe who do them. The gofpel of God is here the gofpel of Chriſt, that which is God's is not another's: Jefus Chriſt is therefore one with the Father, God.

LVI.

"The churches of Chriſt falute you," Rom. xvi. 16. "Paul called to be an apoftle of Jefus Chriſt, through the will of God, and Softhenes our brother, unto the church of God which is at Corinth," 1 Cor. i. 1, 2. It is remarkable that St. Paul wrote from Corinth to Rome, and in his epiftle thence calls the churches there the churches of Chriſt; and that when he is at another time writing to the very fame churches which he had fo

O   deno-

denominated, he addresses himself "to the church of God which is at Corinth," and describes the members of this church to be " sanctified in Christ Jesus, called to be saints, and calling upon the name of the Lord Jesus, both theirs and ours." There is but one church of God, and that is of Christ who is called upon in it: Jesus Christ is therefore one with the Father, God. " Grace be unto you," says St. Paul, immediately after addressing the church which called upon the Lord Jesus, whom he professes to be his Lord and theirs, " and peace from God our Father, and from the Lord Jesus Christ;" and then he proceeds, " I thank my God always on your behalf, for the grace of God which is given you by Jesus Christ," 1 Cor. i. 3, 4. This is a very extraordinary gift for our Saviour to make if it was not his to give; but he has given it. The grace of God is therefore the grace of our Lord Jesus Christ, with the Father, one God.

LVII.

" So that ye come behind in no gift; waiting for the coming of our Lord Jesus Christ: who shall also confirm you unto the end, that ye may be blameless in the day of our Lord Jesus Christ," 1 Cor. i. 7, 8. " He that judgeth me is the Lord. Therefore judge nothing before the time, until the Lord come, who both will bring to light the hidden things of darkness, and will make manifest the counsels of the hearts: and then shall every man have praise of God," 1 Cor. iv. 4, 5. That God, for whose praise Paul is contented to wait, rather than seek the praise of men, is certainly the Lord who will come to judge, and to make manifest the counsels of the hearts. But that the Lord who " judgeth Paul" is the Lord Jesus, whose coming he desires the Corinthians to wait for, that in his day they may be found blameless, is also certain: the conclusion is, that the Lord Jesus is the Lord, and that " the Lord he is God;" and if this needed farther proof, it will appear from the following texts to be the Lord Jesus Christ whose praise he desireth: " we are come as far as to you also, in preaching the gospel of Christ: having hope, when your faith is encreased, that we shall be enlarged by you according to our rule abundantly, to preach the gospel in the regions beyond you, and not to boast in another man's line of things made ready to our hand. But he that glorieth, let him glory in the Lord. For not he that commendeth himself is approved, but whom the Lord commendeth," 2 Cor. x. 14 to 18.

LVIII.

" For it hath been declared unto me, that there are contentions among you. Now this I say, that every one of you saith, I am of Paul, and I of Apollos, and I of Cephas, and I of Christ. Is Christ divided? was Paul crucified for you? or were ye baptized in the name of Paul?" 1 Cor. i. 11, 12, 13. From Christ's not being divided, he dissuades them from divisions, ver. 10. " Who then is Paul, and who is Apollos, but ministers by whom ye believed, even as the Lord gave to every man? I have planted, Apollos watered: but God gave the encrease," 1 Cor. iii. 5, 6. So that God who gave to every man the encrease, that is, assisted them in receiving the gospel, which was planted and watered by Paul and Apollos, is the Lord, according to whose gift they believed. Of Jesus Christ it is said, that " he shall confirm them unto the end," 1 Cor. i. 8. That which was given to every man, confirmation in faith, is then the gift of Jesus Christ the Lord; but God gave the encrease: therefore Jesus Christ, the Lord who gave it, is one with the Father, God.

LIX.

"I thank God, that I baptized none of you, but Crispus and Gaius: left any should say, that I had baptized in my own name," 1 Cor. i. 14, 15. As Jesus Christ had given command to his disciples to baptize "in the name of the Father, the Son, and the Holy Ghost," one God; and as they, in obedience to this command, went forth into all nations, baptizing in the name of Jesus Christ, one with the Father and the Holy Ghost, God, (for I dare not suppose them disobedient to the voice of their ascending Lord) Paul, having reprehended the Corinthians for looking upon him, Apollos, and Cephas, as equally objects of their adherence as Christ, who alone was crucified for them, proceeds to return thanks to God that he had not led such unstable souls into farther errour, and by the exercise of that duty which was to be performed in the name of God, brought them to transfer that divinity to himself which belonged to Christ only: for if their preaching Christ crucified could bring his hearers to conceive the preachers as Christ, he easily saw that baptism in his name would have induced them to look upon them as baptizing in their own name, and assuming to themselves that Godhead, to the belief in which baptism was administered in the name of Christ; an errour of so great magnitude, that the apostle is very happy in not having afforded occasion for it to men, whom he saw so ready to misinterpret the ministry and apostleship of the gospel, which he had preached among them. Mr. Lindsey draws a very extraordinary conclusion from the passage before us, and says, it affords a proof that "baptizing in the name of any one does not of itself imply any divinity in the person in whose name baptism is made." I request that this chapter may be turned to, and refer it to the meanest reader, who shall honour me with a perusal, whether Mr. Lindsey has not fallen into the

very

very errour which St. Paul is here cenfuring in the Corinthians; for at the leaft it muft be admitted that Paul's thankfgiving is made, either that they did not account him as Chrift, or Chrift as him.

LX.

As I have already proved that it was Jefus Chrift who fent forth the apoftles to preach him, and who had chofen thofe veffels which fhould bear his name before the Gentiles, I fhall not now repeat the arguments already made ufe of, but defire my reader may compare the paffages brought together to that purpofe, with the following declaration of St. Paul, "that not many wife men after the flefh, not many mighty, not many noble are called. But God hath chofen the foolifh things of the world, to confound the wife; and God hath chofen the weak things of the world, to confound the things which are mighty; that no flefh fhould glory in his prefence," 1 Cor. i. 26, 27, 28, 29. This he fpeaks of the preachers of the gofpel who had been fent by Jefus Chrift; for he fays, "it pleafed God by the foolifhnefs of preaching to fave them that believe," 1 Cor. i. 21. Jefus Chrift therefore, who chofe them, and "whofe ftrength is perfected in weaknefs," is one with the Father, God; who hath chofen the weak things to confound the mighty. "He that glorieth, let him glory in the Lord," 1 Cor. i. 31, and 2 Cor. x. 17; in which latter place it is evidently fpoken of Jefus Chrift. It is reafonably to be concluded then that he is the Lord, in whom Paul defires us to glory; "as it is written," by Jeremiah, to whom God fpeaks, "let him that glorieth, glory in this; that he underftandeth and knoweth me, that I am the Lord, which exercife loving-kindnefs, judgement, and righteoufnefs in the earth: for in thefe things I delight, faith the Lord," Jer. ix. 24.

"Had

LXI.

"Had they known it, they would not have crucified the Lord of glory," 1 Cor. ii. 8. "Ye killed the Prince of Life," or, as it stands in the margin of the Bible, "the Author of Life." And now, brethren, I wot that through ignorance ye did it, as did also your rulers," Acts iii. 15, 17. "My brethren, have not the faith of our Lord Jesus Christ *the Lord* of glory, with respect of persons," James ii. 1. In this last text the translation has supplied the words "*the Lord*," but the following words "of glory," which express the whole meaning in the Greek, require them, or others to the same purpose, to express it in English; and St. Paul's having used the whole phrase is a sufficient warrant to the translators for preferring that which they have used. And the Lord of glory is a title not very applicable to a creature; for God has said, "I am the Lord, that is my name, and my glory will I not give to another." "Who is this King of glory? the Lord of Hosts, he is the King of glory," Psa. xxiv. 10. Who is this Prince and Author of life? "The Lord God who formed man of the dust of the ground, and breathed into his nostrils the breath of life," Gen. ii. 7.

LXII.

"We speak the wisdom of God in a mystery." "The things of God knoweth no man, but the spirit of God." "But God has revealed them unto us by his spirit:" "we have received, not the spirit of the world, but the spirit which is of God:" "but the natural man receiveth not the things of the spirit of God;" "for who hath known the mind of the Lord, that he may instruct him? but we have the mind of Christ," 1 Cor. ii. 7, to the end. This needs no comment.

LXIII.

That Christ himself spoke by the apostles, is evident from what follows. Paul says to the Corinthians, "Now,

"Now, concerning virgins, I have no commandment of the Lord: yet I give my judgement as one that hath obtained mercy of the Lord to be faithful," 1 Cor. vii. 25. Here the preacher makes a distinction between that effect which the immediate dictate of the spirit had on him, with the authority of speech derived from thence, and the improvement of his natural judgement by the means of habitual faith, through which indeed he became a wiser and a better man, but not more authorized to prescribe. St. Paul often speaks of his having obtained mercy of Jesus Christ, whence it is evident that Christ is the Lord meant here. "To the Lord our God belong mercies, and forgivenesses." Dan. ix. 9. Let him then who extends them be acknowledged to be the God of our salvation.

LXIV.

St. Paul says to the Corinthians, "We know that an idol is nothing in the world, and that there is none other God but one," 1 Cor. viii. 4. This unity of the God, of whom, and by whom he declares all things to be, is opposed to the multitude of idols to which the Corinthians offered sacrifice. These he is about to put down, and in their place to establish the worship of the true God; and now, if ever accuracy of expression be necessary, it was incumbent upon St. Paul to distinguish between the Father and the Son, in terms never to be confounded, to ascribe such attributes to each as must perfectly distinguish him from the other; nay, perhaps he should have gone farther, and have absolutely omitted the name of him, who was not to be considered as a proper object of worship, left his idolatrous hearers, to whom a multitude of gods would not have been exceptionable, should interpret his words into an implication, that he, who was described to them with attributes the very same as those bestowed upon God, was pointed out as an object of adoration, instead of the idols which they heard him object to, and instead of which he was about to substitute a God for them. Has this been the conduct of the apostle? has he diligently withheld the name of Jesus Christ, while he recommends a new worship? If not, I think it reasonably to be concluded, that he did recommend the worship of Jesus Christ to them; to whom he says, "though there be that are called Gods, whether in heaven or in earth, (as there be Gods many, and Lords many) but to us there is but one God, the Father, of whom are all things, and we in him; and one Lord Jesus Christ, by whom are all things, and we by him," 1 Cor. viii. 6. To me this text appears conclusive for the one Godhead of the Father and of the Son. In the same manner Paul and Barnabas, after they had at Lystra "preached the gospel," and, by a miracle of healing, confirmed the testimony which they bore to the truth of their doctrines, and had received divine honours from the idolaters of the country, dissuade them from doing sacrifice unto them, but "preached unto them, that they should turn from these vanities unto the living God, which made heaven and earth, and the sea, and all things that are therein," Acts xiv. 7, 15. I shall here take occasion to observe, upon a very particular mode of argument made use of by Mr. Lindsey, in order to get rid of the conclusion, which naturally follows from the application of the same attributes to the name of the Father, and of the Son, so frequently made by the disciples of our Lord. "The apostles," says this gentleman, Apology, p. 132, "were not so exact in the use of the words, Lord, Saviour, *and the like*, which they indifferently give both to God and to Christ, never supposing that any would mistake their Lord and Master so lately born, and living amongst men, to be the supreme God and object of worship." If the apostles, who, it is allowed, foresaw that men would

would in future time depart from the truth, and, as Mr. Lindsey says, adopt a trinity from Plato, never conceived the possibility of such a mistake; they were, of all men, not only the most careless and inattentive, but the most heinously sinful; for they sinned against the Holy Ghost, whose inspiration had given them a view into futurity, and that for the purpose of making them instrumental to the propagation and support of truth only; but they have most wickedly neglected this first cause of their appointment; and misrepresentation, instead of being the fault of our perverse wills, must hereafter be ascribed to the insufficiency of revelation, to the incompetency of those whom God's choice had pronounced competent, or to their wilful omission of that duty, to which God had been pleased to call them, and assist them with a "guide to all truth", for our instruction. I refer it to reason, whether common attributes do not imply, nay more, do not demonstrate a common nature, and if to be our Lord, and our Saviour, *and the like*, be equally the attributes of God, and of the Son, whether the Son be not therefore God?

But these same apostles, according to Mr. Lindsey, not endowed with a prophetick view, but not even supposing a mistake possible, must have been very extraordinary reasoners, though they even derived their confidence, that, from the circumstances of his having been born, and so lately living amongst men, we should not conclude the Godhead of Christ from their application of the divine attributes to his name. Will any man pretend that the birth and life of our Saviour were such as should mark his nature to be no more than that of the rest of mankind? his death, his resurrection from the dead, and his ascension into heaven, followed immediately by the gift of the Holy
P   Ghost,

Ghoſt, according to his promiſe, might alſo lead the apoſtles to conſider, and preach him as ſomething more than an ordinary man; nay, that very birth which Mr. Lindſey thinks a proof that he was a meer man, the apoſtles, who have related it to us, knew to have been of a Virgin found with child of the Holy Ghoſt, and overſhadowed by the power of the Higheſt, and that the Holy Thing, which was born of that Virgin, was declared to be the Son of God. They alſo knew that life, which he paſt amongſt men, to have been ſpent in daily miracles, to have been ſo interrupted, and ſo reſumed, that it is aſtoniſhing to hear the birth and life of our Saviour made uſe of as a reaſon why we ſhould doubt the veracity of the apoſtles, when they declare him to be God, and why they ſhould not have conceived it neceſſary to mark ſuch a diſtinction as ſhould preclude the poſſibility of ſo momentous an errour, if an errour it be to aſcribe divinity to him, inſtead of uſing an inaccurate expreſſion, whereby we ſhould be led into an opinion that he is God. From that very birth and life, teſtifying whence, and with what endowments he came, I am led to interpret even ambiguous expreſſions as atteſtations of his Godhead, much more to yield my aſſent to ſuch as are perfectly explicit, and declare it without any ambiguity at all; of the latter ſort there are multitudes, from which the former derive their explanation; for if it be in one inſtance declared expreſsly, that " Chriſt is over all, God bleſſed for ever," it will be no difficulty to redeem the names of the diſciples of our Lord from the cruel charge of having lied to the Holy Ghoſt, or neglectingly rejected the conduct of this " guide to all truth;" and when they have uſed the words, Lord, and Saviour, *and the like*, and indifferently given them both to God, and to Chriſt, to declare that they have intentionally done it, in order to inculcate the doctrine of

our

our blessed Redeemer's divinity, instead of imputing to these inspired men a criminal inaccuracy, the consequence of which could not escape the foresight of the meanest human understanding. "Ye know that ye were Gentiles carried away unto these dumb idols, even as ye were led. Wherefore I give you to understand, that no man speaking by the spirit of God, calleth Jesus accursed, and that no man can say that Jesus is the Lord, but by the Holy Ghost," 1 Cor. xii. 2, 3. "God is not the author of confusion," 1 Cor. xiv. 33. I shall therefore rely upon the identity of expression used in speaking of God and of Christ, as evidence of the identity of the Godhead of the Father and of the Son; and as the passages occur, in which such language is used, I shall quote them as testimonies of it.

LXV.

Speaking of the sacrifices of the Gentiles, which he says were offered not to God but to devils, St. Paul says, "Ye cannot drink the cup of the Lord, and the cup of devils: ye cannot be partakers of the Lord's table, and of the table of devils," 1 Cor. x. 20, 21. Here is manifestly a declaration made, that the taking the cup of blessing, and the bread which we break, as the communion of the blood and body of Christ, is an act of worship to him, adequate to that of the Gentiles' sacrifices to their idols. He does not indeed call it a sacrifice, nor intimate that it is one, but says, that it is an ascribing of honour to him, inconsistent with honour being paid to devils. In the same manner as our Saviour himself has said, "Ye cannot serve God and mammon," St. Paul shews, that they cannot, consistently with the worship of the true God, ascribe honour to idols. "What concord hath Christ with Belial? or what part hath he that believeth, with an infidel? and what agreement hath the temple of God with

with idols? for ye are the temple of the living God, &c." 2 Cor. vi. 15, 16.

LXVI.

"We preach not ourselves, but Chrift Jefus the Lord," 2 Cor. iv. 5. Thefe words I produce only to fhew the object of the apoftle's preaching, a circumftance to which I am frequently obliged to refer. Paul has alfo defined the gofpel to be "the teftimony of our Lord Jefus Chrift," 2 Tim. i. 8. The preaching of the gofpel is therefore the bearing teftimony to him, which I wifh to have remembered and carried on in the mind of my reader.

LXVII.

Were I to quote every paffage in the fecond epiftle of St. Paul to the Corinthians that affords a proof of our Saviour's Godhead, I fhould be under a neceffity of tranfcribing the whole epiftle, to which I therefore choofe to refer my reader. One paffage however I muft felect, and fhew its weight in the argument, becaufe Mr. Lindfey has taken fome pains to extricate himfelf from the neceffity of bending under it. It is indeed furprizing, that a man who has fhewed fo evidently his attachment to what he believes the truth, fhould not be more circumfpect in the purfuit of her, but allow himfelf to be deceived by every painted fallacy that fhall appear ever fo little like the original. I am at a lofs to conceive how the following daubed mafk fhould be taken for the native and unadorned fimplicity of truth, by one who profeffes himfelf enamoured of that fimplicity. But upon the 12th chap. and 8, 9 ver. of 2 Cor. a Mr. Beaufobre has afforded the following comment, to which Mr. Lindfey accedes with the moft fupine facility. "For this thing I befought the Lord thrice, that it might depart from me," 2 Cor. xii. 8, 9. "Paul appears here to have directed his prayer to God, the Father, and to have had in his thoughts

thoughts and to have imitated our Lord's prayer in the garden, the night before his suffering, when he prayed to God, that, if it pleased him, the cup of affliction might pass away from him without his drinking it." *Beausobre* on the place. Apology, p. 132. Let us take the whole passage together, and examine it with the context, and then see whether the apostle had any such stuff in his thoughts as the dreams of Mr. Beausobre are made of. St. Paul having said, " of myself I will not glory, but in mine infirmities," proceeds to give an account of those infirmities, and to assign the reason why they are an object of glory to him, saying, " lest I should be exalted above measure through the abundance of the revelations, there was given to me a thorn in the flesh, the messenger of Satan to buffet me, lest I should be exalted above measure. For this thing I besought the Lord thrice, that it might depart from me. And he said unto me, my grace is sufficient for thee: for my strength is made perfect in weakness. Most gladly therefore will I rather glory in mine infirmities, that the power of Christ may rest upon me. Therefore I take pleasure in infirmities, in reproaches, in necessities, in persecutions, in distresses for Christ's sake: for when I am weak, then am I strong," 2 Cor. xii. 5, 7, 8, 9, 10. Wherefore does St. Paul glory? wherefore take pleasure in his infirmities? that the power of Christ may rest upon him; for, by suffering such infirmities as contribute to perfect the strength of the Lord, (to whom he prayed) in weakness, he is then strong when he is weak: but he glories in his infirmities for Christ's sake; it is the strength of Christ then that is perfected in his weakness: but it is the Lord who said, my strength is made perfect in weakness; the Lord therefore who so spoke, is Christ: but of the Lord who so spoke, Paul thrice besought the departure of " this thing." The Lord then being

Christ,

Christ, and Paul having thrice preferred his supplications to him, it necessarily follows, that the Lord Jesus Christ is a proper object of prayer and religious worship, and therefore that he is one with the Father, God. Such is the conclusion from the context; whereas a delusive assertion is inferred by a Mr. Beausobre, from a partial quotation of but one small part of the passage, in itself proving nothing, but made the subject of the weakest comment that ever obtained the acquiescence of a man of virtue; a man, whose errours afflict me, as I honour his worth. I cannot see him turn aside from the study of the word of God itself, to the study of the manner in which partial visionaries have interpreted it, without sensible regret. I do not desire that even my comment should supplant a single inference drawn by a sensible and candid man, from a perusal of the scriptures themselves; it cannot therefore be expected that I shall indulge Mr. Lindsey in laying aside the use of his own better understanding, that he may adopt the doctrines of a multitude of designing or silly men and women upon whom he places such implicit reliance. I only ask of him, and every other reader, that they will take the uncorrupted word of God itself into their own consideration, and with diligence search the scriptures only, and thence infer, for their own use, such tenets as the Holy Spirit shall be found to have testified.

LXVIII.

St. Paul, in his epistle to the Galatians, commences with a declaration that he is " an apostle (not of men, neither by man, but by Jesus Christ, and God the Father,") Gal. i. 1. Here the Father and the Son are put into opposition to man, and declared to be the Being from whom the apostle had his authority; and he declares farther, that " the gospel which was preached of me, is not after man. For I neither received it of man,

neither

neither was I taught it, but by the revelation of Jesus Christ," Gal. i. 11, 12. Who then is Jesus Christ who has thus revealed the gospel to Paul, and whose authority is so very high above that of men? One with the Father, God.

LXIX.

"For do I now persuade men, or God? or do I seek to please men? for if I yet pleased men, I should not be the servant of Christ," Gal. i. 10. This is in context with the last cited passages, and the apostle, still preserving the distinction between God and man, shews the Galatians the authority with which he is about to reprove them, and that they may not expect too great lenity, he shews that he does not seek to please them, but Christ, whose servant he should not be if he neglected to maintain that gospel which some among them had perverted. He distinguishes himself from those who "desire to make a fair shew in the flesh, lest they should suffer persecution for the cross of Christ," Gal. vi. 12; whereas he bore in his body the marks of the Lord Jesus, ver. 17.

LXX.

"God hath sent forth the spirit of his Son into your hearts, crying, Abba, Father," Gal. iv. 6. There is something very remarkable in the course of St. Paul's argument here, and the manner in which he has ascended to the assertion before us. He is shewing that the law was given as "a schoolmaster to bring us unto Christ, that we might be justified by faith," that it was given in the interval of time, between the promise and the time of fulfilling it; but by no means with a view of supplying the place of that which was promised, for it was impossible that a law could be given by which righteousness could come; he farther says, that, being justified by faith, the tuition of the law became unnecessary, and that being therefore emancipated from the
bondage

bondage of the law, " we are made the children of God, by faith in Chrift Jefus:" and now he fays, that the fullnefs of time being come, " God fent forth his Son, made of a woman, made under the law, to redeem them that were under the law, that we might receive the adoption of fons." Is not this affigning a reafon wherefore Chrift took manhood, and particularly why he was fent to the loft fheep of the houfe of Ifrael? But he has, according to " the gofpel, preached before to Abraham," Gal. iii. 8, fuffered, and redeemed them, whereby they have been juftified by faith, and by faith to juftification become Children of God; and what is now the procefs? After we have received the adoption of fons, the fpirit is fent forth into our hearts to make us acknowledge him to be God, whom, till he had fo redeemed us to faith, we had only feen to be a man, " made of a woman, under the law." In the paffage before us, we are told, that God fent forth the fpirit of his Son; and by the fame preacher it is declared to the Romans, that it is by " the fpirit of him that raifed Jefus from the dead, that we are led, in order to be the fons of God, and that by this fpirit of adoption we cry, Abba, Father," Rom. viii. 11, 14, 15. That fpirit, which raifed Jefus from the dead, is therefore that eternal, and invifible, and incomprehenfible God, who was in union with him, while he was living, and who again refumed our nature upon its refurrection from the grave. " No man can fay that Jefus is the Lord but by the Holy Ghoft," 1 Cor. xii. 3. Through faith then, having received the adoption of fons, and by the fpirit of our bleffed Redeemer fent forth into our hearts, let us, without hefitation, cry to him, " Abba, Father," and addrefs the Lord's prayer to him, through whom, and by whom only, we have been called fons, and are enabled to fay, " that Jefus is the Lord," " our Father." I muft obferve here, that as St. Paul was

preach-

preaching to men difpofed to Judaifm and the doctrines of the law, the fpirit of adoption, fent after juftification by faith in Chrift Jefus, was by no means neceffary to induce them to cry Abba, Father, to the God of the Unitarians; for this they were difpofed to do before, and not to recede from it. Somewhat not acceded to by the followers of Mofes was then the doctrine of the apoftle of Jefus Chrift; and he therefore teaches, that by faith in him they are juftified, and thereby receive the fpirit by which they cry to him Abba, Father.

LXXI.

" In whom we have redemption through his blood, the forgivenefs of fins, according to the riches of his grace," Eph. i. 7. " Unto me who am lefs than the leaft of all faints, is this grace given, that I fhould preach among the Gentiles the unfearchable riches of Chrift," Eph. iii. 8. " For this caufe I bow my knees unto the Father of our Lord Jefus Chrift, of whom the whole family in heaven and earth is named, that he would grant you according to the riches of his glory," Eph iii. 14, 15, 16. " Or defpifeft thou the riches of his goodnefs, and forbearance, and long-fuffering; not knowing that the goodnefs of God leadeth thee to repentance?" Rom. ii. 4. " What if God, &c. that he might make known the riches of his glory," Rom. ix. 23. The riches of God and of Chrift are here made fynonimous terms, and furely the riches of grace, and of glory, and of long-fuffering, can only be the attributes of God. But left it fhould be doubted what are the unfearchable riches of Chrift, St. Paul fays, that he prays that his hearers " may be able to comprehend with all faints, what is the breadth, and length, and depth, and height; and to know the love of Chrift, which paffeth knowledge, that ye may be filled with all the fulnefs of God," Eph. iii. 18, 19; fo that all the fulnefs of God, and the knowledge of the love of Chrift, are again made fynonimous terms. But this fulnefs of God is attained to only by having " Chrift to dwell in our hearts by faith," Eph. iii. 17; and then when we have attained to this, and " come in the unity of the faith, and of the knowledge of the Son of God," what is the confequence? are we then " filled with all the fulnefs of God?" moft certainly we are, for we come " unto a perfect man, unto the meafure of the ftature of the fulnefs of Chrift," Eph. iv. 13. Unto himfelf St. Paul fays this knowledge was given, that he might preach the myftery of Chrift to the Gentiles, that they fhould be partakers of the promife in Chrift by the gofpel, " whereof I was made a minifter, according to the gift of the grace of God given unto me," Eph. iii. 7. " But unto every one of us is given grace according to the meafure of the gift of Chrift," Eph. iv. 7. " O the depth of the riches both of the wifdom and knowledge of God! how unfearchable are his judgments, and his ways paft finding out! for who hath known the mind of the Lord, or who hath been his counfellour?" Rom. xi. 33, 34. Thefe laft words afford at once an argument, and no unufeful leffon to a reader of the word of the God of truth.

LXXII.

" When he afcended up on high, he led captivity captive, and gave gifts unto men. (Now that he afcended, what is it but that he alfo defcended firft into the lower parts of the earth? He that defcended, is the fame alfo that afcended up far above all heavens, that he might fill all things,") Eph. iv. 8, 9, 10. St. Paul feems here to enter into the argument, and by the manner in which he puts the above affertions, to have confronted himfelf to Mr. Lindfey; from which I conclude that he had at leaft an equal forefight of the Lindfeian, as of the Platonick fchifm. He forefaw
that

that our Lord's pre-exiftence would be denied, and has therefore made his afcent a proof that he had before defcended to the earth, (for that is all that is meant by the lower parts of the earth) and had again returned to where he had been before, to heaven. (For that in the fame manner is all that is meant by, far above all heavens; and the two terms are ufed in order ftrongly to contraft his dignity and condefcenfion). He forefaw that his divinity would be denied, and has therefore lifted him far above the heavens, and extended him even that he might fill all things. Let us then " henceforth be no more children, toffed to and fro, and carried about with every wind of doctrine, by the fleight of men, and cunning craftinefs, whereby they lie in wait to deceive. But fpeaking the truth in love, grow up into him in all things, which is the Head, even Chrift," Eph. iv. 14, 15.

LXXIII.

" Servants, be obedient to them that are your mafters according to the flefh, with fear and trembling, in finglenefs of your heart, as unto Chrift: not with eye-fervice, as men pleafers, but as the fervants of Chrift, doing the will of God from the heart; with good will doing fervice, as to the Lord, and not to men: knowing that whatfoever good thing any man doeth, the fame fhall he receive of the Lord, whether he be bond or free," Eph. vi. 5, 6, 7, 8. If words could be found more explicitly declaring that the fervant of Chrift and of God is one, whilft " no man can ferve two mafters;" and alfo that the fervice done as to the Lord, is diftinct from that which is done to pleafe men, I fhould endeavour to paraphrafe this paffage. I fhall only now remark, that, in a parallel paffage to the Coloffian fervants, he fays, inftead of " with fear and trembling, in finglenefs of heart, as unto Chrift;" " not with eye-fervice, as men pleafers, but in finglenefs of heart, fearing God," Coloff. iii. 22.

LXXIV.

" Who being in the form of God, thought it not robbery to be equal with God: but made himfelf of no reputation, and took upon him the form of a fervant, and was made in the likenefs of men: and being found in fafhion as a man, he humbled himfelf, and became obedient unto death, even the death of the crofs," Philip. ii. 6, 7. 8. If Mr. Lindfey, who denies not that Jefus Chrift was a man, will not deny that he is here declared to be fuch, I think he cannot deny that he is here declared to be God: for if the words *the form of a fervant, the likenefs of men, and the fafhion of man,* be exactly of the fame import as an affertion that he was actually a man, it neceffarily follows, that the fimilar expreffion, " being in the form of God," muft have a fimilar interpretation, and fignify that he is actually God; and from the whole paffage our Saviour's pre-exiftence (in a ftate of glory) to the time of his being " made man" is fo neceffarily deducible, that it cannot be avoided; the condefcenfion of Chrift, equal with God, in taking on him a nature fo inferior as that of man, being the propofed example of humility, by which we are exhorted to be humble. If this text ftood without another to fupport it, it is conclufive for the Godhead of Jefus Chrift. Being in the form of God, having the fame meaning as the being actually God, we are thereby enabled to interpret St. Paul's affertion that our Saviour " is the image of the invifible God," Coloff. i. 15; and many other paffages declaring him to be " in the form of God."

LXXV.

" For our converfation is in heaven, from whence alfo we look for the Saviour, the Lord Jefus Chrift," Philip. iii. 20. St. Paul having declared that his expectation

pectation of the Saviour is from heaven, pronounces the Saviour to be Jesus Christ; but to Timothy he says, that he is " an apostle of Jesus Christ by the commandment of God our Saviour," 1 Tim. i. 1. That prayers and supplications, and giving of thanks for all men, " is good and acceptable in the sight of God our Saviour," 1 Tim. ii. 3. " We trust in the living God, who is the Saviour of all men, specially of those that believe," 1 Tim. iv. 10. And to Titus he says, that God " hath in due times manifested his word through preaching, which is committed unto me, according to the commandment of God our Saviour," Titus i. 3: so that God our Saviour, is the Saviour whose coming from heaven Paul looked for, even Jesus Christ, one with the Father; that God who committed the preaching of his word, and the manifestation of himself to be made in due time, saying, " I am Jesus whom thou persecutest," Acts ix. 5.

LXXVI.

" Who is the first-born of every creature," Col. i. 15. Instead of conceiving that these words in the least degree derogate from the dignity of Christ as God, or in the least point him out to be even *the first and purest Creature of God*, I believe them to have the very reverse tendency; for from the context we may find St. Paul using the benefit of our redemption thro' the blood of Christ, which he declares to be forgiveness of sins, deliverance from the power of darkness, and translation into the kingdom of the Son, by whom he says, " were all things created that are in heaven, and that are in earth, visible and invisible, whether they be thrones, or dominions, or principalities, or powers: all things were created by him, and for him, and he is before all things, and by him all things consist," Col. i. 16, 17. And this redemption, which is afforded to us, the apostle testifies to be by the blood of the Son, who is the " firſt-born of every creature." By the ſacrifice of Chriſt, and by the ſufficiency of his body once offered, we find the daily ſacrifice for the people taken away, and a full atonement made at once: by his daily prophecies, we find the deſtruction of the Jewiſh temple, and conſequently of the Jewiſh ritual at hand; and the event ſoon juſtified the prophecy; we find their altars and offerings aboliſhed, and their nation ceaſe to be a people peculiar to God: but we find alſo the adoption of all mankind to be, as it were, the children of the promiſe through faith. Now, as the entire hiſtory of the Jewiſh nation is a typical prophecy of our bleſſed Saviour's incarnation, ſufferings, and the adoption of all mankind thro' him, and that their peculiar ſanctity was maintained by blood, and by ſacrifices; ſo we find, that this blood, and theſe ſacrifices were a type of the ſacrifice to be made for all mankind in order to their adoption; for, as the ſacrifice was for an atonement for the ſins and errours of the people, ſo is the ſacrifice of Chriſt, once offered, an atonement for the ſins of thoſe who were thereby adopted. But we find alſo, that the Jews were to be ſanctified by the offering up of the firſt-born to God; and among other parts of their ritual, this ſanctification now no longer ſerviceable, was to be ſet aſide; that event, of which it was a type, having taken place, and our ſanctification to God, by the offering up of Jeſus Chriſt to be " the firſt-born of every creature" being accompliſhed. But it may be ſaid, that the offering of the firſt-born child was long before ſet aſide, and a compenſation taken by God, who accepted of the whole tribe of Levi to be ſervitors in the ſervice of the ark, and afterwards of the temple, inſtead of the firſt-born child through Iſrael. But this very compenſation being now to be ſet aſide, the newly adopted world required a firſt-born after the type of Iſrael, and found it accordingly in Chriſt Jeſus,

who

who not only gave himself for the whole of mankind, to be "the first-born of every creature," but also has, instead of the Levitical priesthood, stood forth himself to be an High-priest for us, whom he hath bought with his blood. If this interpretation of the words before us, which is altogether consonant to the doctrine of St. Paul to the Hebrews, by whose rites he declares our Saviour's sacrifice foreshewed, be not accepted, let the " first-born of every creature" be referred to a declaration in a few verses after, that Jesus Christ is " the first-born from the dead," Col. i. 18. Words spoken with respect to his resurrection, whereby our resurrection to life eternal thro' him is obtained, as he has become the Captain of our salvation, our Leader to a triumph over death and the grave, the first-born of a regenerate world. No man who ever read the context, and saw these words joined to a declaration, that by Jesus Christ all things were made, and that by him all things consist, &c. could conceive them intended to convey an idea that " the Creator of all things that are in heaven, and that are in earth, visible and invisible," was no more than a meer Creature, and the work of his own hands. Some other meaning corresponding to the general sense of the apostle must be sought for, and I sincerely think that I have affixed the true one to the words before us, and am certain that, if I have not, I have not deviated farther from it than they who translate " first-born" into " first-made." Compassion for the unhappy Servetus seems altogether to have absorbed Mr. Lindsey's attention; his death is made into a martyrdom, and his martyrdom into an argument sufficient to make any thing St. Paul says on this subject altogether unnecessary to be enquired into. The little passage is taken apart, and an interpretation fastened upon it, which, when it is restored to its original connection, it altogether rejects.

LXXVII.

The following is an explicit declaration that Jesus Christ is both God and Man, " for in him dwelleth all the fulness of the Godhead bodily," Col. ii. 9.

LXXVIII.

To forgive sins is the peculiar attribute of him to whom belong mercies and forgiveness; and accordingly we are called upon by St. Paul to " put on (as the elect of God, holy and beloved) bowels of mercy, kindess, humbleness of mind, meekness, long-suffering; forbearing one another, and forgiving one another, if any man have a quarrel against any: even as Christ forgave you, so also do ye," Col. iii. 12, 13. This passage is immediately preceded by a declaration, that " Christ is all in all."

LXXIX.

" Of the Lord ye shall receive the reward of the inheritance: for ye serve the Lord Christ. But he that doeth wrong, shall receive for the wrong which he hath done: and there is no respect of persons," Col. iii. 24, 25. Before whom is there no respect of persons? certainly before him who is to deal out the reward impartially, whom we serve; but we are told that " God will render to every man according to his deeds," " for there is no respect of persons with God," Rom. ii. 5, 11. And in the Ephesians, St. Paul says, having called us first servants of Christ," " your Master also is in heaven, neither is there respect of persons with him," Eph. vi. 6, 9. And accordingly we find St. James say, " My brethren, have not the faith of our Lord Jesus Christ, the Lord of glory, with respect of persons," James ii. 1.

LXXX.

To the Thessalonians, St. Paul says, " We were bold in our God, to speak unto you the gospel of God, with much contention," 1 Thess. ii. 2. " We were willing to have imparted unto you, not the gospel of God

God only, but alfo our own fouls," " for labouring night and day, becaufe we would not be chargeable unto any of you, we preached unto you the gofpel of God," 1 Theff. ii. 8, 9. " and fent Timotheus our brother and minifter of God, and our fellow labourer in the gofpel of Chrift, to eftablifh you, and to comfort you concerning your faith," 1 Theff. iii. 2. If Chrift be not God, is this the method of eftablifhing their faith? no, but of fhaking it to its very foundation, for the idea that he is God is fuggefted by it. Either St. Paul intended to inculcate that doctrine, or he did not; if he did, we muft accede to it; if he did not, he has lied to the Holy Ghoft, given " to guide him into all truth," John xvi. 13. or the fpirit of truth has, by inaccuracy, deceived and dealt by our faith with duplicity. But as Paul has declared his exhortation to have been " not of deceit, nor of uncleannefs, nor in guile," 1 Theff. ii. 3, I will believe that this eloquent apoftle fpoke the dictate of the fpirit without ambiguity; and though Mr. Lindfey has charged the appointed witneffes of our bleffed Redeemer with equivocation, I am confident he will not blafphemoufly dare to impute falfehood to the Spirit of truth himfelf. If Paul then fpeaking, with the Holy Ghoft, has fuggefted that Chrift is God, we muft neceffarily believe that he meant to inculcate that doctrine, and therefore that Jefus Chrift is one with the Father, God.

LXXXI.

Reminding the Theffalonians of his former leffons, St. Paul fays, " For ye know what commandments we gave you by the Lord Jefus. For this is the will of God," 1 Theff. iv. 2, 3. He then proceeds to inftruct them in brotherly love, as the will of God, the commandment of the Lord Jefus.

LXXXII.

"It is a righteous thing with God to recompence tribulation to them that trouble you; and to you who are troubled, rest with us, when the Lord Jesus shall be revealed from heaven, with his mighty angels, in flaming fire, taking vengeance on them that know not God, and obey not the gospel of our Lord Jesus Christ: who shall be punished with everlasting destruction from the presence of the Lord, and from the glory of his power; when he shall come to be glorified in his saints, and to be admired in all them that believe (because our testimony among you was believed) in that day," 2 Thess. i. 6, 7, 8, 9, 10. Seeing then that Jesus Christ is revealed from heaven, taking vengeance, and destroying by everlasting expulsion from before the presence of the glory of his power; is not he that God with whom it is a righteous thing to recompence tribulation to them that trouble, to them that know him not to be God in obedience to the gospel of our Lord Jesus Christ, "that the name of our Lord Jesus Christ may be glorified?" See the entire chapter. The glorification of the name of our blessed Lord gives a sanction to our addressing him in these words, "Hallowed be thy name," Matth. vi. 9. "The Lord Jesus shall be revealed, taking vengeance on them that obey not the gospel of our Lord Jesus Christ;" and "what shall the end be of them that obey not the gospel of God?" 1 Pet. iv. 17.

LXXXIII.

"Now our Lord Jesus Christ himself, and God even our Father, which hath loved us, and hath given us everlasting consolation, and good hope thro' grace, comfort your hearts, and establish you in every good word and work," 2 Thess. ii. 16, 17. I am not yet going to enquire into Mr. Lindsey's curious doctrine of pious wishes, but, exclusive of the general sense of this passage,

passage, to make a remark on the great singularity of the expression. Either there are two nominatives joined by the copulative " and," or there is but one preceding the verb in the sentence before us, and in that case, the copulative unites two specific terms put in appofition to the one general nominative; if the former were the case, the verb must necessarily have been put in the plural number, whereas, from its standing in the singular, we must conceive it governed by one nominative only; now, if there be found one term in the sentence including the rest within its general import, that is the nominative case governing the verb: But I have all along asserted, that the Father is God, and that the Son is God, and therefore now say that the word " God," is here that general term comprehending within itself, " our Lord Jesus Christ himself, and even our Father," one God, which *hath* loved us, and *hath* given us everlasting consolation. St. Paul seems to have been diligent to establish this point by the energetick addition of the word " himself" after the name of our Lord; for thus emphatically to dwell upon a word to be dismissed instantly from being of any consequence in the construction of a sentence, is a practice unknown to any writer in any language, and surely not to be imputed to one of the most accurate, concise, and obtrusive speakers that ever forced the meaning of words upon the understanding of mankind; a preacher who gave words only to his ideas, and never sought an expletive to grace, much less to disgrace his language, and distract his argument. After he had thus given them a blessing from his warm and benevolent heart, this excellent man calls upon his hearers for their prayers, and, in consideration of the benediction that he has already bestowed on them, " that God should establish them in every good word and work," he says, " the Lord is faithful, who shall stablish you, and keep you from evil," 2 Thess. iii. 3.

LXXXIV.

"And the Lord direct your hearts into the love of God, and into the patient waiting for Chrift;" or, as it ftands in the margin of the Bible, "the patience of Chrift," 2 Theff. iii. 5. Here is *the Lord*, according to Mr. Lindfey's manner of interpreting, quite neuter, being neither God nor Chrift, for, apart from both, he is to lead to the love of the one, and to the patience of the other. But I believe this gentleman will hardly infift upon it that he is not either in this paffage; and if not here, I refer it to the candour of every advocate of the Unitarian fyftem, whether a diftinction between the Father and Son, as God, is intended to be marked in fuch paffages as the following: "now thanks be to God which always caufeth us to triumph in Chrift," 2 Cor. ii. 14. "In the fight of God fpeak we in Chrift," 2 Cor. ii. 17; and in a multitude of texts, where the diftinction is marked only as in that before us, where the neuter word *Lord* is certainly both that God and Chrift from whom he feems to be diftinguifhed by the action appointed to him.

LXXXV.

"There is one God, and one mediator between God and man, the man Chrift Jefus; who gave himfelf a ranfom for all, to be teftified in due time," 1 Tim. ii. 5, 6. Having already commented on the former part of this paffage, I fhall not now weary my reader by repetition, but remark that, from a declaration that Chrift had given himfelf a ranfom to be teftified in due time, and that that time was now come, in which God our Saviour will have all men come to the knowledge of the truth by the teftimony of the apoftolical preaching, with the Holy Ghoft, Paul inftantly paffes on to fay, that having been himfelf appointed a witnefs of our Saviour, a preacher, and an apoftle, teaching of the Gentiles in faith and verity, "I will therefore that men pray every where, lifting up holy hands,

without

without wrath and doubting," 1 Tim. ii. 7, 8. Wherefore? becaufe he is a witnefs to teftify of Chrift who gave himfelf a ranfom for all. And how does this authorize him to will that all men fhould pray? there can be but one anfwer given to this, namely, that he, whom he teftified, was the proper object of that prayer which he defired fhould be preferred, even Jefus Chrift, one with the Father, God.

LXXXVI.

St. Paul, about to fend Timothy to preach "found doctrine, according to the glorious gofpel of the bleffed God, which was committed to his truft," 1 Tim. i. 10, 11. gives him the following epitome of what he would have him promulgate and teftify; " Now, without controverfy, great is the myftery of godlinefs: God was manifeft in the flefh, juftified in the fpirit, feen of angels, preached unto the Gentiles, believed on in the world, received up into glory," 1 Tim. iii. 16. What can more demonftrate the Godhead of him who, having been manifeft in the flefh, was witneffed by the apoftles to have afcended into heaven, and who, by them, was now preached unto the Gentiles, than this direct affertion, that he, of whom it was afferted, was, and is God. And fhall we now deny that the revelation of godlinefs is a myftery?

LXXXVII.

Forewarning Timothy of future defection from the truth, and recommending perfeverance, St. Paul fays, " We both labour, and fuffer reproach, becaufe we truft in the living God, who is the Saviour of all men, 1 Tim. iv. 10. " This" he declares to be "a faithful faying, and worthy of all acceptation;" and in fo many words he has afferted the fame thing of the following fact, that " Jefus Chrift came into the world to fave finners," 1 Tim. i. 15. To be the Saviour then is the common attribute of God and of Chrift, who is therefore God; for Jefus Chrift is not faid to have been the means of falvation, which would have better defcribed the inftrument of God in our redemption, but he is one and the fame Saviour with God. Of the man Chrift Jefus of the feed of David, it is indeed faid that he was raifed from the dead, 2 Tim. ii. 8. But Jefus Chrift as God, clothed with eternal glory, is he by whom we have obtained eternal falvation, 2 Tim. ii. 10.

LXXXVIII.

" I give thee charge in the fight of God, who quickeneth all things, and before Chrift Jefus, who before Pontius Pilate witneffed a good confeffion; that thou keep this commandment without fpot, unrebukeable, until the appearing of our Lord Jefus Chrift: which in his times he fhall fhew, who is the bleffed and only potentate, the King of kings, and Lord of lords; who only hath immortality, dwelling in the light which no man can approach unto, whom no man hath feen, nor can fee: to whom be honour and power everlafting. Amen," 1 Tim. vi. 13, 14, 15, 16. Here even the glory of God, unapproachable by man, is afcribed to Jefus Chrift; and this is only afcribable to his divinity, as many men had feen the man Jefus; and St. Paul fays, " yea, though we have known Chrift after the flefh, yet now henceforth know we him no more," 2 Cor. v. 16. That he is the King of kings, and Lord of lords, is not only afferted here, but is in fo many terms declared to be the name of Jefus Chrift by St. John, Rev. xix. 16. His Godhead is therefore incontrovertibly eftablifhed here. That St. Paul fhould fpeak of the Son only, is an inference naturally refulting from the confideration that he was making out an appointment to Timothy to go and to preach Jefus Chrift, of whom he fpeaks in fuch terms in the firft chapter of this epiftle, that I choofe to refer to it,

rather

rather than make a partial quotation, and the whole is too long to infert. The *pious* wifh, or rather let me have liberty to call it the benediction of the apoftle, is " grace, mercy, and peace from God our Father, and Jefus Chrift our Lord;" a wifh, which I cannot well imagine how he fhould expect to have gratified by a mere creature; nay, he fays more, that the grace of our Lord was exceeding abundant, fets forth, that to his truft was committed the glorious gofpel of God, and inftantly thanks Jefus for putting him into the miniftry; declares Jefus Chrift to have come into the world (a phrafe extraordinary, if the commencement of our Saviour's life was in the flefh) to fave finners; and having recounted the particular mercy and long-fuffering of Jefus Chrift toward himfelf, his gratitude breaks out into a doxology, the object of which muft evidently appear to be the fame as the Being from whom he received the benefits that invite his praife. " And now" he fays " unto the King eternal, immortal, invifible, the only wife God, be honour and glory, for ever and ever. Amen." He muft be a perverfe interpreter who can underftand thefe words in any other fenfe than that of a declaration that the merciful and long-fuffering Jefus, the abundance of whofe grace had pardoned his multitudinous perfecutions and blafphemies, for a pattern to all who fhould hereafter believe to life everlafting, " is the King eternal, the only wife God, to whom he afcribes honour and glory, in confideration of the exceedingly great benefits which he had received of him, and which were now fo ftrongly impreffed upon his mind, as at once to call forth his acknowledgments and his exulting praife."

LXXXIX.

St. Paul fays to Timothy, whom he is fending to " do the work of an Evangelift," " I charge thee therefore before God and the Lord Jefus Chrift, who fhall judge the quick and the dead at his appearing,

and

and his kingdom: preach the word, &c." 2 Tim. iv. 1. And "unto all them that love his appearing," he says, "the Lord the righteous Judge shall give a crown of righteousness at that day," ver. 8. Here the kingdom, the judgement-seat, and the appearing, are assigned to Jesus Christ, and the crown of righteousness is conferred on all those who love his appearing, according to what he says to Titus, to whom he is giving a like charge: " looking for that blessed hope, and the glorious appearing of the great God, and our Saviour Jesus Christ," Titus ii. 13. That these then are all synonimous terms I shall not affront the understanding of my reader by an attempt to make more evident than it must at once appear; and our Saviour Jesus Christ is therefore one with the Father, God.

XC.

In the charge to Titus last cited, St. Paul holds out " this blessed hope, and glorious appearing of the great God, and our Saviour Jesus Christ," to such as deny worldly lusts, and who, by so doing, " adorn the doctrine of God our Saviour," Titus ii. 10. Jesus Christ was the doctrine committed to Titus, and more particularly " how our salvation arose from his having given himself for us, that he might redeem us from all iniquity;" " that having been disobedient, serving lusts and pleasures, not our merits, but his mercy shone forth in saving us:" that therefore, " Jesus Christ having loved us, and washed us from our sins in his blood," Rev. i. 5. " the kindness and love of *God our Saviour* appeared, by washing of regeneration, and renewing of the Holy Ghost; which was shed on us abundantly, thro' *Jesus Christ our Saviour*," Titus iii. 4, 5, 6. Here, speaking to a man who was to act under him, and whose discharge of the office conferred on him, must in a great measure depend upon the accuracy of St. Paul's expression, this apostle, preaching that which was committed to him, according to the com-

commandment of God our Saviour," falls into a mode of expreffion, which, if Jefus Chrift be not God, muft perpetually miflead Titus, keep him wandering in continual errour, and utterly incapacitate him to " exhort and convince by found doctrine." That mankind had obtained falvation, is the committed doctrine; that God is our Saviour, and that Jefus Chrift is our Saviour, are fentences occurring every where through the epiftle, nay, in contiguous verfes; for, after declaring himfelf an apoftle by the commandment of *God our Saviour*, St. Paul proceeds to fay, " To Titus mine own Son after the common faith: grace, mercy, and peace from God the Father, and the *Lord Jefus Chrift our Saviour*," Titus i. 3, 4. Did he mean to diftract him? if not, he is very defective in his addrefs; but if he meant to inculcate the divinity of Chrift, and to fhew that the Father and the Son are one God, our Saviour, he has fpoken to the purpofe, and confiftently with the coherent ftile that fo exceedingly diftinguifhes the writings of St. Paul.

XCI.

" Verily, he took not on him the nature of angels; but he took on him the feed of Abraham," Heb. ii. 16. This is urged as a perfuafive to us to lay hold of and embrace the great falvation, afforded to us by fo wonderful an inftance of condefcenfion as that of our Saviour's having taken our nature upon him, which he is declared to have done, that he might, as man, become the Captain of our falvation, by fuffering death for all men. But St. Paul fays, that he took not on him the nature of angels, but defcended a little lower: What is this but faying, that out of two things equally poffible to him, he has made a choice? and to that which is not yet ufhered into being, we know that there is not any thing poffible; therefore Jefus Chrift had pre-exiftence to the time he came in the flefh: But he verily

rily took not on him the nature of angels; therefore, in his pre-exiftent ftate, he was not an angel. But while the power of making choice among all inferior natures which he would take was his, he affumed that in which a purpofe beneficial to mankind was to be anfwered; and we are accordingly invited to offer up the tribute of our gratitude and confidence to him who had been thus merciful. But who was he to whom fuch a choice belonged? Certainly God, to whom alone all things are fubfervient, "by whom and for whom all things were created, that are in heaven, and that are in earth," Col. i. 16. who can exalt, as well as debafe, the works of his own hands, and take into himfelf whatfoever nature it fhall pleafe him to honour. This ftupendous dignity he has conferred upon ours; and for our advantage has become man, even the man Jefus Chrift. This adopted nature, this progeny of his power and mercy he has declared his Son; and for the fake of this his "holy child Jefus," who, notwithftanding that he was in all points tempted like as we are, continued to the end doing the will of God, fpotlefs, without fin, became obedient to the death for our redemption, and having fuffered, thereby to become the Author and Captain of our falvation, accompanied the * reafcending God into heaven, there for ever to remain our Mediator and Interceffor; for his fake, I fay, has God been pleafed to extend falvation to us; "for this beloved Son, in whom he is well pleafed," and whom therefore he has eternally united with himfelf, has undertaken the caufe of our infirmities, and has gracioufly condefcended to call us brethren; he has even called us fons; and having taken part in that flefh and blood whereof we are partakers, pronounced

us

---

* "Now, that he afcended, what is it but that he alfo defcended firft into the lower parts of the earth?" Eph. iv. 8.

us his children; and with more than paternal kindnefs bowed himfelf down to death for our fanctification, " that he might thereby deftroy him that had the power of death, that is the devil, and deliver them that, through fear of death, were all their life time fubject to bondage." See Heb. ii. throughout. Let us then, in memory of that fellowfhip which God himfelf has with us, having been " partaker of that flefh and blood," through the mercies which he has thereby vouchfafed us, approach the throne of his grace with confidence, " knowing that we have a new and living way confecrated to us, through the vail, that is to fay, his flefh," Heb. x. 20. " And having," therefore, "an high prieft over the houfe of God, let us draw near with a true heart, in full affurance of faith," " without wavering;" for if we fin wilfully, after that we have received the knowledge of the truth, " of the offering of the body of Jefus Chrift once," " there remaineth no more facrifice for fin, but a fiery indignation fhall devour the adverfary, who hath trodden under foot the Son of God, and counted the blood of the covenant wherewith he was fanctified an unholy thing, and hath done defpite unto the fpirit of grace; for we know him that hath faid, vengeance belongeth unto me, I will recompence, faith the Lord. And again the Lord fhall judge his people," Heb. x. throughout.

Where now is Mr. Lindfey's analogy between the offering up of prayer and religious worfhip to Aaron the high prieft of the Jews, and to our great high prieft Jefus Chrift? between the prieft " that ftandeth daily miniftering and offering oftentimes the fame facrifices which can never take away fin," and this Man, who, after he had offered one facrifice for fins, for ever fat down at the right hand of God; who, by one offering, hath perfected for ever them that are fanctified? " For the law maketh men high priests; but the word of the oath which was since the law, maketh the Son, who is consecrated for evermore;" "who, having as a priest, once made sacrifice, having offered up himself," is set on the right hand of the throne of the majesty in the heavens, where he has become the mediator of the new covenant; in which he has declared, "I will put my laws into their minds, and write them in their hearts, and I will be to them a God, and they shall be to me a people," Heb. vii. and viii. chap. And he, who has, by his flesh, broken down the partition wall that divided God and man, and whose human nature, perfected by sufferings for an atonement to reconcile man to God, is now in eternal union with the divine nature, and clothed with the one glory, is surely a mediator, a high priest, of a dignity to which the posterity of Aaron never aspired; "he is a high priest in things pertaining to God, to make reconciliation for the sins of the people;" and he is an object of our adoration and religious worship; "for in that he himself hath suffered, being tempted, he is able to succour them that are tempted," Heb. ii. 17, 18. To this high honour the glorified body of Christ is called, after it had been made perfect, and thence become the author of our salvation: whereas of Aaron's priesthood it is said, that "the sacrifices which were offered year by year continually," under it, "could never make the comers thereunto perfect," Heb x. 1. Are Aaron and Jesus Christ now equally objects of our adoration? or are we equally to withhold our worship from both, him who cannot, and him who can succour us? from him who daily shed the insufficient blood of bulls and goats, for the errours of the people, and from him who abolished the sacrifice and offering by the one sacrifice, the one offering of his own " prepared body, which came and bled for us, that we might be enabled to do

thy

thy will, O God," Heb. x. 5, 6. that we might be a party to the new covenant? The doctrine of the apostle is therefore here manifestly, that, inasmuch as the flesh and blood of the man Jesus is now in union with the eternal Godhead, and that in the world he had suffered so much for us, and had called us brethren, we may entertain great hope in the mercy of him, whose experience of human infirmities and temptations, can cause him to have compassion on us; and therefore we are desired to call upon God through these mercies, through Jesus Christ, his name, as our ransom from death, abolished by the death of his human body. It is not to " the unlearned reader" that I refer what I have now written, for I do not expect it to have any weight with such as have not read the law of Moses, and compared the types of the Jewish ritual with the great event of which it was the shadow; and also attended to the course of the apostle's argument throughout his epistle to the Hebrews. Before I conclude this comment I must insist upon the circumstance of the law having been no more than a shadow of the things to come, and not the exact portraiture; and therefore cannot refrain from expressing my surprize at seeing Aaron and our blessed Lord so closely brought together and assimilated by Mr. Lindsey, who will not admit of even a shadowy representation, throughout the law, of that which was to come, when it happens to typify that which opposes his own system. But as I have the word of God for it, I shall venture to assert, that the government of the Jews, by God, was an epitome of the government of the afterwards adopted world; that the selection of the Jews, for the faith of Abraham their father, was an instance of the value of faith in the pure eyes of God, and an epitome of the adoption " of many sons," to be elected thro' faith in Jesus Christ; that the purifications by blood, and the atonement,

by

by sacrifices for the people, were a type of that great sacrifice of the body of our Lord, offered once for our atonement, by which we are reconciled and restored to that blessed hope of everlasting life, which we had forfeited as heirs to the transgression of Adam; for as in Adam all men died, and as the law was given that sin might abound, so by Jesus Christ are all men made alive, and by the abundance of sin, his grace has the more abounded to us, by faith in our redemption, by the blood of the new covenant, to which the old covenant was a guide, that new covenant, of which the man Jesus perfected by death, and in eternal union with God, is the mediator. Let us then, on our part, declare, that we will be to him a people, as he has, upon his, promised, that he will be to us a God; and let us, when we hear the voice of " the Son of God" from our graves, acknowledge " the God who quickeneth the dead," and " rejoice in the appearing of the Son of man coming in the clouds of heaven;" when we consider that for our sakes he took our nature upon him, that he might have compassion upon our infirmities; and that he is our appointed judge, " because he is the Son of man."

XCII.

As it is already laid down, and, I presume, well remembered, that all are to be judged by our Lord Jesus Christ, when he shall come in his glory on his own day, with the holy angels, bringing his reward with him, and recompensing every man according to his works, I shall not repeat the proofs of it. " Of the Lord then, whose coming draweth nigh," St. James says, " be ye patient therefore brethren unto the coming of the Lord; the judge standeth before the door; we count them happy which endure; ye have heard of the patience of Job, and have seen the end of the Lord: that the Lord is very pitiful and of tender mercy," James v. 8.

8, 9, 10, 11. The patience of Job is here urged as an example to them who were defirous of haftening the day of the Lord; but the patience of Job was in waiting the end of God, whofe pity and tender mercy at length amply rewarded his refignation. The pitiful and tenderly merciful Lord, who fhall recompenfe them who, after the example of Job, and " the prophets, who fpoke in the name of the Lord," with patience wait for his own appointed day, is therefore the fame God who rewarded Job, and for whofe coming the prophets waited. But St. James goes on and fays, that with refpect to fick perfons the elders of the church are to be called for, and to pray over them, " and the prayer of faith fhall fave the fick, and the Lord fhall raife him up," James v. 14, 15. This is in context with the preceding paffage, which renders it manifeft who the Lord is that fhall hear the prayer of faith, and heal the fick; even the fame Lord of whom St. Peter faid to Eneas, at Lydda, " Jefus Chrift maketh thee whole, arife," Acts ix. 34; who faid himfelf to her that, with full affurance of his power, touched but his garment, and had her iffue of blood ftaunched, " daughter, be of good comfort: thy faith hath made thee whole," Luke viii. 48; and who, without the intermediate ufe of any other name, faid to the leper who befought him with a prayer of faith, * " I will; be thou clean," Luke v. 13: of Jefus Chrift then we are to afk and have. He therefore is one with the Father, God.

XCIII.

In the commencement of his epiftle, James calls himfelf " a fervant of God, and of the Lord Jefus Chrift," James i. 1. As a reafon why we fhould " not have

* Quere, How does this ftand in the French? is it *je fouhaite?* or if it be, what does it fignify? See *Apology, note, p, 5.*

have the faith of our Lord Jesus Christ, the Lord of glory, with respect of persons," James ii. 1, he says, " hearken, my beloved brethren, hath not God chosen the poor of this world, rich in faith, and heirs of the kingdom which he hath promised to them that love him?" James ii. 5. " If ye have respect to persons, ye commit sin," James ii. 9. " For he shall have judgement without mercy, that hath shewed no mercy; and mercy rejoiceth against judgement," ii. 13.

XCIV.

In order to avoid repetition of arguments already used, I shall observe upon but one passage in St. Peter's first general epistle in its course.

" The elders which are among you, I exhort, who am also an elder, and a witness of the sufferings of Christ, and also a partaker of the glory that shall be revealed: feed the flock of God which is among you," " neither as being lords over God's heritage, but being ensamples to the flock. And when the chief shepherd shall appear, ye shall receive a crown of glory that fadeth not away," 1 Pet. v. 1, 2, 3, 4. If it be remembered that this charge comes from St. Peter to men engaged in the same occupation as himself, it is but reasonable to suppose that he had in mind those words of our blessed Lord when he conferred the charge of his flock upon him, which were so emphatically spoken, and so affectingly received by him. After his resurrection from the dead, Jesus having on the third time shewed himself to his disciples " when they had dined, saith to Simon Peter, Simon son of Jonas, lovest thou me more than these? he saith unto him, yea, Lord; thou knowest that I love thee. He saith unto him, feed my lambs. He saith to him again the second time, Simon son of Jonas, lovest thou me? he saith unto him, yea, Lord; thou knowest that I love thee. He saith unto him,

him, feed my sheep. He saith unto him the third time, Simon son of Jonas, lovest thou me? Peter was grieved, becaufe he faid unto him the third time, loveſt thou me? and he faid unto him, Lord, thou knoweſt all things; thou knoweſt that I love thee. Jeſus faith unto him, feed my ſheep," John xxi. 14, 15, 16, 17. A charge attended by ſuch circumſtances, and repeatedly conveyed in ſuch terms, muſt neceſſarily have been deeply impreſſed on the memory of Peter, who was grieved that he who knew all things ſhould think it neceſſary to renew it a third time. That Peter ſhould therefore ever afterwards conſider the office conferred upon him as that of a ſhepherd, and thoſe to whom he was ſent as the flock of the chief ſhepherd who had committed them to him, is not to be wondered at; and accordingly we find him in another place ſay of him, who had declared himſelf " no hireling, but the ſhepherd, whoſe own the ſheep are; the good ſhepherd, who giveth his life for the ſheep," John x. 13, 14. " Ye were as ſheep going aſtray; but are now returned unto the ſhepherd and biſhop of your ſouls," 1 Pet. ii. 25. So that here is that flock of Jeſus Chriſt, the good ſhepherd, whoſe own the ſheep are, expreſsly declared to be the flock of God. St. Paul too has called " Jeſus Chriſt, that great ſhepherd of the ſheep, Heb. xiii. 20; and ſpeaking to the Epheſian Elders, he deſires them to " take heed to all the flock, over the which the Holy Ghoſt had made them overſeers, to feed the church of God," Acts xx. 28. From the chief ſhepherd alſo, when he ſhall appear, we are to receive a crown of glory which fadeth not away. " Bleſſed is the man that endureth temptation; for when he is tried, he ſhall receive the crown of life; which the Lord hath promiſed to them that love him," James i. 12. This promiſe is explained; " Hath not God choſen the poor of this world, rich in faith, and heirs of the kingdom,

which

which he hath promised to them that love him?" James ii. 5. From whom now are we "* to obtain an incorruptible crown," "a crown of righteousness, which the Lord, the righteous Judge, shall give at that day, unto all them that love his appearing? †" Certainly from that God who hath promised the kingdom; that Lord who hath promised the crown of life to them that love him, shall we receive a crown of glory which fadeth not away, when the chief shepherd shall appear as a righteous judge to give an incorruptible crown of righteousness to all them that love his appearing. This chief shepherd is therefore that righteous Judge, that Lord, that God who hath promised, and will give a crown of glory to all that love him, even Jesus Christ, one with the Father, God; "to whom be praise and dominion for ever and ever. Amen." 1 Pet. iv. 11.

XCV.

The first verse of the first chapter of St. Peter's second epistle general, has these remarkable words, as literally translated in the margin of our Bible. "Simon Peter, a servant and apostle of Jesus Christ, to them that have obtained like precious faith with us, through the righteousness of our God and Saviour Jesus Christ," 2 Pet. i. 1. Paul to Timothy, also calls himself "an apostle by the commandment of God our Saviour, and Lord Jesus Christ, which is our hope," 1 Tim i. 1.

XCVI.

"An entrance shall be ministered unto you abundantly, into the everlasting kingdom of our Lord and Saviour Jesus Christ," 2 Pet. i. 11.

XCVII.

"The day of the Lord will come as a thief in the night; in the which the heavens shall pass away with a great noise, and the elements shall melt with fervent heat;

* 1 Cor. ix. 25. † 2 Tim. iv. 8.

heat, the earth alſo and the works that are therein ſhall be burnt up. Seeing then that all theſe things ſhall be diſſolved, what manner of perſons ought ye to be in all holy converſation and godlineſs, looking for and haſting unto the coming of the day of God, wherein the heavens being on fire ſhall be diſſolved, and the elements ſhall melt with fervent heat?" 2 Pet. iii. 10, 11, 12. As there is but one day mentioned in this paſſage, it is evident that the Lord, whoſe day it is called in the firſt, is the ſame as the God, whoſe day it is ſaid to be in the laſt verſe; one and the ſame God. But, that the ſpecified Lord, who is God, is our Lord Jeſus Chriſt, the context, to which I refer, ſhews beyond contradiction. Beſides other circumſtances evincing this fact throughout the whole chapter, the apoſtle ſays, " the long-ſuffering of our Lord is to be accounted ſalvation; even as our beloved brother Paul alſo hath written unto you," 2 Pet. iii. 15. Now the words of Paul, to which St. Peter here refers, are, " For this cauſe I obtained mercy, that in me firſt Jeſus Chriſt might ſhew forth all long-ſuffering, for a pattern to them which ſhould hereafter believe on him to life everlaſting," 1 Tim. i. 16. Here then, mercy and life everlaſting, which are ſalvation, are preached to all thro' the long-ſuffering of Jeſus Chriſt, after the pattern of Paul, to which Peter has referred, calling him, who is by Paul called Jeſus Chriſt, Lord; and immediately after calling him, whom he had himſelf named Lord, God. Let us not therefore " fall from our ſtedfaſtneſs, but grow in grace, and in the knowledge of our Lord and Saviour Jeſus Chriſt: to him be glory both now and for ever. Amen." 2 Pet. iii. 18.

XCVIII.

" He is Antichriſt, that denieth the Father and the Son," 1 John ii. 22. How is he who denieth the Father, Antichriſt? How is he who denieth Jeſus to be

the

the Chrift, and " confeffeth not that he is come in the flefh," to be confidered as denying the Father? For this plain reafon, that the Son is one with the Father, God; and confequently the Father is denied upon the denial of him who is with him, one.

XCIX.

" Every fpirit that confeffeth not that Jefus Chrift is come in the flefh, is not of God," 1 John iv. 3. Though the apoftle's intention in this verfe be to fhew that Jefus Chrift was truly man, yet it is no ftrained inference to fay, that the Being, who came in the flefh, had pre-exiftence to the time of taking it upon him; and this indeed follows the more naturally, when we confider that this denial is made " by the fpirit of Antichrift," which denieth the Father and the Son.

C.

As I do believe the 7th verfe of the 5th chapter of St. John's 1ft epiftle to be at the beft a very dubious text, I refign all advantage that might accrue to my caufe, from its having come from his infpired pen. But I fhall beg leave to exprefs myfelf in the words of it, which very well comprize the conclufion following from the whole of facred writ, and which I hope I have rendered obvious by this time. In my own perfon then I fay that I believe in " the Father, the word, and the Holy Ghoft, and thefe three are one."

CI.

If words could be found more directly enjoining prayer to Jefus Chrift than thofe which follow, I fhould endeavour to enlarge on the fubject; but as the beloved difciple of our Redeemer has given us the precept, I fhall leave it to Mr. Lindfey to draw the conclufion, for which he ftands engaged, and to acknowledge that Jefus Chrift is one with the Father, God. " Thefe things have I written unto you that believe on the name of the Son of God; that ye may know ye
have

have eternal life, and that ye may believe on the name of the Son of God. And this is the confidence that we have in him, that if we afk any thing according to his will, he heareth us. And if we know that he hear us, whatfoever we afk, we know that we have the petitions that we defired of him," 1 John v. 13, 14, 15. " Beloved, if our heart condemn us not, then have we confidence towards God. And whatfoever we afk, we receive of him, becaufe we keep his commandments," 1 John iii. 21, 22. Here exactly the fame precept is repeated; but the one Godhead is named in the latter, inftead of the fecond perfon of the Trinity fpecified in the former paffage.

CII.

" And we know that the Son of God is come, and hath given us an underftanding, that we may know him that is true: and we are in him that is true, even in his Son Jefus Chrift. This is the true God and eternal life," 1 John v. 20. It is remarkable that this declaration is followed by a defire to " keep from idols," to the overthrow of whofe worfhip he preaches the Godhead of Jefus Chrift, the Son. But left it fhould be faid that the elder was inattentive to the confequence of fpeaking in ambiguous language to idolaters, concerning the God whom he preached to them, I will produce proofs from the context to teftify that Chrift is here fpoken of, and pointed out for adoration. " He that hath the Son, hath life," and " God hath given us eternal life, and this life is in his Son," and " thefe things have I written unto you that believe on the name of the Son of God; that ye may know that ye have eternal life," 1 John v. 11, 12, 13. Thefe words explain who is the true God in whom we have this eternal life; befides, the gift of underftanding is an act of Godhead, and is here made to us by the Son. Suppofe for a moment with Mr. Lindfey that the prophetick

eyes

eyes of the apostles were blinded to the opinion afterwards to be entertained by mankind, who have since their day believed Jesus Christ to be God, notwithstanding that they had seen him a man born and living amongst men, even this absurd supposition would not extend to St. John, nor indeed to St. Paul, who were themselves witnesses of that early heresy by which the manhood of Jesus Christ was denied, and had heard that body which he had come in, declared only to have been an appearance; so that their own living experience might have given them a hint, that accuracy in the application of the terms Lord, and Saviour, and *the like*, was necessary, if they had not been the most stupid as well as wicked men that ever lived on the earth. They were accurate men, they were honest men; and by the application of those terms to both the Father and the Son, they have left us an irrefragable proof that the Father and the Son are one God.

The goodness of God, and that gracious indulgence with which he has consulted the infirmities of our state, is, in this respect also, very strongly displayed, that he took manhood on him, in order to give a sensible object of worship to mankind, incapable of forming any adequate idea of the abstract God, whose qualities are of a nature incomprehensible by our minds; and not only our natural incapacity to conceive a God purely spiritual was considered, but the world, merged in idolatry at the time of his incarnation, was mercifully indulged with an object of sense, to which men could look according to habit also, and to whom, even by the exertion of the same faculties by which they had adopted and adored idols, they could prefer worship without the imputation of idolatry. A resting place is hereby given to the mind, instead of its being continued

nued under the neceffity of launching out into vaft infinity and eternity, and vainly endeavouring to engage itfelf in the contemplation of matters, of which it can form no idea at all.

CIII.

"Whofoever tranfgreffeth, and abideth not in the doctrine of Chrift, hath not God: he that abideth in the doctrine of Chrift, he hath both the Father and the Son," 2 John 9. After having fhewed who had not God, the elder goes on to fhew of the direct contrary character, that he hath the Father and the Son, who are therefore that God which abideth in him. "Whofoever denieth the Son, the fame hath not the Father," 1 John ii. 23. But "whofoever fhall confefs that Jefus is the Son of God, God dwelleth in him, and he in God," 1 John iv. 15. "If we love one another, God dwelleth in us," 1 John iv. 12. Who now is the Father and the Son, who dwelleth in us if we abide in the doctrine of Chrift?

CIV.

"Jude, a fervant of Jefus Chrift, and brother of James; to them that are fanctified by God the Father," Jude 1. Paul, who has frequently called himfelf both the fervant of God and of Jefus Chrift, (fee Philip. i. 1, and Titus i. 1.) has in like manner addreffed the Corinthians, "to them that are fanctified in Chrift Jefus," 1 Cor. i. 1.

CV.

Speaking of the judgement that awaits "ungodly men, turning the grace of God into lafcivioufnefs, and denying the only Lord God, and our Lord Jefus Chrift," "who fpeak evil of thofe things which they know not," Jude fays, that "Enoch alfo, the feventh from Adam, prophefied of thefe, faying, behold, the Lord cometh with ten thoufands of his faints, to execute judgement upon all, and to convince all that are un-

ungodly among them, of all their ungodly deeds, which they have ungodly committed, and of all their hard speeches, which ungodly sinners have spoken against him." Now we know very well that Jesus Christ is to come to judgement, with the holy angels; that to those who work iniquity he shall give everlasting punishment, but unto the righteous, eternal life. We must therefore conclude him to have been the object of Enoch's prophecy; and the more so, as the apostle proceeds to recommend the remembrance and observation of what " the apostles of our Lord Jesus Christ had spoken, that in the latter times there should be mockers, sensual, not having the spirit," and to desire that they to whom he writes, " building up themselves in our most holy faith, should pray in the Holy Ghost, keep themselves in the love of God, looking for the mercy of our Lord Jesus Christ, unto eternal life. Now unto him that is able to keep us from falling, to present us faultless before the presence of his glory with exceeding joy; to the only wise God, our Saviour, be glory and majesty, dominion and power, both now and ever. Amen." See Jude throughout. A comment must be unnecessary here.

As I prescribed to myself the order in which the books of the scripture are arranged, and had determined to enquire of the testimony afforded by each in its course; and as I had but one conclusion in view, to the evidence of which alone proofs were to be brought, my intelligent reader will see the impossibility of steping from proof to proof in a mathematical process, or of producing an encreasing testimony commencing at a partial, and, in the end, resulting in a full demonstration of the truth of that one proposition, which must be rendered equally manifest by the first, as by the last argument in its behalf. That the scriptures have declared

clared the divinity of our Lord, it is my office to show, and that this declaration is true, if made, must necessarily follow, upon the conceffion that the fcriptures are the word of God, and therefore true; and as this conceffion is made, I am only to produce fuch declarations as are contained in them: this muft be at once feen to preclude progreffive enquiry. I have, however, for the gratification of my reader, referved a very few paffages, in which it is more directly and literally afferted that Jefus Chrift is one with the Father, God; and with thefe I fhall clofe the evidence of the apoftles, the appointed witneffes of our bleffed Redeemer.

CVI.

"Hereby perceive we the love of God, becaufe he laid down his life for us," 1 John iii. 16. The name of "Jefus Chrift" does not once occur in the preceding part of the chapter, of which this is the 16th verfe, fo that it cannot poffibly be referred to by the pronoun "he;" our Lord and Saviour is therefore literally declared to be God. The courfe of the argument alfo makes a literal interpretation abfolutely neceffary, for the beloved difciple is perfuading us to love one another in confequence of our brotherhood, a motive which God could not have, to love beings fo infinitely inferior to him; but that God loved us, is manifefted by his having rendered himfelf fubject to death for our fake; we are therefore defired to love one another, from the equality and fympathy of our nature: the love of God is perceived, becaufe he laid down his life for us; and therefore, "we ought to lay down our lives for the brethren," 1 John iii. 16.

CVII.

St. Paul preaches thus to the Ephefians, whom he had called to Miletus, and whom he appointed elders over the church to preach the gofpel.

"Take heed therefore unto yourselves, and to all the flock over the which the Holy Ghost hath made you overseers, to feed the church of God, which he hath purchased with his own blood," Acts xx. 28. What can convince if this be unable? Shall we see the blood of God himself streaming for our redemption, and still deny that God and man are one Christ? or shall we not rather seek to be of the fold, "return to the shepherd of our souls," to the "Lord God, who shall feed his flock like a shepherd? who shall gather the lambs with his arm, and carry them in his bosom," Isaiah xl. 11. But St. Paul foresaw that men would look upon this position, which he has laid down, as a difficulty, which would turn aside such as yielded not their faith, but should proceed to enquire of the hidden mystery, and withdraw from the acknowledgment of spiritual things, because they were not in possession of spiritual things to compare with them, whereby they should comprehend the things of God, into which the natural man is unable to enquire; and therefore he has said even to these elders to whom he directs his charge, "For I know this, that after my departing, shall grievous wolves enter in among you, not sparing the flock. Also of yourselves shall men arise, speaking perverse things, to draw away disciples after them," Acts xx. 29, 30. I wish that St. Paul may not have had our present day in view when he spoke thus.

CVIII.

To the Hebrews, St. Paul says, that the address from the Majesty on high to him, "by whom he made the worlds," is, "Thy throne, O God, is for ever and ever; a sceptre of righteousness is the sceptre of thy kingdom: And, thou Lord, in the beginning hast laid the foundation of the earth; and the heavens are the works of thy hands. They shall perish, but thou remainest: and they all shall wax old as doth a garment;

and

and as a vesture shalt thou fold them up, and they shall be changed: but thou art the same, and thy years shall not fail," Heb. i. 8, 10, 11, 12. That the attributes here ascribed, are ascribable only to God, I believe will not be denied; but they are ascribed by God himself, and to whom? To Jesus Christ, after he had laid aside the form of a servant, and again taken upon him the form of God, the express image of his person; when he had by himself purged our sins; and, being the brightness of his glory, sat down on the right-hand of the Majesty on high. They are ascribed to Jesus Christ, upon the reassumption of that glory which he had laid down, when he was made a little lower than the angels, that, by the grace of God, he might taste death for every man; that, by suffering, he might be made perfect, to lead mankind to salvation; to him who had called us brethren, and had now taken up his anointed body, "anointed with the oil of gladness above his fellows;" that body, by which he became our fellow, our brother, and our Saviour; and by the ascent of which he has marshalled our way to his eternal kingdom. To him, I say, who had been partaker of our flesh and blood, and who, having made himself acquainted with our infirmities, has taken into heaven that nature, by which he can be touched with a compassionate feeling of them; and has therefore become our "merciful high priest and intercessor," are these attributes ascribed, this address of exultation is made; it is (if I may so say) the welcome of God to the captain and leader of mankind to glory. And, if I may dare to use the expression, we find, as it were, a passion of joy in the great God of our salvation, at seeing the means of his grace take effect in restoring mankind to that forfeited happiness, from which by transgression he had fallen; in reconciling him to himself; in seeing that a passage is now opened into his own eternal happinefs to man, by the taking the manhood into God, as the Godhead had before on earth rendered one man a worthy and fufficient atonement for all men. His grace is now perfected; our nature is feated in heaven; and the glory which Chrift had with the Father before the foundations of the world were laid, is now afcribed to him; the Father has glorified him with his own felf; he is, by the majefty moft high, declared to be one with him, declared to be God, whofe throne endureth for ever, and whofe years fhall never fail; the man was feen to afcend; but the God is acknowledged by him to whom alone the God is comprehenfible, " who only knoweth who the Son is." I do not fee how it is poffible to avoid, or evade, the ftrength of this proof, refulting from the application of thefe words of David to the Son, of whofe Godhead they are as exprefs a declaration as words can convey. God himfelf acknowledges and declares the fecond perfon in himfelf; and this in exact conformity with our Lord's own words, upon feeing Judas go out with a refolution to betray him; his hour he knew was now come, and, " therefore, when he (Judas) was gone out, Jefus faid, now is the Son of man glorified, and God is glorified in him. If God be glorified in him, God fhall alfo glorify him in himfelf, and fhall ftraightway glorify him," John xiii. 31, 32. And as fuch a doxology, according to this prediction, comes from God himfelf to Chrift, I own that to me it appears an impious perverfenefs to withhold prayer, an impious ingratitude to withhold our praife and thankfgiving from him. When we fee our own falvation the fource of fuch joy in heaven; when we fee the infinitely great " maker of all things that are in heaven, and that are in the earth," take fuch an intereft in the happinefs of us his very little creatures, we have an additional encouragement to approach the throne of his

mercy

mercy with thanfgiving for our redemption; for which he not only fuffered, but rejoiced in his fufferings, and efteemed them glory for our fake. " Of Jefus Chrift, the fame yefterday, and to day, and for ever," Heb. xiii. 8. Let us then acknowledge, that " of the Jews, as concerning the flefh, Chrift came, but that he is over all, God bleffed for ever, Amen." Rom. ix. 5.——

I now come to the fourth kind of teftimony borne to the divinity of our Lord and Saviour Jefus Chrift, that which he has afforded himfelf, by the revelation made to St. John, after his afcenfion, and in which he has, in his glorified ftate, declared his own nature. I do not mean to difcufs the prophecy contained in the apocalypfe, but to produce fuch evidence as the book affords to my point only; fuch other proofs as are referable to this head, I have noted, as they have occurred in the former parts of this enquiry.

CIX.

Jefus Chrift reveals himfelf to St. John in the following words: " thefe things faith the firft and the laft, which was dead, and is alive," Rev. ii. 8. God fays to Ifaiah, " I am the firft, and I am the laft, and befides me there is no God," If. xliv. 6. Hence we fee, that befides the firft and the laft, there is no God: but Jefus Chrift fays, " I am the firft, and I am the laft;" the conclufion is, that befides Jefus Chrift, one with the Father, there is no God, and he is the " alpha and omega, the beginning and the ending, which is, and which was, and which is to come, the Almighty," Rev. i. 8, and xxii. 13.

CX.

Jefus Chrift fays, " I am he that fearcheth the reins and hearts: and I will give unto every one of you according to your works," Rev. ii. 23. God fays to Jeremiah,

remiah, "I the Lord search the heart, I try the reins, even to give every man according to his ways, and according to the fruit of his doings," Jer. xvii. 10. Here God has declared himself the searcher of hearts. Is there any other searcher of hearts? None. But Jesus Christ declares that he is he that searcheth the hearts: as there is none other that searcheth, and that Jesus Christ has declared that he searcheth, Jesus Christ is none other than God Almighty, one with the Father; "the Lord of hosts, that judgeth righteously, and trieth the reins and the heart," Jer. xi. 20; "the Lord of hosts, that trieth the righteous, and seeth the reins and the heart," Jer. xx. 12. And the unity of the Godhead of the Lord, the King of Israel, and his Redeemer the Lord of hosts, is thus asserted by the one first and last; "Thus saith the Lord the King of Israel, and his Redeemer, the Lord of hosts, I am the first, and I am the last, and besides me there is no God," Isa. xliv. 6.

CXI.

"I am alpha and omega, the beginning and the ending, saith the Lord, which is, and which was, and which is to come, the Almighty," Rev. i. 8. To the proof already given, that these words are spoken by Jesus Christ, I will add this, that the declaration follows a description of the coming of the Lord, exactly corresponding to that given by our Saviour of the coming of the Son of man; "then shall all the tribes of the earth mourn, and they shall see the Son of man coming in the clouds of heaven, with power and great glory," Matth. xxiv 30. "Behold, he cometh with clouds; and every eye shall see him, and they also which pierced him: and all kindreds of the earth shall wail because of him," Rev. i. 7. He then proceeds to declare himself to be the Lord, which is, and which was,

was, and which is to come: to Jesus Christ the Lord, then, the four beasts " rest not day and night, saying, holy, holy, holy, Lord God Almighty, which was, and is, and is to come," Rev. iv. 8.

CXII.

"I am he that liveth, and was dead; and behold, I am alive for evermore. Amen." Rev. i. 18. That these words are spoken by Jesus Christ, cannot admit of a doubt. "And when those beasts give glory, and honour, and thanks to him who sat on the throne, who liveth for ever and ever, the four and twenty elders fall down before him that sat on the throne, and worship him that liveth for ever and ever, and cast their crowns before the throne, saying, thou art worthy, O Lord, to receive glory, and honour, and power: for thou hast created all things, and for thy pleasure they are, and were created," Rev. iv. 9, 10, 11. Such is the honour ascribed in heaven to him who is " alive for evermore. Amen." And shall we, who are a part of his creation, " by whom are all things, and we by him," alone withdraw ourselves from the worship of the " one Lord, Jesus Christ," " by whom all things consist?" And shall we not rather join our voice to the voices in heaven, and say, " hallowed be thy name. Thy will be done in earth, as it is in heaven?" Matth. vi. 9, 10; see also 1 Cor. viii. 6, and Col. i. 17.

CXIII.

The following words of our Saviour to St. John, to be delivered by him to the church of Philadelphia, warrant our preferring that petition of the Lord's prayer to him, " lead us not into temptation, but deliver us from evil," Matth vi. 13. " I will also keep thee from the hour of temptation, which shall come upon all the world, to try them that dwell upon the earth," Rev. iii. 10.

"As

CXIV.

"As many as I love, I rebuke and chaften," says Jefus Chrift to St. John, Rev. iii. 19. "Behold, happy is the man whom God correcteth," Job v. 17. "For whom the Lord loveth he chafteneth, and fcourgeth every fon whom he receiveth. If ye endure chaftening, God dealeth with you as with fons: for what fon is he whom the Father chafteneth not?" Heb. xii. 6, 7.

CXV.

"Grace be unto you, and peace from him which is, and which was, and which is to come; and from the feven fpirits which are before his throne; and from Jefus Chrift, who is the faithful witnefs, and the firft-begotten of the dead, and the Prince of the kings of the earth: unto him that loved us, and wafhed us from our fins in his own blood, and hath made us kings and priefts unto God and his Father; to him be glory and dominion for ever and ever. Amen." Rev. i. 4, 5, 6. If it be allowed that there is an errour in the manufcript whence our tranflation of the firft chapter and fifth verfe of the apocalypfe was taken, there is but very little loft by the conceffion; for fubftituting the words τῷ αγαπήσαντος καὶ λύσαντος inftead of the accepted reading τῷ αγαπήσαντι καὶ λύσαντι, and then adopting Mr. Lindfey's own tranflation, I do not fee that the doxology contained in the paffage, is by any means turned away from its proper object, Jefus Chrift; for, taking the whole together, it runs thus, "grace be unto you, and peace from him which is, and which was, and which is to come; and from the feven fpirits which are before his throne; and from Jefus Chrift, who is the faithful witnefs, and the firft-begotten of the dead, and the Prince of the kings of the earth, *who hath* loved us, and wafhed us from our fins, in his own blood, and hath made us kings and priefts unto God and his Father; to him be glory and dominion for ever and ever. Amen." Rev. i. 5, 6. It is difficult to imagine how any man should conceive "him" to be referable to any preceding term in the sentence, besides that to which the multitude of epithets is referred; and that this is Jesus Christ, does not admit of a doubt. This I say even upon a supposition that Mr. Lindsey has taken the text as it was actually written; but I will now withdraw that concession, upon an assurance that the commonly accepted reading is supported by at least equal authority as that of Dr. Mill, and that the translators of our Bible have thought it the preferable one. But if I were altogether to relinquish this text, which will however admit of no other sense than that I have ascribed to it, it would avail this gentleman but very little, for the 13th verse of the 5th chapter affords a doxology which I will not resign so easily as he may expect. "Blessing and honour, and glory, and power be unto him that sitteth upon the throne, and unto the Lamb for ever and ever," Rev. v. 13. Is this doubtful? No, nor a doubt pretended: but Jesus Christ is in sight, and therefore, says Mr. Lindsey, an object of worship. God only, says this gentleman in another part of his book, is the proper object of worship; but here Jesus Christ in sight is a proper object of worship. I will draw the necessary conclusion; therefore Jesus Christ in sight is God. And, "am I a God at hand, saith the Lord, and not a God afar off?" Jer. xxiii. 23. Is this to be acceded to? If Jesus Christ be a creature, he is not an object of worship; and my turning my eye upon him can never confer infinity and eternity on that which was before local and temporary; but Mr. Lindsey persisting in it that he is a creature, has given the beholders a power of *looking him* into the one Creator. This is too absurd to dwell on. I shall only ask, if Jesus Christ has not any right to our adoration, how he is authorized

authorized to demand it on fight? and, if he be in any cafe entitled to our adoration, " the incommunicable honour and prerogative of God alone *," and that therefore he be God, whether it be not the depth of ftupidity, as well as impiety, to deny that our Lord and Saviour Jefus Chrift is one with the Father, God? " Grow in grace, and in the knowledge of the Lord and Saviour Jefus Chrift: to him be glory both now and for ever. Amen." fays St. Peter; and one fuch declaration, that glory is his for ever and ever, is equal to a thoufand; and, were every other one to be given up, this would remain a fufficient eftablifhment of the eternal glory of Jefus Chrift; but, when we find glory once fo afcribed, I do not fee any reafon for doubting fuch doxologies as repeat the praifes of our Lord and Saviour; for, one eftablifhing the right, it is but reafonable to believe, that men, who faw with the fame enlightened underftanding as Peter did, fhould equally afcribe to him the glory which they muft have equally feen to be his due.

CXVI.

" The kings of the earth, &c. hid themfelves in the dens, and in the rocks of the mountains; and faid to the mountains and rocks, fall on us, and hide us from the face of him that fitteth on the throne, and from the wrath of the Lamb: for the great day of his wrath is come; and who fhall be able to ftand?" Rev. vi. 15, 16. This fpeaks for itfelf. There is in context with it a remarkable paffage, by which Jefus Chrift, coming to judgement, acts exactly in correfpondence with thofe words which are addreffed to him by the Father upon his afcenfion into heaven; " The heavens fhall perifh, and wax old as doth a garment, and as a vefture fhalt thou fold them up," Heb. i. 12. " And the ftars of heaven fell unto

---

* Apology, p. 137.

unto the earth, even as a fig-tree casteth her untimely figs when she is shaken of a mighty wind: and the heaven departed as a scrowl when it is rolled together," Rev. vi. 13, 14.

CXVII.

" And I saw another angel fly in the midst of heaven, having the everlasting gospel to preach unto them that dwell on the earth, and to every nation, and kindred, and tongue, and people, saying with a loud voice, Fear God, and give glory to him, for the hour of his judgement is come: and worship him that made heaven and earth, and the sea, and the fountains of waters," Rev. xiv, 6, 7. Paul, who had often termed himself " a prisoner of Jesus Christ," Philemon 9. and who tells the Romans, " I am not ashamed of the gospel of Christ," Rom. i. 16. says to Timothy, " Be not thou therefore ashamed of the testimony of our Lord, nor of me his prisoner," 2 Tim. i. 8; and also says to the Philippians, that though some do preach Christ out of contention, and some of love; yet, being " set for the defence of the gospel; what then? Notwithstanding every way, whether in pretence, or in truth, Christ is preached; and I therein do rejoice; yea, and will rejoice," Phil i. 17, 18. These passages precisely ascertain the meaning of the words *preaching the gospel*, and shew them to be of the same import as *preaching Christ*, or *bearing the testimony of Christ*. Now, in the text before us, we see an angel flying in the midst of heaven *to preach the everlasting gospel*. And, as we well know that it is " the Lord Jesus Christ, who shall judge the quick and the dead at his appearing, and his kingdom," 2 Tim. iv. 1. what does this cœlestial harbinger of our Judge proclaim? " Fear God and give glory to him, for the hour of his judgement is come." " We have one Lord Jesus Christ, by whom are all things, and we by him," 1 Cor. viii. 6.

" All things were created by him, and for him, and he is before all things, and by him all things confift," Col. i. 16, 17. But the angel proceeds, " worfhip him that made heaven and earth, and the fea, and the fountains of waters." A new and heavenly preacher of the gofpel, that is, of Chrift, here directly afcribes to our Judge the name and attributes of God: let us then, upon the teftimony of this herald, " fear and give glory to the Lord Jefus Chrift," the final preacher of whofe gofpel has declared him to be one with the Father, God.

CXVIII.

" The lamb fhall overcome them: for he is the Lord of Lords, and King of kings," Rev. xvii. 14. " The King of kings, and Lord of lords" appears again in the 19th chapter and 16th verfe, mounted upon a white horfe, and followed by the armies in heaven; he is affailed by the beaft, and the kings of the earth, and their armies; but the beaft is taken, and his armies are overcome; and " the remnant were flain with the fword of him that fat upon the horfe; and all the fowls were filled with their flefh," Rev. xix. 21. In the 17th verfe of this chapter, before the war, in which the King of kings and Lord of Lords overcame and flew the beaft, and the armies, and the kings, " an angel cried with a loud voice, faying to all the fowls that fly in the midft of heaven, come and gather yourfelves together unto the fupper of the great God; that ye may eat the flefh of kings, and the flefh of captains, and the flefh of mighty men, and the flefh of horfes, and of them that fit on them, and the flefh of all men, both free and bond, both fmall and great," Rev. xix. 17, 18. The war immediately enfues; and he that fat upon the horfe, having overcome and flain thofe who came againft him, " filled all fowls with their flefh;" fo that we find that fupper given to them by the King
of

of kings, and Lord of lords, to which they are invited by an angel as to the fupper of the great God. Him then we muft believe to be the great God, who fupplied it to them who were called to come to it: but Jefus Chrift fupplied it to them; Jefus Chrift is therefore one with the Father, that great God.

CXIX.

" His name (that fat upon the horfe) is called the Word of God," Rev. xix. 13. As there is not the leaft doubt that it is Jefus Chrift who fat upon the horfe, we may venture to explain the beginning of the firft chapter of St. John's gofpel by this declaration, that " his name is called the Word of God;" and whatfoever is there fpoken of the Word of God, muft be allowed to have been faid of him who fat upon the horfe, even Jefus Chrift, " the victorious Lamb, the King of kings, and Lord of lords;" and there it is exprefsly declared that " the Word was God," John i. 1; that " the Word was made flefh, and dwelt among us, and we beheld his glory," John i. 14; that " the fame (Word) was in the beginning with God, and that by him, who was in the world, and who came unto his own, the world was made," John i. 2, 10, 11. And as " in the beginning God created the heaven and the earth," Gen. i. 1. " that all things were made by him (the Word); and without him was not any thing made that was made;" that " in him was life, and the life was the light of men," John i. 3, 4. To the fame purpofe are the following texts: " I am the light of the world," fays our Lord; and " he that followeth me, fhall not walk in darknefs, but fhall have the light of life," John viii. 12. " We declare unto you, that God is light," fays the fame Evangelift, 1 John i. 5. " We have looked upon, and our hands have handled of the Word of life; (for the life was manifefted, and we have feen it, and bear witnefs, and

fhew

shew unto you that eternal life which was with the Father, and was manifested unto us)" 1 John i. 1, 2. "God was manifest in the flesh," says St. Paul, 1 Tim. iii. 16; and that "the Word of God liveth and abideth for ever," is the declaration of St. Peter, 1 Pet. i. 23. "Through faith we understand that the worlds were framed by the Word of God," Heb. xi. 3. "By whom also he made the worlds," Heb. i. 2. Here every attribute of God is ascribed to the Word of God, to have been from the beginning; to have been the original and author of all created things; or, to use St. John's expression, "the beginning of the creation of God," Rev. iii. 14; to have life in him, and to be the light. But it is farther added, that this Word came in the flesh, in which it was manifest, seen, and handled in the world; this therefore is evidently spoken of Jesus Christ. But the Word of God (here seated on a horse, and declared to be Jesus Christ himself under that appellation) is expressly said to be God: Jesus Christ therefore being that Word manifest in the flesh, and that Word being God, Jesus Christ is therefore one with the Father, God. The gospel is the testimony of Christ, "but the Word of the Lord endureth for ever. And this is the Word which by the gospel is preached unto you," 1 Pet. i. 25. John Baptist was certainly the appointed forerunner of our Lord, and it was of him therefore that John gave testimony. "John bare witness of him," John i. 15. It is very remarkable that these words are not once preceded, in St. John's gospel, by the name of Jesus Christ; but that they immediately follow a declaration, that "the Word was made flesh and dwelt among us;" the Word therefore is Jesus Christ, and "the Word was God;" Jesus Christ is therefore one with the Father, God.

As to Mr. Lindſey's laborious diſſertation on the Chaldee Targums and the word Mimra, I have nothing to ſay to it, it does not properly come within my province; one ſhort remark, however, I will make on it. If the word Mimra ſignify both " word and ſelf," as it is certain that Jeſus Chriſt is " the word of God," the word being the ſame as the ſelf of God, Jeſus Chriſt is therefore the " ſelf of God; or, to uſe a more common expreſſion, Jeſus Chriſt is therefore God's own ſelf *. This I infer from Mr. Lindſey's own premiſes; and ſo obvious is the concluſion from the manner in which he has ſupplied them from half a dozen writers, that I wonder how it eſcaped even his own obſervation. I will take occaſion here to ſay, that I wave all advantage that I might derive from the idiomatick plurals of the Hebrew language (if only idiomatick they be) preceding verbs of the ſingular number. They may afford argument to thoſe who, with better knowledge than I am poſſeſſed of, ſhall look for it among them: but I am in purſuit of truth, and not of ſyſtem; I am in purſuit of truth too momentous to be trifled with, and, while I call upon men to yield their aſſent to a propoſition eſſential to the happineſs of their immortal ſouls, God forbid that I ſhould knowingly call one ſophiſm into proof, or offer that as argument to my readers, which did not carry conviction to my own breaſt. At the ſame time that I relinquiſh this argument, it is but for myſelf I do, or can relinquiſh it.

CXX.

When Mr. Lindſey has declared the office of a prieſt to be " to offer up the prayers of others," Apol. p. 127, he ſhould not therefore have precluded prayer to Chriſt, and the practice of making him the object of religious worſhip, unleſs he were very certain that no prieſthood had been appointed to him; but " they ſhall be prieſts of God and of Chriſt," Rev. xx. 6. I have brought this

---

* Glorify thou me with thine own ſelf, John xvii. 5.

this verse to establish the Divinity of our blessed Redeemer, upon a foundation which negligence or blinded prejudice overlooked; but upon which I now demand the acquiescence of the Unitarians in the Godhead of Jesus Christ; we see it allowed an argument if it can be brought, and here it is for them. It is remarkable also that these priests of Christ are those who are partakers of the first resurrection, of whom it is said "that they are blessed and holy:" to those then who are blessed and holy we have reason to conclude, that this mystery of the Godhead of Christ will be more manifestly displayed than to us, who are yet to taste of death. Surely there can be no more uncomfortable conviction than that all the stores of God's wisdom are open to us here, and that in a future state there can be found nothing to add to knowledge; the very expectation of seeing farther into the government of the universe, directed by power and wisdom that are infinite, is a motive to obedience; and a full insight into a mystery which is the means of our own entrance into eternal happiness, is a hope so delightful in itself, that it should make us thankful for such a revelation as intimates it to us, yet withholds the full manifestation for a part of our reward "who wait patiently the coming of the Lord," "for behold, we count them happy which endure," James v.

Jesus Christ was indeed on earth a priest, and accordingly here discharged his sacerdotal office, by offering up the one sufficient sacrifice of himself for all mankind, and "by the blood of sprinkling, that speaketh better things, than that of Abel," which cried from the ground, he has made us a party to the covenant of which he is himself the mediator; and by his blood which does not cry against us, but on the contrary maketh intercession for us, (that body from which it was poured out being our expiation) he has extended salvation

tion to all that believe on him. The writer to the Hebrews has so clearly pointed out to them how their own ritual was a type of Christ's prepared body and blood shed as a sacrifice for the sins of all men; so literally pronounced him our atonement; and so explicitly laid open the nature of his priesthood, and the subsequent mediation of his sufferings in our behalf; that I should ask my reader's forgiveness for so frequently entering into that subject: but when the whole doctrine of atonement by the death of our Saviour is denied, and that he is declared to have died only as a proof that he had lived, I cannot but think it necessary to speak of it, as the occasion offers, in the course of my enquiry; and the rather, when I consider how vastly more probable it is, that even my book shall be read by the Unitarians than the Bible.

CXXI.

"And I saw the dead, small and great, stand before God; and the books were opened: and another book was opened, which is the book of life: and the dead were judged out of those things which were written in the books, according to their works. And the sea gave up the dead which were in it; and death and hell delivered up the dead which were in them: and they were judged every man according to their works. And death and hell were cast into the lake of fire; this is the second death. And whosoever was not found written in the book of life, was cast into the lake of fire," Rev. xx. 12, 13, 14, 15. I need not repeat the numerous passages in which it is set forth, that "the Son of man shall come in his glory, and all the holy angels with him, then shall he sit upon the throne of his glory. And before him shall be gathered all nations; and he shall separate them one from another," Matth. xxv. 31, 32. "Then shall he (the Son of man) reward every man according to his works," Matth. xvi. 27; and that

that "things which offend, and them that do iniquity; he (the Son of man) shall cast into a furnace of fire; there shall be wailing and gnashing of teeth," Mat. xiii. 41, 42. Here every act of our Saviour's office as the judge of the world, who has declared his own determination to call all flesh to account, is given to God, before whom St. John sees the dead, small and great, stand, and all nations gathered to receive judgement, "every man according to his works," and by whom "they that do iniquity" "are cast into a furnace of fire." There can be no truth in such a vision, if it be not that the very same thing is presented to the view of St. John, which is foretold by our Saviour; and that he who declared that he would judge, even Jesus Christ, has, according to his declaration, proceeded to judge, and to testify himself to be one with the Father, God. The book of life is said, in another place, to be "the Lamb's book of life," Rev. xxi. 27. It is declared that, "the Father judgeth no man, but hath committed all judgement unto the Son," John v. 22. And a reason is given for this appointment, "(the Father) hath given him (the Son) authority to execute judgement also, because he is the Son of man." As the Son of man only he could receive an appointment, and to him who, as a Son of man, has called us brethren, and can have a feeling of our infirmities, it is most mercifully made. All men are here assembled to judgement before the great God; but "the Father judgeth no man;" before the Son then are they assembled: but they are before God; the Son therefore is one with the Father, God.

CXXII.

"The Lamb which is in the midst of the throne, shall feed them, and shall lead them unto living fountains of waters," Rev. vii. 17. Jesus said to John, "I am alpha and omega, the beginning and the end,

the

the firſt and the laſt," Rev. xxii. 13. " And he (that fat upon the throne) faid unto me it is done. I am alpha and omega, the beginning and the end: I will give unto him that is athirſt, of the fountain of the water of life freely. He that overcometh, ſhall inherit all things, and I will be his God, and he ſhall be my Son," Rev. xxi. 6, 7. Here every attribute of him who has called us, if we ſhall prove victorious, his fons, is equally the Son's as the Father's; he is enthroned; he leads to the living fountains of water, and he is the one firſt and laſt; therefore he is with the Father, one God. What an invitation do the Unitarians decline!

CXXIII.

In the holy Jeruſalem, " I faw no temple therein: for the Lord God Almighty and the Lamb, are the temple of it. And the city had no need of the fun, neither of the moon to ſhine in it: for the glory of God did lighten it, and the Lamb is the light thereof," Rev. xxi. 22, 23. " For the Lord God giveth them light," Rev. xxii. 5. " The throne of God and of the Lamb ſhall be in it; and his ſervants ſhall ſerve him, and they ſhall fee his face; and his name ſhall be in their foreheads," Rev. xxii. 3, 4. Here God and the Lamb are but one temple, ſhed one light, which is the one incommunicable glory of God, and poſſeſs one throne, preſent one face to the view of *his* ſervants, and *his* ſervants ſerve *him*, that is God and the Lamb, ſpoken of in the ſingular number as but one God. To the trinal unity of God, then I am not afraid to aſcribe the excellent doxology of Dr. Tucker, who, when he uſed it, remembered that there *is* but one God, and that there *are* three perſons; " to *him* therefore, Father, Son, and Holy Ghoſt, let theſe miracles of divine mercy be ever aſcribed; and to *them* be glory, praiſe, majeſty, and dominion, both now and for evermore."
" The perſonal pronoun *him*," ſays Mr. Lindſey, "evidently

dently points to one person, one individual intelligent agent *;" so that as God and the Lamb are, in the passage before us, pointed to by this same personal pronoun *him*, let God and the Lamb, even Jesus Christ, be acknowledged to be one individual intelligent agent, one God blessed for ever. " I will write upon him my new name," says our Saviour, Rev. iii. 12. " A Lamb stood on the mount Sion, and with him an hundred forty and four thousand, having his Father's name written in their foreheads," Rev. xiv. 1. Conformable to the superscription of the name of the Father, and the new name of the Son, our Lord says, " I will write upon him the name of my God," Rev. iii. 12.

CXXIV.

The angel who spoke to John, and signified to him those things which he was sent by Jesus Christ to reveal to his servant John, Rev. i. 1. testifies as follows, " the Lord God of the holy prophets sent his angel to shew unto his servants the things which must shortly be done," Rev. xxii. 6. And our Saviour immediately after, speaking of this very angel, which has said that he was sent by, and has called himself the angel of the Lord, declares, " I Jesus have sent mine angel to testify unto you, these things in the churches," Rev. xxii. 16. Jesus Christ, who sent his angel, which was sent by the Lord God, is therefore one with the Father, the Lord God.

CXXV.

Such farther evidence as I mean to produce from the holy scriptures, to prove the Godhead of our gracious Redeemer, I shall reserve till I come to consider and confute the arguments by which Mr. Lindsey has endeavoured to depose him from the throne of his glory: and as I closed the apostolical testimony of our Saviour's divinity, by shewing that the appointed witnesses of Jesus

---

* Apology, p. 199.

fus Chrift had brought God himfelf to fpeak the fact, and to pronounce that he who had been flain, and had taken that body, by the blood of which we are cleanfed, into heaven, there for ever to remain, is one with himfelf, " God Almighty, whofe throne endureth for ever and ever, and the fceptre of whofe kingdom is a fceptre of righteoufnefs;" fo I fhall conclude this chapter by bringing together thofe doxologies with which all things both in heaven and in earth have glorified the Son of man; and if by thefe alfo, the kingdom, and the power, and the glory be afcribed to him, who, of ranfomed mankind, admitted to fellowfhip with him, can then refufe to " magnify the name of the Lord Jefus," and to unite his voice with " ten thoufand times ten thoufand, and thoufands of thoufands of angels, who reft not day and night, faying, holy, holy, holy, Lord God Almighty, which was, and which is, and which is to come," " worthy art thou, O Lord, to receive glory, and honour, and power *," " worthy is the Lamb that was flain to receive power, and riches, and wifdom, and ftrength, and honour, and glory, and bleffing †," " and with every creature which is in heaven and in earth, and under the earth, and fuch as are in the fea, and all that are in them, faying, Bleffing, and honour, and glory, and power, be unto him that fitteth on the throne, and unto the Lamb for ever and ever, Amen ‡." " Salvation to our God which fitteth on the throne, and unto the Lamb §," " which is in the midft of the throne ‖ ?" for fuch is the fong of angels, and of every creature " created by him, and for him **; fuch are the grateful hymns of thofe who are redeemed by the blood of the " flaughtered Lamb ††," which have come out of great tribulation, and have wafhed their robes, and made them white in the blood
of

* Rev. iv. 8, 11. † Rev. v. 12. ‡ Rev. v. 13.
§ Rev. vii. 10. ‖ Rev. vii. 17. ** Coloff. i. 16. †† If. liii. 7.

of the Lamb," and who " therefore are before the throne of God, and serve him night and day in his temple," " a great multitude, which no man could number, of all nations, and kindreds, and people, and tongues standing before the throne, and before the Lamb clothed with white robes *". To these the glorious company of the apostles have added their praise, saying " to the King of kings, and Lord of lords †," " who only hath immortality, dwelling in the light which no man can approach unto, whom no man hath seen, nor can see, be honour and power everlasting. Amen ‡." " To our Lord and Saviour Jesus Christ be glory both now and for ever. Amen § :" " to whom be praise and dominion both now and for ever. Amen ‖." " Wherefore seeing we also are compassed about with so great a cloud of witnesses, let us lay aside every weight, and the sin which doth so easily beset us, and let us run with patience the race that is set before us, looking unto Jesus, the author and finisher of our faith, who, for the joy that was set before him, endured the cross, despising the shame **," which was undergone for our redemption; and let us " with every tongue confess that Jesus Christ is Lord, with every knee, of things in heaven, and things in earth, and things under the earth, bow our knee also at the name of Jesus ††;" and knowing that the same Lord over all is rich unto all that call upon him, let us also call upon the name of the Lord, and be saved; and to him that sitteth on the throne, and the Lamb, one God, the Father and the Son, with the whole host of heaven and earth, and all created beings, join in ascribing " blessing and honour, and glory, and power. Amen."

CHAP.

* Rev. vii. 9, 14, 15. † Rev. xvii. 14. ‡ 1 Tim. vi. 15, 16.
§ 2 Pet. iii. 18. ‖ 1 Pet. iv. 11. ** Heb. xii. 1. †† Phil. ii. 10.

CHAP. IV.

Controverted Evidence of our Saviour's Divinity established.—Objections answered.—The Divinity of the Holy Ghost proved from the Scriptures.

"Religious worship," says Mr. Lindsey, "is the incommunicable honour and prerogative of God alone," Apology, p. 137. Among the multitudinous proofs which I have already given of our Lord's divinity, I have produced many instances of prayer, of praise, and thanksgiving, preferred to him both in earth and in heaven; by angels and those who have already become partakers of the benefits of his passion in heaven; and in earth, by men filled with the Comforter, the holy spirit of truth, to whom " the testimony of Jesus" * was given. These I look upon to be acts of religious worship; but this honour and prerogative of God alone is ascribed to Jesus Christ; it is incommunicable, and must therefore perfectly and essentially distinguish the possessour; but Jesus Christ is the possessour; Jesus Christ is therefore one with the Father, that God alone whose incommunicable honour and prerogative it is to be the object of our religious worship and adoration.

Mr. Lindsey is so exceedingly anxious to emancipate himself from the service of Jesus Christ, whose servant and Prisoner Paul declares it is his joy and glory to be; he bends so reluctantly under the easy yoke, the light burden of the gospel; he so boisterously dashes about the bonds of peace, and so fretfully endeavours to cast the cords from him; and with such a foaming hydrophobia flies from " the fountains of living waters," that he has really become a very melancholy spectacle, and therefore

* Rev. xix. 10.

fore I feel it a duty incumbent upon me to force, as strongly as I can, this conviction upon him, that if he will drink of these waters, they will refresh him, and he shall not thirst again; that if he return to Christ, the great shepherd and bishop of our souls, however sorrowful and heavily laden he may be, he shall find rest to his soul; that if he knock, Christ shall open; and, that " if he ask any thing according to his will, the Son of God will hear him, and he shall have the petition that he desired of him *," Let me therefore now, presuming that Christ at hand is not different from Christ afar off; and that no merits can put any created being into possession of the incommunicable prerogatives of God, or render inferior natures worthy of the honour which belongs to God alone, recapitulate, and once again present him with an instance of each; of prayer, by that of Stephen, " Lord Jesus receive my spirit;" " Lord, lay not this sin to their charge." Of praise, by that in the Revelation, " Blessing, and honour, and glory, and power, be unto him that sitteth upon the throne, and unto the Lamb for ever and ever;" " salvation to our God which sitteth upon the throne, and unto the Lamb;" and of thanksgiving, by that of St. Paul, " I thank Christ Jesus our Lord, for that he counted me faithful, putting me into the ministry."

There is yet another species of religious worship, which I have intentionally omitted to take notice of in its course; it is Benediction; and my reason for deferring to observe upon it, is, that it demanded a separate consideration, on account of Mr. Lindsey's doctrine concerning it. He denies benediction to be any evidence at all; and, till I had established its competency, it is therefore easy to see I should have produced it out of its place before. Mr. Lindsey's assertion, Apology, p. 131,

* 1 John v. 14.

p. 131, concerning such passages as 1 Cor. i. 3. * is, "that they are only pious wishes, not prayers." Admitting for a moment only this distinction between prayers and pious wishes, and the conclusion thence inferred, I believe these same pious wishes will be found to be very impious wishes, and a wish that God should have an assistant in conferring blessings on mankind, be acknowledged rather derogatory from the all-sufficiency of his power: but I do not see how any inference can be drawn from a wish different from that which follows from a prayer, they both equally acknowledge the power which they desire to have put into exertion; and if the power be acknowledged by a declaration of it to a third person, entrusted with an assurance that I wish it to be exerted, I cannot imagine why the possessor of it should not be addressed and let into the secret also, he may not else know my mind, and the power may not therefore be quite so beneficially exerted as I could piously wish. Is it that a Being, whose power is to be acknowledged adequate to the gift of blessings, is unintelligent and unable to hear our prayers? or are we not to address him, because he is unable to grant them? If the latter, we reject our own conclusion, and waste our wishes; and I believe the inconsistency of the former supposition is too apparent to require a comment. The same consequence is inferred, I say, by our wishes as by our prayers, and if the power of God is acknowledged by prayer to be in Jesus Christ, by our wishes also that he would exert that power, it is equally acknowledged; so that even this (I think disingenuous) evasion will not invalidate the force of that testimony which is afforded to this dreaded position, that Jesus Christ is one with the Father, God, by the benedictions of the apostles, the appointed witnesses of our Lord.

Z Of

* "Grace be unto you, and peace from God our Father, and from the Lord Jesus Christ."

Of thefe benedictions I need only produce one from St. Paul, becaufe it comprehends in it the fubftance of all the reft, which he has beftowed upon his hearers, " Grace, mercy, and peace from God the Father, and the Lord Jefus Chrift our Saviour," Titus i. 4. From God alone can the bleffings of grace, mercy, and peace proceed; but I will fhew that they have all proceeded from Jefus Chrift; for St. Paul himfelf, who knew the ability of him whom he thus invoked, and that " he is able to fuccour," fays, " I thank Jefus Chrift our Lord, who hath enabled me, for that he counted me faithful, putting me into the miniftry; who was before a blafphemer, and a perfecutor, and injurious. But I obtained *mercy*, becaufe I did it ignorantly in unbelief: and *the grace of our Lord* was exceeding abundant," 1 Tim. i. 12, 13, 14. Here we find grace and mercy beftowed by the fearcher of hearts, who, thro' the veil of blafphemy and perfecution, diftinguifhed that faith which enabled Paul to be put into the miniftry by the Lord Jefus Chrift. We do not find this accurate apoftle ever fay grace, mercy, and peace from Apollos or Cephas; he knew that they, on whom he beftowed his bleffing, were not of Apollos nor of Cephas, who were only fellow-labourers with himfelf; and that, had he been to the end of time calling down grace and mercy from them, they had it not to impart; from Chrift, that God who gave the encreafe, when they watered what he himfelf planted, he called for bleffings; from God alone, to whom belong mercies, it was fit that he fhould call them down, becaufe that he alone could anfwer and confer them. " My peace I give you," fays Jefus Chrift, " not as the world giveth give I," John xiv. 27. If grace, mercy, and peace then be in the power of our gracious and merciful Redeemer to beftow, every benediction of the apoftle of the gofpel of peace is to be confidered as a fhort prayer preferred

ferred to him; and benedictions being thus considered as a part of religious worship, it is easy to see the conclusion, that Jesus Christ, to whom it is offered, is one with the Father, that God, whose incommunicable prerogative and honour religious worship is. " Let us therefore, beloved," " being called unto the grace of Christ," Gal i. 6. " not separate ourselves, having not the spirit, but building up ourselves on our most holy faith, praying in the Holy Ghost, keep ourselves in the love of God, looking for the mercy of our Lord Jesus Christ unto eternal life," Jude 19, 20, 21; and " believe that through the grace of our Lord Jesus Christ we shall be saved," Acts xv. 11.

But it has been said that the interposal of the conjunctive *and*, enumerates distinct natures between the Father *and* Son; and that grace, mercy, and peace may proceed from, or glory, honour, and dominion be ascribed to one part of the subject, without affecting the other. Not to insist on the absurdity of introducing a name, to say nothing about it, in any proposition; on other grounds also, the distinction between God *and* Lord, how well soever it may have been supported by an epigram *, seems to me not only weak but insincere. " From God the Father *and* our Lord Jesus Christ," are words that occur perpetually in St. Paul's epistles; and I think that candour will allow that " the Father, and our Lord Jesus Christ," are, in such passages, put in apposition to " God," and mark a distinction of persons indeed, but undoubtedly an unity, an identity of Godhead; for, were that copulative *and* to be taken as a mark of any other distinction, and insisted on as introductory of a second power, however subordinate it may be to the Father, and acting under him; the consequences of such a manner of understanding it might prove very fatal to the cause it is brought to support; for the same copulative is used by St. James,

Apology, p. 6.

in a manner that would deſtroy the Godhead of the Father himſelf; for by it the word " Father" is ſet apart from God. He ſays, " true religion, and undefiled before God *and* the " Father," where the copulative is uſed exactly in the ſame manner as by St. Paul: If it be admitted then that the perſonal terms ſtand in appoſition to the general name of " God," all is at once accounted for; whereas, on the other hand, if it be inſiſted upon, that, in the one caſe, the conjunctive enumerates diſtinct natures, a conſequence will neceſſarily follow, which even an Unitarian would ſtart at drawing from it. St. James does not ſtand alone in this manner of diſtinguiſhing between God *and* the Father; St. Paul has afforded many inſtances of a like nature, " giving thanks to God and the Father," Col. iii. 17. " Now, God himſelf, and our Father, and our Lord Jeſus Chriſt, direct our way unto you," 1 Theſſ. iii. 11. " In the ſight of God and the Father," 1 Theſſ. i. 3. How uncandidly then does even this honeſt and diſintereſted man deal by himſelf, in making uſe of, or yielding his aſſent to ſuch weak ſophiſms; but I am ſorry to ſay that every thing ſeems an argument in his eyes, that only appears to make againſt " the acknowledgment of the myſtery of God, and of the Father, and of Chriſt," Col. ii. 2. " Now, unto God and our Father, be glory for ever and ever. Amen." Phil. iv. 20*.

In

* If it be inſiſted upon, that the following words, " Peace from God our Father, and the Lord Jeſus Chriſt," have any other meaning than that the Father and the Lord Jeſus Chriſt are the one God, by which name the three perſons of the Trinity is comprehended, I ſhall inſiſt upon the diſtinction between " God and the Father" here, and maintain that they have diſtinct meanings alſo, and that the Father is therefore not intended by the word God in this doxology.—But in that caſe the word God is without any meaning at all. To this I anſwer, that it has a meaning, and ſignifies the Son, our Lord Jeſus Chriſt, to whom, as well as to the Father, glory is aſcribed. I give Mr. Lindſey his choice how he will interpret; for, let him take it either way, the divinity of our Lord follows.

In the Jewish ritual, the necessity of repeating the sacrifice is made use of as a proof of the insufficiency of any single victim, to establish those who came to the altar: for, had any one offering been answerable to so great an end, the daily sacrifice had been taken away, that work for which it had been appointed being finished. Just such is the case with Mr. Lindsey's arguments; the sacrifice of to-day manifested the weakness of the sacrifice of yesterday; and the offering now made upon the altar of sophistry, manifests the insufficiency of that which has preceded it, to establish the votary, that doctrine, of which he stands the priest; it acknowledges the weakness of the priesthood, and that it is not faultless; like that of the Jews, therefore, I entertain a chearful hope that the whole shall at length vanish away. This gentleman, accordingly, very justly considering all that he has already urged as no argument at all, proceeds to insinuate, rather than say, (for he has not put it into so many words) that the junction of the name of Christ, in doxologies and benedictions, with the name of God, which is invoked or glorified in them, does not afford any proof that Jesus Christ is God, because that to their names sometimes other names also are joined. Had the fact been as here stated, I should have allowed it some weight, and therefore looking on it as material, I did literally " search the scriptures," and throughout could find but that one instance in which Mr. Lindsey has exemplified the rule. It is the benediction of St. John in the first chapter and fourth verse of the Revelation, " Grace be unto you, and peace from him which was, and which is, and which is to come, and from the seven spirits, which are before his throne; and from Jesus Christ," Rev. i. 4, 5. And here it must be granted, that unless the seven spirits be God also, the junction of the name of Jesus Christ is not a proof that he is God; but I

may

may possibly surprize Mr. Lindsey by an assurance that these seven spirits also are God; and this is a position easily explained to any man who remembers that " Noah found grace in the eyes of the Lord *;" " The seven spirits are the eyes of the Lamb †;" and grace, in the eyes of the Lamb, is surely a blessing devoutly to be implored, when we consider who that Lamb is, even our Lord Jesus Christ himself, " the Lord of Lords;" and when we reflect on the advantages that accrued to Noah from his having found favour in his eyes before. According to Mr. Lindsey's mode of arguing, we might as well declare that St. Paul meant to distinguish between God and the hands of God, when he says, " It is a fearful thing to fall into the hands of the living God," Heb. x. 31. For, if these terms be not only different appellations of the same Being, I will then allow that to find grace from God, and from the eyes of God, have likewise distinct meanings.

This is the only benediction against which this charge is brought, and I hope I have shewed its inability to affect the Godhead of our blessed Lord; had it been proved I should have allowed it an argument, as it is true that God alone is the fountain whence grace and mercy can flow, and from which alone the apostles, with the spirit of truth, could seek to draw them: but surely if the names of other Beings be found joined with that of God in the performance of actions, of which other Beings are capable, it can never be admitted an argument against the divinity of Christ, whose name is often found joined with God, and invoked to perform actions of which God alone is capable. To Timothy St. Paul says, " I charge thee before God and the Lord Jesus Christ, and the elect angels," 1 Tim. v. 21; and on this passage Mr. Lindsey

* Gen. vi. 8.   † Rev. v. 6.

fey makes the fame obfervation as that above, faying, " the angels being here joined with God and Chrift, fhews that when God is joined with other Beings in the moft folemn manner, no equality can be inferred from fuch a conjunction;" Apology, p. 107. Now I deny that God is in this inftance joined with other Beings in the moft folemn manner, the conferring of a charge upon Timothy was an act of which every Being, upon whom God had beftowed the powers of difcernment, was a proper and competent witnefs before whom he fhould confer it, and therefore, had the apoftle joined man and every intelligent nature to the name of God, and of Jefus Chrift, and the elect angels, it could not in the leaft derogate from the dignity of God, or ever be interpreted as conferring upon them a claim to Godhead. That it fhould argue againft Chrift's divinity, it is neceffary to fhew that it proves too much, and therefore nothing, and that too-much, which it is fuppofed to prove, is, that the angels are God alfo; but does any fuch confequence follow? Certainly not; and therefore this moft folemn conjunction cannot impeach the divinity of our Lord. I do not defire the aid of this verfe in proof of our Saviour's Godhead, there being no greater power called into exercife than that of witneffing a charge to which the witnefs of God will add folemnity indeed, but which is an act that he has given power to inferior natures to perform. " Ye are my witneffes, and God alfo," 1 Theff. ii. 10, fays St. Paul: now which does this moft folemn conjunction of God and the Theffalonians prove, the Theffalonians to be God, or God a Theffalonian? Neither one nor the other; for the conduct of Paul, which he called upon God and them to teftify to be juft and holy, was performed equally before God and them, and they being endowed with adequate faculties, were therefore equally competent witneffes of it. But with refpect to

the

the passage before us, the apostle, about to send forth a preacher of the gospel of Jesus Christ, and recommending perseverance and constancy in "the testimony of our Lord," has, with peculiar accuracy, selected the witnesses to his charge to Timothy, remembering that Jesus Christ, coming to judgement, is to be attended by the holy angels, who are therefore on that day, when all flesh shall be assembled before God, to be witnesses to the manifestation of all the hidden things, and the counsels of all hearts: before them therefore Paul has judiciously chosen to give his charge, as in their presence Timothy well knew he should in the end render an account of his apostleship, and, according to the discharge of his holy function, "have praise of God," or "be made a spectacle to angels," 1 Cor. iv. 9; for Jesus Christ has himself said, "whosoever shall confess me before men, him shall the Son of man also confess before the angels of God," Luke xii. 8. &c.

I have now brought to an end, not indeed the whole of the evidence of our Saviour's divinity afforded by the scriptures, but the whole of that which I intend to produce; for, "if they should be written every one, I suppose that even the world could not contain the books that should be written." Somewhere however I must pause, and therefore consider myself as well warranted to do so now, as I should be after a much more voluminous work: for, to my apprehension, I have already exhibited proof amply sufficient to establish my point, and therefore sincerely hope for the concurrence of my intelligent, and not "unlearned reader," in this conclusion from the whole, namely, that our Lord and Saviour Jesus Christ is with the Father the one "first and last, which was dead and is
alive

alive for evermore, the Almighty, besides whom there is no God," If. xliv. 6. Rev. i. 8, and ii. 8.

I by no means consider every one of the scriptural proofs which I have made use of, as equally able to sustain the argument by itself; for some among them may be of disputable interpretation, but at the same time, being united with such as are incontrovertible, (for many such I am bold to declare there are) they borrow light from them, and strength to support their part of the burden: but let me carry this idea to the utmost, and suppose every assertion that Christ is God, which I have brought from scripture, confuted and shewed to be misapplied, one only excepted, that one to which no answer can be given must remain as compleat a proof of our Saviour's divinity as ten thousand repetitions of it could afford; for all scriptures being written by inspiration, there is no assertion for the truth of which God himself is not responsible, and that which God has once said requires no farther confirmation: but if it be found that he has once declared the Godhead of Jesus Christ, that fact is immutably established; and being established, may well be allowed a matter of sufficient importance to be frequently referred to, nay, (though not necessarily for the confirmation of God's truth, yet for the more extensive information of mankind) to be frequently repeated. If then many texts in scripture, upon incontestible proof of Christ's Godhead from any one, admit of an easy interpretation by referring them to that great truth, why should we hesitate to interpret them by it, instead of wresting them to senses that they will not endure; Procrustes-like, torturing them down to the diminutive bulk of our own imaginations; and thereby rendering the word of God, which alone is true and wise, inexplicable and inconsistent with itself?

It is only the facts which are revealed, and not the manner of relating the facts contained in scripture, that are said to be to the Greeks foolishness; were the relation inconsistent with itself, it would be justly chargeable with folly before God himself, who cannot lye. That folly which St. Paul apprehends the Greeks will lay to the charge of his gospel, is, that it did not coincide with their doctrines. Inconsistency with itself is inconsistency with God, who sees things only as they really are, and consequently not as they are not; whereas inconsistency with my opinion may be wisdom, though to me foolishness; for I may have seen things as they are not, or not have seen them as they really are. What God relates cannot be but true; he cannot relate contradictions; our belief therefore is not required to contradictions. A God crucified in the flesh, in which he had humbly taken the form of a servant, and submitted to feel the infirmities of man, was, to the philosophical religion of the Greeks, foolishness indeed; for, with it, it was altogether inconsistent; but it was nevertheless the wisdom of God, and the power of God unto salvation to every one that believeth. To the Jews, who had long known the one true God, and who had experienced prosperity or adversity as his mighty arm was stretched out to lead or to chastise them, the bleeding body of our Lord suffering death under their own hands, was indeed a stumbling-block; for it was altogether inconsistent with their idea of the Almighty Jehovah. A plurality of persons in the God who had declared his name to be "one," was to the Jews an unsurmountable difficulty; it transcended their faculties; and, as they conceived themselves in possession of a full acquaintance with the incomprehensible nature of their Maker, it was altogether inconsistent with their vain presumptions. To the Jew and to the Unitarian it is alike a stumbling-block, "For unquestionably the Trinity is one of those doctrines that prejudice them most against christianity," Apology, p. 88.

If it be asked, as indeed it is, though not in direct terms, why a fact of such great importance to us to believe is not laid down in so many words, by the witnesses of our Lord, in any of their epistles? it is not difficult to give an answer to such as will consider, that the epistles were written to men already in possession of it; not with a view of introducing them to a new object of faith, but of establishing them in a faith already imparted; for, not to insist upon the circumstance of Paul's having visited all those people to whom he afterwards addressed his epistles, the Romans and the Colossians excepted; nor to weary my less active reader by taking him in pursuit of this vigilant apostle through all the dangers that he encountered for the sake of propagating "the gospel of God our Saviour" in every region; I can prove, from internal evidence, that he only wrote to those who had already obtained grace to be faithful, and who therefore needed not that he should now instruct them in the object of their faith. From Corinth, where he had first known and taught Aquila and Priscilla, he wrote to the Romans; and when he wrote his epistle to them, Aquila and Priscilla were at Rome, for he salutes them there. To these fellow labourers of Paul, Apollos was indebted for his knowledge of the gospel: it is therefore highly probable that so faithful and diligent preachers of the word had not been inactive in bearing the testimony of our Lord to the Romans also; for Paul directs his letter to them in the following terms: "To all that be at Rome, beloved of God, called to be saints, and whose faith is spoken of throughout the whole world," Rom, i. 7, 8. If such was their faith already, to what end should the object of it be pointed out anew; but perseverance and constancy were indeed properly to be recommended, and a stedfast adherence to that which they had known. He had already planted; his object now was to water only; to cultivate and assist the growth of the infant gospel; to cause it to extend its boughs; to gather the faithful under its peaceful shade; and to point out to their observation the blessed fruit with which the branches of this tree of life were laden, saying, in the day that thou eatest hereof thou shalt surely LIVE. To the Corinthians he wrote from Philippi, and addresses himself " to them that are sanctified in Christ Jesus, called to be saints with all that in every place call upon the name of Jesus Christ our Lord, both theirs and ours," 1 Cor. i. 2. Is not this a direct acknowledgment that they were already well informed, and needed not now to be told that he, on whose name they called, the object of their religious worship, even Jesus Christ, their Lord and ours, was one with the Father, God? This he had taught them before when he was present, and had baptized Crispus and Gaius among them; and to what end should he now renew the superfluous information? The Galatians he chides, not indeed for having relinquished the gospel which he had before preached to them, but for having listened to some who had endeavoured to introduce the ceremonies of the law into the practice of christianity. To these therefore he is more explicit, as they were perverted, and that it was necessary to bring them back; and though he does not, in direct terms, declare the Godhead of our Saviour, he uses words very nearly synonimous, words fully sufficient to recall former knowledge, and revive the memory of what he had before communicated; for he says, that " he was not taught the gospel of Christ by man, but by the revelation of Jesus Christ; that he had himself once been as zealous of the law, as they could now be, but that, notwithstanding

he

he had, through Zeal for the traditions of the Jews, perfecuted the church of God: being now called to be a fervant of Jefus Chrift, he faw and preached that juftification came by faith in Chrift, and not by fuch works as are enjoined by the flefhly ordinances of the law," Gal. i. In his epiftle to the Ephefians, to whom he wrote from Rome, after he had been tranfmitted thither by Feftus, and fome years after his laft vifit to them, he fays, " I ceafe not to give thanks for you, after I heard of your faith in the Lord Jefus," Eph i. For the faith of the Philippians alfo he thanks God, and directs his epiftle " to all the faints in Chrift Jefus, which are at Philippi," Philip. i. To them and to the Coloffians he wrote while a prifoner at Rome, and to thefe latter he addreffes himfelf " to the faints and faithful brethren in Chrift, which are at Coloffe," " we give thanks to God fince we heard of your faith in Chrift Jefus," Colof. i. *At Theffalonica Paul was feverely treated by the unbelieving Jews, who, after his departure, not only purfued him to Berea, but continued to perfecute the few of their own countrymen who had believed, and " conforted with Paul and Silas :" to this little " church of the Theffalonians, which is in God the Father, and in the Lord Jefus Chrift;" it is that St. Paul writes, " remembering without ceafing their work of faith, as they had become followers of the Lord, having received the word with much affliction, wherefore they were enfamples to all that believe," 1 Theff. i. 1. Now the word of God which Paul had preached at Theffalonica, and for which he was driven out, was charged againft him by his perfecutors, to have been his " faying, contrary to the decree of Cæfar, that there is another *King*, one Jefus;" fo that we find, that, though to a faithful people, he did not think it neceffary to tell what was the object of their faith, which it is probable Paul was of opinion they

* Acts xvii.   knew

knew themselves; he neverthelefs on his firft vifit let them into an acquaintance with the one meaning of the words *God* and *Chrift*, and that Jefus Chrift is with the Father, the one God, the Lord of hofts, the *King* of glory. Timothy and Titus he calls " his own fons after the faith;" and we well know that they had accompanied, and affifted him in diffufing the light of the gofpel; his epiftles to them contain a charge to " bear the teftimony of our Lord," and a rule for their demeanor as men appointed to fo great a truft. His letter to Philemon, " his dearly beloved fellow labourer," feems little more than of a private nature. The object of this " Jew of Tarfus," in writing to his own countrymen the Hebrews, is to remove their adherence to the law of Mofes, which was the grand obftruction to their belief, and to fhew that it was not, as they conceived, altogether profitable, and therefore not immutably permanent, but that it might be done away; and this even according to their own prophets, to which he therefore refers them. It is not my purpofe here to paraphrafe the epiftles of this great preacher of Jefus Chrift; it anfwers my end to fhew that there is a fufficient reafon for his not having fummed the doctrine, which he conveys in them, into the one fhort propofition, that " Jefus Chrift is one with the Father, God." It feems to be the intention of " James, a fervant of God, and of the Lord Jefus Chrift," to comment on the epiftles of St. Paul, and to ftand up againft the mifreprefentations of the unlearned and unftable, who wrefted fuch things as were hard to be underftood in them to their own deftruction. He did not undertake to point out an object of faith, but to fhew " with what refpect we fhould have the faith of our Lord Jefus Chrift, the Lord of glory;" he prefuppofes the faith of his hearers, and is grafting the morality of a Chriftian upon it; he oppofes himfelf to

fome-

something very like modern methodism, built upon an erroneous acceptation of St. Paul's doctrine of justification by faith alone; shews that the works which that apostle precludes are the ceremonies of the law, as inconsistent with the liberty of the gospel, but that, by works of "pure and undefiled religion, spotless and benevolent *before God*, the faith in our blessed Redeemer is made perfect," he prescribes, not what faith we should entertain, but how we should entertain that of which we were before possessed. Peter writes to the "elect, who, not having seen Christ, yet love him; who believe, and therefore rejoice with unspeakable joy full of glory;" and this "servant of Jesus Christ" addresses his second epistle "to them that have obtained like precious faith with us, through the righteousness of our God and Saviour Jesus Christ," 2 Pet i. 1. For so it stands (not in the French perhaps, but) in the Greek, as the margin of our Bible also acknowledges. St. John writes his first epistle, "not because ye know not the truth, but because ye know it," 1 John ii. 21; and then proceeds to establish his hearers against those who seduce them, by doctrines which hardly differ from the direct proposition; but of which I have already taken notice. He rejoices greatly that the "elect lady," to whom he directs his second epistle, and Gaius, to whom he addresses his third, "walk in the truth." "St. Jude, the servant of Jesus Christ," writes "to them that are sanctified by God the Father, and preserved in Jesus Christ, and called," and declares the sufficiency of once delivering the faith. To what end now should any one of the apostles, in direct terms impart the divinity of our blessed Lord, when every person, to whom they wrote, was already apprized of the fact? But it may be said that they wrote for the information of posterity, as well as of those to whom they more immediately addressed themselves, and that therefore they should have done it. And have they not sufficiently done it? have they not sufficiently revealed it to such as will, in obedience to the precept of our Lord himself, "search the scriptures"? When I hear that there is but one God; when I hear our Saviour, in the vail of the flesh, say, " Father, if it be possible let this cup pass away from me;" and when knowing that Jesus Christ died for our redemption, I hereby " perceive the love of God, because he laid down his life for us," 1 John iii. 16: what need have I of a farther explanation to enable me to form the proposition myself, and say that as the Father is God, and as the Son is God, and yet as there is but one God, the Son, even our Lord Jesus Christ, is therefore one with the Father, that one God. But it may still be objected, that we see the apostles frequently, on their first appearance among the different people to whom they preached, and that therefore we might expect to hear the fact related expressly in their Acts; and do we not? has not Paul charged the Ephesian elders at Miletus " to feed the church of God, which he hath purchased with his own blood?" Acts xx. 28. Was not every prescript made by the apostles, made to all that would hear the word? and were not the doctrines delivered by them to any one church, written for the profit of all? and was not that which was delivered to all of that generation, written in one code, and transmitted through time for our use and information? That code is the Bible; and from the whole of the Bible, this one proposition is to be deduced; the whole Bible therefore, and nothing less than the whole, is to be pronounced the gospel or testimony of our Saviour Jesus Christ, and thence it is, that this proposition is as deducible as any conclusion resulting from any premises, even in the mathematical Elements of Euclid, namely, that Jesus Christ is one with the Father, God.

I shall, for the future, consider my point as proved, and therefore admitted, and henceforward address myself more directly to Mr. Lindsey's book, and weigh the objections which he has made to our Saviour's Divinity; and as I have but little doubt that I shall be able to shew these wanting in the balance, I shall dismiss them with what expedition I possibly can. He tells us that there were very early heresies in the church; and in the next passage says, that " all *Christian people for upwards of three hundred years after Christ, till the council of Nice, were generally Unitarians* *." I do not mean to enter the lists with this gentleman on the ground of ecclesiastical history in general; but in this point I will dare to meet him, and I will not use " the authorities of men, which are nothing. It is holy scripture alone which can decide this important point, and to that we must make our final appeal †." To that I do appeal; and thence I learn, and think that even I have thence rendered it evident, that not one of the apostles of our Lord was an Unitarian. The first of these three centuries then I must use the liberty of taking away from Mr. Lindsey's bold and unsupported assertion; for to the close of it was the life of the beloved disciple of Jesus Christ extended; and therefore *all* Christian men were not Unitarians: but perhaps the less extensive word " *generally*" came into the latter end of the sentence as a saving term, and with intention to subtract from " *all*" in the commencement of it, and so to leave St. John the remainder; a single instance of a retrograde character, who, notwithstanding the weight of general example, very obstinately

B b

* Apology, p. 24.   † Apology, p. 23.

ſtinately perſiſted in the belief of the ſpirit of truth, from whom he had learned a contrary doctrine. Holy ſcripture is ſilent with reſpect to the two ſucceeding centuries; I ſhall therefore here decline the combat, and ſuppoſe the fact to be as this gentleman has ſtated it, and, on that ſuppoſition, refer to what he has himſelf ſaid, that, "at the firſt planting of the goſpel a crop of evil weeds, and wild opinions grew up, together with the plant of heavenly *truth*," Apology, p. 20*.

"Diſbelief of the Trinity, no blameable hereſy," is the marginal title of a ſhort ſection of Mr. Lindſey's Apology. I ſhall not enlarge on the merit or demerit of belief in the doctrines of Chriſtianity, but muſt ſay, that I look upon a diſbelief in the Trinity to be the ſame with a diſbelief in Jeſus Chriſt, as revealed to us in the holy ſcriptures.

I ſhould be ſorry that any reader of my book ſhould impute a ſpirit of intolerance to me, becauſe I altogether reject the teſtimony of fire and faggot, undergone by ſome Unitarians in maintenance of their tenets. I have at leaſt equal compaſſion for their ſufferings, with that which Mr. Lindſey can feel; but as I cannot infer the truth of their profeſſion from their miſeries, ſo neither can I admit the cruelty which inflicted them to be any argument of the falſehood of the religion embraced, or rather profeſſed by their barbarous tormentors; for, if this be inſiſted on to be of weight againſt the profeſſion of faith in the Trinity, "the tranſitory triumphs of the Arians," notwithſtanding the brevity of their proſperous

---

* I ſhould here aſk Mr. Lindſey's pardon for the abridgment of his beautiful metaphor, in which he has ſowed *light* upon a buſy mind, and, inſtead of reaping a fine crop of young luminaries, has, on account of the rankneſs of the ſoil, only been able to gather in evil weeds and wild opinions of baleful *ſhade*.

rous days, can furnish me with means to make the opposite scale greatly preponderate. Were recrimination my object, or were I to admit but for a moment, that sufferings are of any value in evidence, good God! how many witnesses might I call to prove the truth of the doctrines which I maintain! But why should I call? from whom shall I receive my answer? They are for ever silent who should have rendered it; the poor dumb mouths, which once eloquently poured forth the doctrines of our Redeemer, now tongueless, can only pour forth that blood which they have shed to testify their belief in him. Yet even here I seek not a testimony of the truth of my own tenets, nor of the falsehood of theirs, who, to shun the confutation, put those to silence who could have uttered it. But as I have treated of this mode of argument before, I shall now finally dismiss it, with an assurance to Mr. Lindsey, that I do, as warmly as he can, compassionate all men who have suffered for their sincerity, and as utterly abhor the execrable zeal of their infatuated persecutors as he can possibly do.

The immutable nature of truth can never be affected, she remains equally spotless, whether she be assailed by an ingenious opponent, or an absurd advocate. The ingenuity of sophism is in like manner unable to alter the nature of falsehood, neither can she borrow strength from the weakness of her adversary. To this short position I refer that great body of human authority cited by Mr. Lindsey, and to which, however able the men who compose it may be, I cannot pay any respect while they stand opposed to the word of God. To this head I also refer such absurdities as that uttered by Anselm, Archbishop of Canterbury; the truth remained unchanged, even tho' he abetted it with violence. I do not desire to have it considered that every man who believes with me is therefore wife, and can give a reason for the faith that is in him. If I be found a defective advocate myself, let not my deficiency be transferred to my cause.

Mr. Lindsey says, " Authorities of men are nothing: It is holy scripture alone which can decide this important point, and to that we must make our final appeal," Apology, p. 23. After this assertion one might expect a candid enquiry into what the apostles have said upon this important point. But here we are severely disappointed, and scarce find a text quoted throughout his book but at second hand; nay, scarce a page of original writing through the whole work. Holy scripture is not once appealed to; and this same Nothing, the authorities of men, is the foundation of his system; and such as the foundation is, such indeed is the superstructure. But all this is very soon accounted for, and a perfectly new mode of argument is most ingeniously devised and introduced; and in the very next sentence to that in which he makes the scripture the final appeal, he proposes that " the matter is to be put to the vote, as it were." Now, though he never appeals to his final appeal, he does not in the same manner desert his own darling invention; but has instant recourse to as very an electioneering trick as ever was played at Brentford or Shoreham; for he flatly assures " the less learned" reader, that, upon enquiry, he shall find that to be undeniably true, which I have already shewed to be undeniably false; namely, that " all christian people for upwards of three hundred years after Christ, till the council of Nice, were generally Unitarians." This is a method of procuring votes with a witness; the whole interest of " the less learned" is obtained at one bold stroke; and in another passage of his book he has solicited the suffrages of the absolutely " unlearned;" and

having

having thus obtained the ear of the populace, he trumpets forth a multitude of names of men, and sacrifices every confideration of the authority of fcripture to the eftablifhment of their authority with the unlearned reader. To fome of thefe I will allow that he may have done but juftice, and I will not difturb the afhes of thofe on whom he has poured unmerited incenfe. I fear not his hoft of Unitarians, fo long as I am abetted by the word of God, againft which he has arrayed them. But in his diligent canvafs I am furprized that he fhould think of the names of the Voltaires, the Morgans, and the St. Johns: does he mean to poll thefe men too? Are thefe the apoftles of the gofpel to which Mr. Lindfey appeals? But errour cannot, forfooth, efcape their quick-fighted eyes; I fincerely believe it; they are active in purfuing and embracing errour, and I fhall therefore allow them well qualified to vote with him on this occafion. But when did their quick-fighted eyes difcover or purfue truth? In a few pages after we are aftonifhed at feeing David Hume advance to give his fuffrage in the conteft; his vote, however, I muft admit to be unexceptionable; he is excellently qualified to abet Mr. Lindfey's tenets, having undertaken to fubvert the religion and liberties of this country. Whenever the bonds of religion are loofed, and the reftrictions of confcience taken away, a fubftitute muft be found to controul mankind, and an earthly tyrant be eftablifhed on the throne of a depofed God, to bind in fetters thofe hands which have rejected the eafy yoke of their Creator, and emancipated themfelves from obedience to the mild fway of their merciful Redeemer. Thus far the cunning, for I cannot call it the manly underftanding, of Mr. Hume, has been able to penetrate; and accordingly, when with talents exactly adequate to mifchief, propenfities to put them into exercife, and a difpofition to enjoy the perpetrated

petrated crime, he has, by shallow sophistry, seduced mankind into the paths of vice; he rushes on the villain he has made, and, like Jonathan Wild, consigns to chains the wretch who has deserved them from his own persuasion. When, as an essayest, with just enough of art to withhold a fraud from the eyes of an indolent or willing reader, he has obliterated every virtue by which we can deserve or enjoy freedom, and has rendered the heart of an Englishman no strenuous foe to despotism, he becomes the voluminous pamphleteer of the Stuarts, and, with just enough of plausibility to conceal a falsehood from one who has no longer an interest in detecting it, to the consenting slave points out the acceptable tyrant, and to the tyrant the hands which he has fitted to his chains *.

Mr.

* I may seem here to have stepped out of my way unnecessarily; I cannot, however, admit that I have. The peace and tranquillity of mankind are my object, and to the maintenance of them it is necessary that I should strike at their enemies as they cross me, and put my fellow creatures on their guard against the invader of their happiness; such I consider Mr. Hume to be, and accordingly point him out as a Being that has waged eternal war with the welfare of mankind, both here and hereafter; who has untied, or, rather like a rat, nibbled at, the bonds of religious duty, that a necessity might thence arise of imposing the manacles of civil slavery; who frees us from our God that he may enthral us to man; inflicts the heaviest ills upon us in this life, and with a merciless hand tears away that hope of a future recompense, which was the only consolation that remained to the wretch he had enslaved.—Let it not be said that, in what he has done to these ends, he is himself also deceived. No man can ignorantly falsify in the relation of important historical facts; he therefore who has so falsified must have done it knowingly, and he who is capable of imposing known falsehood upon the public ear, is capable of broaching known sophisms: but this man has by falsehood struck at our liberties, and, by premeditated sophistry, at our religion. The necessity of their aid to the promotion of his design, is no mean proof of our right to enjoy the invaluable blessings of freedom and hope, and argues them to stand upon the firm basis of truth; and surely that he has had recourse to them for such a purpose as that of subverting all human felicity, is a sufficient reason for us to despise the wretch whose treachery and malice prepense has aimed a blow against our religious and civil rights.—When I have just repeated that I look upon our liberty to be so intimately connected with our virtue, and our virtue with the religion of the gospel, that, on the

over-

Mr. Whiston may give his voice for Mr. Lindsey; he preferred the *apostolical* constitutions to the canonical books of the New Testament, declared them more sacred and quite divine, because they favoured his Arian sentiments *. This book was written in the fourth century; and, as it teaches a doctrine not found in the scriptures, has, from this *apostolic* old man, obtained a preference. But I shall cease to pursue this idea farther; for, however deserving of ridicule Mr. Lindsey's argument may be, the subject calls on me to be serious.

Mr. Lindsey dwells upon the prejudices of mankind taken in with their nurses milk, upon doctrines darkened and perplexed by early prepossessions. It is true, and I thank God and my pious parents for it, that, with my nurse's milk, I did imbibe the doctrine which I now maintain; and at the same time I embibed a belief, that grass was green, that fire was hot, that snow was cold, and that two and two make four. With such various errours was my infancy turned aside from truth, and so radically have they been established in my mind by education, that I have never since that fatal time, when my instructors cruelly took advantage of my susceptible and tender years, been able to comprehend that clear evidence which is of force to set aside such absurdities. This childish and commonplace objection to the truth, because it was early known, does not deserve a serious refutation. If the scriptures afford a sufficient testimony now, is it an argument to the contrary of that which they testify, that our teachers have read and assented to them, and that they have thought the word of God fit to be

com-

overthrow of the latter, one undistinguished ruin must overwhelm them all together, my indignation will probably meet not the pardon only, but the approbation of *some* of my countrymen.

* Apology, p. 68.

communicated to their children? But I will now put a question to Mr. Lindsey, to which, if he does not find the answer on the surface of his heart, let him search the inmost recesses of it, and thence inform me; whether even his disinterested conduct, whether the doctrine of Unitarianism, of which he is the strenuous advocate, are pursued by him without one prejudice? I do not speak of those which are instilled by education, but others which, perhaps, he has not found so conquerable. This, however, is a delicate point, and must not be pursued farther. I mean not to wound nor diminish the public regard of this worthy gentleman, but choosing to put my rule by an instance, rather than in a general way, have fixed upon his name, as affording me an argument *à fortiori* in its behalf.

Such objections as turn meetly upon words I shall leave unanswered, they merit contempt and not consideration; but I must show that, upon such a supposition as the existence of the Trinity, that chain of absurdities and contradictions, which Mr. Lindsey thinks would follow, are by no means the natural consequence of the doctrine: there may be much that Mr. Lindsey cannot look into, I grant it; but did God take council of Mr. Lindsey; or has he revealed himself to him as he did to the apostles and prophets? Bishop Pearson's words keep the first and second persons in the Trinity distinct; the Father and the Son are not said in the scriptures to be jointly one Father, or one Son, but they are declared to be one God. And as to the assertion, that we who join in the four invocations, at the beginning of the litany, can be but ill defended against the charge of holding four Gods, to wit, the Father, the Son, the Holy Ghost, and the Trinity, (declared by him to be a fourth intelligent agent); it is about as wisely put as if we should

say,

say, that the government of Rome was administered, not by three, but by four men, to wit, Octavius, Lepidus, Anthony, and the Triumvirate, " which is the utmost confusion imaginable." Apology, p. 124.

To the consequences of offering up divine honour to Jesus Christ our Lord, which are brought together in the 136th page of the Apology, I oppose all that I have already brought in proof of the one Godhead of the Father and the Son; for this one position being admitted, our Saviour has directed prayer to be made to himself.—There is authority for so doing in the writings of the apostles.—The object of our worship is not inferior to the Father, with whom he is one God;—and therefore there never can be a distraction in the mind of the sober worshipper, who, holding in sane memory the unity of the Godhead of the Father, and of our Lord Jesus Christ, will never entertain " a doubt, when he is to pray to God, and when to Christ, when it is right, and when amiss to do it;" he will always find one God the object of his adoration, who, remembering his mercies vouchsafed to man in the flesh, will hear the prayer preferred to him, with gratitude and reliance upon him, who has already so graciously redeemed him by laying down his own life for him, 1 John iii. 16.

Mr. Lindsey, having allowed that it is Jesus Christ who is to judge the world, by disallowing his Godhead, and consequently the direction of prayer to him, has actually conferred upon God the Father, the office of Mediator with Jesus Christ, who is to judge us: for if the Godhead be not in Christ, our merits, of which no creature can have cognizance, are to be handed over for his information; and God the Father, to whom alone they can be known, is to stand forth before the seat of judgement, as our accuser or excuser: so that here we find a change of office between the Father and the Son; an absurdity at least as great as any that appears to Mr. Lindsey's reason, on the establishment of my tenets; an absurdity, in which no man can acquiesce, because it contradicts the principles whence our argument proceeds, and directly opposes itself to revelation: whereas the difficulties arising from an acquiescence in the doctrine of our Saviour's divinity, are only in matters not submitted to reason, and upon which we never should pronounce that the facts are not so, because we do not see how they are so with faculties not equal to the intuition.

The argumentum ad absurdum to which Mr. Lindsey's authors have frequent recourse, is to be judged of according to the nature of the absurdity which it would point out, as a consequence of admitting the fact it is opposed to; and if that be only such, or said to be such, because our reason cannot solve it from its incomprehensibility, it affords no confutation of the position it tries to confute: whereas, if the absurdity result from inconsistency with revelation, which must fall upon its establishment, it is a good argument; nothing being to be admitted which can militate against the truth of God. This general rule, (a rule so obvious, that nothing but having seen a book written without any regard to it, could have induced me to set it down) the reader of Mr. Lindsey's Apology will do well to hold constantly in mind, for by referring what he reads there to it, there is very little contained in the book to which it does not afford a compleat answer.

Having believed the scriptures to be the revelation of God, I have ever avoided the glosses of commentators, influenced by interest or prejudice, and have made the unperverted

unperverted original my study, in order thence to derive a religion for myself, and I must acknowledge that I have often conceived, both from St. John's first epistle, and from several passages in the epistles of St. Paul, that they particularly opposed themselves to an opinion, prevalent in their day, that Jesus Christ had not come in the flesh; that he had not like infirmities and temptations as we have, but that the senses of mankind were imposed upon by the appearance of a body only. But as I have said that the truth most difficult to be conceived by mankind is, not that God had descended to dwell on earth, or that a man Jesus had lived on earth; but that an union of the two natures of God and of man had subsisted in Jesus Christ, a man living among them, I inferred the following conclusion, " that the apostles had preached him as God only, leaving it to their own knowledge of him, to prove that he was man; that having seen the power with which the testimony of the apostles was attended, the hearers yielded credit to that which they witnessed, and forthwith acknowledged Jesus Christ to be God: but that not being able to understand the compatibility of divine perfection and human imperfection, and therefore concluding that such an union could not have subsisted, they considered their senses imposed upon by an apparent body only, and rejected their belief in the manhood of Christ, not believing him to be man, whom they had acknowledged to be God; and that the apostles, on seeing such a doctrine arise, found themselves now under a necessity of preaching him as man, whom they had already taught to be God, and obliged to make use of the testimony of the Holy Ghost, to re-establish a fact which they had at first left to the testimony of the senses; a testimony which they had considered as sufficient then, but now saw superseded by that of their preaching."
Mr. Lindsey has proved that I was not mistaken in this;

and his account of these erroneous tenets is very correspondent to the idea which I had formed of them from scripture: for, of those who entertained them, he says, "They could not allow that a pure emanation of deity, such as they presumed Christ to be, could have any connection with so impure a substance as a human material body; and so they invented this solution of the difficulty, that he was a man in appearance only, and not in reality." Apology, p. 154. I cannot, for my part, exceedingly wonder at the errour into which these hearers fell; for I frankly acknowledge, that had I been a witness of the birth, life, death, burial, resurrection, and reascension of Jesus Christ into heaven; and had I afterwards heard him, by the assisted preaching of the apostles, declared to be God; the reality of that body, in which I had seen him, and in which I had seen him act such a part, would have come into suspicion with me; I should have doubted of the reality of a body so differently endowed from the bodies of all other men: " metuissem credere in carne natum, ne credere coactus fuissem ex carne inquinatum," St. Austin, quoted by Mr. Lindsey, Apology, p. 158, and I should have believed that he was all God without manhood. But I sincerely return thanks to the divine spirit that has testified of the flesh of our blessed atonement, and redeemed me from an errour whereby my spirit would have been proved not to have been of God. I care not to what Genus this Linnæus of divinity, who has so skilfully classed the opinions of mankind, will refer me; let him only remember that I do not now embrace such errours; for that philosophy, by which I should have said that he who is God, is therefore not man, is superseded; and I yield my faith obedient to his word, whose word alone is true; and, by consequence, I believe that Jesus Christ is come." a man

as

as concerning the flesh," and that he is also "over all, God blessed for ever."

The truth as set forth in the scriptures, I have all along acknowledged my reason incapable to comprehend; but Mr. Lindsey thinks it ought to be comprehensible, and will not allow that God had a right to retain a power greater than he has given us abilities to search into; or wisdom, the exercise of which he has not endowed us with a capacity to understand; and therefore he thinks we had better reject all that surpasses our faculties; for, by so doing, he is of opinion that we should have a perfect union in the church. Let us for a moment grant that we should obtain this union; what is it? An union in errour; and is such an union to be desired? is this the object of his wishes? does he look upon a concurrence in falsehood as a compensation for rejected truth? But the ruin of truth, he says, and quotes Dr. Clayton for it, is not likely to result; for the gates of hell shall never prevail against the Christian religion. That they never will is my sincere belief, and therefore it is my sincere belief, that Mr. Lindsey's proposed union in errour will never take place; for, is the rejection of a point, on which nothing less than the essence of Christianity depends, is the denial of his divinity, whom we worship, no subversion of his religion? I think that the object of my worship, and of my religion is one; and if my worship be deprived of its object, I know not where to find that of my religion; and should, on seeing "the King of kings" degraded from the throne of his glory, the "God who purchased us with his own blood," torn from the supplication of his adorers, then say that the gates of hell had prevailed against his church; an event which I trust that, of his infinite mercy, and according to his immutable

mutable promife, he will avert. But I fhall now re-fume the conceffion I made, for a while, and oppofe Mr. Lindfey's affertion, that union would be the confequence of a legal eftablifhment, or admiffion of his tenets; for we of the church, as now eftablifhed, might, in that cafe, think fit to be diffenters from his doctrines, as he diffents now from ours. I know that, for my part, I fhould oppofe them to the utmoft of my power. But the true meaning of his words is eafily comprized in this fhort but profound propofition, That if all mankind will agree with Mr. Lindfey, Mr. Lindfey will not difagree with all mankind: yet even this I muft take the liberty to doubt.

It is a very weak affertion, that faith in the divinity of Jefus Chrift leads to the admiffion of many objects of worfhip, and that the church of Rome has thence taken occafion to adore the Virgin Mary, the apoftles, and martyrs, and fuch other perfons as her own favour has been pleafed to rank among her faints: for as the ground of faith in Jefus Chrift, as God, is by no means pretended to be the ground for the adoration of any befides him, it is not true that the faints are worfhipped, becaufe he is revealed to be God. Jefus Chrift is revealed to be God; the faints are not revealed to be God: does it therefore follow that the faints are to be worfhipped? Certainly not. But very particular care has been taken to guard againft the adoration of the Virgin Mary, and the apoftles, and to prevent their being confidered as proper objects of worfhip, though fhe was declared bleffed among women, and they were highly favoured above men, having been entrufted with the teftimony of Jefus Chrift, who alfo wrought many miracles by their hands in fupport of their witnefs. It feems to have been with a view of preventing mankind from looking upon fuch circumftances as a ground of worfhip, worship, that our Saviour has, in more passages than one, spoken with seeming disrespect (if I may dare to use the expression of him who was without sin) to his mother: " woman, what have I to do with thee?" John ii. 4. " Who is my mother?" Mark iii. 33. Peter, when Cornelius met him and fell down at his feet, and worshipped him, " took him up, saying, stand up, I myself also am a man," Acts x. 25, 26. And Paul and Barnabas, when they heard that the priest of Jupiter, with the people at Lystra, would have done sacrifice unto them, " rent their cloaths, and ran in among the people, crying out, and saying, Sirs, why do ye these things? We also are men of like passions with you; and yet with these sayings scarce restrained they the people, that they had not done sacrifice unto them," Acts xiv. 14, 15, 18. And even the angel, than whom man is made a little lower, declined the worship of St. John, saying, " I am thy fellow servant, and of thy brethren that have the testimony of Jesus, worship God," Rev. xix. 10. From the exercise of miraculous power, from supernatural endowments, we find mankind easily persuaded to conclude divinity, or at least an adorable superiority in those who are so endowed. To guard against this facility of superstition, and to shew that from an absolute revelation only we are to believe the divinity of any, the several texts which I have cited, seem to have been written. It is true a revelation that Jesus Christ is God, one with the Father, conveys an idea different from that of Mr. Lindsey, that the Father only is God, and so may afford an analogy, by which, faith, in a multitude of persons in the Godhead, might be facilitated, if revealed; but by no means a proof that there are more persons than are revealed: let us still remember the limits of reason, and not perpetually fly beyond her confines: she will conduct us very safely, if we do

not

not obtrude premises upon her which are not within her district: with respect to scripture truths, the peremptory word of the God of truth, is the ultimate boundary of her province. Our terms of salvation are prescribed, and God does not require our ingenuity in finding more points of faith than he has offered for our assent in order to secure it; and if he has not revealed, he does not need our belief, however like we may conclude our own suggestions to be to that which he has made known. Analogy may indeed facilitate conception, and make us more readily enter into a position laid down; yet it is but a bad ground to argue upon, for no certain conclusion can ever follow from it. I shall myself use it now to illustrate; and as I have denied that it can, from the divinity of Jesus Christ, shew the divinity of any other not revealed to be divine, I only ask its assistance in procuring a more easy assent to the divinity of that which is revealed to be divine; and this will, I presume, not be withheld by those who have carried its use so much higher than I dare to do. If then the Holy Ghost be revealed to be one with the Father, and the Son, God, it may be some ease to the mind in giving its assent to the existence of a third person in the Godhead, to reflect that it has already acquiesced in the admission of a second. It is not my intention to examine into the evidence of the divinity of the Holy Spirit so extensively as I have already done into that which is afforded to the Godhead of our blessed Redeemer; it is not so strenuously opposed; besides my attentive reader has, in all probability, inferred it for himself, from several contexts which I have laid down already, though I have not directly pointed it out as a conclusion. I shall therefore now content myself with a very few passages proving the Holy Ghost to be God also, reminding my reader of what I have already offered

fered concerning the sufficiency of any one assertion, for the truth of which God himself is responsible.

" He shall be great, and shall be called the Son of the Highest." " The Holy Ghost shall come upon thee, and the power of the Highest shall overshadow thee: therefore also that Holy Thing which shall be born of thee, shall be called the Son of God," Luke i. 31, 35. That which is conceived in her, is of the Holy Ghost," Matth. i. 20. That which is conceived of the Holy Ghost, is therefore called the Son of God; the Holy Ghost therefore, of whom the Son of God is conceived, is one with the Father and the Son, " the Highest."

" I will pray the Father, and he shall give you another Comforter, that he may abide with you for ever, even the Spirit of Truth." " I will not leave you comfortless: I will come to you." " If a man love me, he will keep my words: and my Father will love him, and we will come unto him, and make our abode with him," John xiv. 16, 17, 18, 23. Here the Father, Son, and Holy Ghost, one God, are, or is, the Comforter, the witness to the truth, which shall come and abide, or make abode with him who loveth the Son, and keepeth his words. The identity of the Godhead of the Holy Spirit with that of the Father, and of the Son, is here expressly declared.

" Why hath Satan filled thine heart to lie to the Holy Ghost?" " thou hast not lied unto men but unto God," Acts v. 3, 4. Here also the Holy Ghost is directly pronounced to be one, with the Father and the Son, God.

" The things of God, knoweth no man but the Spirit of God;" "which things also we speak, not in

D d   the

the words which man's wisdom teacheth, but which the Holy Ghost teacheth," 1 Cor. ii. 11, 13. Here the Holy Ghost is one and the same with the Spirit of God; and in the 16th verse he is called " the mind of Christ;" he is therefore one in Godhead with the Father and the Son, from both of whom, one God, he equally proceeds.

" What, know ye not that ye are the temple of the Holy Ghost which is in you, which ye have of God; and ye are not your own? For ye are bought with a price," 1 Cor. vi. 19. What now is the price paid for this purchase wherewith we are bought? are we not " the church of God which he hath purchased with his own blood?" Acts xx. 28. Being then redeemed by the blood of Jesus Christ shed for our ransom, we have therefore become the temple of the Holy Ghost. But " know ye not that ye are the temple of God, and that the Spirit of God dwelleth in you? If any man defile the temple of God, him shall God destroy; for the temple of God is holy; which temple ye are," 1 Cor. iii. 16, 17. The Father is God, and the Son is " God, who purchased us with his own blood;" and the Holy Ghost, whose temple we are, is here declared to be God. But there is but one God; the Father, Son, and Holy Ghost are therefore that one God, that Trinity in Unity which is to be worshipped. This may seem to 'the natural man', Mr. Lindsey, to be *hay and stubble*; but let him lay aside the vanity of thinking himself in the least degree a judge of spiritual things, and believe that which God has witnessed; " Let him become a fool, that he may be wise, for the wisdom of this world is foolishness with God," 1 Cor. iii. 18, 19; " Let him account of the apostles as stewards of the mysteries of God," 1 Cor. iv. 1. " and not be taken as wise in his own craftiness." " We are the

the houſe of Chriſt, if we hold faſt the confidence and the rejoicing of the hope firm unto the end," Heb. iii. 6. "Know ye not your ownſelves that Jeſus Chriſt in you, except ye be reprobates?" 2 Cor. xiii. 5. "Ye are the temple of the Holy Ghoſt which is in you." "Ye are the temple of the living God; as God hath ſaid, I will dwell in them, and walk in them; and I will be their God, and they ſhall be my people," 2 Cor. vi. 16. Is this to be reſiſted?

That it was God who ſpoke by the prophets, is not denied. But by the mouth of the prophet David God has ſaid, "To-day if ye will hear his voice, harden not your hearts as in the provocation, and as in the day of temptation in the wilderneſs: when your fathers tempted me, proved me, and ſaw my work. Forty years long was I grieved with this generation, and ſaid, it is a people that do err in their heart, and they have not known my ways. Unto whom I ſware in my wrath, that they ſhould not enter into my reſt," Pſ. xcv. 7, 8, 9, 10, 11. Of him who has thus ſworn, and who was thus provoked for forty years in the wilderneſs, even that God who led the children of Iſrael out of the land of Egypt, and out of the houſe of bondage, and ſaid, "I am the Lord thy God," it is thus declared by St. Paul, "the Holy Ghoſt faith, to-day if you will hear his voice, harden not your hearts, &c," Heb. iii. 7, 8, 9, 10, 11.

Our Saviour himſelf ſays, "The ſpirit of truth, which proceedeth from the Father, he ſhall teſtify of me," John xv. 26; and accordingly St. Paul having declared to the Hebrews, that they who had heard the Lord confirmed his great ſalvation unto us, "God alſo bearing them witneſs," Heb. ii. 3. proceeds to preach the ſufficiency of the one ſacrifice of Chriſt's body once offered for ſins, and the kingdom of heaven

opened

opened to all believers by his having overcome the sharpness of death, and "an entrance into the holiest by the blood of Jesus, by a new and living way which he hath consecrated for us," "whereof the Holy Ghost is a witness to us," Heb. x. 15. "It is the Spirit that beareth witness, because the spirit is truth." "If we receive the witness of men, the witness of God is greater: for this is the witness of God, which he hath testified of his Son. He that believeth on the Son of God, hath the witness in himself: he that believeth not God, hath made him a liar, because he believeth not the record that God gave of his Son;" 1 John v. 9, 10. These words amply explain the meaning of St. Paul's direction to the Thessalonians, "Quench not the Spirit," 1 Thess. v. 19; and, upon the whole, we so frequently find the testimony of Jesus Christ borne by God and by the Holy Ghost, that we must conclude the Holy Ghost, who "is a witness unto us," to be one with the Father and with the Son, God, who hath given the record of his Son, "that witness who is in him that believeth on the Son of God." This may perhaps afford more provender for Mr. Lindsey. I should hope however that he may, by this time at least, have begun to doubt the tenets which he has professed, and reflect on the very destructive consequences of his errour, if he can be persuaded to consider his doctrine to be such. To this purpose, and as the last argument which I shall produce to the divinity of the Holy Ghost, and his unity with the Father and Son, I shall add the declaration of our Saviour himself, who declared to the Scribes, who said, "He hath Beelzebub, and by the prince of the devils casteth he out devils;" "all sins shall be forgiven to the sons of men, and blasphemies, wherewith soever they shall blaspheme: but he that shall blaspheme against the Holy Ghost hath never forgiveness, but is in danger

of

of eternal damnation: becaufe they faid, he hath an unclean fpirit," Mark iii. 22 to 30. Here the context requires the following interpretation, 'Ye have faid that I have a devil; it fhall neverthelefs be forgiven you: but if ye fhall hereafter ufe like blafphemy, ye fhall never have forgivenefs: I came not to bear record of myfelf, and therefore difpenfe with your unbelief; whereas, when the Holy Ghoft fhall in due time bear witnefs, that ultimate teftimony upon which the faith of mankind is to be required; when the whole of that evidence fhall be afforded to the world, upon which God has thought right to demand the faith of men, and to which he will not add; then, if ye blafpheme, or lay fuch a charge againft the Son of man, declared by the Holy Ghoft to be God, ye refift the united Trinity, and fin againft God, who fhall bear me witnefs; and whofe witnefs is greater than that of man, which as yet ye are pardonable for conceiving me only to be.' The manner in which St. Luke has related the fame event, greatly corroborates this manner of underftanding the declaration of our Lord, "He that denieth me before men, fhall be denied before the angels of God. And whofoever fhall fpeak a word againft the Son of man, it fhall be forgiven him: but unto him that blafphemeth againft the Holy Ghoft, it fhall not be forgiven;" for our Saviour is in context with the declaration appointing the apoftles to be witneffes unto him; and for the purpofe of rendering them competent and irrefiftible without fin, he goes on to fay, "Take ye no thought how or what thing ye fhall anfwer, or what ye fhall fay: for the Holy Ghoft fhall teach you in the fame hour what ye ought to fay," Luke xii. 9, 10, 11, 12. On this place it is to be remarked, that our Lord has declared of him who fhall fpeak againft the Son of man, that he fhall be forgiven; and alfo, that he who denieth him,

him, shall be denied also. Here are two contradictory assertions made, and consequently two distinct circumstances are to be understood for the sake of reconciling them to truth, and to sense, which easily results, upon admitting that two distinct times are intended; and that "he who now denies me is pardonable; but that he who shall hereafter deny me, shall himself also be denied. Ye have not now the manifest testimony of God; but hereafter the Holy Ghost shall bear me witness: and in the hour when the Holy Ghost shall teach my appointed witnesses what they ought to say: ye shall not be forgiven if ye withhold belief." I desire my reader will refer this argument to the doctrine of my second chapter.

I have now proved to my own, and I hope also to my reader's, entire satisfaction, that the Son is God, and that the Holy Ghost is God: that the Father is God, and that there is but one God, are conceded points; and, having been admitted, I have been exempted from the necessity of proving them. But as there is but one God, and that each of the three persons is God, does not a Trinity in unity necessarily follow? But Mr. Lindsey does not find this conclusion drawn in so many words, and so will not believe that it results. Had Mr. Lindsey told me how many miles it measured from Richmond to Catterick, I apprehend he would charge me with great stupidity if I could not conclude for myself how many miles from Catterick to Richmond; and yet even this obvious inference does not offer itself more perspicuously to the understanding than that with which he quarrels. The premises are all fairly stated; and which am I to charge it to, the account of obstinacy, want of discernment, or a composition of both, that he will not look upon the necessary conclusion, which is, that the object

of

of our religious worſhip is a holy, bleſſed, and glorious Trinity, three perſons and one God?

That each of the three perſons is God, ſeems to me a fully ſufficient reaſon why I ſhould prefer to each my prayer, my praiſe, and my thankſgiving; that the three perſons are one God, is in like manner a reaſon why I ſhould addreſs my adoration to this trinal unity. That this is a ſtumbling-block to the Unitarians and to the Jews, I grant; that to the Greeks it is fooliſhneſs, I grant alſo; that it altogether ſurpaſſes my own faculties, I as freely acknowledge; but that it is revealed by the God of truth I know, and therefore I yield my faith to what he has declared concerning his own inſcrutable nature,

AND WHERE I CAN'T UNRIDDLE LEARN TO TRUST.
PARNELL.

I can clearly ſee that the inſolence of reaſon, or rather of pride under her abuſed name, meets in this point the object of its contempt; but " behold ye deſpiſers, and wonder and periſh; for I work a work in your days, a work which ye ſhall in nowiſe believe, though a man declare it unto you," Acts xii. 41. I do not apply theſe words uncharitably, I uſe them to ſhew that God had beforehand ordained a difficulty to the conceptions of mankind, that they who withſtand his teſtimony, becauſe they have not been admitted of his council, are impeached of contempt, and threatened with eternal deſtruction. " Knowing therefore the terrour of the Lord," I would perſuade men to humility, to obedience, to faith unto ſalvation; that they may eſcape the " vengeance taken upon them that obey not the goſpel of Jeſus Chriſt."

It is not my office to ſtand forth the panegyriſt of the liturgy of the eſtabliſhed church, and therefore I refrain from entering into a ſcriptural vindication of

it's

it: if it indeed remain neceſſary now, I have taken a great deal of pains to very little purpoſe; for I ſhould conceive an intelligent reader of the arguments I have already cited in proof of the divinity of Jeſus Chriſt and of the Holy Ghoſt, muſt, without any more particular diſcuſſion of the point, be very well able to vindicate it himſelf, and to ſet forth the propriety of offering up his adoration to them with the Father, one God. Were I diſpoſed ſo to do, I could draw together alſo the opinions of ſome of the wiſeſt men that have ever adorned our iſlands; who have conceived our book of common prayer one of the fineſt compoſitions that has flowed from the pen of man: but even this human compoſition I ſhall not maintain by human authority, though I could bring ſtronger hands to ſupport the fabric of our church, than thoſe of either Dr. Clarke or Mr. Lindſey; which have been deſperately employed in dilapidating; or, to uſe Mr. Lindſey's leſs-confuſed metaphor, in *ſmothering the fabric.*

This gentleman, after he had deprecated all human authority as a ground of faith, we have already ſeen making uſe of it, and nothing elſe, in ſupport of his doctrines. But he has attacked human authority in another ſenſe of the words alſo; and, to the great conſternation of every Briton, who ſhall meet it in his way, has emphatically and concluſively pronounced it A MONSTER. But the terrified reader of his book may calm his breaſt when he comes to know that this ſame monſter is nothing worſe than "a legal eſtabliſhment of the church of England." An eſtabliſhment, the neceſſity of which, I am ſorry to ſay, grows every day more and more obvious; and to whoſe good purpoſes, Mr. Lindſey's own conduct bears an incontrovertible teſtimony. A farther vindication of this alſo exceeds the limits of my deſign; but methinks a gentleman, who has experienced ſuch lenity from our eſtabliſhment, blifhment, fhould at leaft acknowledge, from the tolerated altar of his new fynagogue, that the church of England is not a very fierce monfter.

As the limits are, however, of my own appointment, I will take the liberty of tranfgreffing them a little here. The articles of religion, when firft prefcribed, were chiefly intended as a barrier to divide our new reformation from Popery, which it had juft efcaped, many of the particular tenets of which are formally abjured in them. Though accefs to the fcriptures were now permitted to all men, it was thought neceffary to affift the weak, in forming their conclufions upon the whole, and to fum up in brief thofe doctrines which lie diffufed in the facred writings. Moderation appears alfo to have been a principal object in forming them; for as abhorrence muft naturally fucceed the detection of the felf-interefted frauds of the church of Rome, it feems a reafonable apprehenfion, that every tenet which it had held, would fall into contempt, if not confpicuoufly held forth, as retained by the leaders of reformation; hence the Trinity is formally avowed, in which we continued our agreement. I am far from maintaining that the body of the people fhould be obliged to fubfcribe to any articles of faith; but it appears to me abfolutely neceffary that certain articles of faith fhould be fubfcribed by the paftors in our church, otherwife we muft ceafe to be a church; and, inftead of a general amity amongft men, the gofpel will be converted into a fource of univerfal difcord, and bring indeed, not peace, but a fword; we fhall, inftead of a church of England, have as many churches as parifh minifters; every parifh, zealous to maintain the doctrines of its polemic paftor, will war on its neighbour, and think they do God fervice by reducing thofe, who diffent from them, to opinions which they have been in-

E e ftructed

structed to esteem necessary to be entertained. Subscription to these doctrines, as a security for the maintenance of the imposed faith, will be required, and that which is now established in peace, will be, if relinquished, again exacted by the very consequences of having relinquished it; for, however exceptionable those articles which are now subscribed may be thought, I greatly doubt whether they who complain would agree together in forming a set that would be less liable to objection; and that subscription would again be required and submitted to, as the purchase of tranquillity, I do not entertain the smallest doubt. Articles, summing up in few words the essential doctrines diffused in the scriptures, ought to be prescribed to those who are authorized to teach; and these alone should they be permitted to promulgate, whatever they might privately think. It is true the conscientious man who does not acquiesce in their truth, and therefore cannot subscribe to them, is excluded from the office of a teacher, and withheld: but from what? from an opportunity of propagating opinions contrary to those which the wisest men have conceived deducible from scripture, for by such I conceive these articles to be formed. It is to be hoped that many a weak man has a tender conscience; by this then he is restrained from uttering his trifling suggestions; while he who has less scrupulously acquiesced in what he doubted, has, by his subscription, given security to mankind that he will not propagate pernicious or silly tenets. I do not wish to confine the private sentiments of the heart, but I do to restrain the liberty of teaching and imparting such notions as a weak man may instill into a credulous or unthinking congregation. Anabaptism itself pretended to the sanction of scripture, and may again, to the utter subversion of all religion and virtue. The church of Catterick may set up against that of Northallerton, and

who

who shall decide which is right, if there be no prescript? The more extensive diocesan churches may disagree, and when the church of Carlisle shall make inroads into the neighbouring churches of Durham and Chester, who shall restrain the arm that declares itself raised for the propagation of truth? Intestine wars and universal confusion may at length leave the decision in the hands of victory, and vanquished truth shall then subscribe to articles dictated by its erroneous conquerour. Such would be the process: and let not those who now complain of the necessity of subscribing the articles of the church of England, flatter themselves that matters would be rendered more agreeable even to themselves, if they should be indulged in their desires. Perhaps, when every species of disturbance and puritanical absurdity had raged through the nation, and robbed them of their tranquillity, they would then begin to acknowledge the happiness they enjoyed when protected by that barrier which they had themselves broken down, and become the first to replace it; the want would teach the value of that which they now overlook, because they possess it. But the subscription of articles of faith is no such mighty grievance as some would intimate; it may be a severity to a few who are not admitted into the pulpit, because they cannot accede to them: but surely it is a great happiness to the body of the people that they are under the guardianship of an establishment that protects them from the necessity of listening to the whimsical interpretation of weak teachers. It is therefore necessary, so long as there is no compulsion on the laity to learn and give their faith to the doctrines of the clergy, that the conclusions which are to be drawn from holy writ should be prescribed to those who are appointed to teach: if they cannot subscribe, let them let it alone, a church with which they cannot concur, is even better without them.

them. Is it for the admiffion of a few individuals that a door is to be opened, by which every fpecies of abufe may enter?

I honour and concur with Mr. Lindfey's patriot wifh, that England fhould ever fet the example of improvement; but it is very weakly urged, that religion fhould keep pace with fcience in improvement, and that a fubfcription to articles muft always impede its progrefs; for nothing can be more abfurd than the idea of a progreffive religion, which, being founded upon the declared, not the imagined will of God, muft, if it attempt to proceed, relinquifh that revelation which is its bafis, and fo ceafe to be a religion founded upon God's word. God has revealed himfelf, and all that he has fpoken, and confequently all that is demanded of us to accede to, is declared in one book, from which nothing is to be retrenched, and to which nothing can be added. All that it contains was as perfpicuous to thofe who firft perufed it, after the rejection of the Papal yoke, as it can be to us now, or as it can be to our pofterity in the fiftieth generation. If we look for any thing new, it is not in the fcriptures that it is to be found; and if we add, it is not religion that has improved, for truth will never defert her own foundations, nor follow our fantaftic imaginations. The progrefs of every fcience has been to the difcovery of fomething new, derived from new combinations of principles within our comprehenfion, and confequently capable of being compared for the fake of additional knowledge. Is fuch a progrefs to be defired in religon? What novelty do we feek for, or what advantage do we propofe from the introduction of novelty into religion? Such an idea feems to intimate

As if religion were intended

For nothing elfe but to be mended. HUDIBRAS.

CHAP,

CHAP. V.*

ΤΩ͂Ν ΠΕΡΙ᾽ ῾ΕΑΥΤΟ῀Υ.

MY name appearing prefixed to this edition will put it out of doubt that I am in truth, as I formerly stated myself, a Layman, and I conceive that my book has rendered it unneceſſary for me to ſay that I am altogether unread in theological diſputations; of theſe two circumſtances, however, I am now about to make my advantage, for I ſtill deſire to have the end kept in view, and to convert even myſelf into ſome ſort of argument in behalf of it.

On the publication of Mr. Lindſey's Apology, as I have already ſaid, I was drawn by curioſity to look into it; but finding it to contain a doctrine which I had not in the leaſt ſuſpected, (as I really had never known any thing of the gentleman before) I placed the Bible by my ſide, happy in finding the beſt, the only evidence in this caſe offered to the examination of every man. With perfect freedom from prejudice, nay, I am almoſt aſhamed to confeſs it, with the firſt ſerious conſideration of ſo important a point that I had ever entered into†, I ſat down to read Mr. Lindſey's book, and, for the truth of every poſition contained in it, appealed to the word of God himſelf, that I might thence learn how truly it was advanced; when, to my utter aſtoniſhment, I ſoon found that this was the only book upon the ſubject, which the diligent Apologiſt had not critically read, and that in every particular it directly oppoſed itſelf to him, and to his frequent quotations. It grew into a

matter

---

* This chapter is for the moſt part a parody of Mr. Lindſey's concluding chapter, and title is the ſame with his.

† I would not have it underſtood that I had never read the Bible before, but that I never read it to this point, or in a like inquiſitive manner as now,

matter of wonder with me, what could influence a man to furrender his worldly competence in defence of a contradiction to the only witnefs that bears any teftimony concerning the fact which he contradicts. As I had received an education among men not unlettered, I was not altogether unacquainted with the laws of argument, and foon perceived his errour to proceed from his having drawn from a wrong fource, from his having laid afide the Bible, and faid, " my reafon does not acquiefce in a Trinity of Perfons in the one God, and my reafon is competent; this is a matter fubmitted to my faculties, and I am fkilled to affirm or deny concerning a comprehenfible God." As I found difficulties in lifting up my own faculties to God, I conceived Mr. Lindfey's no better able to foar to fuch unfurmountable heights; and having found that my Maker *had* fpoken, looked upon his word as the fountain from which all argument concerning him fhould flow, and accordingly I have ftated my own idea of the manner of purfuing this enquiry in my firft chapter. Under this perfuafion I noted my Bible, and to what purpofe my reader is empowered to judge from my third and fourth chapters: but, as I went along, the degrees or different fpecies of teftimony afforded to the divinity of our Lord and Saviour Jefus Chrift, offered themfelves to my obfervation; and this alfo I have in my fecond chapter fubmitted to public cenfure. Such was the procefs of an enquiry entered into by a man who fet about it for his own information only; but the fubftance of which, as it has afforded perfect conviction to himfelf, he has at length decided to be due to mankind; at length decided, I fay, becaufe that many fcruples delayed my determination. Firft it occurred to me that, being a Layman, it was, properly fpeaking, no bufinefs of mine; that an eftablifhed clergy was appointed for the defence of religion; that at the head of this Clergy there was a refpectable and venerable body of

learned

learned Bishops, who were daily acquiring more weight by the accession of a numerous Nobility to their bench; by which accession, if the body should lose (as in all human probability they will) on the side of learning, they were sure of obtaining consequence on the side of fashion, and therefore that it was not to be supposed that the conduct of one country clergyman could long continue of any national importance. But when, on the other hand, I considered how ready the world was to impute partiality to any body of men who should write on a subject in which their private interest was so deeply concerned, and that their own silence shewed they were themselves aware of this, I thought that a Layman writing upon the subject, a man totally unconnected with their profession, would probably be more attended to. Another objection which occurred to me, was my entire ignorance of controversial theology, and particularly my having never looked into any controversy upon the Trinity, except what I have seen in Mr. Lindsey's book; but being by Mr. Lindsey's book convinced that the Bible was the only guide to be depended upon, I then thought that the reading that with attention would be a sufficient preparative for writing; that my very ignorance in controversy would turn to account, and that it might be considered as a corroborating proof of the truth of what I should write, that the Bible alone had been found sufficient to convince *one young man*; and accordingly, thro' the whole course of my enquiry, the Bible alone have I consulted, and this (notwithstanding that I have acknowledged myself educated in these doctrines) without a single prejudice, either my own, or borrowed from any other. Perhaps I have been too nicely scrupulous in this respect; for, through the fear of imbibing one prejudice on so important a question, I have worked only on my own ideas derived from scripture, shunned the superior suggestions of wiser men, and diligently withheld myself from an acquaintance with any thing
that

that had ever been faid upon the fubject before. I knew not thro' what foul or crooked channels the courfe of the ftream had been turned, but was very certain that the well-head was pure, and thence only I therefore determined to draw. From this circumftance I alfo entertained fome hope, that, being totally unbiaffed, I might poffibly ftrike out fome new lights; or, where I fhould accidentally agree with any former writers, put an old argument in fo different a manner, that it fhould convey a new impreffion, and convince fuch of my readers as affect novelty; for of novelty, if that be a recommendation, they have undoubtedly a chance, as all contained in my work is my own, whether any of it may have been ftated before or not.

May I have leave to fay, without blame, that having been born a gentleman, a farther difficulty oppofed my refolution to publifh; the inconfiftency of fuch doctrines as I was about to maintain, with the modifh practices and eafy principles of the polite world fuggefted itfelf to me; why then, it often occurred to me, why muft I be fo fingularly nice and fcrupulous as not to comply with what men of fafhion accommodate themfelves to? why difturb others, and not give way to a more chearful way of thinking; why promulgate that veneration for a Deity which a free communication with the world may difperfe or remove? and why render myfelf obnoxious to men who muft deteft the doctrines which reftrain their will, and not rather wait patiently for a change in the morals of the age? Thefe confiderations altogether were of weight to divert me for a while from the thought of publication; not that I now juftify myfelf therein: yea rather I condemn myfelf, and have at length decided to offer to mankind thofe arguments which have already afforded conviction to myfelf *.

I

---

* See Apology, p. 216, of which this paragraph is only a parody.

I am very confcious that my ftyle would admit of great improvement; but if it be confidered that I did not fee Mr. Lindfey's book till * late in the month of January, I fhall readily be forgiven by the ingenuous and candid reader, who will fee that I have employed that time in the purfuit of matter, which, had I lefs regard to an argument of fo high importance to him and myfelf, I might have beftowed in polifhing a lefs convincing work. But why then fhould I not have withheld it longer from the world, and rendered it better able to fuftain their criticifm ? For this fhort reafon: a deadly poifon has been adminiftered to the publick, I have hafted to prepare the antidote, and have not paufed to fugar over the brim of the veffel in which I offer it to their lips. He muft love the poifon who rejects the antidote that is not feafoned to his palate. I am as fenfible of the charms of language as my faftidious reader may be, and could perhaps, even without his affiftance, have rendered my own ftyle more agreeable to his ear, and greatly fhortened what I have been forced, thro' hafte, to exprefs in unfelected terms. If, however, he be fuch a man as cannot pardon me, I do not afk his pardon.

I fhall here take occafion to explain what I have written with refpect to Mr. Lindfey himfelf. I have heretofore confidered him in the character of a Sectary and Writer only; and confequently have been under a neceffity of fpeaking concerning him in terms, which I have always uttered with regret. I am not, however, going to retract a fingle fyllable which can only affect him in his public character; but, on the contrary, more fummarily to avow the fubftance of what I have already laid down. As a Sectary then, I think he would be a dangerous man, had he not himfelf diminifhed

---

* I did not fee it till the 21ft of January, and the former edition of this volume was finifhed from the prefs May 5, 1774.

nifhed his importance by becoming the advocate of his own tenets; for as a Writer, I confider him to be perfectly harmlefs; yet ftill from that character, in which I fhall henceforward addrefs him, I dread the Schifmatick, and have therefore oppofed myfelf to a book, which, had it not come from the felf-denying hand of this gentleman, might, for me, have gradually fubfided in its congenial oblivion. His conduct, however, might fupport it for a time; my effort therefore is more expeditioufly to difmifs it from exiftence.

It may look a little quarrelfome, that I cannot let even fo much of his book, as correfponds with the title page, pafs without a cenfure. But this gentleman has thought it neceffary to make an apology for the moft unexceptionable conduct that he could poffibly have purfued; for a fincere obedience to the dictates of his confcience; for having made a facrifice to what he efteemed the truth, however miftaken; for having looked upon pardon as inconfiftent with the retained offence; and for having convinced mankind that "he had efcaped the pollutions of the world by his former knowledge of the Lord and Saviour Jefus Chrift," 2 Pet. ii. 20. Had he indeed purfued a contrary courfe, and continued to profefs when he had ceafed to believe, then would an apology have been truly neceffary, and we fhould not perhaps have admitted it to be fatisfactory, though he had even yielded to the importunity of ftronger motives than thofe which he has refifted. Had his power of doing good been far more extenfive, and had the fubfcription of a doctrine, which he did not believe, afforded his benevolent propenfities an opportunity of propagating the oppofite tenet which he did believe, and think neceffary to be received by all men, not even fo good an end fhould exempt the means from the charge of falfehood, nor the perpetrator from

from the imputation of holding " the damnable doctrine of doing evil that good may come of it." Had a dignified character extended his influence still wider; had the pastoral office been committed to his hand; and had the emblem of the descending spirit sat upon him, he could but ill defend himself from the justice of universal condemnation, though thus, meditating, he should address his mitre, the symbol of a cloven tongue, " thou art the symbol of a double tongue, and thou shalt sanctify duplicity; thou shalt be my warrant for *hypocrisy and prevarication*; for thee will *I keep up all these forms* of subscribing what I do not believe, *till relieved by proper authority*, and vested with dignities without the necessity of falsifying, in order to obtain them; for thee *I will ministerially comply with what I am not able to remove, and patiently remain in my post, however invidiously misrepresented*; for thee, and under thy sanction, I will utter two languages; I will tell a lye for the sake of telling truth; enter into terms for the purpose of infringing them; and comply with such proposed conditions as shall afford me an occasion of shewing that they ought not to be complied with. At the door of the vineyard I will say that *the wild branches* are but the fine luxuriance of nature, and that their growth ought to be encouraged, so shall I obtain the power of *pruning them away*; I shall create to myself an opportunity of *rooting out some of* what I take to be *the rankest weeds*, by telling the owner of the vineyard that I think them the most beautiful plants, and engaging that I will diligently cultivate them: thus shall I trick him into his own advantage, and prove, by having dispensed with truth in order to get admission, that his service, and not my profit, was the only motive to the fraud, the pious fraud by which I induced him to admit me †. Had Mr. Lindsey, I say, thus pondering, lulled himself

† See considerations on the propriety of requiring a subscription to articles of faith.

himself into a hope that none *would suspect him of hypocrisy and prevarication*, he should have found it vain; every whisper would be interpreted into censure, and every breeze of opinion, prove a storm sufficient to disturb the tranquillity of his soul. Is there any man who can have thus dealt by himself? To him I call to descend from his throne, to seek for happiness in self-approbation, and for public applause, by conspicuous and exemplary virtue; let him place the mitre upon other brows, and put upon his own " the helmet of salvation." There are men in England who can profess with sincerity, and maintain what they have professed; who do not need the picklock of equivocation, nor the burglary of more open falsehood, to obtain an entrance into the ministry, from which I thus boldly call, in the name of each man's conscience, upon every person, whether he be Archbishop, Bishop, Priest, or Deacon, who has subscribed with insincerity, or who cannot now overcome his scruples, to retire, and follow the worthy example which is afforded them by Mr. Lindsey.

As a good man, I honour Mr. Lindsey; as a man strenuous in the maintenance of his faith, though I believe it erroneous, I respect him; and if his understanding were but nearly commensurate with his honesty, I believe that the church which he has deserted, would have found in him, who is now her weak opponent, an advocate truly able to maintain her cause; for I do not remember in my life to have met with a man, in whom the excellencies of head and heart had united, who did not submit his own understanding to the word of his Maker, and believe, because that his immutable truth is a fully sufficient ground of faith.

As I am now about to conclude, I must call back the mind of my reader, and having brought my argument

ment to an end, refer to him the issue upon which he is to determine.

Either Jesus Christ is one with the Father, God, or he is not; either the Holy Ghost is one with the Father and the Son, God, or he is not.—On supposing that the negative side of this dilemma can be assumed, (and for argument's sake it must be supposed, however irksome) a consequence ensues, horrible to thought. The God of peace becomes a firebrand of contention; tenfold confusion proceeds from God, " who is not the author of confusion;" the Spirit of truth is a lyar; the simple and guileless zeal of the apostles, is crafty and designing duplicity; the wisdom of God, folly, beneath the foolishness of men; and the revelation of the God of truth, from end to end, scarce the word of designing falsehood, it must have proceeded from a dupe to his own artifices. I shudder while I write: but it is acknowledged that the scriptures are the word of God, and the application of this description to them I will leave with men who can persist in the denial of this great mystery: Whereas, on the other hand, three persons and one God being acknowledged, a fact is established concerning the things of God, incomprehensible to us, who have not spiritual things to compare with spiritual, and which therefore, though it may transcend, can never contradict our reason. Our belief, which is all that is required, may be yielded to the evidence of the fact without any violence offered to our understanding; and therefore, however incomprehensible the object of the testimony may be, there can be no difficulty in making the affirmative, which does not equally attend upon pronouncing the negative of the proposition, and one of the two we are under an absolute necessity of adopting.

In whatsoever God acts, he must condescend. The whole extent of created nature bears to him but a like proportion as an atom; he is equally the God of a fraction as of the universe; and a fraction is as commensurate to his infinity as the universe. But his love is infinite, and we have been the object of it, an object as observable by him as all worlds; for, little as we are, we bear the same proportion to him. Let us then lay aside that pride, which, in the pretence of humility, withdraws mankind from the eye of his Maker; from that microscopick eye, by which even the hairs of our head are numbered; that equal and all-pervading eye, which as accurately sees and marks the fall of a sparrow, as the crush of worlds. When we thus consider him, doubts will vanish; we shall see that we may possibly be within his contemplation, the objects of his favour; we shall acquiesce in a revelation of the benefits he has conferred upon us, and acknowledge that we *have been* the objects of his favour; our ignorance shall be dissipated, our pride deposed; and reason (rightly so called) assuming her proper dignity, conduct us with certainty so far as her own prescribed boundaries extend; instruct us where to pause; teach us the limits of our own faculties, and the illimitable extent of our Maker's; put an end to idle speculation; point out God as our revealed Benefactor, not the subject of our inquisitive curiosity; dictate confidence and hope in him; and make us, because he has revealed it, " to acknowledge the mystery of God, and of the Father, and of Christ."

F I N I S.

INDEX

TO THE

Texts *of* Scripture *quoted in the third Chapter, according to the Order in which they stand compared.*

I.

	Ch. V. Page
Isaiah	vii. 14. 50

II.

Isaiah	ix. 6. 50

III.

Isaiah	xliv. 6 } 50
Revelation	ii. 8 }

IV.

Isaiah	li. 9
	10
	15
Isaiah	lii. 10
Isaiah	liii. 1 } 51
Luke	iii. 6
John	xii. 38
	41
1 Corinthians	x. 9

V.

Isaiah	xl. 10
	11
Revelation	xxii. 12 } 52
John	x. 11
Hebrews	xiii. 20
	21

VI.

Isaiah	lii. 7 } 52
Romans	x. 15 }

VII.

Psalm	viii. 2 }
	1 } 53
Matthew	xxi. 16 }

VIII.

Psalm	xliv. 22 } 53
Romans	viii. 35 }

IX.

Matthew	vi. 10 }
	13 } 54
Matthew	xxiv. 30 }
	31 }

	Ch. V. Page
Matthew	xxv. 31
	32
	33
Mark	viii. 34
	38
Matthew	xiii. 41
Matthew	xvi. 27 } 54
Luke	ix. 26
Ephesians	v. 5
2 Timothy	iv. 1
2 Peter	i. 11
Luke	xvii. 20 to 30

X.

Matthew	xi. 27 } 56
Luke	x. 22 }

XI.

Matthew	xxviii. 20
Mark	xvi. 20 } 57
Hebrews	ii. 3
	4

XII.

Mark	ix. 24 57

XIII.

Luke	v. 20 to 25 }
Isaiah	xliii. 25 } 57
Nehemiah	ix. 17 }

XIV.

Luke	vi. 22
	23
Acts	vii. 52 } 58
	59
1 Peter	iv. 13
	14

XV.

Luke	viii. 38
	39
Mark	v. 19 } 59
	20
John	xi. 35

XVI.

	Ch. V. Page		Ch. V. Page
XVI.		**XXIII.**	
Luke — xxiii. 42 ⎫		John — xiv. 8 ⎫	
43 ⎬ 60		9 ⎬ 68	
Luke — xxiv. 26 ⎭		10	
		11 ⎭	
XVII.		**XXIV.**	
John — ii. 19 ⎫		John — xiv. 12 ⎫	
21 ⎬ 61		13	
Acts — ii. 32 ⎭		14	
XVIII.		John — xvi. 23 ⎬ 69	
John — iv. 10 ⎫		Exodus — iii. 15	
14		1 Timothy — iii. 16	
Jeremiah — xvii. 13		1 John — i. 1	
Revelation — xxii. 1		John — i. 1 ⎭	
17		**XXV.**	
John — iv. 14		John — xvi. 7 ⎫	
Isaiah — lv. 1 ⎬ 61		John — xiv. 26	
Isaiah — xliv. 3		John — xv. 26	
John — vii. 37		2 Peter — i. 21 ⎬ 72	
38		1 Peter — i. 11	
Acts — xx. 28		John — xvi. 14	
John — iv. 42		15 ⎭	
Isaiah — xii. 3 ⎭		**XXVI.**	
XIX.		John — xvii. 1	
John — v. 17 ⎫		Hebrews — ix. 24 ⎬ 73	
18		John — xvii. 5	
John — v. 26		24 ⎭	
27		**XXVII.**	
Hebrews — ii. 18		John — xviii. 37 ⎫	
Hebrews — iv. 15 ⎬ 63		1 Timothy — vi. 13 ⎬ 74	
John — v. 21		John — i. 49 ⎭	
25		**XXVIII.**	
28		John — xx. 28 ⎫	
John — vi. 69		29 ⎬ 75	
John — ix. 38 ⎭		John — xx. 16 ⎭	
XX.		**XXIX.**	
John — v. 24 ⎫		Acts — i. 24	
John — iii. 18		John — xv. 27	
John — iii. 13		Mark — xvi. 15	
John — iii. 31 ⎬ 65		Romans — i. 5	
John — vi. 62		John — ii. 25	
John — xvi. 28		Acts — i. 21	
29 ⎭		22	
XXI.		Acts — ix. 5	
John — viii. 58 ⎫		6 ⎬ 76	
Revelation — i. 4 ⎬ 66		13	
Exodus — iii. 14		14	
John — iv. 26 ⎭		15	
XXII.		1 Corinthians — i. 17	
John — x. 30 ⎫		Luke — xi. 49	
John — x. 33 ⎬ 67		Mattthew — xxiii. 34	
John — x. 38 ⎭		Acts — ix. 20	
		21 ⎭	

Acts

	Ch.	V.	Page		Ch.	V.	Page
Acts	ix.	2		Matthew	xxviii.	20	
		15		Mark	xvi.	20	
Acts	xxii.	14	76	Hebrews	ii.	4	89
John	xxi.	17		Acts	xix.	10	
John	xiii.	37				11	
		38					

XXX.

XXXV.

	Ch.	V.	Page		Ch.	V.	Page
Acts	iii.	12		Acts	xvi.	14	
Acts	iv.	10				15	
		21	81			16	
Acts	ix.	34				17	
		35		Luke	xxiv.	45	92
				Mark	i.	34	
				Romans	i.	1	
				Philippians	i.	1	
				Titus	i.	1	

XXXI.

XXXVI.

	Ch.	V.	Page		Ch.	V.	Page
Acts	vii.	54		Acts	xvi.	30	
		55				31	
		56				32	93
		57				33	
		58				34	
		59					
		60					

XXXVII.

John	xvi.	13			Ch.	V.	Page
Psalm	xxxi.	5		Acts	xvii.	18	
Revelation	xxii.	9	82	Acts	xvii.	23	
Jeremiah	xxiii.	23				24	
Acts	vii.	56				28	94
		57		Colossians	i.	16	
Matthew	xxvi.	64				17	
		65		Isaiah	xlii.	8	
		67					
Matthew	xiv.	61					
		to					
		65					

XXXVIII.

	Ch.	V.	Page
Acts	xviii.	8	
		9	
		10	95
		11	

XXXII.

| Acts | ix. | 40 | 88 | Acts | xxiii.| 11 | |
| | | 42 | | | | | |

XXXIII.

XXXIX.

Acts	xi.	18		Acts	xviii.	24	
		20				to	96
		21	89			28	
		22					
		23					
Acts	xv.	11					

XL.

Acts	xix.	10	
Acts	xix.	17	
		18	97
		19	
		20	

XXXIV.

Acts	xiii.	45	
		46	
		47	
Isaiah	xlix.	6	
Matthew	xv.	24	89
Acts	xiii.	48	
		49	
Acts	xiv.	1	
		3	

XLI.

Acts	xxi.	11	
		to	97
		14	
Matthew	vi.	10	

XLII.

| Acts | xxii. | 16 | 98 |

INDEX

	Ch.	V.	Page
XLIII.			
Acts		xxii.	17, 18 } 98
Acts		xxii.	19, 20
XLIV.			
Acts		xxiv.	5, 14 } 99
John		v.	39
XLV.			
Romans		i.	1, 9 } 99
XLVI.			
Romans		ii.	3
John		v.	22 } 100
Matthew		xvi.	27
Romans		ii.	6
XLVII.			
Romans		ii.	4
Acts		xi.	18
1 Timothy		i.	16 } 100
2 Peter		iii.	15, 9
XLVIII.			
Romans		iii.	
Romans		iv.	} 101
Hebrews		xi. xii.	
The whole of each chapter referred to.			
XLIX.			
Romans		viii.	9, 11 } 101
L.			
Romans		ix.	5 102
LI.			
Romans		x.	12, 13 } 102
LII.			
Romans		xiv.	6 to 9 } 103
1 Corinthians		x.	31, 28
LIII.			
Romans		xiv.	10, 11, 12
Isaiah		xlv.	23, 21, 22 } 103
2 Corinthians		v.	10
Hebrews		x.	31

	Ch.	V.	Page
LIV.			
Romans		xiv.	14 104
LV.			
Romans		xv.	16, 19 } 105
LVI.			
Romans		xvi.	16
1 Corinthians		i.	1, 2, 3, 4 } 105
LVII.			
1 Corinthians		i.	7, 8
1 Corinthians		iv.	5 } 106
2 Corinthians		x.	14 to 18
LVIII.			
1 Corinthians		i.	11, 12, 13
1 Corinthians		i.	10 } 107
1 Corinthians		iii.	5, 6
1 Corinthians		i.	8
LIX.			
1 Corinthians		i.	14, 15 } 108
LX.			
1 Corinthians		i.	26, 27, 28, 29
1 Corinthians		i.	21, 31 } 109
2 Corinthians		x.	17
Jeremiah		ix.	24
LXI.			
1 Corinthians		ii.	8
Acts		iii.	15, 17
James		ii.	1 } 110
Psalm		xxiv.	10
Genesis		ii.	7
LXII.			
1 Corinthians		ii.	7 to the end. } 110
LXIII.			
1 Corinthians		vii.	25 } 110.
Daniel		ix.	9

LXIV

INDEX.

	Ch.	V.	Page
LXIV.			
1 CORINTHIANS	viii.	4	
1 Corinthians —	viii.	6	
Acts ———	xiv.	7	
		15	111
1 Corinthians —	xii.	2	
		3	
1 Corinthians —	xiv.	33	
LXV.			
1 CORINTHIANS	x.	20	
		21	
2 Corinthians —	vi.	15	115
		16	
LXVI.			
2 CORINTHIANS	iv.	5	116
2 Timothy —	i.	8	
LXVII.			
2 CORINTHIANS	xii.	5	
		7	
		8	116
		9	
		10	
LXVIII.			
GALATIANS —	i.	1	
Galatians —	i.	11	118
		12	
LXIX.			
GALATIANS —	i.	10	
Galatians —	vi.	12	119
		17	
LXX.			
GALATIANS —	iv.	6	
Galatians —	iii.	8	
Romans. —	viii.	11	119
		14	
		15	
1 Corinthians —	xii.	3	
LXXI.			
EPHESIANS —	i.	7	
Ephesians —	iii.	8	
		14	
		15	
		16	
Romans —	ii.	4	
Romans —	ix.	23	
Ephesians —	iii.	18	121
		19	
		17	
Ephesians —	iv.	13	
Ephesians —	iii.	7	
Ephesians —	iv.	7	
Romans —	xi.	33	
		34	

	Ch.	V.	Page
LXXII.			
EPHESIANS —	iv.	8	
		9	
		10	122
Ephesians —	iv.	14	
		15	
LXXIII.			
EPHESIANS —	vi.	5	
		6	
		7	123
		8	
Colossians —	iii.	22	
LXXIV.			
PHILIPPIANS —	ii.	6	
		7	124
		8	
Colossians —	i.	15	
LXXV.			
PHILIPPIANS —	iii.	20	
1 Timothy —	i.	1	
1 Timothy —	ii.	3	124
1 Timothy —	iv.	10	
Titus —	i.	3	
Acts ———	ix.	5	
LXXVI.			
COLOSSIANS —	i.	15	
		16	125
		17	
		18	
LXXVII.			
COLOSSIANS —	ii.	9	128
LXXVIII.			
COLOSSIANS —	iii.	11	
		12	128
		13	
LXXIX.			
COLOSSIANS —	iii.	24	
		25	
Romans —	ii.	5	
		11	128
Ephesians —	vi.	6	
		9	
James —	ii.	1	
LXXX.			
1 THESSALONIANS	ii.	2	
1 Thessalonians —	ii.	8	
		9	128
1 Thessalonians —	iii.	2	
John —	xvi.	13	
1 Thessalonians —	ii.	3	
LXXXI.			
1 THESSALONIANS	iv.	2	129
		3	

	Ch.	V.	Page
LXXXII.			
2 Thessalonians	i.	6	}130
		7	
		8	
		9	
		10	
Matthew	vi.	9	
1 Peter	iv.	17	
LXXXIII.			
2 Thessalonians	ii.	16	}130
		17	
2 Thessalonians	iii.	3	
LXXXIV.			
2 Thessalonians	iii.	5	}132
2 Corinthians	ii.	14	
		17	
LXXXV.			
1 Timothy	ii.	5	}132
		6	
		7	
		8	
LXXXVI.			
1 Timothy	iii.	16	}133
1 Timothy	i.	10	
		11	
LXXXVII.			
1 Timothy	iv.	10	}133
1 Timothy	i.	15	
2 Timothy	ii.	8	
		10	
LXXXVIII.			
1 Timothy	vi.	13	}134
		14	
		15	
		16	
2 Corinthians	v.	16	
Revelation	xix.	16	
LXXXIX.			
2 Timothy	iv.	1	}135
		8	
Titus	ii.	13	
XC.			
Titus	ii.	13	}136
		10	
Revelation	i.	5	
Titus	iii.	4	
		5	
		6	
Titus	i.	3	
		4	

	Ch.	V.	Page
XCI.			
Hebrews	ii.	16	}137
Colossians	i.	16	
Hebrews	x.		
Hebrews	vii.		
Hebrews	viii.		
Hebrews	ii.		
XCII.			
James	v.	8	}142
		9	
		10	
		11	
James	v.	14	
		15	
Acts	ix.	34	
Luke	viii.	48	
Luke	v.	13	
XCIII.			
James	i.	1	}143
James	ii.	1	
		5	
		9	
		13	
XCIV.			
1 Peter	v.	1	}144
		2	
		3	
		4	
John	xxi.	14	
		15	
		16	
		17	
John	x.	13	
		14	
1 Peter	ii.	25	
Hebrews	xiii.	20	
Acts	xx.	28	
James	i.	12	
James	ii.	5	
1 Corinthians	ix.	25	
2 Timothy	iv.	8	
1 Peter	iv.	11	
XCV.			
2 Peter	i.	1	}146
1 Timothy	i.	1	
XCVI.			
2 Peter	i.	11	146
XCVII.			
2 Peter	iii.	10	}146
		11	
		12	
2 Peter	iii.	15	
1 Timothy	i.	16	
2 Peter	iii.	18	
XCVIII.			

XCVIII.
1 John — ii. 22 148

XCIX.
1 John — iv. 3 148

C.
1 JOHN — v. 7 148

CI.
2 John — v. 13 }
                14
                15 } 148
1 John — iii. 21
                22

CII.
1 John — v. 20 }
1 John — v. 11 }
                12 } 149
                13

CIII.
2 John — 9 }
1 John — ii. 23 }
1 John — iv. 15 } 151
                12

CIV.
Jude — 1 }
Philippians — i. 1 }
Titus — i. 1 } 151
1 Corinthians — i. 1

CV.
Jude — 151

CVI.
1 John — iii. 16 153

CVII.
Acts — xx. 28 }
Isaiah — xl. 11 }
Acts — xx. 29 } 153
                30

CVIII.
Hebrews — i. 8 }
                10
                to 12 } 154
Hebrews — i. 9
Romans — ix. 5
Hebrews — xiii. 8

CIX.
Revelation — ii. 8 }
Isaiah — xliv. 6 }
John — xiii. 31 }
                32 } 157
Revelation — i. 8
Revelation — xxii. 13

CX.
Revelation — ii. 23 }
Jeremiah — xvii. 10 }
Jeremiah — xi. 20 } 157
Jeremiah — xx. 12 }
Isaiah — xliv. 6

CXI.
Revelation — i. 8 }
Matthew — xxiv. 30 }
Revelation — i. 7 } 158
Revelation — iv. 8

CXII.
Revelation — i. 18 }
Revelation — iv. 9 }
                10 }
                11 }
Matthew — vi. 9 } 159
                10 }
1 Corinthians — viii. 6 }
Colossians — i. 17

CXIII.
Revelation — iii. 10 } 159
Matthew — vi. 13

CXIV.
Revelation — iii. 19 }
Job — v. 17 }
Hebrews — xii. 6 } 160
                7

CXV.
Revelation — v. 13 }
Revelation — i. 4 }
                5 } 160
                6 }
Jeremiah — xviii. 23

CXVI.
Revelation — vi. 15 }
                16 }
Hebrews — i. 12 } 162
Revelation — vi. 13 }
                14

CXVII.
Revelation — xiv. 6 }
                7 }
Philemon — 9 }
Romans — i. 16 }
2 Timothy — i. 8 }
Philippians — i. 17 } 163
                18 }
2 Timothy — iv. 1 }
1 Corinthians — viii. 6 }
Colossians — i. 16 }
                17

CXVIII.

INDEX

CXVIII.
	Ch.	V.	Page
REVELATION	—	xvii.	14 ⎫
Revelation	—	xix.	21 ⎪
			16 ⎬ 164
			17 ⎪
			18 ⎭

CXIX.
	Ch.	V.	Page
REVELATION	—	xix.	13 ⎫
John	—	i.	1
			14
			2
			10
			11
Genesis	—	i.	1
John	—	i.	3
			4
John	—	viii.	12 ⎬ 165
1 John	—	i.	5
			1
			2
1 Timothy	—	iii.	16
1 Peter	—	i.	23
Hebrews	—	xi.	3
Hebrews	—	i.	2
Revelation	—	iii.	14
1 Peter	—	i.	25
John	—	i.	15 ⎭

CXX.
	Ch.	V.	Page
REVELATION	—	xx.	6 ⎫ 167
James	—	v.	⎭

CXXI.
	Ch.	V.	Page
REVELATION	—	xx.	12 ⎫
			13
			14
			15
Matthew	—	xxv.	31
			32 ⎬ 169
Matthew	—	xvi.	27
Matthew	—	xiii.	41
			42
Revelation	—	xxi.	27
John	—	v.	22 ⎭

CXXII.
	Ch.	V.	Page
REVELATION	—	xxii.	13 ⎫
Revelation	—	vii.	17 ⎬ 170
Revelation	—	xxi.	6
			7 ⎭

CXXIII.
	Ch.	V.	Page
REVELATION	—	xxi.	22 ⎫
			23
Revelation	—	xxii.	5 ⎬ 171
			3
			4
Revelation	—	iii.	12
Revelation	—	xiv.	1 ⎭

CXXIV.
	Ch.	V.	Page
REVELATION	—	xxii.	6 ⎫
Revelation	—	i.	1 ⎬ 172
Revelation	—	xxii.	16 ⎭

CXXV.
	Ch.	V.	Page
REVELATION	—	iv.	8 ⎫
			11
Revelation	—	v.	12
			13
Revelation	—	vii.	10
			17
Colossians	—	i.	16
Isaiah	—	liii.	7
Revelation	—	vii.	9 ⎬ 172
			14
			15
Revelation	—	xvii.	14
1 Timothy	—	vi.	15
			16
2 Peter	—	iii.	18
1 Peter	—	iv.	11
Hebrews	—	xii.	1
Philippians	—	ii.	10 ⎭

INDEX

TO THE

TEXTS of SCRIPTURE *quoted in the third Chapter according to the Order in which they stand in the Bible.*

	Page
GENESIS i. 1	165
—— ii. 7	110
EXODUS iii. 14	66
—— iii. 15	71
NEHEMIAH ix. 17	58
JOB v. 17	160
PSALMS viii. 1	53
—— viii. 2	53
—— xxiv. 10.	110
—— xxxi. 5	85
—— xliv. 22	53
ISAIAH vii. 14	50
—— ix. 6	50
—— xii. 3	62
—— xl. 10, 11	52
—— xlii. 8	95
—— xliii. 25	58
—— xliv. 3	62
—— xliv. 6	50, 157, 158
—— xlv. 21, 22, 23	104
—— xlix. 6	90
—— li. 9, 10, 15	51
—— lii. 7, 10	51
—— liii. 1	51
—— 7	173
—— lv. 1	62
JEREMIAH ix. 24	61
—— xi. 20	158
—— xvii. 10	158
—— xvii. 13	61
—— xx. 12	158
—— xxiii. 23	86, 161
DANIEL ix. 9	111
MATTHEW vi. 9	130, 159
—— vi. 10	54, 98, 159
—— vi. 13	54, 159
—— xi. 27	56
—— xiii. 41	55, 170
—— xiii. 42	170

	Page
MATTHEW xiv. 61 to 65	82
—— xv. 24	91
—— xvi. 27	55, 100, 169
—— xxi. 16	53
—— xxiii. 34	78
—— xxiv. 30	158
—— 31	54
—— xxv. 31, 32, 33, 34	54, 169
—— xxvi. 64, 65, 67	87
—— xxviii. 20	57, 92
MARK i. 34	93
—— v. 19	59
—— viii. 38	55
—— ix. 24	57
—— xvi. 15	77
—— xvi. 20	57, 92
LUKE iii. 6	51
—— v. 13	143
—— v. 20 to 25	58
—— vi. 22, 23	58
—— viii. 38, 39	59
—— viii. 48	143
—— ix. 26	55
—— x. 22	56
—— xi. 49	78
—— xvii. 20 to 30	55
—— xxiii. 42, 43	60
—— xxiv. 26	60
—— xxiv. 45	92
JOHN i. 1	71

JOHN

	Page		Page
John i. 1 to 14	165	John xvi. 7	72
—— i. 15	166	—— 13	84, 129
—— i. 49	74	—— 14, 15	73
—— ii. 19, 21	61	—— 23	70
—— 25	77	—— 28	66
—— iii. 13		—— 29	66
—— 18	65	—— xvii. 5, 24	73
—— 31		—— xviii. 37	74
—— iv. 10, 14	61	—— xx. 16, 28, 29	75
—— iv. 42	62	—— xxi. 14, 15, 16, 17	145
—— iv. 26	67		
—— v. 17, 18, 26, 27	63	Acts i. 21, 22	77
—— v. 21, 25, 28	64	—— 24, 25	76
		—— ii. 32	61
—— v. 22	100, 170	—— iii. 12	81
—— v. 24	65	—— 15, 17	110
—— v. 39	99	—— iv. 10, 21	81
—— vi. 62	65	—— vii. 51	59
—— vi. 69	64	—— 52	58, 59
—— vii. 37, 38	62	—— 53	53
—— viii. 12	165	—— 54	59, 82
—— viii. 58	66	—— 55	59, 82
—— ix. 38	65	—— 56	59, 82
—— x. 11	52	—— 57	59, 82
—— x. 13, 14	145	—— 58	59, 82
—— x. 30	67	—— 59	59, 82
—— x. 33	67	—— 60	82
—— x. 38	68	—— ix. 2	79
—— xi. 35	60	—— 5	77, 125
—— 38	52	—— 6	77
—— xii. 41	52	—— 13	78
—— 12, 13, 14	69	—— 14	78
		—— 15	78
—— xiii. 31	156	—— 20	78
—— 32	156	—— 21	77, 78
—— xiv. 8 to 11	68	—— 22	77
—— xiv. 12 to 14	68	—— 26	78
		—— 34	82, 143
		—— 35	82
		—— 40	88
		—— 42	88
—— xiv. 26	72	—— xi. 18	89, 100
—— xv. 26	72	—— 20	89
—— xv. 27	77	—— 21	89
		—— 22	89

Acts

INDEX.

		Page
Acts xi.	23	89
— xiii.	45	90
	46	90
	47	90
	48	91
	49	91
— xiv.	1	91
	3	91
	7	112
	15	112
— xv.	11	89
— xvi.	14	93
	15	93
	16	93
	17	93
	30	93
	31	93
	32	93
	33	93
	34	93
— xvii.	18	94
	23	94
	24	95
	28	95
— xviii.	8	95
	9	95
	10	95
	11	95
	24	97
	25	97
	26	97
	27	97
	28	97
— xix.	10	92, 97
	11	92
	17	97
	18	97
	19	97
	20	97
— xx.	28	62, 145, 154
	29	154
	30	154
— xxi.	11	97
	12	97
	13	97
	14	97
— xxii.	14	80
	16	98
	17	98
	18	98
	19	98
	20	98
— xxiv.	5	99
	14	99
Romans i.	1	93, 99
	5	77

		Page
Romans i.	9	100
	16	163
— ii.	3	100
	4	100, 125
	5	128
	6	100
	11	128
— iii.	26	101
— iv.		101
— viii.	9	101
	11	101, 120
	14	120
	15	120
	35	53
— ix.	5	102, 157
	23	121
— x.	12	102
	13	102
	15	53
— xi.	33	122
	34	122
— xiv.	6	103
	7	103
	8	103
	9	103
	10	103
	11	103
	12	103
	14	104
— xv.	16	105
	19	105
— xvi.	16	105
1 Corinthians i.	1	105, 157
	2	105
	3	106
	4	106
	7	106
	8	106, 107
	10	107
	11	107
	12	107
	13	107
	14	108
	15	108
	17	78
	21	109
	26	109
	27	109
	28	109
	29	109
	31	109
— ii.	7 to the end	110
	8	110
— iii.	5	107
	6	107
— iv.	5	106

H h   1 Corinthians

	Page			Page
1 CORINTHIANS vii. 25	111	EPHESIANS vi.	6 —	123, 128
——— viii. 4 —	111		7 —	123
6 —	112, 159, 163		8 —	123
——— ix. 25 —	146		9 —	128
——— x. 9 —	52	PHILIPPIANS i.	1	93, 151
20 —	115		17	163
21 —	115		18	163
28 —	103	——— ii.	6	124
31 —	103		7	124
——— xii. 2 —	115		8	124
3 —	115, 120		10	174
——— xiv. 33 —	115	——— iii.	20	124
2 CORINTHIANS ii. 14	132	COLOSSIANS i.	15	124, 125
17	132		16	95, 125, 138, 163, 173
——— iv. 5	116		17	95, 125, 159, 163
——— v. 10	104		18	127
16	134	——— ii.	9	128
——— vi. 15	115	——— iii.	11	128
16	115		12	128
——— x. 14	107		13	128
15	107		22	123
16	107		24	128
17	107, 109		25	128
18	107	1 THESSALONIANS ii.	2	128
——— xii. 5	117		3	129
7	117		8	129
8	117		9	129
9	117	——— iii.	2	129
10	117	——— iv.	2	129
GALATIANS i. 1 —	118		3	129
10 —	119	2 THESSALONIANS i.	6	130
11 —	119		7	130
12 —	119		8	130
——— iii. 8 —	120		9	130
——— iv. 6 —	119		10	130
——— vi. 12 —	119	——— ii.	16	130
17 —	119		17	130
EPHESIANS i. 7 —	121	——— iii.	3	131
——— iii. 7 —	122		5	132
8 —	121	1 TIMOTHY i.	1	125, 146
14 —	121		10	133
15 —	121		11	133
16 —	121		15	133
17 —	122		16	100, 147
18 —	121	——— ii.	3	125
19 —	121		5	132
——— iv. 7 —	122		6	132
8 —	122		7	132
9 —	122		8	132
10 —	122	——— iii.	16	71, 133, 166
13 —	122	——— iv.	10	125, 133
14 —	123	——— vi.	13	74, 134
15 —	123		14	134
——— v. 5 —	55		15	134, 174
——— vi. 5 —	123		16	134, 174

1 TIMOTHY

INDEX.

Reference	Page
2 Timothy i. 8	116, 163
—— ii. 8	134
10	134
—— iv. 1	55, 135, 163
8	136, 146
Titus i. 1 —	93, 151
3 —	125, 137
4 —	137
—— ii. 10 —	136
13 —	136
—— iii. 4 —	136
5 —	136
6 —	136
Philemon 9 —	163
Hebrews i. 2	166
8	155
9	155
10	155
11	155
12	155, 162
—— ii.	139
The whole referred to.	
3	57
4	57, 92
16	137
17	140
18	63, 140
—— iv. 15	63
—— vii.	140
The whole referred to.	
—— viii.	140
The whole referred to.	
—— ix. 24	73
—— x.	139
The whole referred to.	
1	140
5	140
6	140
20	139
31	104
—— xi.	101
The whole referred to.	
3	166
—— xii.	101
The whole referred to.	
1	174
6	160
7	160
—— xiii. 8	157
20	52, 145
21	52
James i. 1 —	143
12 —	145
—— ii. 1 —	110, 128, 144
5 —	144, 146
9 —	144

Reference	Page
James ii. 13 —	144
—— v.	168
The whole referred to.	
8 —	142
9 —	142
10 —	142
11 —	142
14 —	143
15 —	143
1 Peter i. 11	73
23	166
25	166
—— ii. 25 —	145
—— iv. 11	146, 174
13	59
14	59
17	131
—— v. 1	144
2	144
3	144
4	144
2 Peter i. 1	146
11	55, 146
21	72
—— iii. 9	101
10	146
11	147
12	147
15	100, 147
18	147, 174
1 John i. 1	71, 165
2	165
5	165
—— ii. 22 —	147
23 —	151
—— iii. 16 —	153
21 —	149
22 —	149
—— iv. 3 —	148
12 —	151
15 —	151
—— v. 7 —	148
11 —	149
12 —	149
13 —	149
14 —	149
15 —	149
20 —	149
2 John 9 —	151
Jude, the whole,	151
Revelation i. 1	172
4	66, 160
5	136, 160
6	157, 160
7	158
8	157, 158

REVE-

INDEX

		Page				Page
REVELATION	i. 18	159	REVELATION	xix.	13	165
	ii. 8	51, 157			16	134, 164
	23	157			17	164
	iii. 10	159			18	164
	12	172			21	164
	14	166		xx.	6	167
	19	160			12	169
	iv. 8	159, 173			13	169
	9	159			14	169
	10	159			15	169
	11	159, 173		xxi.	6	171
	v. 12	173			7	171
	13	161, 173			22	171
	vi. 13	163			23	171
	14	163			27	169
	15	162		xxii.	1	62
	16	162			3	171
	vii. 9	174			4	171
	10	173			5	171
	14	174			6	172
	15	174			9	85
	17	170, 173			12	52
	xiv. 1	172			13	157, 170
	6	163			16	172
	7	163			17	62
	xvii. 14	164, 174				

ERRATA.

Page.	line.	for.	read.
19	17	the inscrutable	his inscrutable
33	23	the Lord shall	the Lord God shall
101	32	synonimous.	*dele* the full point
160	31	?ã	?ã
164	12	the Lord	*dele* the

There are, besides, a few typographical errours of less importance, which are therefore left unnoticed. The reader is requested to pardon these, and the omission or misplacing (if any there be) of the inverted commas, by which quotations are marked.

PAGE 40—Pliny's Epistle to Trajan, giving him an account of the professours of Christianity, is alluded to; in which he says of them, "Carmenque Christo quasi "Deo dicere secum invicem."

PAGE 195—The horrid persecution carried on in Africa, against the Believers in the Godhead of our Saviour, by the Arian tyrant HUNERIC, in the fifth century, is alluded to—See Mosheim's Ecclesiastical History, Vol. I. p. 401, Octavo, 1768.

PAGE 198—In support of what I have said concerning Mr. Hume, see his works *passim*. Or rather save yourself the disagreeable labour, and attentively read Dr. Beattie's manly and convincing *Essay on the Nature and Immutability of Truth, in opposition to Sophistry and Scepticism*; in which you will find Mr. Hume already detected. — See also Harris's well-authenticated *Historical and Critical Account of Charles* I. p. 264, Octavo, 1758, where the Infidelity of the Historian is pointed out.

www.ingramcontent.com/pod-product-compliance
Lightning Source LLC
Chambersburg PA
CBHW030546300426
44111CB00009B/878